The Editor

Judith L. Raiskin is Associate Professor and Director of Women's Studies at the University of Oregon. She is the author of *Snow on the Cane Fields: Women's Writing and Creole Subjectivity*.

A NORTON CRITICAL EDITION

Jean Rhys

WIDE SARGASSO SEA

BACKGROUNDS

CRITICISM

Edited by

JUDITH L. RAISKIN

UNIVERSITY OF OREGON

W • W • NORTON & COMPANY • *New York* • *London*

This title is printed on permanent paper containing 30 percent post-consumer waste recycled fiber.

Copyright © 1999 by W. W. Norton & Company, Inc.

Wide Sargasso Sea copyright © 1966 by Jean Rhys. Published by arrangement with the Wallace Literary Agency, Inc.

The text of this book is composed in Electra with the display set in Bernhard Modern. Composition by PennSet, Inc. Manufacturing by Courier Companies.

Cover illustration: Watercolor by Brenda Lockhart. Reproduced by permission of Brenda Lockhart and the Jean Rhys Collection, University of Tulsa, Oklahoma.

Library of Congress Cataloging-in-Publication Data
Rhys, Jean.
    Wide Sargasso Sea / Jean Rhys ; background, criticism edited by
Judith L. Raiskin.
        p.   cm. — (A Norton critical edition)
    Prequel to: Jane Eyre / Charlotte Brontë.
    Includes bibliographical references.

    ISBN 0-393-96012-9 (pbk.)

    1. Man-woman relationships — West Indies — Fiction.   2. British —
West Indies — Fiction.   3. Historical fiction. gsafd.   4. Love
stories. gsafd.   I. Brontë, Charlotte, 1816–1855.   Jane Eyre.
II. Raiskin, Judith L.   III. Title.   IV. Series.
PR6035.H96W5   1998
823'.912 — DC21   98-14266
                                                                          CIP

W. W. Norton & Company, Inc., 500 Fifth Avenue, New York, N.Y. 10110
http://www.wwnorton.com
W. W. Norton & Company Ltd., 10 Coptic Street, London WC1A 1PU

7 8 9 0

Contents

v

Criticism   157

List of Illustrations

Jean Rhys, photograph by Ander Gunn.

Preface

Several years after *Wide Sargasso Sea* was published, A. Alvarez declared in the *New York Times Book Review* that Jean Rhys was the "best living English novelist," a claim that simultaneously validated and misrepresented Rhys's literary standing. Indeed, after a lifetime of writing and struggling to write while suffering the miseries of poverty, isolation, alcoholism, and illness, Rhys was gratified by the widespread recognition of her work that finally came to her late in life. But it is an irony that Rhys, who always hated England and English culture and who perceived herself to be, as a displaced colonial, the object of English disdain and hatred, should be declared a light of English culture and made, at the age of 88, a Commander of the Order of the British Empire for her contributions to literature. Jean Rhys was born in 1890 on the Caribbean island of Dominica to a Welsh father and a "white Creole" mother whose family had had great influence on the island for generations. In 1907 Rhys left Dominica, as did many colonial children, to pursue her education in England. Although she never returned to the Caribbean, except for a short trip in 1936, and although she spent most of her life in small, remote English villages, she never considered herself to be English and remained throughout her life an incisive and bitter critic of what she perceived to be English values. The circumstances that made it impossible to return to Dominica— lack of money, two world wars, several marriages, a tendency toward despondency and despair, and the changing political and cultural status of the English colonies—were also the circumstances that made it difficult for Rhys to write, particularly when she dedicated herself to *Wide Sargasso Sea*, which deals directly with colonialism, European dominance in the Caribbean, and the hypocrisies of English culture. It took Rhys twenty-one years to write this short novel, years that we can see with hindsight were crucial to the development of feminist, anticolonial, postmodern perspectives that would permit critics to recognize Rhys as one of the foremost novelists, English or not, of her time.

The Text

Jean Rhys first mentions working on what was to become *Wide Sargasso Sea* in October 1945. Although the book was not finished and published in full until 1966, she knew immediately the power of her ideas and believed that this book "might be the one book I've written that's much use."[1] Rhys was a painstakingly careful writer, never completely satisfied with her work despite her meticulous honing. As her editor Diana Athill wrote in her forward to Rhys's unfinished autobiography, *Smile Please*, "Jean Rhys allowed no piece of writing to leave her hands until it was finished except for the very smallest details. An example of her perfectionism: some five years after the publication of *Wide Sargasso Sea*, she said to me out of the blue: 'There is one thing I've always wanted to ask you. Why did you let me publish that book?' . . . I was indignant when I asked her what on earth she meant. 'It was not finished,' she said coldly. She then pointed out the existence in the book of two unnecessary words. One was 'then,' the other 'quite.' "

A version of Part One was published in 1964 in the first issue of *Art and Literature*, a journal edited by Francis Wyndham and dedicated to showcasing new and "in-progress" literary works. Rhys's revisions of that version are mostly the addition of several key passages (such as the poisoning of the horse, Antoinette's visit to her mother after the fire, and Mr. Mason's discussion with Antoinette in the convent) and smaller changes that affect the feeling but not the sense of the narrative (see illustrations, pp. 146 and 147). While these revisions were not received in time to be included in the issue, they were included in the completed novel published by André Deutsch with a preface by Francis Wyndham in 1966. These revisions and the manuscripts of *Wide Sargasso Sea* housed in the British Library show Rhys's long process of composition and her fierce attention to mood, rhythm, and historical detail. What read in the final version as simple, perfectly crafted descriptions, interior monologues, and dialogues, begin in exercise books and on loose pieces of paper as repetitions of key words and phrases worked in slightly different combinations, highlighted by slightly different tenses, word order, and the deletion or addition of adjectives. As Rhys commented on her own writing, "I know it seems stupid to fuss over a few lines or words, but I've never got over my longing for clarity, and a smooth firm foundation underneath the sound and the fury. I've learned one generally gets this by cutting, or by very slight shifts and changes . . ." (Nov. 9, 1949; *LJR*, 60). Her persistent desire that the novel be accurate motivated her revisions: "I've always *known* that this book must be done as well as I could—(*no* margin of error) or that it would be unconvincing" (March 3, 1964; *LJR*, 253). Instead of distracting readers with footnotes referring to the numerous slight changes Rhys made while editing her novel, I have selected a number of letters she wrote that address her process of composition and the stakes she

---

1. Francis Wyndham and Diana Melly, eds., *The Letters of Jean Rhys* (hereafter, *LJR*) p. 39.

saw in her literary choices. The text presented here is the one published in 1966, the only version of the complete novel.

Critical Approaches

Particularly since the publication of *Wide Sargasso Sea*, Rhys's work has challenged easy definition and has invited intense debate. This was a surprising novel for a variety of reasons: It appeared twenty-seven years after Rhys's last novel, *Good Morning, Midnight*, which was published on the eve of World War II and had sunk, along with its author, into obscurity (many had assumed that Rhys had died sometime during or shortly after the war); unlike her earlier novels, which had all been set in England and France in the 1920s and 1930s, *Wide Sargasso Sea* was set in the 1840s in the West Indies; with an unremitting determination it rewrote the English classic, Charlotte Brontë's *Jane Eyre*, and by shifting the focus from Jane to Bertha it challenged an array of accepted truths from the glories of Empire and English culture to the celebrations of liberal feminism.

The novel lends itself to a variety of critical approaches that have become over the past thirty years increasingly sophisticated. *Wide Sargasso Sea* has served as a touchstone text for critics interested in modernism, feminism, and postcolonial theory. This slim novel has generated an enormous amount of critical discussion, in large part because it is not easily categorized. For critics interested in modernism and postmodernism, Rhys's last novel raises some interesting questions about literary periods and style. To a great extent, modernist literature has been defined by the stylistic conventions and urban settings of the interwar period typical of Rhys's earlier four novels and short stories. While her writing shared the harsh portrayal of urban modern life with that of many of her contemporaries, critics have also read her earlier novels as a postmodern critique of the modernist visions themselves, which often were based in a nostalgia for a past that Rhys repudiated. *Wide Sargasso Sea*, appearing so many years later, retains the modernist sparseness of Rhys's pre-war work but is set a century earlier, in a time and place distinctly nonindustrial, and exploits the tropes of early nineteenth-century romanticism (passion, supernatural beauty, magic) as much as those of modernism and postmodernism.

Similarly, feminist critics have been challenged by a novel that rewrites an English classic long touted for its feminist vision. Interested in Rhys's unrelenting portrayal of the economic and sexual exploitation of her women characters in her earlier fiction, feminist critics find that the issues of race and slavery raised in *Wide Sargasso Sea* complicate not only many evaluations of *Jane Eyre* but also the readings of Rhys's "European fiction" that analyze exploitation in terms of gender only.

Some feminist critics have found recent psychoanalytic theory useful in debating the status of Rhys's heroines and understanding in particular Antoinette's disastrous choices.

Perhaps the most active and heated debate has involved critics interested in postcolonial theory who have sought to place Rhys and *Wide Sargasso Sea* in geographical, national, cultural, or racial categories to interpret the novel's representation of colonial relations. Rhys's personal history—the fact that she was born in the Caribbean but was fairly insulated within the white community that made up only one percent of the island population and that she left the Caribbean forever at the age of seventeen—has led critics to argue for and against Rhys's inclusion in collections of writings by or theoretical discussions about Caribbean, postcolonial, or "Third World" writers. Since the novel focuses on the white Creole character, these critics have debated whether that focus recognizes or silences the historic resistance of black Caribbeans to European domination. Edward Kamau Brathwaite has recently called Rhys the "Helen of our wars," underscoring the political implications of claiming Rhys and her fiction. The exercise of placing Rhys and her work invites a larger discussion about the changing definitions of national literatures and cultural territories in a world where information, music, fashions, and money travel faster than they ever have before.

Backgrounds and Criticism

I have divided the materials in this edition into Backgrounds and Criticism. For those who have not read Brontë's novel and for those who would find a comparison useful, I have included several key scenes from *Jane Eyre* that are crucial to Rhys's revision. I have selected sections from her unfinished autobiography, *Smile Please*, to give a sense of Rhys's childhood in Dominica and her process of using that material in her fiction. The letters selected pertain primarily to Rhys's writing of *Wide Sargasso Sea*, her feelings about *Jane Eyre* and its significance, her struggles with the narrative voices of the novel and its structure, and her understanding of the role of a writer and her own contribution to literature. The unpublished essay "The Bible is Modern" articulates Rhys's belief that artistic style is inseparable from cultural training and reveals her suspicion about English culture and her understanding of herself as not-English.

In selecting critical essays for this edition, I have tried to give a sense of the wide interest this novel has generated and the variety of interpretations it has inspired. I have introduced this section with the poem "Jean Rhys" by Derek Walcott, Nobel Laureate from the Caribbean nation St. Lucia, since it offers a tribute to Rhys's vision, which was sharpened by her own status as both native and alien, as well as a contemporary view of the Victorian white settler class Rhys preserved in her novel. Michael Thorpe's essay was one of the first of many articles to focus on the relationship between Charlotte Brontë's *Jane Eyre* and Jean Rhys's use of that material in *Wide Sargasso Sea*. The work of Wilson Harris, Sandra Drake, and Mary Lou Emery has contributed to placing Rhys's novel in the context of Caribbean cosmology and intellectual traditions. Lee Erwin, Caroline Rody, and Mona Fayad focus on the relationship among narrative form, female subjectivity, and feminist theory. The selections by Gayatri Chakravorty Spivak, Benita Parry, and myself highlight a variety of questions regarding colonial domination and resistance. Although I have not been able to include many important essays, I hope that references made to them in the essays I have selected will provide guidance for further reading. For instance, Kenneth Ramchand's article refers to the important issues raised by Edward Kamau Brathwaite, Wally Look Lai, and John Hearn about the meaning of Caribbean identity and the definition of Caribbean literature. The selected bibliography is designed to direct readers to other important articles about *Wide Sargasso Sea* and to books that treat the novel in the context of the full body of Rhys's work.

Faculty summer grants from the University of Oregon and the University of California at Santa Barbara allowed me the time to complete this edition. I am most grateful to Francis Wyndham for his permission to reprint the novel, letters, and excerpts from *Smile Please* and to publish material from the Jean Rhys Collection held in the McFarlin Library at the University of Tulsa. Lori Curtis, curator of Special Collections at the McFarlin Library, was particularly helpful during my visit and later in locating specific materials and photographs for this edition. Valerie Francis at the National Library of Jamaica helped locate and reproduce the plate "A Treadmill Scene in Jamaica." Recent scholarship by Peter Hulme, Veronica Marie Gregg, Teresa O'Connor, and Carole Angier concerning the historic background of the novel and the biographical specificities of Rhys's West Indian family history has been especially useful to me in glossing the text. I am grateful to Susan Johnson-Roehr and Rachel Adams, who provided superb research assistance. For their help in identifying various references in the text I thank June Bobb, Jessica Harris, Peter Hulme, Steven Kruger, Daniel Pope, and Angela Smith. I have appreciated the opportunity to work on this edition and thank Carol Bemis and Kate Lovelady at W. W. Norton for their expertise and their careful attention to detail. I am grateful as always to Mary Wood and Eli Raiskin-Wood for giving me the space and time to think and write about literature as provocative as this novel.

The Text of
WIDE SARGASSO SEA*

---

* The Sargasso Sea is an oval-shaped area of the North Atlantic Sea, bordered by the Gulf
Stream and encompassing the Bermuda Islands. It is characterized by weak currents, very
little wind, and a free-floating mass of seaweed called Sargassum. It was mentioned by Chris-
topher Columbus, who crossed it in 1492. The area gave rise to many legends surrounding
the fate of ships that supposedly lost their way in the weeds, became entangled, and were
never heard from again. In contrast to the unfounded fears of later navigators, Columbus
interpreted the floating vegetation as a sign that land was near (see Carson, pp. 117–19).
Rhys also considered naming the novel "Gold Sargasso Sea," after the title of a Creole song
written by her cousin from St. Lucia.

Introduction

Francis Wyndham

Jean Rhys was born at Roseau, Dominica, one of the Windward Islands, and spent her childhood there. Her father was a Welsh doctor and her mother a Creole—that is, a white West Indian. At the age of sixteen she came to England, where she spent the First World War. Then she married a Dutch poet and for ten years lived a rootless, wandering life on the Continent, mainly in Paris and Vienna. This was during the 1920s, and the essence of the artist's life in Europe at that time is contained in her first book, *The Left Bank* (Cape, 1927), which was described on the dust-jacket as 'sketches and studies of present-day Bohemian Paris'. In an enthusiastic preface, Ford Madox Ford comments on 'a terrifying instinct and a terrific—an almost lurid!—passion for stating the case of the underdog . . .' He goes on: 'When I, lately, edited a periodical, Miss Rhys sent in several communications with which I was immensely struck, and of which I published as many as I could. What struck me on the technical side . . . was the singular instinct for form possessed by this young lady, an instinct for form being possessed by singularly few writers of English and by almost no English women writers.' There is something patronizing about this preface (Ford was, in literal fact, her patron) but he must be credited with recognizing, so early in her career, the main elements which (increasing in intensity as her art developed) were to place her among the purest writers of our time. These are her 'passion for stating the case of the underdog' and her 'singular instinct for form'—a rare, but necessary combination. Without the instinct, the passion might so easily be either sentimental or sensational; without the passion, the instinct might lead to only formal beauty; together, they result in original art, at the same time exquisite and deeply disturbing.

It is likely that Ford Madox Ford was somewhat taken aback by his protégée's next book, a novel published in England as *Postures* (Chatto & Windus, 1928) and in the USA as *Quartet* (Simon & Schuster)—it is the American title that Miss Rhys prefers. The character of H. J. Heidler, a cold-eyed anglicized German dilettante, may have been in part suggested by Ford himself. In *Quartet* we find the first embodiment of the Jean Rhys heroine: for essentially the first four novels deal with

3

the same woman at different stages of her life, although her name and minor details of her circumstances alter from volume to volume. Marya Zelli has been a chorus girl in England and is now (the year is 1926) adrift in Montparnasse with a charming, feckless Pole whom she has married. This aimless, passive existence is suddenly disrupted when her husband is sent to prison. She is befriended by the Heidlers: a middle-aged picture-dealer and his very English, rather bossily 'emancipated' wife. It is taken for granted by this couple that Marya should become the husband's mistress. She is at first revolted by him, and then falls passionately in love with him: throughout she views him with a kind of hypnotized terror. The story describes the grisly *ménage à trois* that ensues (briskly broadminded wife, selfish petulant lover and their be-wildered, uncomfortably candid victim) until the husband comes out of prison. Numbed by misery, Marya mismanages the situation and loses both men. The actual writing of *Quartet* betrays a few uncertain-ties that were later eliminated from Miss Rhys's style, but it is conceived with that mixture of quivering immediacy and glassy objectivity that is among her most extraordinary distinctions.

After Leaving Mr Mackenzie (Cape, 1930) also starts in Paris, about the year 1928. Julia Martin has been pensioned off by an ex-lover and is leading a lonely, dream-like life in a cheap hotel. One morning the weekly cheque from Mr Mackenzie's solicitor arrives with a letter ex-plaining that it is to be the last. Julia has no money, and is losing confidence in her power to attract men. She decides to visit London, to look up former lovers and ask them for money. The visit (spent in boarding-houses at Bayswater and Notting Hill Gate) is not a success. She is met with patronizing incomprehension, with exasperation and moral disapproval. She has an affair with a young man called Mr Hors-field which goes farcically wrong; she returns to Paris to face an empty, threatening future. The novel is written in the third person; it has a clear, bitter quality, but it does not reach so deep into the central char-acter as the two that followed it, in which the heroines tell their own stories.

Jean Rhys returned to England after writing this book, and it is there that *Voyage in the Dark* (Constable, 1934) is set: the date, however, revealed casually half-way through, is 1914. Anna Morgan, who is nine-teen, is touring the provinces in the chorus of a pantomime. Memories of her childhood on a West Indian island, of kind coloured servants and tropical beauty, form a poignant accompaniment to her adventures in an icy, suspicious land. At Southsea she is picked up by a man called Walter Jeffries; he seduces her and offers to keep her. She falls in love with him ('You shut the door and you pull the curtains and then it's as long as a thousand years and yet so soon ended'); she moves, a shivering dreaming creature, to rooms near Chalk Farm. But her lover's house in Green Street is 'dark and cold and not friendly to me. Sneering faintly, sneering discreetly, as a servant would. Who's this? Where on earth did he pick her up?' And Mr Jeffries is clearly made uneasy by her absent manner, and sometimes shocked by her sudden directness. When he is tired of her, his handsome cousin Victor tells her so in a letter. 'My dear Infant, I am writing this in the country, and I can assure you that when you get into a garden and smell the flowers and all that all this rather beastly sort of love simply doesn't matter. However, you will think I am preaching at you, so I will shut up. . . . Have you kept any of the letters Walter wrote to you? If so you ought to send them back.' Stunned by this *coup de grâce* (although she has always expected it), Anna drifts into prostitution: in its treatment of a subject often falsified in fiction, this part of the book stands comparison with the novels of Charles Louis Philippe, and with Godard's film *Vivre sa Vie*. The story ends with Anna recovering from an abortion to hear the doctor say, 'She'll be all right. Ready to start all over again in no time, I've no doubt.'

In the next and most alarming instalment, *Good Morning, Midnight* (Constable, 1939), we see Sasha Jansen revisiting Paris in 1937, over forty, mistrustful of the men she tries to attract, expecting insults but unarmed against them, trying, as she says, to drink herself to death. Some restaurants may not be entered, because of the memories they inspire; the atmosphere of others is subtly hostile; the effort needed to buy a hat she cannot afford, to dye her hair, to follow up a promising encounter, is almost too much for her. Sasha meets a young man who turns out to be a gigolo, deceived by her fur coat into thinking her a rich woman. They embark on a complicated relationship, both at cross purposes. Sasha wants to work off on this boy her resentment at all men; she enjoys watching his desperate anxiety to please her, planning her revenge. 'This is where I might be able to get some of my own back. You talk to them, you pretend to sympathize; then, just at the moment when they are not expecting it, you say: "Go to Hell".' The gigolo is not so easy to shake off; he seems to be planning some sort of revenge of his own. What starts as mutual teasing becomes mutual torture. This involved episode is worked out with great subtlety; its climax, which brings the novel to an end, is brilliantly written and indescribably unnerving to read.

Sasha is the culmination of Jean Rhys's composite heroine. Although she is aggressively unhappy, she is always good company; her self-knowledge is exact, her observation of others comical and freezing. She is often unreasonable, and at moments one even pities the well-meaning men who found her so difficult to deal with. But she is not malicious: pity extends beyond herself to embrace all other sufferers. For her suffering transcends its cause. This is not only a study of a lonely, ageing woman, who has been deserted by husbands and lovers and has taken to drink; it is the tragedy of a distinguished mind and a generous nature that have gone unappreciated in a conventional, uni-maginative world. A victim of men's incomprehension of women, a symptom of women's mistrust of men, Sasha belongs to a universal type that is seldom well written about; for the writer must treat her, as Miss Rhys does, with understanding and restraint.

After *Good Morning, Midnight*, Jean Rhys disappeared and her five books went out of print. Although these had enjoyed a critical success, their true quality had never been appreciated. The reason for this is simple: they were ahead of their age, both in spirit and in style. One has only to compare Miss Rhys's early books, written during the 1920s, with contemporary work by Katherine Mansfield, Aldous Huxley, Jean Cocteau, and other celebrated writers of the period, to be struck by how little the actual text has 'dated': the style belongs to today. More important, the novels of the 1930s are much closer in *feeling* to life as it is lived and understood in the 1960s than to the accepted attitudes of their time. The elegant surface and the paranoid content, the brutal honesty of the feminine psychology and the muted nostalgia for lost beauty, all create an effect which is peculiarly modern.

The few people who remembered their admiration for these books, and those even fewer who (like myself) were introduced to them later and with great difficulty managed to obtain second-hand copies, for a while formed a small but passionate band. But nobody could find her; and nobody would reprint the novels. Then, as the result of a dra-matized version of *Good Morning, Midnight* broadcast on the Third Programme in 1958, she was finally traced to an address in Cornwall. She had a collection of unpublished stories, written during and im-mediately after the Second World War, and she was at work on a novel.

Of these stories, *Till September Petronella, The Day They Burned the Books* and *Tigers are Better Looking* have since been published in *The London Magazine* (which also printed a new, long story, *Let Them Call it Jazz*, written in 1961); *Outside the Machine* appeared in the sixth edition of *Winter's Tales* (Macmillan, 1960) and *A Solid House* in an anthology entitled *Voices* (Michael Joseph, 1963). *I Spy a Stranger, The Sound of the River, The Lotus* and *Temps Perdi* were published in the eighth, ninth, eleventh and twelfth editions of *Art and Literature*.

For many years, Jean Rhys has been haunted by the figure of the first Mrs Rochester—the mad wife in *Jane Eyre*. The present novel—completed at last after much revision and agonized rejection of earlier versions—is her story. Not, of course, literally so: it is in no sense a pastiche of Charlotte Brontë and exists in its own right, quite inde-pendent of *Jane Eyre*. But the Brontë book provided the initial inspi-ration for an imaginative feat almost uncanny in its vivid intensity. From her personal knowledge of the West Indies, and her reading of their history, Miss Rhys knew about the mad Creole heiresses in the early nineteenth century, whose dowries were only an additional burden to them: products of an inbred, decadent, expatriate society, re-sented by the recently freed slaves whose superstitions they shared, they languished uneasily in the oppressive beauty of their tropical surround-ings, ripe for exploitation. It is one of these that she has chosen for her latest heroine: and Antoinette Cosway seems a logical development of Marya, Julia, Anna and Sasha, who were also alienated, menaced, at odds with life.

The novel is divided into three parts. The first is told in the heroine's own words. In the second the young Mr Rochester describes his arrival in the West Indies, his marriage and its disastrous sequel. The last part is once more narrated by his wife: but the scene is now England, and she writes from the attic room in Thornfield Hall. . . .

All Jean Rhys's books to date have shared a modern, urban back-ground: Montparnasse cafés, cheap Left Bank hotels, Bloomsbury boarding-houses, furnished rooms near Notting Hill Gate are evoked with a bitter poetry that is entirely her own. Only the West Indian flashbacks in *Voyage in the Dark* and some episodes in *The Left Bank* strike a different note—one of regret for innocent sensuality in a lush, beguiling land. In *Wide Sargasso Sea*, which is set in Jamaica and Dominica during the 1830s, she returns to that spiritual country as to a distant dream: and discovers it, for all its beauty (and she conjures up this beauty with haunting perfection) to have been a nightmare.

F.W.

Part One

They say when trouble comes close ranks, and so the white people did. But we were not in their ranks. The Jamaican ladies had never approved of my mother, 'because she pretty like pretty self' Christophine said.[1]

She was my father's second wife, far too young for him they thought, and, worse still, a Martinique girl.[2] When I asked her why so few people came to see us, she told me that the road from Spanish Town[3] to Coulibri Estate[4] where we lived was very bad and that road repairing was now a thing of the past. (My father, visitors, horses, feeling safe in bed—all belonged to the past.)

Another day I heard her talking to Mr Luttrell, our neighbour and her only friend. 'Of course they have their own misfortunes. Still waiting for this compensation the English promised when the Emancipation Act was passed. Some will wait for a long time.'[5]

How could she know that Mr Luttrell would be the first who grew tired of waiting? One calm evening he shot his dog, swam out to sea and was gone for always. No agent came from England to look after

1. "Self" provides emphasis in Caribbean English: "She is pretty like prettiness itself."
2. In 1839 Martinique was a French colony and Jamaica was an English colony. France and England were political, economic, cultural, and religious rivals both in Europe and in the Caribbean.
3. Spanish Town, named for its Spanish founders in 1525, was the capital of Jamaica from 1534 to 1872, when the capital became Kingston. Jamaica was captured from the Spanish in 1655 and became a British colony in 1670.
4. Although this fictional estate is set in Jamaica, Rhys knew a Coulibri Estate in Dominica next to Geneva, her great-grandmother's ancestral home. The name Coulibri derives from a Carib word for the Antillean Crested Hummingbird, and it is used generally for several varieties of hummingbirds. At the time the Spanish arrived, the Caribs, native to northern South America, had driven the more peaceful indigenous Arawaks out of the Lesser Antilles and were expanding their conquest with attacks on other islands. Unlike the Arawaks, the Caribs, depicted by the Europeans as a savage, ferocious, and cannibalistic people, were able to maintain territory for centuries. Because of its mountainous terrain, Dominica became a stronghold for Carib resistance.
5. Although Britain ended its slave trade in 1807, slavery itself was not abolished until Britain's Parliament approved the Emancipation Act in 1833 outlawing slavery in Britain and all its colonies. The Act took effect a year later. Between 1834 and 1838 former slaves in the colonies were forced to work under a so-called apprenticeship system, after which slave-owners were compensated monetarily for each slave; considered to be property, the slaves themselves received no compensation. Jean Rhys's mother's family, the Lockharts, also waited in vain for compensation, and the family plantation in Dominica, Geneva, decayed after losing its slave labor. About her Scottish great-grandfather, James Lockhart, Rhys wrote, "He died before the Emancipation Act was passed and as he was a slave owner the Lockharts, even in my day, were never very popular. That's putting it mildly" (Jean Rhys, *Smile Please* [hereafter referred to as *SP*], p. 25).

9

his property—Nelson's Rest it was called—and strangers from Spanish Town rode up to gossip and discuss the tragedy.

'Live at Nelson's Rest? Not for love or money. An unlucky place.'

Mr Luttrell's house was left empty, shutters banging in the wind. Soon the black people said it was haunted, they wouldn't go near it. And no one came near us.

I got used to a solitary life, but my mother still planned and hoped—perhaps she had to hope every time she passed a looking glass.

She still rode about every morning not caring that the black people stood about in groups to jeer at her, especially after her riding clothes grew shabby (they notice clothes, they know about money).

Then one day, very early, I saw her horse lying down under the frangipani tree.[6] I went up to him but he was not sick, he was dead and his eyes were black with flies. I ran away and did not speak of it for I thought if I told no one it might not be true. But later that day, Godfrey found him, he had been poisoned. 'Now we are marooned,'[7] my mother said, 'now what will become of us?'

Godfrey said, 'I can't watch the horse night and day. I too old now. When the old time go, let it go. No use to grab at it. The Lord make no distinction between black and white, black and white the same for Him. Rest yourself in peace for the righteous are not forsaken.' But she couldn't. She was young. How could she not try for all the things that had gone so suddenly, so without warning. 'You're blind when you want to be blind,' she said ferociously, 'and you're deaf when you want to be deaf. The old hypocrite,' she kept saying. 'He knew what they were going to do.' 'The devil prince of this world,' Godfrey said, 'but this world don't last so long for mortal man.'

She persuaded a Spanish Town doctor to visit my younger brother Pierre who staggered when he walked and couldn't speak distinctly. I don't know what the doctor told her or what she said to him but he never came again and after that she changed. Suddenly, not gradually. She grew thin and silent, and at last she refused to leave the house at all.

Our garden was large and beautiful as that garden in the Bible—the

<hr/>

6. Also called *Plumieria*, a small tree native to the West Indies with flowers that smell very sweet, especially at night.

7. In Jamaica, the word "maroons" referred to the runaway slaves and their descendants who escaped to the mountains and lived free in small communities; due to successful guerrilla techniques by these fugitives, British soldiers called the Cockpit Country region of Jamaica "The Land of Look Behind." The English term "maroons" comes from the Spanish "cimarrones," which means "wild and untamed," or from "marrano," meaning "wild boar." Annette's feeling of isolation can be understood by looking at the Jamaican population census of 1844 in which out of 377,433 people only 15,776, or 4 percent, were identified as white. When Rhys grew up in Dominica whites were 1 percent of the total population.

tree of life grew there.[8] But it had gone wild. The paths were overgrown and a smell of dead flowers mixed with the fresh living smell. Underneath the tree ferns, tall as forest tree ferns, the light was green. Orchids flourished out of reach or for some reason not to be touched. One was snaky looking, another like an octopus with long thin brown tentacles bare of leaves hanging from a twisted root. Twice a year the octopus orchid flowered—then not an inch of tentacle showed. It was a bell-shaped mass of white, mauve, deep purples, wonderful to see. The scent was very sweet and strong. I never went near it.

All Coulibri Estate had gone wild like the garden, gone to bush. No more slavery—why should *anybody* work? This never saddened me. I did not remember the place when it was prosperous.

My mother usually walked up and down the *glacis*, a paved roofed-in terrace which ran the length of the house and sloped upwards to a clump of bamboos. Standing by the bamboos she had a clear view to the sea, but anyone passing could stare at her. They stared, sometimes they laughed. Long after the sound was far away and faint she kept her eyes shut and her hands clenched. A frown came between her black eyebrows, deep—it might have been cut with a knife. I hated this frown and once I touched her forehead trying to smooth it. But she pushed me away, not roughly but calmly, coldly, without a word, as if she had decided once and for all that I was useless to her. She wanted to sit with Pierre or walk where she pleased without being pestered, she wanted peace and quiet. I was old enough to look after myself. 'Oh, let me alone,' she would say, 'let me alone,' and after I knew that she talked aloud to herself I was a little afraid of her.

So I spent most of my time in the kitchen which was in an outbuilding some way off. Christophine slept in the little room next to it.

When evening came she sang to me if she was in the mood. I couldn't always understand her patois songs—she also came from Martinique—but she taught me the one that meant 'The little ones grow old, the children leave us, will they come back?' and the one about the cedar tree flowers which only last for a day.

The music was gay but the words were sad and her voice often quavered and broke on the high note. 'Adieu.' Not adieu as we said it, but *à dieu*,[9] which made more sense after all. The loving man was lonely, the girl was deserted, the children never came back. Adieu.

8. The Garden of Eden. From Columbus's writings on, the New World was often described as "the Terrestrial Paradise," the Garden eastward of Eden. The "precivilized" topos inspired ambivalent descriptions by European writers ranging from the idyllic to the monstrous. Two supernatural trees, one of knowledge and the other of life, are mentioned in the biblical description of the garden of Eden (Genesis 2:8–3:24). The tree of life bestowed immortality on those who ate from it. Adam and Eve were banished from Eden after eating from the tree of knowledge.
9. "To God," as opposed to "farewell."

Her songs were not like Jamaican songs, and she was not like the other women.

She was much blacker—blue-black with a thin face and straight features. She wore a black dress, heavy gold ear-rings and a yellow handkerchief—carefully tied with the two high points in front. No other negro woman wore black, or tied her handkerchief Martinique fashion. She had a quiet voice and a quiet laugh (when she did laugh), and though she could speak good English if she wanted to, and French as well as patois,[1] she took care to talk as they talked. But they would have nothing to do with her and she never saw her son who worked in Spanish Town. She had only one friend—a woman called Maillotte,[2] and Maillotte was not a Jamaican.

The girls from the bayside who sometimes helped with the washing and cleaning were terrified of her. That, I soon discovered, was why they came at all—for she never paid them. Yet they brought presents of fruit and vegetables and after dark I often heard low voices from the kitchen.

So I asked about Christophine. Was she very old? Had she always been with us?

'She was your father's wedding present to me—one of his presents. He thought I would be pleased with a Martinique girl. I don't know how old she was when they brought her to Jamaica, quite young. I don't know how old she is now. Does it matter? Why do you pester and bother me about all these things that happened long ago? Christophine stayed with me because she wanted to stay. She had her own very good reasons you may be sure. I dare say we would have died if she'd turned against us and that would have been a better fate. To die and be forgotten and at peace. Not to know that one is abandoned, lied about, helpless. All the ones who died—who says a good word for them now?'

'Godfrey stayed too,' I said. 'And Sass.'

'They stayed,' she said angrily, 'because they wanted somewhere to sleep and something to eat. That boy Sass! When his mother pranced off and left him here—a great deal *she* cared—why he was a little skeleton. Now he's growing into a big strong boy and away he goes. We shan't see him again. Godfrey is a rascal. These new ones aren't too kind to old people and he knows it. That's why he stays. Doesn't do a

1. A French word also used in English to refer to any dialect that develops out of contact between the language of a colonizing people (i.e., the English, French, Spanish, Portuguese, or Dutch) and that of a colonized people (i.e., West Africans or Native Americans). Until recently, "patois" was viewed as any non-Standard variety of a European language and the term was usually derogatory, implying low social status of the speaker and of the dialect. In both English and French, "Creole" is a word carrying similar connotations, although it also refers to people themselves (see note 7, p. 10).
2. In Rhys's 1934 novel *Voyage in the Dark*, the character Anna remembers reading on an old slave list, "Maillotte Boyd, aged 18, mulatto, house servant."

thing but eat enough for a couple of horses. Pretends he's deaf. He isn't deaf—he doesn't want to hear. What a devil he is!'

'Why don't you tell him to find somewhere else to live?' I said and she laughed.

'He wouldn't go. He'd probably try to force us out. I've learned to let sleeping curs lie,' she said.

'Would Christophine go if you told her to?' I thought. But I didn't say it. I was afraid to say it.

It was too hot that afternoon. I could see the beads of perspiration on her upper lip and the dark circles under her eyes. I started to fan her, but she turned her head away. She might rest if I left her alone, she said.

Once I would have gone back quietly to watch her asleep on the blue sofa—once I made excuses to be near her when she brushed her hair, a soft black cloak to cover me, hide me, keep me safe.

But not any longer. Not any more.

These were all the people in my life—my mother and Pierre, Christophine, Godfrey, and Sass who had left us.

I never looked at any strange negro. They hated us. They called us white cockroaches. Let sleeping dogs lie. One day a little girl followed me singing, 'Go away white cockroach, go away, go away.' I walked fast, but she walked faster. 'White cockroach, go away, go away. Nobody want you. Go away.'

When I was safely home I sat close to the old wall at the end of the garden. It was covered with green moss soft as velvet and I never wanted to move again. Everything would be worse if I moved. Christophine found me there when it was nearly dark, and I was so stiff she had to help me to get up. She said nothing, but next morning Tia was in the kitchen with her mother Maillotte, Christophine's friend. Soon Tia was my friend and I met her nearly every morning at the turn of the road to the river.

Sometimes we left the bathing pool at midday, sometimes we stayed till late afternoon. Then Tia would light a fire (fires always lit for her, sharp stones did not hurt her bare feet, I never saw her cry). We boiled green bananas in an old iron pot and ate them with our fingers out of a calabash[3] and after we had eaten she slept at once. I could not sleep, but I wasn't quite awake as I lay in the shade looking at the pool—deep and dark green under the trees, brown-green if it had rained, but a bright sparkling green in the sun. The water was so clear that you could see the pebbles at the bottom of the shallow part. Blue and white and striped red. Very pretty. Late or early we parted at the turn of the

---

3. A large dried gourd of the local calabash tree; they were used as bowls.

road. My mother never asked me where I had been or what I had done.

Christophine had given me some new pennies which I kept in the pocket of my dress. They dropped out one morning so I put them on a stone. They shone like gold in the sun and Tia stared. She had small eyes, very black, set deep in her head.

Then she bet me three of the pennies that I couldn't turn a somersault under water 'like you say you can.'

'Of course I can.'

'I never see you do it,' she said. 'Only talk.'

'Bet you all the money I can,' I said.

But after one somersault I still turned and came up choking. Tia laughed and told me that it certainly look like I drown dead that time. Then she picked up the money.

'I did do it,' I said when I could speak, but she shook her head. I hadn't done it good and besides pennies didn't buy much. Why did I look at her like that?

'Keep them then, you cheating nigger,' I said, for I was tired, and the water I had swallowed made me feel sick. 'I can get more if I want to.'

That's not what she hear, she said. She hear all we poor like beggar. We ate salt fish[4]—no money for fresh fish. That old house so leaky, you run with calabash to catch water when it rain. Plenty white people in Jamaica. Real white people, they got gold money. They didn't look at us, nobody see them come near us. Old time white people nothing but white nigger now, and black nigger better than white nigger.[5]

I wrapped myself in my torn towel and sat on a stone with my back to her, shivering cold. But the sun couldn't warm me. I wanted to go home. I looked round and Tia had gone. I searched for a long time before I could believe that she had taken my dress—not my underclothes, she never wore any—but my dress, starched, ironed, clean that morning. She had left me hers and I put it on at last and walked home in the blazing sun feeling sick, hating her. I planned to get round the back of the house to the kitchen, but passing the stables I stopped to stare at three strange horses and my mother saw me and called. She was on the *glacis* with two young ladies and a gentleman. Visitors! I dragged up the steps unwillingly—I had longed for visitors once, but that was years ago.

They were very beautiful I thought and they wore such beautiful clothes that I looked away down at the flagstones and when they laughed—the gentleman laughed the loudest—I ran into the house, into my bedroom. There I stood with my back against the door and I

4. Salted, dried cod imported from Canada as standard food for slaves and wages for apprentices. The colloquial connotations of the term "salt fish" include low-class status and low quality of character, as well as a poor diet.
5. Refers to the drop in economic and social status of former slave-owners and challenges the myths of racial purity maintained by the settler class.

could feel my heart all through me. I heard them talking and I heard
them leave. I came out of my room and my mother was sitting on the
blue sofa. She looked at me for some time before she said that I had
behaved very oddly. My dress was even dirtier than usual.

'It's Tia's dress.'

'But why are you wearing Tia's dress? Tia? Which one of them is
Tia?'

Christophine, who had been in the pantry listening, came at once and
was told to find a clean dress for me. 'Throw away that thing. Burn it.'

Then they quarrelled.

Christophine said I had no clean dress. 'She got two dresses, wash
and wear. You want clean dress to drop from heaven? Some people
crazy in truth.'

'She must have another dress,' said my mother. 'Somewhere.' But
Christophine told her loudly that it shameful. She run wild, she grow
up worthless. And nobody care.

My mother walked over to the window. ('Marooned,' said her straight
narrow back, her carefully coiled hair. 'Marooned.')

'She has an old muslin dress. Find that.'

While Christophine scrubbed my face and tied my plaits[6] with a fresh
piece of string, she told me that those were the new people at Nelson's
Rest. They called themselves Luttrell, but English or not English they
were not like old Mr Luttrell. 'Old Mr Luttrell spit in their face if he
see how they look at you. Trouble walk into the house this day. Trouble
walk in.'

The old muslin dress was found and it tore as I forced it on. She
didn't notice.

No more slavery! She had to laugh! 'These new ones have Letter of
the Law. Same thing. They got magistrate. They got fine. They got jail
house and chain gang. They got tread machine to mash up people's
feet. New ones worse than old ones—more cunning, that's all.'[7]

All that evening my mother didn't speak to me or look at me and I
thought, 'She is ashamed of me, what Tia said is true.'

I went to bed early and slept at once. I dreamed that I was walking
in the forest. Not alone. Someone who hated me was with me, out of
sight. I could hear heavy footsteps coming closer and though I struggled

6. Braids.
7. The emancipation legislation imposed upon newly freed slaves a so-called apprenticeship
period. Their former masters were required to provide apprentice laborers with food, clothing,
housing, and medical care or to give land on which apprentices could cultivate their own
produce during their "free time." Apprentice laborers were not free to chose their "employers"
or to negotiate their wages. The apprenticeship was, in fact, a new form of slavery under the
jurisdiction of special magistrates paid by the government, and the punishments for alleged
infractions were severe, at times more so than under slavery (see note 9, p. 96). "These new
ones" refers to English entrepreneurs who came to the West Indies to take advantage of the
depressed sugar market and to buy the estates and plantations being sold cheaply after
emancipation.

and screamed I could not move. I woke crying. The covering sheet was on the floor and my mother was looking down at me.

'Did you have a nightmare?'

'Yes, a bad dream.'

She sighed and covered me up. 'You were making such a noise. I must go to Pierre, you've frightened him.'

I lay thinking, 'I am safe. There is the corner of the bedroom door and the friendly furniture. There is the tree of life in the garden and the wall green with moss. The barrier of the cliffs and the high mountains. And the barrier of the sea. I am safe. I am safe from strangers.'

The light of the candle in Pierre's room was still there when I slept again. I woke next morning knowing that nothing would be the same. It would change and go on changing.

I don't know how she got money to buy the white muslin and the pink. Yards of muslin. She may have sold her last ring, for there was one left. I saw it in her jewel box—that, and a locket with a shamrock inside. They were mending and sewing first thing in the morning and still sewing when I went to bed. In a week she had a new dress and so had I.

The Luttrells lent her a horse, and she would ride off very early and not come back till late next day—tired out because she had been to a dance or a moonlight picnic. She was gay and laughing—younger than I had ever seen her and the house was sad when she had gone.

So I too left it and stayed away till dark. I was never long at the bathing pool, I never met Tia.

I took another road, past the old sugar works and the water wheel that had not turned for years. I went to parts of Coulibri that I had not seen, where there was no road, no path, no track. And if the razor grass cut my legs and arms I would think 'It's better than people.' Black ants or red ones, tall nests swarming with white ants, rain that soaked me to the skin—once I saw a snake. All better than people.

Better. Better, better than people.

Watching the red and yellow flowers in the sun thinking of nothing, it was as if a door opened and I was somewhere else, something else. Not myself any longer.

I knew the time of day when though it is hot and blue and there are no clouds, the sky can have a very black look.

I was bridesmaid when my mother married Mr Mason[8] in Spanish Town. Christophine curled my hair. I carried a bouquet and everything

8. In *Jane Eyre*, Mr. Mason is Bertha's biological father and Richard Mason is her biological brother. By creating the new character of Mr. Cosway, Rhys introduces a distinction between the pre-emancipation plantocracy and the English who brought new capital to the ruined estates previously maintained by slave labor. By creating this new character, Rhys also introduces into the story Antoinette's larger "colored" family, including Mr. Cosway's sons Alexander and (perhaps) Daniel Cosway, who are Antoinette's half-brothers, and Sandi Cosway, her father's grandson, whom she calls "cousin."

I wore was new—even my beautiful slippers. But their eyes slid away from my hating face. I had heard what all these smooth smiling people said about her when she was not listening and they did not guess I was. Hiding from them in the garden when they visited Coulibri, I listened.

'A fantastic marriage and he will regret it. Why should a very wealthy man who could take his pick of all the girls in the West Indies, and many in England too probably?' 'Why *probably?*' the other voice said. '*Certainly.*' 'Then why should he marry a widow without a penny to her name and Coulibri a wreck of a place? Emancipation troubles killed old Cosway? Nonsense—the estate was going downhill for years before that. He drank himself to death. Many's the time when—well! And all those women! She never did anything to stop him—she encouraged him. Presents and smiles for the bastards every Christmas. Old customs? Some old customs are better dead and buried. Her new husband will have to spend a pretty penny before the house is fit to live in—leaks like a sieve. And what about the stables and the coach house dark as pitch, and the servants' quarters and the six-foot snake I saw with my own eyes curled up on the privy seat last time I was here. Alarmed? I screamed. Then that horrible old man she harbours came along, doubled up with laughter. As for those two children—the boy an idiot kept out of sight and mind and the girl going the same way in my opinion—a *lowering* expression.'

'Oh I agree,' the other one said, 'but Annette is such a pretty woman. And what a dancer. Reminds me of that song "light as cotton blossom on the something breeze", or is it air? I forget.'

Yes, what a dancer—that night when they came home from their honeymoon in Trinidad[9] and they danced on the *glacis* to no music. There was no need for music when she danced. They stopped and she leaned backwards over his arm, down till her black hair touched the flagstones—still down, down. Then up again in a flash, laughing. She made it look so easy—as if anyone could do it, and he kissed her—a long kiss. I was there that time too but they had forgotten me and soon I wasn't thinking of them. I was remembering that woman saying 'Dance! He didn't come to the West Indies to dance—he came to make money as they all do. Some of the big estates are going cheap, and one unfortunate's loss is always a clever man's gain. No, the whole thing is a mystery. It's evidently useful to keep a Martinique obeah woman[1] on

9. The most southerly of the Caribbean islands, fifteen miles from the north coast of Venezuela, governed by Britain from 1802 until independence in 1962. Throughout the colonial period many plantation owners were absentee landlords of properties in a number of Caribbean islands.
1. A woman who practices obeah as a secret profession and has paying clients. Obeah is a system of beliefs and practices, African in origin, through which a practitioner works to gain for her/ his client success, money, love, cures for illnesses, and protection, as well as cause trouble for the client's enemies. As a white Creole, Rhys was introduced to the symbols and beliefs of obeah, Vodou, and zombis early in her life by the cook at Bona Vista, Ann Tewitt, and her nurse, Meta, who introduced her to the stories and rituals of obeah (*SP*, pp. 15–16, 23).

the premises.' She meant Christophine. She said it mockingly, not meaning it, but soon other people were saying it—and meaning it.

While the repairs were being done and they were in Trinidad, Pierre and I stayed with Aunt Cora in Spanish Town.

Mr Mason did not approve of Aunt Cora, an ex-slave-owner who had escaped misery, a flier in the face of Providence.

'Why did she do nothing to help you?'

I told him that her husband was English and didn't like us and he said, 'Nonsense.'

'It isn't nonsense, they lived in England and he was angry if she wrote to us. He hated the West Indies. When he died not long ago she came home, before that what could she do? *She* wasn't rich.'

'That's her story. I don't believe it. A frivolous woman. In your mother's place I'd resent her behaviour.'

'None of you understand about us,'[2] I thought.

Coulibri looked the same when I saw it again, although it was clean and tidy, no grass between the flagstones, no leaks. But it didn't feel the same. Sass had come back and I was glad. They can *smell* money, somebody said. Mr Mason engaged new servants—I didn't like any of them excepting Mannie the groom. It was their talk about Christophine that changed Coulibri, not the repairs or the new furniture or the strange faces. Their talk about Christophine and obeah changed it.

I knew her room so well—the pictures of the Holy Family and the prayer for a happy death.[3] She had a bright patchwork counterpane, a broken-down press for her clothes, and my mother had given her an old rocking-chair.[4]

Yet one day when I was waiting there I was suddenly very much afraid. The door was open to the sunlight, someone was whistling near the stables, but I was afraid. I was certain that hidden in the room (behind the old black press?) there was a dead man's dried hand, white chicken feathers, a cock with its throat cut, dying slowly, slowly. Drop by drop the blood was falling into a red basin and I imagined I could hear it. No one had ever spoken to me about obeah—but I knew what I would find if I dared to look. Then Christophine came in smiling and pleased to see me. Nothing alarming ever happened and I forgot, or told myself I had forgotten.

Mr Mason would laugh if he knew how frightened I had been. He

2. "Us" here refers to white Creoles. At this time "Creole" was used in the British Caribbean islands to refer to those of English or European descent born in the Caribbean (see note 7, p. 39).
3. This icon and prayer indicate that Christophine is a Catholic. Colonists and their descendants from the French colonies tended to be Catholic and gave their slaves religious instruction; the English colonists and their descendants tended to be Anglican, and while the planters were wary of teaching slaves Christian beliefs, nonconformist missionaries promoted their beliefs among the slaves.
4. A counterpane is a bedspread; a press is a dresser.

would laugh even louder than he did when my mother told him that she wished to leave Coulibri.

This began when they had been married for over a year. They always said the same things and I seldom listened to the argument now. I knew that we were hated—but to go away . . . for once I agreed with my stepfather. That was not possible.

'You must have some reason,' he would say, and she would answer 'I need a change' or 'We could visit Richard.' (Richard, Mr Mason's son by his first marriage, was at school in Barbados. He was going to England soon and we had seen very little of him.)

'An agent could look after this place. For the time being. The people here hate us. They certainly hate me.' Straight out she said that one day and it was then he laughed so heartily.

'Annette, be reasonable. You were the widow of a slave-owner, the daughter of a slave-owner, and you had been living here alone, with two children, for nearly five years when we met. Things were at their worst then. But you were never molested, never harmed.'

'How do you know that I was not harmed?' she said. 'We were so poor then,' she told him, 'we were something to laugh at. But we are not poor now,' she said. 'You are not a poor man. Do you suppose that they don't know all about your estate in Trinidad? And the Antigua property? They talk about us without stopping. They invent stories about you, and lies about me. They try to find out what we eat every day.'

'They are curious. It's natural enough. You have lived alone far too long, Annette. You imagine enmity which doesn't exist. Always one extreme or the other. Didn't you fly at me like a little wild cat when I said nigger. Not nigger, nor even negro. Black people I must say.'

'You don't like, or even recognize, the good in them,' she said, 'and you won't believe in the other side.'

'They're too damn lazy to be dangerous,' said Mr Mason. 'I know that.'

'They are more alive than you are, lazy or not, and they can be dangerous and cruel for reasons you wouldn't understand.'

'No, I don't understand,' Mr Mason always said. 'I don't understand at all.'

But she'd speak about going away again. Persistently. Angrily.

Mr Mason pulled up near the empty huts on our way home that evening. 'All gone to one of those dances,' he said. 'Young and old. How deserted the place looks.'

'We'll hear the drums if there is a dance.' I hoped he'd ride on quickly but he stayed by the huts to watch the sun go down, the sky and the sea were on fire when we left Bertrand Bay at last. From a long way off I saw the shadow of our house high up on its stone foundations. There was a smell of ferns and river water and I felt safe again, as if I was one of the righteous. (Godfrey said that we were not righteous. One day when he was drunk he told me that we were all damned and no use praying.)

'They've chosen a very hot night for their dance,' Mr Mason said, and Aunt Cora came on to the *glacis*. 'What dance? Where?'

'There is some festivity in the neighbourhood. The huts were abandoned. A wedding perhaps?'

'Not a wedding,' I said. 'There is never a wedding.' He frowned at me but Aunt Cora smiled.

When they had gone indoors I leaned my arms on the cool *glacis* railings and thought that I would never like him very much. I still called him 'Mr Mason' in my head. 'Goodnight white pappy,'[5] I said one evening and he was not vexed, he laughed. In some ways it was better before he came though he'd rescued us from poverty and misery. 'Only just in time too.' The black people did not hate us quite so much when we were poor. We were white but we had not escaped and soon we would be dead for we had no money left. What was there to hate?

Now it had started up again and worse than before, my mother knows but she can't make him believe it. I wish I could tell him that out here is not at all like English people think it is. I wish . . .

I could hear them talking and Aunt Cora's laugh. I was glad she was staying with us. And I could hear the bamboos shiver and creak though there was no wind. It had been hot and still and dry for days. The colours had gone from the sky, the light was blue and could not last long. The *glacis* was not a good place when night was coming, Christophine said. As I went indoors my mother was talking in an excited voice.

'Very well. As you refuse to consider it, I will go and take Pierre with me. You won't object to that, I hope?'

'You are perfectly right, Annette,' said Aunt Cora and that did surprise me. She seldom spoke when they argued.

Mr Mason also seemed surprised and not at all pleased.

'You talk so wildly,' he said. 'And you are so mistaken. Of course you can get away for a change if you wish it. I promise you.'

'You have promised that before,' she said. 'You don't keep your promises.'

He sighed. 'I feel very well here. However, we'll arrange something. Quite soon.'

'I will not stay at Coulibri any longer,' my mother said. 'It is not safe. It is not safe for Pierre.'

Aunt Cora nodded.

---

5. Jamaican slaves often referred to their masters as "father" or "big Pappy," not so much as a sign of respect as a veiled but mocking form of aggression. This term of address was usually reserved for the most naive of the masters, who would be flattered by it.

As it was late I ate with them instead of by myself as usual. Myra, one of the new servants, was standing by the sideboard, waiting to change the plates. We ate English food now, beef and mutton, pies and puddings.

I was glad to be like an English girl but I missed the taste of Christophine's cooking.

My stepfather talked about a plan to import labourers—coolies he called them—from the East Indies.[6] When Myra had gone out Aunt Cora said, 'I shouldn't discuss that if I were you. Myra is listening.'

'But the people here won't work. They don't want to work. Look at this place—it's enough to break your heart.'[7]

'Hearts have been broken,' she said. 'Be sure of that. I suppose you all know what you are doing.'

'Do you mean to say—'

'I said nothing, except that it would be wiser not to tell that woman your plans—necessary and merciful no doubt. I don't trust her.'

'Live here most of your life and know nothing about the people. It's astonishing. They are children—they wouldn't hurt a fly.'

'Unhappily children do hurt flies,'[8] said Aunt Cora.

Myra came in again looking mournful as she always did though she smiled when she talked about hell. Everyone went to hell, she told me, you had to belong to her sect to be saved and even then—just as well not to be too sure.[9] She had thin arms and big hands and feet and the handkerchief she wore round her head was always white. Never striped or a gay colour.

So I looked away from her at my favourite picture, 'The Miller's Daughter',[1] a lovely English girl with brown curls and blue eyes and a dress slipping off her shoulders. Then I looked across the white tablecloth and the vase of yellow roses at Mr Mason, so sure of himself, so without a doubt English. And at my mother, so without a doubt not English, but no white nigger either. Not my mother. Never had been. Never could be. Yes, she would have died, I thought, if she had not met him. And for the first time I was grateful and liked him. There are more ways than one of being happy, better perhaps to be peaceful and

---

6. Thirty-three thousand indentured laborers from East India were brought to Jamaica between 1839 and 1844. The conditions of such employment were at times very close to those of slavery.
7. Historical evidence shows that after emancipation the ex-slaves were extremely productive, many becoming small proprietors and landholders, contributing to the diversification of the British West Indian economy. Based on the decline of sugar production alone, the sugar planters began a campaign disparaging black labor and calling for the importation of mostly East Indian immigrant indentured laborers.
8. Cf. Shakespeare's King Lear (4.1.36–37): "As flies to wanton boys are we to th'gods: They kill us for their sport."
9. Like many of the ex-slaves in Jamaica, and unlike Christophine and Maillotte, Myra belongs to a nonconformist Christian sect.
1. After the popular 1832 poem by Alfred, Lord Tennyson, Poet Laureate of England from 1850 until his death in 1892.

contented and protected, as I feel now, peaceful for years and long years, and afterwards I may be saved whatever Myra says. (When I asked Christophine what happened when you died, she said, 'You want to know too much.') I remembered to kiss my stepfather goodnight. Once Aunt Cora had told me, 'He's very hurt because you never kiss him.'

'He does not look hurt,' I argued. 'Great mistake to go by looks,' she said, 'one way or the other.'

I went into Pierre's room which was next to mine, the last one in the house. The bamboos were outside his window. You could almost touch them. He still had a crib and he slept more and more, nearly all the time. He was so thin that I could lift him easily. Mr Mason had promised to take him to England later on, there he would be cured, made like other people. 'And how will you like that' I thought, as I kissed him. 'How will you like being made exactly like other people?' He looked happy asleep. But that will be later on. Later on. Sleep now. It was then I heard the bamboos creak again and a sound like whispering. I forced myself to look out of the window. There was a full moon but I saw nobody, nothing but shadows.

I left a light on the chair by my bed and waited for Christophine, for I liked to see her last thing. But she did not come, and as the candle burned down, the safe peaceful feeling left me. I wished I had a big Cuban dog to lie by my bed and protect me, I wished I had not heard a noise by the bamboo clump, or that I were very young again, for then I believed in my stick. It was not a stick, but a long narrow piece of wood, with two nails sticking out at the end, a shingle, perhaps. I picked it up soon after they killed our horse and I thought I can fight with this, if the worst comes to the worst I can fight to the end though the best ones fall and that is another song. Christophine knocked the nails out, but she let me keep the shingle and I grew very fond of it, I believed that no one could harm me when it was near me, to lose it would be a great misfortune. All this was long ago, when I was still babyish and sure that everything was alive, not only the river or the rain, but chairs, looking-glasses, cups, saucers, everything.

I woke up and it was still night and my mother was there. She said, 'Get up and dress yourself, and come downstairs quickly.' She was dressed, but she had not put up her hair and one of her plaits was loose. 'Quickly,' she said again, then she went into Pierre's room, next door. I heard her speak to Myra and I heard Myra answer her. I lay there, half asleep, looking at the lighted candle on the chest of drawers, till I heard a noise as though a chair had fallen over in the little room, then I got up and dressed.

The house was on different levels. There were three steps down from my bedroom and Pierre's to the dining-room and then three steps from the dining-room to the rest of the house, which we called 'downstairs.'

The folding doors of the dining-room were not shut and I could see that the big drawing-room was full of people. Mr Mason, my mother, Christophine and Mannie and Sass. Aunt Cora was sitting on the blue sofa in the corner now, wearing a black silk dress, her ringlets were carefully arranged. She looked very haughty, I thought. But Godfrey was not there, or Myra, or the cook, or any of the others.

'There is no reason to be alarmed,' my stepfather was saying as I came in. 'A handful of drunken negroes.' He opened the door leading to the *glacis* and walked out. 'What is all this,' he shouted. 'What do you want?' A horrible noise swelled up, like animals howling, but worse. We heard stones falling on to the *glacis*. He was pale when he came in again, but he tried to smile as he shut and bolted the door. 'More of them than I thought, and in a nasty mood too.[2] They will repent in the morning. I foresee gifts of tamarinds in syrup and ginger sweets tomorrow.'[3]

'Tomorrow will be too late,' said Aunt Cora, 'too late for ginger sweets or anything else.' My mother was not listening to either of them. She said, 'Pierre is asleep and Myra is with him, I thought it better to leave him in his own room, away from this horrible noise. I don't know. Perhaps.' She was twisting her hands together, her wedding ring fell off and rolled into a corner near the steps. My stepfather and Mannie both stooped for it, then Mannie straightened up and said, 'Oh, my God, they get at the back, they set fire to the back of the house.' He pointed to my bedroom door which I had shut after me, and smoke was rolling out from underneath.

I did not see my mother move she was so quick. She opened the door of my room and then again I did not see her, nothing but smoke. Mannie ran after her, so did Mr Mason but more slowly. Aunt Cora put her arms round me. She said, 'Don't be afraid, you are quite safe. We are all quite safe.' Just for a moment I shut my eyes and rested my head against her shoulder. She smelled of vanilla, I remember. Then there was another smell, of burned hair, and I looked and my mother was in the room carrying Pierre. It was her loose hair that had burned and was smelling like that.

I thought, Pierre is dead. He looked dead. He was white and he did not make a sound, but his head hung back over her arm as if he had no life at all and his eyes were rolled up so that you only saw the whites. My stepfather said, 'Annette, you are hurt—your hands . . .' But

2. Perhaps a reference to the 1844 census riots, called by the whites the "guerre nègre," which resulted from the belief that the census was to be used to reintroduce slavery as had been done in Haiti. In her autobiography, *Smile Please*, Rhys refers to her grandfather's estate house being burned by freed slaves in the 1830s after the Emancipation Act. Historical evidence, however, suggests that the house may have been looted then but not burned until 1932.

3. The tamarind tree, imported from Africa, produces pods whose pulp and seeds are boiled in sugar for a treat. There is a popular Barbadian legend of a tamarind tree that produced seeds in the shape of a human head following the hanging of a slave from that tree.

she did not even look at him. 'His crib was on fire,' she said to Aunt
Cora. 'The little room is on fire and Myra was not there. She has gone.
She was not there.'

'That does not surprise me at all,' said Aunt Cora. She laid Pierre
on the sofa, bent over him, then lifted up her skirt, stepped out of her
white petticoat and began to tear it into strips.

'She left him, she ran away and left him alone to die,' said my
mother, still whispering. So it was all the more dreadful when she began
to scream abuse at Mr Mason, calling him a fool, a cruel stupid fool.
'I told you,' she said, 'I told you what would happen again and again.'
Her voice broke, but still she screamed, 'You would not listen, you
sneered at me, you grinning hypocrite, you ought not to live either,
you know so much, don't you? Why don't you go out and ask them to
let you go? Say how innocent you are. Say you have always trusted
them.'

I was so shocked that everything was confused. And it happened
quickly. I saw Mannie and Sass staggering along with two large earth-
enware jars of water which were kept in the pantry. They threw the
water into the bedroom and it made a black pool on the floor, but the
smoke rolled over the pool. Then Christophine, who had run into my
mother's bedroom for the pitcher there, came back and spoke to my
aunt. 'It seems they have fired the other side of the house,' said Aunt
Cora. 'They must have climbed that tree outside. This place is going
to burn like tinder and there is nothing we can do to stop it. The sooner
we get out the better.'

Mannie said to the boy, 'You frightened?' Sass shook his head. 'Then
come on,' said Mannie. 'Out of my way,' he said and pushed Mr Mason
aside. Narrow wooden stairs led down from the pantry to the outbuildings, the kitchen, the servants' rooms, the stables. That was where they
were going. 'Take the child,' Aunt Cora told Christophine, 'and come.'

It was very hot on the *glacis* too, they roared as we came out, then
there was another roar behind us. I had not seen any flames, only smoke
and sparks, but now I saw tall flames shooting up to the sky, for the
bamboos had caught. There were some tree ferns near, green and
damp, one of those was smouldering too.

'Come quickly,' said Aunt Cora, and she went first, holding my hand.
Christophine followed, carrying Pierre, and they were quite silent as
we went down the *glacis* steps. But when I looked round for my mother
I saw that Mr Mason, his face crimson with heat, seemed to be dragging
her along and she was holding back, struggling. I heard him say, 'It's
impossible, too late now.'

'Wants her jewel case?' Aunt Cora said.

'Jewel case? Nothing so sensible,' bawled Mr Mason. 'She wanted to
go back for her damned parrot. I won't allow it.' She did not answer,
only fought him silently, twisting like a cat and showing her teeth.

Our parrot was called Coco, a green parrot. He didn't talk very well, he could say *Qui est là? Qui est là?* and answer himself *Ché Coco, Ché Coco*.[4] After Mr Mason clipped his wings he grew very bad tempered, and though he would sit quietly on my mother's shoulder, he darted at everyone who came near her and pecked their feet.

'Annette,' said Aunt Cora. 'They are laughing at you, do not allow them to laugh at you.' She stopped fighting then and he half supported, half pulled her after us, cursing loudly.

Still they were quiet and there were so many of them I could hardly see any grass or trees. There must have been many of the bay people but I recognized no one. They all looked the same, it was the same face repeated over and over, eyes gleaming, mouth half open to shout. We were past the mounting stone[5] when they saw Mannie driving the carriage round the corner. Sass followed, riding one horse and leading another. There was a ladies' saddle on the one he was leading.

Somebody yelled, 'But look the black Englishman! Look the white niggers!', and then they were all yelling. 'Look the white niggers! Look the damn white niggers!' A stone just missed Mannie's head, he cursed back at them and they cleared away from the rearing, frightened horses. 'Come on, for God's sake,' said Mr Mason. 'Get to the carriage, get to the horses.' But we could not move for they pressed too close round us. Some of them were laughing and waving sticks, some of the ones at the back were carrying flambeaux[6] and it was light as day. Aunt Cora held my hand very tightly and her lips moved but I could not hear because of the noise. And I was afraid, because I knew that the ones who laughed would be the worst. I shut my eyes and waited. Mr Mason stopped swearing and began to pray in a loud pious voice. The prayer ended, 'May Almighty God defend us.' And God who is indeed mysterious, who had made no sign when they burned Pierre as he slept— not a clap of thunder, not a flash of lightning—mysterious God heard Mr Mason at once and answered him. The yells stopped.

I opened my eyes, everybody was looking up and pointing at Coco on the *glacis* railings with his feathers alight. He made an effort to fly down but his clipped wings failed him and he fell screeching. He was all on fire.

I began to cry. 'Don't look,' said Aunt Cora. 'Don't look.' She stooped and put her arms round me and I hid my face, but I could feel that they were not so near. I heard someone say something about bad luck and remembered that it was very unlucky to kill a parrot, or even to see a parrot die. They began to go then, quickly, silently, and those that were left drew aside and watched us as we trailed across the grass. They were not laughing any more.

4. "Who's there?" / "Dear Coco."
5. Stone from which to mount a horse.
6. Flaming torches.

'Get to the carriage, get to the carriage,' said Mr Mason. 'Hurry!' He went first, holding my mother's arm, then Christophine carrying Pierre, and Aunt Cora was last, still with my hand in hers. None of us looked back.

Mannie had stopped the horses at the bend of the cobblestone road and as we got closer we heard him shout, 'What all you are, eh? Brute beasts?' He was speaking to a group of men and a few women who were standing round the carriage. A coloured man with a machete in his hand was holding the bridle. I did not see Sass or the other two horses. 'Get in,' said Mr Mason. 'Take no notice of him, get in.' The man with the machete said no. We would go to police and tell a lot of damn lies. A woman said to let us go. All this an accident and they had plenty witness. 'Myra she witness for us.'

'Shut your mouth,' the man said. 'You mash centipede, mash it, leave one little piece and it grow again . . . [7]What you think police believe, eh? You, or the white nigger?'

Mr Mason stared at him. He seemed not frightened, but too astounded to speak. Mannie took up the carriage whip but one of the blacker men wrenched it out of his hand, snapped it over his knee and threw it away. 'Run away, black Englishman, like the boy run. Hide in the bushes. It's better for you.' It was Aunt Cora who stepped forward and said, 'The little boy is very badly hurt. He will die if we cannot get help for him.'

The man said, 'So black and white, they burn the same, eh?'

'They do,' she said. 'Here and hereafter, as you will find out. Very shortly.'

He let the bridle go and thrust his face close to hers. He'd throw her on the fire, he said, if she put bad luck on him. Old white jumby,[8] he called her. But she did not move an inch, she looked straight into his eyes and threatened him with eternal fire in a calm voice. 'And never a drop of sangoree[9] to cool your burning tongue,' she said. He cursed her again but he backed away. 'Now get in,' said Mr Mason. 'You, Christophine, get in with the child.' Christophine got in. 'Now you,' he said to my mother. But she had turned and was looking back at the house and when he put his hand on her arm, she screamed.

One woman said she only come to see what happen. Another woman began to cry. The man with the cutlass said, 'You cry for her—when she ever cry for you? Tell me that.'

---

7. In her autobiography Rhys writes about her nurse teaching her about centipedes, "Meta also told me that if a centipede was killed all the different bits would be alive and run into the corners to become bigger, stronger centipedes. It must be crushed. She said 'mashed up' " (SP, p. 23).
8. An evil spirit raised from the dead that may take a variety of forms.
9. A mulled drink made from lime, sugar, water, and Madeira wine; "sangoree" refers to its blood-red color.

But now I turned too. The house was burning, the yellow-red sky was like sunset and I knew that I would never see Coulibri again. Nothing would be left, the golden ferns and the silver ferns, the orchids, the ginger lilies and the roses, the rocking-chairs and the blue sofa, the jasmine and the honeysuckle, and the picture of the Miller's Daughter. When they had finished, there would be nothing left but blackened walls and the mounting stone. That was always left. That could not be stolen or burned.

Then, not so far off, I saw Tia and her mother and I ran to her, for she was all that was left of my life as it had been. We had eaten the same food, slept side by side, bathed in the same river. As I ran, I thought, I will live with Tia and I will be like her. Not to leave Coulibri. Not to go. Not. When I was close I saw the jagged stone in her hand but I did not see her throw it. I did not feel it either, only something wet, running down my face. I looked at her and I saw her face crumple up as she began to cry. We stared at each other, blood on my face, tears on hers. It was as if I saw myself. Like in a looking-glass.

'I saw my plait, tied with red ribbon, when I got up,' I said. 'In the chest of drawers. I thought it was a snake.'

'Your hair had to be cut. You've been very ill, my darling,' said Aunt Cora. 'But you are safe with me now. We are all safe as I told you we would be. You must stay in bed though. Why are you wandering about the room? Your hair will grow again,' she said. 'Longer and thicker.'

'But darker,' I said.

'Why not darker?'

She picked me up and I was glad to feel the soft mattress and glad to be covered with a cool sheet.

'It's time for your arrowroot,'[1] she said and went out. When that was finished she took the cup away and stood looking down at me.

'I got up because I wanted to know where I was.'

'And you do know, don't you?' she said in an anxious voice.

'Of course. But how did I get to your house?'

'The Luttrells were very good. As soon as Mannie got to Nelson's Rest they sent a hammock and four men. You were shaken about a good deal though. But they did their best. Young Mr Luttrell rode alongside you all the way. Wasn't that kind?'

'Yes,' I said. She looked thin and old and her hair wasn't arranged prettily so I shut my eyes, not wanting to see her.

'Pierre is dead, isn't he?'

'He died on the way down, the poor little boy,' she said.

1. Indigenous medicinal herb.

'He died before that,' I thought but was too tired to speak.

'Your mother is in the country. Resting. Getting well again. You will see her quite soon.'

'I didn't know,' I said. 'Why did she go away?'

'You've been very ill for nearly six weeks. You didn't know anything.'

What was the use of telling her that I'd been awake before and heard my mother screaming *'Qui est là? Qui est là?'*, then 'Don't touch me. I'll kill you if you touch me. Coward. Hypocrite. I'll kill you.' I'd put my hands over my ears, her screams were so loud and terrible. I slept and when I woke up everything was quiet.

Still Aunt Cora stayed by my bed looking at me.

'My head is bandaged up. It's so hot,' I said. 'Will I have a mark on my forehead?'

'No, no.' She smiled for the first time. 'That is healing very nicely. It won't spoil you on your wedding day,' she said.

She bent down and kissed me. 'Is there anything you want? A cool drink to sip?'

'No, not a drink. Sing to me. I like that.'

She began in a shaky voice.

> *'Every night at half past eight*
> *Comes tap tap tapping—'*

'Not that one. I don't like that one. Sing *Before I was set free*.'[2]

She sat near me and sang very softly, 'Before I was set free.' I heard as far as 'The sorrow that my heart feels for—' I didn't hear the end but I heard that before I slept, 'The sorrow that my heart feels for.'

I was going to see my mother. I had insisted that Christophine must be with me, no one else, and as I was not yet quite well they had given way. I remember the dull feeling as we drove along for I did not expect to see her. She was part of Coulibri, that had gone, so she had gone, I was certain of it. But when we reached the tidy pretty little house where she lived now (they said) I jumped out of the carriage and ran as fast as I could across the lawn. One door was open on to the veranda. I went in without knocking and stared at the people in the room. A coloured[3] man, a coloured woman, and a white woman sitting with her head bent so low that I couldn't see her face. But I recognized her hair, one plait much shorter than the other. And her dress. I put my arms round her and kissed her. She held me so tightly that I couldn't breathe and I thought, 'It's not her.' Then, 'It must be her.' She looked at the door, then at me, then at the door again. I could not say, 'He is dead,' so I shook my head. 'But I am here, I am here,' I said, and she

---

2. A black spiritual; also what Rhys at times called the novel when she was working on it (*Letters of Jean Rhys* [hereafter, *LJR*], p. 215).

3. Of mixed white and black (Anglo-European and African) racial ancestry.

said, 'No,' quietly. Then 'No no no' very loudly and flung me from
her. I fell against the partition and hurt myself. The man and the
woman were holding her arms and Christophine was there. The
woman said, 'Why you bring the child to make trouble, trouble, trouble? Trouble enough without that.'

All the way back to Aunt Cora's house we didn't speak.

The first day I had to go to the convent, I clung to Aunt Cora as
you would cling to life if you loved it. At last she got impatient, so I
forced myself away from her and through the passage, down the steps
into the street and, as I knew they would be, they were waiting for me
under the sandbox tree. There were two of them, a boy and a girl. The
boy was about fourteen and tall and big for his age, he had a white
skin, a dull ugly white covered with freckles, his mouth was a negro's
mouth and he had small eyes, like bits of green glass. He had the eyes
of a dead fish. Worst, most horrible of all, his hair was crinkled, a
negro's hair, but bright red, and his eyebrows and eyelashes were red.
The girl was very black and wore no head handkerchief. Her hair had
been plaited and I could smell the sickening oil she had daubed on it,
from where I stood on the steps of Aunt Cora's dark, clean, friendly
house, staring at them. They looked so harmless and quiet, no one
would have noticed the glint in the boy's eyes.

Then the girl grinned and began to crack the knuckles of her fingers.
At each crack I jumped and my hands began to sweat. I was holding
some school books in my right hand and I shifted them to under my
arm, but it was too late, there was a mark on the palm of my hand and
a stain on the cover of the book. The girl began to laugh, very quietly,
and it was then that hate came to me and courage with the hate so
that I was able to walk past without looking at them.

I knew they were following, I knew too that as long as I was in sight
of Aunt Cora's house they would do nothing but stroll along some
distance after me. But I knew when they would draw close. It would
be when I was going up the hill. There were walls and gardens on
each side of the hill and no one would be there at this hour of the
morning.

Half-way up they closed in on me and started talking. The girl said,
'Look the crazy girl, you crazy like your mother. Your aunt frightened
to have you in the house. She send you for the nuns to lock up. Your
mother walk about with no shoes and stockings on her feet, she *sans
culottes*.[4] She try to kill her husband and she try to kill you too that
day you go to see her. She have eyes like zombie[5] and you have eyes

4. Without underpants.
5. A person whose soul has been stolen or put to sleep by a bokor, or sorcerer, who takes full
   command of the body for his own purposes. Belief in this living-dead creature is of African
   origin but became more important in the Caribbean, where the alienation of the zombi
   provided a powerful metaphor for the experience of plantation slaves.

like zombie too. Why you won't look at me.' The boy only said, 'One day I catch you alone, you wait, one day I catch you alone.' When I got to the top of the hill they were jostling me, I could smell the girl's hair.

A long empty street stretched away to the convent, the convent wall and a wooden gate. I would have to ring before I could get in. The girl said, 'You don't want to look at me, eh, I make you look at me.' She pushed me and the books I was carrying fell to the ground.

I stooped to pick them up and saw that a tall boy who was walking along the other side of the street had stopped and looked towards us. Then he crossed over, running. He had long legs, his feet hardly touched the ground. As soon as they saw him, they turned and walked away. He looked after them, puzzled. I would have died sooner than run when they were there, but as soon as they had gone, I ran. I left one of my books on the ground and the tall boy came after me.

'You dropped this,' he said, and smiled. I knew who he was, his name was Sandi, Alexander Cosway's son. Once I would have said 'my cousin Sandi' but Mr Mason's lectures had made me shy about my coloured relatives.[6] I muttered, 'Thank you.'

'I'll talk to that boy,' he said. 'He won't bother you again.'

In the distance I could see my enemy's red hair as he pelted along, but he hadn't a chance. Sandi caught him up before he reached the corner. The girl had disappeared. I didn't wait to see what happened but I pulled and pulled at the bell.

At last the door opened. The nun was a coloured woman and she seemed displeased. 'You must not ring the bell like that,' she said. 'I come as quick as I can.' Then I heard the door shut behind me.

I collapsed and began to cry. She asked me if I was sick, but I could not answer. She took my hand, still clicking her tongue and muttering in an ill-tempered way, and led me across the yard, past the shadow of the big tree, not into the front door but into a big, cool, stone-flagged room. There were pots and pans hanging on the wall and a stone fireplace. There was another nun at the back of the room and when the bell rang again, the first one went to answer it. The second nun, also a coloured woman, brought a basin and water but as fast as she sponged my face, so fast did I cry. When she saw my hand she asked if I had fallen and hurt myself. I shook my head and she sponged the stain away gently. 'What is the matter, what are you crying about? What has happened to you?' And still I could not answer. She brought me a glass of milk, I tried to drink it, but I choked. 'Oh la la,' she said, shrugging her shoulders and went out.

6. See note 8, p. 16.

When she came in again, a third nun was with her who said in a calm voice, 'You have cried quite enough now, you must stop. Have you got a handkerchief?'

I remembered that I had dropped it. The new nun wiped my eyes with a large handkerchief, gave it to me and asked my name.

'Antoinette,' I said.

'Of course,' she said. 'I know. You are Antoinette Cosway, that is to say Antoinette Mason. Has someone frightened you?'

'Yes.'

'Now look at me,' she said. 'You will not be frightened of me.'

I looked at her. She had large brown eyes, very soft, and was dressed in white, not with a starched apron like the others had. The band round her face was of linen and above the white linen a black veil of some thin material, which fell in folds down her back. Her cheeks were red, she had a laughing face and two deep dimples. Her hands were small but they looked clumsy and swollen, not like the rest of her. It was only afterwards that I found out that they were crippled with rheumatism. She took me into a parlour furnished stiffly with straight-backed chairs and a polished table in the middle. After she had talked to me I told her a little of why I was crying and that I did not like walking to school alone.

'That must be seen to,' she said. 'I will write to your aunt. Now Mother St Justine will be waiting for you. I have sent for a girl who has been with us for nearly a year. Her name is Louise—Louise de Plana. If you feel strange, she will explain everything.'

Louise and I walked along a paved path to the classroom. There was grass on each side of the path and trees and shadows of trees and sometimes a bright bush of flowers. She was very pretty and when she smiled at me I could scarcely believe I had ever been miserable. She said, 'We always call Mother St Justine, Mother Juice of a Lime. She is not very intelligent, poor woman. You will see.'

Quickly, while I can, I must remember the hot classroom. The hot classroom, the pitchpine desks, the heat of the bench striking up through my body, along my arms and hands. But outside I could see cool, blue shadow on a white wall. My needle is sticky, and creaks as it goes in and out of the canvas. 'My needle is swearing,' I whisper to Louise, who sits next to me. We are cross-stitching silk roses on a pale background. We can colour the roses as we choose and mine are green, blue and purple. Underneath, I will write my name in fire red, Antoinette Mason, née Cosway, Mount Calvary Convent, Spanish Town, Jamaica, 1839.[7]

7. A year after full emancipation. Rhys has changed the time period of *Jane Eyre* to coincide with emancipation. *Jane Eyre* is narrated in 1818 or 1819 and describes events taking place between 1798 and 1808.

As we work, Mother St Justine reads us stories from the lives of the Saints, St Rose, St Barbara, St Agnes.[8] But we have our own Saint, the skeleton of a girl of fourteen under the altar of the convent chapel. The Relics. But how did the nuns get them out here, I ask myself? In a cabin trunk? Specially packed for the hold? How? But here she is, and St Innocenzia is her name. We do not know her story, she is not in the book. The saints we hear about were all very beautiful and wealthy. All were loved by rich and handsome young men.

'. . . more lovely and more richly dressed than he had ever seen her in life,' drones Mother St Justine. 'She smiled and said, "Here Theophilus is a rose from the garden of my Spouse,[9] in whom you did not believe." The rose he found by his side when he awoke has never faded. It still exists.' (Oh, but where? Where?) 'And Theophilus was converted to Christianity,' says Mother St Justine, reading very rapidly now, 'and became one of the Holy Martyrs.' She shuts the book with a clap and talks about pushing down the cuticles of our nails when we wash our hands. Cleanliness, good manners and kindness to God's poor. A flow of words. ('It is her time of life,' said Hélène de Plana, 'she cannot help it, poor old Justine.') 'When you insult or injure the unfortunate or the unhappy, you insult Christ Himself and He will not forget, for they are His chosen ones.' This remark is made in a casual and perfunctory voice and she slides on to order and chastity, that flawless crystal that, once broken, can never be mended. Also deportment. Like everyone else, she has fallen under the spell of the de Plana sisters and holds them up as an example to the class. I admire them. They sit so poised and imperturbable while she points out the excellence of Miss Hélène's coiffure, achieved without a looking-glass.

'Please, Hélène, tell me how you do your hair, because when I grow up I want mine to look like yours.'

'It's very easy. You comb it upwards, like this and then push it a little forward, like that, and then you pin it here and here. Never too many pins.'

'Yes, but Hélène, mine does not look like yours, whatever I do.'

Her eyelashes flickered, she turned away, too polite to say the obvious thing. We have no looking-glass in the dormitory, once I saw the new

---

8. St. Rose of Lima (1586–1617), the first saint of America, named patron of South America and the Philippine Islands. According to legend, St. Barbara was shut up in a tower by her father so that no man should see her. Her usual emblem is a tower. After condemning her to die as a Christian, Barbara's father was killed by lightning. St. Barbara is the patron of those in danger of sudden death, particularly by lightning. Also a virgin martyr, Agnes refused marriage at age thirteen because of her dedication to Christ, preferring death to any violation of her consecrated virginity. As a child Rhys attended a convent school in Dominica for a short time. Most of the whites in Dominica were Anglican, so the majority of the students were "colored" or black. Rhys felt very close to the Superior, Mother Mount Calvary, after whom she names this convent.

9. Christ.

young nun from Ireland looking at herself in a cask of water, smiling to see if her dimples were still there. When she noticed me, she blushed and I thought, now she will always dislike me.

Sometimes it was Miss Hélène's hair and sometimes Miss Germaine's impeccable deportment, and sometimes it was the care Miss Louise took of her beautiful teeth. And if we were never envious, they never seemed vain. Hélène and Germaine, a little disdainful, aloof perhaps, but Louise, not even that. She took no part in it—as if she knew that she was born for other things. Hélène's brown eyes could snap, Germaine's grey eyes were beautiful, soft and cow-like, she spoke slowly and, unlike most Creole girls, was very even-tempered.[1] It is easy to imagine what happened to those two, bar accidents. Ah but Louise! Her small waist, her thin brown hands, her black curls which smelled of vetiver,[2] her high sweet voice, singing so carelessly in Chapel about death. Like a bird would sing. Anything might have happened to you, Louise, anything at all, and I wouldn't be surprised.

Then there was another saint, said Mother St Justine, she lived later on but still in Italy, or was it in Spain. Italy is white pillars and green water. Spain is hot sun on stones, France is a lady with black hair wearing a white dress because Louise was born in France fifteen years ago, and my mother, whom I must forget and pray for as though she were dead, though she is living, liked to dress in white.

No one spoke of her now that Christophine had left us to live with her son. I seldom saw my stepfather. He seemed to dislike Jamaica, Spanish Town in particular, and was often away for months.

One hot afternoon in July my aunt told me that she was going to England for a year. Her health was not good and she needed a change. As she talked she was working at a patchwork counterpane. The diamond-shaped pieces of silk melted one into the other, red, blue, purple, green, yellow, all one shimmering colour. Hours and hours she had spent on it and it was nearly finished. Would I be lonely? she asked and I said 'No', looking at the colours. Hours and hours and hours I thought.

This convent was my refuge, a place of sunshine and of death where very early in the morning the clap of a wooden signal woke the nine of us who slept in the long dormitory. We woke to see Sister Marie Augustine sitting, serene and neat, bolt upright in a wooden chair. The long brown room was full of gold sunlight and shadows of trees moving

1. The description refers to the metropolitan belief that Creoles were, having been "tropicalized" by their environments, emotionally high-strung, lazy, and sexually excessive. In an attempt to encourage Englishmen to marry English Creole women, Thomas Atwood wrote in 1791 a refutation "of that too generally received notion, that women in particular, in warm climates, are given to inordinate desires" (The History of the Island of Dominica, p. 213).
2. An essential oil made from a grass plant and used in perfumes, cosmetics, and soaps.

quietly. I learnt to say very quickly as the others did, 'offer up all the prayers, works and sufferings of this day.' But what about happiness, I thought at first, is there no happiness?[3] There must be. Oh happiness of course, happiness, well.

But I soon forgot about happiness, running down the stairs to the big stone bath where we splashed about wearing long grey cotton chemises which reached to our ankles. The smell of soap as you cautiously soaped yourself under the chemise, a trick to be learned, dressing with modesty, another trick. Great splashes of sunlight as we ran up the wooden steps of the refectory. Hot coffee and rolls and melting butter. But after the meal, now and at the hour of our death, and at midday and at six in the evening, now and at the hour of our death. Let perpetual light shine on them.[4] This is for my mother, I would think, wherever her soul is wandering, for it has left her body.[5] Then I remembered how she hated a strong light and loved the cool and the shade. It is a different light they told me. Still, I would not say it. Soon we were back in the shifting shadows outside, more beautiful than any perpetual light could be, and soon I learnt to gabble without thinking as the others did. About changing now and the hour of our death for that is all we have.

Everything was brightness, or dark. The walls, the blazing colours of the flowers in the garden, the nuns' habits were bright, but their veils, the Crucifix hanging from their waists, the shadow of the trees, were black. That was how it was, light and dark, sun and shadow, Heaven and Hell, for one of the nuns knew all about Hell and who does not? But another one knew about Heaven and the attributes of the blessed, of which the least is transcendent beauty. The very least. I could hardly wait for all this ecstasy and once I prayed for a long time to be dead. Then remembered that this was a sin. It's presumption or despair, I forget which, but a mortal sin. So I prayed for a long time about that too, but the thought came, so many things are sins, why? Another sin, to think that. However, happily, Sister Marie Augustine says thoughts are not sins, if they are driven away at once. You say Lord save me, I perish.[6] I find it very comforting to know exactly what must be done. All the same, I did not pray so often after that and soon, hardly at all. I felt bolder, happier, more free. But not so safe.

During this time, nearly eighteen months, my stepfather often came to see me. He interviewed Mother Superior first, then I would go into the parlour dressed ready for a dinner or a visit to friends. He gave me

3. "Joy" is a usual offering in the Morning Offering, a popular Catholic devotion.
4. The last phrase of the Hail Mary, a Roman Catholic prayer repeated as part of the Rosary, is "Hail Mary, Mother of God, pray for us sinners now and at the hour of our death." "Let Perpetual Light shine on them" is a phrase from the Prayer for the Dead.
5. See note 5, p. 29.
6. Cf. Matthew 8:25.

presents when we parted, sweets, a locket, a bracelet, once a very pretty dress which, of course, I could not wear.

The last time he came was different. I knew that as soon as I got into the room. He kissed me, held me at arm's length looking at me carefully and critically, then smiled and said that I was taller than he thought. I reminded him that I was over seventeen, a grown woman. 'I've not forgotten your present,' he said.

Because I felt shy and ill at ease I answered coldly, 'I can't wear all these things you buy for me.'

'You can wear what you like when you live with me,' he said.

'Where? In Trinidad?'

'Of course not. Here, for the time being. With me and your Aunt Cora who is coming home at last. She says another English winter will kill her. And Richard.[7] You can't be hidden away all your life.'

'Why not?' I thought.

I suppose he noticed my dismay because he began to joke, pay me compliments, and ask me such absurd questions that soon I was laughing too. How would I like to live in England? Then, before I could answer, had I learnt dancing, or were the nuns too strict?

'They are not strict at all,' I said. 'The Bishop who visits them every year says they are lax. Very lax. It's the climate he says.'

'I hope they told him to mind his own business.'

'She did. Mother Superior did. Some of the others were frightened. They are not strict but no one has taught me to dance.'

'That won't be the difficulty. I want you to be happy, Antoinette, secure, I've tried to arrange, but we'll have time to talk about that later.'

As we were going out of the convent gate he said in a careless voice, 'I have asked some English friends to spend next winter here. You won't be dull.'

'Do you think they'll come?' I said doubtfully.

'One of them will. I'm certain of that.'

It may have been the way he smiled, but again a feeling of dismay, sadness, loss, almost choked me. This time I did not let him see it.

It was like that morning when I found the dead horse. Say nothing and it may not be true.

But they all knew at the convent. The girls were very curious but I would not answer their questions and for the first time I resented the nuns' cheerful faces.

They are safe. How can they know what it can be like *outside*?

This was the second time I had my dream.

Again I have left the house at Coulibri. It is still night and I am walking towards the forest. I am wearing a long dress and thin slippers,

---

7. His son, Antoinette's stepbrother.

so I walk with difficulty, following the man who is with me and holding up the skirt of my dress. It is white and beautiful and I don't wish to get it soiled. I follow him, sick with fear but I make no effort to save myself; if anyone were to try to save me, I would refuse. This must happen. Now we have reached the forest. We are under the tall dark trees and there is no wind. 'Here?' He turns and looks at me, his face black with hatred, and when I see this I begin to cry. He smiles slyly. 'Not here, not yet,' he says, and I follow him, weeping. Now I do not try to hold up my dress, it trails in the dirt, my beautiful dress. We are no longer in the forest but in an enclosed garden surrounded by a stone wall and the trees are different trees. I do not know them. There are steps leading upwards. It is too dark to see the wall or the steps, but I know they are there and I think, 'It will be when I go up these steps. At the top.' I stumble over my dress and cannot get up. I touch a tree and my arms hold on to it. 'Here, here.' But I think I will not go any further. The tree sways and jerks as if it is trying to throw me off. Still I cling and the seconds pass and each one is a thousand years. 'Here, in here,' a strange voice said, and the tree stopped swaying and jerking.

Now Sister Marie Augustine is leading me out of the dormitory, asking if I am ill, telling me that I must not disturb the others and though I am still shivering I wonder if she will take me behind the mysterious curtains to the place where she sleeps. But no. She seats me in a chair, vanishes, and after a while comes back with a cup of hot chocolate.

I said, 'I dreamed I was in Hell.'

'That dream is evil. Put it from your mind—never think of it again,' and she rubbed my cold hands to warm them.

She looks as usual, composed and neat, and I want to ask her if she gets up before dawn or hasn't been to bed at all.

'Drink your chocolate.'

While I am drinking it I remember that after my mother's funeral, very early in the morning, almost as early as this, we went home to drink chocolate and eat cakes. She died last year, no one told me how, and I didn't ask. Mr Mason was there and Christophine, no one else. Christophine cried bitterly but I could not. I prayed, but the words fell to the ground meaning nothing.

Now the thought of her is mixed up with my dream.

I saw her in her mended habit riding a borrowed horse, trying to wave at the head of the cobblestoned road at Coulibri, and tears came to my eyes again. 'Such terrible things happen,' I said. 'Why? Why?'

'You must not concern yourself with that mystery,' said Sister Maria Augustine. 'We do not know why the devil must have his little day. Not yet.'

She never smiled as much as the others, now she was not smiling at all. She looked sad.

She said, as if she was talking to herself, 'Now go quietly back to bed. Think of calm, peaceful things and try to sleep. Soon I will give the signal. Soon it will be tomorrow morning.'

Part Two

So it was all over, the advance and retreat, the doubts and hesitations.[1] Everything finished, for better or for worse. There we were, sheltering from the heavy rain under a large mango tree, myself, my wife Antoinette and a little half-caste[2] servant who was called Amélie. Under a neighbouring tree I could see our luggage covered with sacking, the two porters and a boy holding fresh horses, hired to carry us up 2,000 feet to the waiting honeymoon house.

The girl Amélie said this morning, 'I hope you will be very happy, sir, in your sweet honeymoon house.'[3] She was laughing at me I could see. A lovely little creature but sly, spiteful, malignant perhaps, like much else in this place.

'It's only a shower,' Antoinette said anxiously. 'It will soon stop.'

I looked at the sad leaning cocoanut palms, the fishing boats drawn up on the shingly beach, the uneven row of whitewashed huts, and asked the name of the village.

'Massacre.'[4]

'And who was massacred here? Slaves?'

'Oh no.' She sounded shocked. 'Not slaves. Something must have happened a long time ago. Nobody remembers now.'

The rain fell more heavily, huge drops sounded like hail on the leaves of the tree, and the sea crept stealthily forwards and backwards.

So this is Massacre. Not the end of the world, only the last stage of

1. Although the character who speaks in this section is often referred to in criticism as Brontë's Mr. Rochester, he remains unnamed in this novel. As Rhys wrote in a letter, "I carefully haven't named the man at all" (*LJR*, p. 297).
2. Of mixed racial ancestry.
3. Based on Rhys's father's estate, Amalia. Rhys wrote, ". . . I tried to put some of my love of the place where I was born (I shifted their honeymoon to Dominica). . . ." (*LJR*, p. 172).
4. A fishing village on the leeward coast of Dominica, just north of Roseau, Rhys's birthplace. The village is at the foot of the climb to the holiday cottage Rhys's father built in the mountains. The massacre here refers to the treacherous murder in 1674 of a party of 60–70 Carib men, women, and children including Thomas "Indian" Warner, the supposed half-Carib son of one of the foremost English colonists in the West Indies, Sir Thomas Warner, Governor of St. Kitts. "Indian" Warner and his Carib allies were killed by his half-brother, Philip, the legitimate son of Sir Thomas. Raised by his father, yet mistreated by his stepmother after his father's death, "Indian" Warner chose to live with his mother's family, becoming a Carib leader who often negotiated between the English and the Caribs. The reference is significant here because "Indian" Warner represents in Caribbean history and mythology a position between two cultures, a space of alienation and possibility.

our interminable journey from Jamaica, the start of our sweet honey-moon. And it will all look very different in the sun.

It had been arranged that we would leave Spanish Town immediately after the ceremony and spend some weeks in one of the Windward Islands,[5] at a small estate which had belonged to Antoinette's mother. I agreed. As I had agreed to everything else.

The windows of the huts were shut, the doors opened into silence and dimness. Then three little boys came to stare at us. The smallest wore nothing but a religious medal round his neck and the brim of a large fisherman's hat. When I smiled at him, he began to cry. A woman called from one of the huts and he ran away, still howling.

The other two followed slowly, looking back several times.

As if this was a signal a second woman appeared at her door, then a third.

'It's Caro,' Antoinette said. 'I'm sure it's Caro. Caroline,' she called, waving, and the woman waved back. A gaudy old creature in a brightly flowered dress, a striped head handkerchief and gold ear-rings.

'You'll get soaked, Antoinette,' I said.

'No, the rain is stopping.' She held up the skirt of her riding habit and ran across the street. I watched her critically. She wore a tricorne hat[6] which became her. At least it shadowed her eyes which are too large and can be disconcerting. She never blinks at all it seems to me. Long, sad, dark alien eyes. Creole of pure English descent she may be, but they are not English or European either.[7] And when did I begin to notice all this about my wife Antoinette? After we left Spanish Town I suppose. Or did I notice it before and refuse to admit what I saw? Not that I had much time to notice anything. I was married a month after I arrived in Jamaica and for nearly three weeks of that time I was in bed with fever.

The two women stood in the doorway of the hut gesticulating, talking not English but the debased French patois they use in this island. The rain began to drip down the back of my neck adding to my feeling of discomfort and melancholy.

I thought about the letter which should have been written to England a week ago. Dear Father . . .

5. The southeast group of Caribbean islands ranging from Dominica to Grenada.
6. A hat with three corners fashionable during the eighteenth century in Europe.
7. The term has a variety of contradictory meanings. It originally referred to those of Anglo-European descent born in the colonies and was used to indicate so-called racial purity. The term was also used to refer to slaves and animals locally born, rather than imported, and so the adjective "white" was later added to distinguish white from black Caribbeans. Beginning in the nineteenth century, "Creole" was increasingly used to indicate racial mixture, linguistic mixture of African and European languages, or food or cultural forms associated with black West Indians. Rhys changed her working title for the novel from "Creole" because "that has a different meaning now" (LJR, pp. 153–54). The narrator here agrees with the earlier state-ments of Antoinette, Annette, and Cora that the white settler class had, over several genera-tions, developed a distinct culture. The narrator hints at the metropolitan suspicion that the differences between the English and the Creoles are racial as well as cultural.

'Caroline asks if you will shelter in her house.'

This was Antoinette. She spoke hesitatingly as if she expected me to refuse, so it was easy to do so.

'But you are getting wet,' she said.

'I don't mind that.' I smiled at Caroline and shook my head.

'She will be very disappointed,' said my wife, crossed the street again and went into the dark hut.

Amélie, who had been sitting with her back to us, turned round. Her expression was so full of delighted malice, so intelligent, above all so intimate that I felt ashamed and looked away.

'Well,' I thought. 'I have had fever. I am not myself yet.'

The rain was not so heavy and I went to talk to the porters. The first man was not a native of the island. 'This a very wild place—not civilized. Why you come here?' He was called the Young Bull he told me, and he was twenty-seven years of age. A magnificent body and a foolish conceited face. The other man's name was Emile, yes, he was born in the village, he lived there. 'Ask him how old he is,' suggested the Young Bull. Emile said in a questioning voice, 'Fourteen? Yes I have fourteen years master.'

'Impossible,' I said. I could see the grey hairs in his sparse beard.

'Fifty-six years perhaps.'[8] He seemed anxious to please.

The Young Bull laughed loudly. 'He don't know how old he is, he don't think about it. I tell you sir these people are not civilized.'

Emile muttered, 'My mother she know, but she dead.' Then he produced a blue rag which he twisted into a pad and put on his head.

Most of the women were outside their doors looking at us but without smiling. Sombre people in a sombre place. Some of the men were going to their boats. When Emile shouted, two of them came towards him. He sang in a deep voice. They answered, then lifted the heavy wicker basket and swung it on to his head-pad singing. He tested the balance with one hand and strode off, barefooted on the sharp stones, by far the gayest member of the wedding party. As the Young Bull was loaded up he glanced at me sideways boastfully and he too sang to himself in English.

The boy brought the horses to a large stone and I saw Antoinette coming from the hut. The sun blazed out and steam rose from the green behind us. Amélie took her shoes off, tied them together and hung them round her neck. She balanced her small basket on her head and swung away as easily as the porters. We mounted, turned a corner and the village was out of sight. A cock crowed loudly[9] and I remembered the night before which we had spent in the town. Antoinette had

---

8. This discrepancy makes sense if Emile had been born on February 29 of a leap year.
9. In the Gospels the cock's crowing is linked to Peter's denial and Judas's betrayal of Jesus (Matthew 26:23–35).

a room to herself, she was exhausted. I lay awake listening to cocks
crowing all night, then got up very early and saw the women with trays
covered with white cloths on their heads going to the kitchen. The
woman with small hot loaves for sale, the woman with cakes, the
woman with sweets. In the street another called *Bon sirop, Bon sirop*,[1]
and I felt peaceful.

The road climbed upward. On one side the wall of green, on the
other a steep drop to the ravine below. We pulled up and looked at
the hills, the mountains and the blue-green sea. There was a soft warm
wind blowing but I understood why the porter had called it a wild
place. Not only wild but menacing. Those hills would close in on you.
'What an extreme green,' was all I could say, and thinking of Emile
calling to the fishermen and the sound of his voice, I asked about him.
'They take short cuts. They will be at Granbois long before we are.'
Everything is too much, I felt as I rode wearily after her. Too much
blue, too much purple, too much green. The flowers too red, the
mountains too high, the hills too near. And the woman is a stranger.
Her pleading expression annoys me. I have not bought her, she has
bought me, or so she thinks. I looked down at the coarse mane of the
horse . . . Dear Father. The thirty thousand pounds have been paid to
me without question or condition. No provision made for her (that
must be seen to). I have a modest competence now. I will never be a
disgrace to you or to my dear brother the son you love. No begging
letters, no mean requests. None of the furtive shabby manœuvres of a
younger son.[2] I have sold my soul or you have sold it, and after all is
it such a bad bargain? The girl is thought to be beautiful, she is beautiful. And yet . . .
Meanwhile the horses jogged along a very bad road. It was getting
cooler. A bird whistled, a long sad note. 'What bird is that?' She was
too far ahead and did not hear me. The bird whistled again. A mountain bird. Shrill and sweet. A very lonely sound.
She stopped and called, 'Put your coat on now.' I did so and realized
that I was no longer pleasantly cool but cold in my sweat-soaked shirt.

1. A refreshing drink made of sweet syrup.
2. Refers to the uniquely severe English common law of patrilineal inheritance that granted all
   land to the eldest son. Primogeniture, as this law of real property was called, was considered
   by landowners to be essential for the continuity of the aristocracy, the British constitution,
   and English culture. Nevertheless, fathers usually exercised their right to settle some portion
   of their estate on younger sons and daughters. Younger sons often married heiresses to support
   themselves. In *Jane Eyre*, Rochester received £30,000 through an arranged marriage with
   Bertha, the daughter of a West Indian plantation owner. The narrator's belief that this wealth
   comes at the cost of his soul is a reference to the legend in which Faust sells his soul to the
   devil in exchange for the fulfillment of all his worldly desires. The sum of £30,000 would be
   about £1,500,000—or $2,400,000—today. Rhys's father, William Rees Williams, a less-favored
   second son of a clergyman, traveled from Wales to Dominica as a young man and married
   into a Creole family.

We rode on again, silent in the slanting afternoon sun, the wall of trees on one side, a drop on the other. Now the sea was a serene blue, deep and dark.

We came to a little river. 'This is the boundary of Granbois.' She smiled at me. It was the first time I had seen her smile simply and naturally. Or perhaps it was the first time I had felt simple and natural with her. A bamboo spout jutted from the cliff, the water coming from it was silver blue. She dismounted quickly, picked a large shamrock-shaped leaf to make a cup, and drank. Then she picked another leaf, folded it and brought it to me. 'Taste. This is mountain water.' Looking up smiling, she might have been any pretty English girl and to please her I drank. It was cold, pure and sweet, a beautiful colour against the thick green leaf.

She said, 'After this we go down then up again. Then we are there.'

Next time she spoke she said, 'The earth is red here, do you notice?'

'It's red in parts of England too.'

'Oh England, England,' she called back mockingly, and the sound went on and on like a warning I did not choose to hear.

Soon the road was cobblestoned and we stopped at a flight of stone steps. There was a large screw pine to the left and to the right what looked like an imitation of an English summer house—four wooden posts and a thatched roof. She dismounted and ran up the steps. At the top a badly cut, coarse-grained lawn and at the end of the lawn a shabby white house. 'Now you are at Granbois.' I looked at the mountains purple against a very blue sky.

Perched up on wooden stilts the house seemed to shrink from the forest behind it and crane eagerly out to the distant sea. It was more awkward than ugly, a little sad as if it knew it could not last. A group of negroes were standing at the foot of the veranda steps. Antoinette ran across the lawn and as I followed her I collided with a boy coming in the opposite direction. He rolled his eyes, looking alarmed and went on towards the horses without a word of apology. A man's voice said, 'Double up now double up. Look sharp.' There were four of them. A woman, a girl and a tall, dignified man were together. Antoinette was standing with her arms round another woman. 'That was Bertrand who nearly knocked you down. That is Rose and Hilda. This is Baptiste.'

The servants grinned shyly as she named them.

'And here is Christophine who was my da, my nurse long ago.'[3]

Baptiste said that it was a happy day and that we'd brought fine

---

3. After emancipation in Jamaica, Christophine cannot return to her home island, Martinique, as it did not free its slaves until 1848. Phyllis Shand Allfrey, another white Creole writer from Dominica, published a novel called *The Orchid House* in 1953 that she sent to Rhys in England. There are two characters in Allfrey's novel who are named Christophine and Baptiste. Allfrey was also a politician and owned and edited the opposition Dominican newspaper *The Star*, copies of which she sent to Rhys over the years in Devonshire. Rhys had promised to write a forward for the reprint of *The Orchid House* but died before she could do so.

weather with us. He spoke good English, but in the middle of his address of welcome Hilda began to giggle. She was a young girl of about twelve or fourteen, wearing a sleeveless white dress which just reached her knees. The dress was spotless but her uncovered hair, though it was oiled and braided into many small plaits, gave her a savage appearance. Baptiste frowned at her and she giggled more loudly, then put her hand over her mouth and went up the wooden steps into the house. I could hear her bare feet running along the veranda.

'Doudou, ché cocotte,'[4] the elderly woman said to Antoinette. I looked at her sharply but she seemed insignificant. She was blacker than most and her clothes, even the handkerchief round her head, were subdued in colour. She looked at me steadily, not with approval, I thought. We stared at each other for quite a minute. I looked away first and she smiled to herself, gave Antoinette a little push forward and disappeared into the shadows at the back of the house. The other servants had gone.

Standing on the veranda I breathed the sweetness of the air. Cloves I could smell and cinnamon, roses and orange blossom. And an intoxicating freshness as if all this had never been breathed before. When Antoinette said 'Come, I will show you the house' I went with her unwillingly for the rest of the place seemed neglected and deserted. She led me into a large unpainted room. There was a small shabby sofa, a mahogany table in the middle, some straight-backed chairs and an old oak chest with brass feet like lion's claws.

Holding my hand she went up to the sideboard where two glasses of rum punch were waiting for us. She handed me one and said, 'To happiness.'

'To happiness,' I answered.

The room beyond was larger and emptier. There were two doors, one leading to the veranda, the other very slightly open into a small room. A big bed, a round table by its side, two chairs, a surprising dressing-table with a marble top and a large looking-glass. Two wreaths of frangipani lay on the bed.

'Am I expected to wear one of these? And when?'

I crowned myself with one of the wreaths and made a face in the glass. 'I hardly think it suits my handsome face, do you?'

'You look like a king, an emperor.'

'God forbid,' I said and took the wreath off. It fell on the floor and as I went towards the window I stepped on it. The room was full of the scent of crushed flowers. I saw her reflection in the glass fanning herself with a small palm-leaf fan coloured blue and red at the edges. I felt sweat on my forehead and sat down, she knelt near me and wiped my face with her handkerchief.

---

4. An endearment, "darling little ducky."

'Don't you like it here? This is my place and everything is on our side. Once,' she said, 'I used to sleep with a piece of wood by my side so that I could defend myself if I were attacked. That's how afraid I was.'

'Afraid of what?'

She shook her head. 'Of nothing, of everything.'

Someone knocked and she said, 'It's only Christophine.'

'The old woman who was your nurse? Are you afraid of her?'

'No, how could I be?'

'If she were taller,' I said, 'one of these strapping women dressed up to the nines, I might be afraid of her.'

She laughed. 'That door leads into your dressing-room.'

I shut it gently after me.

It seemed crowded after the emptiness of the rest of the house. There was a carpet, the only one I had seen, a press made of some beautiful wood I did not recognize. Under the open window a small writing-desk with paper, pens, and ink. 'A refuge' I was thinking when someone said, 'This was Mr Mason's room, sir, but he did not come here often. He did not like the place.' Baptiste, standing in the doorway to the veranda, had a blanket over his arm.

'It's all very comfortable,' I said. He laid the blanket on the bed.

'It can be cold here at night,' he said. Then went away. But the feeling of security had left me. I looked round suspiciously. The door into her room could be bolted, a stout wooden bar pushed across the other. This was the last room in the house. Wooden steps from the veranda led on to another rough lawn, a Seville orange tree grew by the steps. I went back into the dressing-room and looked out of the window. I saw a clay road, muddy in places, bordered by a row of tall trees. Beyond the road various half-hidden outbuildings. One was the kitchen. No chimney but smoke was pouring out of the window. I sat on the soft narrow bed and listened. Not a sound except the river. I might have been alone in the house. There was a crude bookshelf made of three shingles strung together over the desk and I looked at the books, Byron's poems, novels by Sir Walter Scott, *Confessions of an Opium Eater*, some shabby brown volumes, and on the last shelf, *Life and Letters of* . . . The rest was eaten away.[5]

---

5. Lord Byron (1788–1824) and Sir Walter Scott (1771–1832) were English writers of the Romantic tradition. Both wrote and had political visions about the conquest of the Middle East for the British Empire. *Confessions of an English Opium-Eater* was written by Thomas de Quincey (1785–1859). The library of Rhys's childhood home was similarly stocked with English encyclopedias and histories and tales of travel and Empire: *Robinson Crusoe, Treasure Island, Gulliver's Travels, The Arabian Nights* (SP, pp. 20–21). Rhys's great-grandfather, James Potter Lockhart, was a cousin of Sir Walter Scott's son-in-law and biographer, James Gibson Lockhart.

Dear Father, we have arrived from Jamaica after an uncomfortable few days. This little estate in the Windward Islands is part of the family property and Antoinette is much attached to it. She wished to get here as soon as possible. All is well and has gone according to your plans and wishes. I dealt of course with Richard Mason. His father died soon after I left for the West Indies as you probably know. He is a good fellow, hospitable and friendly; he seemed to become attached to me and trusted me completely. This place is very beautiful but my illness has left me too exhausted to appreciate it fully. I will write again in a few days' time.

I reread this letter and added a postscript:

I feel that I have left you too long without news for the bare announcement of my approaching marriage was hardly news. I was down with fever for two weeks after I got to Spanish Town. Nothing serious but I felt wretched enough. I stayed with the Frasers, friends of the Masons. Mr Fraser is an Englishman, a retired magistrate, and he insisted on telling me at length about some of his cases. It was difficult to think or write coherently. In this cool and remote place it is called Granbois (the High Woods I suppose) I feel better already and my next letter will be longer and more explicit.

A cool and remote place . . . And I wondered how they got their letters posted. I folded mine and put it into a drawer of the desk.

As for my confused impressions they will never be written. There are blanks in my mind that cannot be filled up.

It was all very brightly coloured, very strange, but it meant nothing to me. Nor did she, the girl I was to marry. When at last I met her I bowed, smiled, kissed her hand, danced with her. I played the part I was expected to play. She never had anything to do with me at all. Every movement I made was an effort of will and sometimes I wondered that no one noticed this. I would listen to my own voice and marvel at it, calm, correct but toneless, surely. But I must have given a faultless performance. If I saw an expression of doubt or curiosity it was on a black face not a white one.

I remember little of the actual ceremony. Marble memorial tablets on the walls commemorating the virtues of the last generation of planters. All benevolent. All slave-owners. All resting in peace. When we came out of the church I took her hand. It was cold as ice in the hot sun.

Then I was at a long table in a crowded room. Palm leaf fans, a mob of servants, the women's head handkerchiefs striped red and yellow, the

men's dark faces. The strong taste of punch, the cleaner taste of champagne, my bride in white but I hardly remember what she looked like.
Then in another room women dressed in black. Cousin Julia, Cousin
Ada, Aunt Lina. Thin or fat they all looked alike. Gold ear-rings in
pierced ears. Silver bracelets jangling on their wrists. I said to one of
them, 'We are leaving Jamaica tonight,' and she answered after a
pause, 'Of course, Antoinette does not like Spanish Town. Nor did her
mother.' Peering at me. (Do their eyes get smaller as they grow older?
Smaller, beadier, more inquisitive?) After that I thought I saw the same
expression on all their faces. Curiosity? Pity? Ridicule? But why should
they pity me. I who have done so well for myself?

The morning before the wedding Richard Mason burst into my room
at the Frasers as I was finishing my first cup of coffee. 'She won't go
through with it!'

'Won't go through with what?'

'She won't marry you.'

'But why?'

'She doesn't say why.'

'She must have some reason.'

'She won't give a reason. I've been arguing with the little fool for an
hour.'

We stared at each other.

'Everything arranged, the presents, the invitations. What shall I tell
your father?' He seemed on the verge of tears.

I said, 'If she won't, she won't. She can't be dragged to the altar. Let
me get dressed. I must hear what she has to say.'

He went out meekly and while I dressed I thought that this would
indeed make a fool of me. I did not relish going back to England in
the role of rejected suitor jilted by this Creole girl. I must certainly
know why.

She was sitting in a rocking chair with her head bent. Her hair was
in two long plaits over her shoulders. From a little distance I spoke
gently. 'What is the matter, Antoinette? What have I done?'

She said nothing.

'You don't wish to marry me?'

'No.' She spoke in a very low voice.

'But why?'

'I'm afraid of what may happen.'

'But don't you remember last night I told you that when you are my
wife there would not be any more reason to be afraid?'

'Yes,' she said. 'Then Richard came in and you laughed. I didn't like
the way you laughed.'

'But I was laughing at myself, Antoinette.'

She looked at me and I took her in my arms and kissed her.

'You don't know anything about me,' she said.

'I'll trust you if you'll trust me. Is that a bargain? You will make me very unhappy if you send me away without telling me what I have done to displease you. I will go with a sad heart.'

'Your sad heart,' she said, and touched my face. I kissed her fervently, promising her peace, happiness, safety, but when I said, 'Can I tell poor Richard that it was a mistake? He is sad too,' she did not answer me. Only nodded.

Thinking of all this, of Richard's angry face, her voice saying, 'Can you give me peace?', I must have slept.

I woke to the sound of voices in the next room, laughter and water being poured out. I listened, still drowsy. Antoinette said, 'Don't put any more scent on my hair. He doesn't like it.' The other: 'The man don't like scent? I never hear that before.' It was almost dark.

The dining-room was brilliantly lit. Candles on the table, a row on the sideboard, three-branch candlesticks on the old sea-chest. The two doors on to the veranda stood open but there was no wind. The flames burned straight. She was sitting on the sofa and I wondered why I had never realized how beautiful she was. Her hair was combed away from her face and fell smoothly far below her waist. I could see the red and gold lights in it. She seemed pleased when I complimented her on her dress and told me she had it made in St Pierre, Martinique. 'They call this fashion *à la Joséphine*.'[6]

'You talk of St Pierre as though it were Paris,' I said.

'But it is the Paris of the West Indies.'[7]

There were trailing pink flowers on the table and the name echoed pleasantly in my head. Coralita Coralita.[8] The food, though too highly seasoned, was lighter and more appetizing than anything I had tasted in Jamaica. We drank champagne. A great many moths and beetles found their way into the room, flew into the candles and fell dead on the tablecloth. Amélie swept them up with a crumb brush. Uselessly. More moths and beetles came.

'Is it true,' she said, 'that England is like a dream? Because one of my friends who married an Englishman wrote and told me so. She said this place London is like a cold dark dream sometimes. I want to wake up.'

6. After Joséphine deBeauharnais, a white Creole Martinican who married Napoleon Bonaparte in 1796, became Empress of France in 1804, and was divorced by Napoleon in 1809. Like Antoinette's mother, Annette, Joséphine was a white Creole from Martinique and, like Antoinette, she was the daughter of a plantation family.
7. Former capital of Martinique, St. Pierre was destroyed by the volcano Mount Pelée in 1902; the entire population of 30,000 died, except one man imprisoned in an underground jail. The eruption was widely interpreted as divine punishment for the decadence and immorality of the French settler class.
8. A climbing vine with bright pink heart-shaped flowers.

'Well,' I answered annoyed, 'that is precisely how your beautiful island seems to me, quite unreal and like a dream.'

'But how can rivers and mountains and the sea be unreal?'

'And how can millions of people, their houses and their streets be unreal?'

'More easily,' she said, 'much more easily. Yes a big city must be like a dream.'

'No, this is unreal and like a dream,' I thought.

The long veranda was furnished with canvas chairs, two hammocks, and a wooden table on which stood a tripod telescope. Amélie brought out candles with glass shades but the night swallowed up the feeble light. There was a very strong scent of flowers—the flowers by the river that open at night she told me—and the noise, subdued in the inner room, was deafening. 'Crac-cracs,' she explained, 'they make a sound like their name, and crickets and frogs.'

I leaned on the railing and saw hundreds of fireflies—'Ah yes, fireflies in Jamaica, here they call a firefly La belle.'[9]

A large moth, so large that I thought it was a bird, blundered into one of the candles, put it out and fell to the floor. 'He's a big fellow,' I said.

'Is it badly burned?'

'More stunned than hurt.'

I took the beautiful creature up in my handkerchief and put it on the railing. For a moment it was still and by the dim candlelight I could see the soft brilliant colours, the intricate pattern on the wings. I shook the handkerchief gently and it flew away.

'I hope that gay gentleman will be safe,' I said.

'He will come back if we don't put the candles out. It's light enough by the stars.'

Indeed the starlight was so bright that shadows of the veranda posts and the trees outside lay on the floor.

'Now come for a walk,' she said, 'and I will tell you a story.'

We walked along the veranda to the steps which led to the lawn.

'We used to come here to get away from the hot weather in June, July and August. I came three times with my Aunt Cora who is ill. That was after . . .' She stopped and put her hand up to her head.

'If this is a sad story, don't tell it to me tonight.'

'It is not sad,' she said. 'Only some things happen and are there for always even though you forget why or when. It was in that little bedroom.'

I looked where she was pointing but could only see the outline of a narrow bed and one or two chairs.

'This night I can remember it was very hot. The window was shut

9. A crac-crac is a cricketlike insect; La belle ("Beautiful one") is a large species of firefly found in Dominica. The flowers that open at night are called moonflowers.

but I asked Christophine to open it because the breeze comes from the hills at night. The land breeze. Not from the sea. It was so hot that my night chemise[1] was sticking to me but I went to sleep all the same. And then suddenly I was awake. I saw two enormous rats, as big as cats, on the sill staring at me.'

'I'm not astonished that you were frightened.'

'But I was not frightened. That was the strange thing. I stared at them and they did not move. I could see myself in the looking-glass the other side of the room, in my white chemise with a frill round the neck, staring at those rats and the rats quite still, staring at me.'

'Well, what happened?'

'I turned over, pulled up the sheet and went to sleep instantly.'

'And is that the story?'

'No, I woke up again suddenly like the first time and the rats were not there but I felt very frightened. I got out of bed quickly and ran on to the veranda. I lay down in this hammock. This one.' She pointed to a flat hammock, a rope at each of the four corners.

'There was full moon that night—and I watched it for a long time. There were no clouds chasing it, so it seemed to be standing still and it shone on me. Next morning Christophine was angry. She said that it was very bad to sleep in the moonlight when the moon is full.'[2]

'And did you tell her about the rats?'

'No, I never told anyone till now. But I have never forgotten them.'

I wanted to say something reassuring but the scent of the river flowers was overpoweringly strong. I felt giddy.

'Do you think that too,' she said, 'that I have slept too long in the moonlight?'

Her mouth was set in a fixed smile but her eyes were so withdrawn and lonely that I put my arms round her, rocked her like a child and sang to her. An old song I thought I had forgotten:

> 'Hail to the queen of the silent night,
> Shine bright, shine bright Robin as you die.'

She listened, then sang with me:

> 'Shine bright, shine bright Robin as you die.'

There was no one in the house and only two candles in the room which had been so brilliantly lit. Her room was dim, with a shaded candle by the bed and another on the dressing-table. There was a bottle of wine on the round table. It was very late when I poured out two glasses and told her to drink to our happiness, to our love and the day

1. Long loose gown.
2. Refers to the belief that looking at the full moon for extended periods or sleeping under the full moon will cause madness. The term "lunacy" originally described a kind of insanity interrupted by lucid intervals that was supposedly influenced by changes in the moon.

without end which would be tomorrow. I was young then. A short youth mine was.

I woke next morning in the green-yellow light, feeling uneasy as though someone were watching me. She must have been awake for some time. Her hair was plaited and she wore a fresh white chemise. I turned to take her in my arms, I meant to undo the careful plaits, but as I did so there was a soft discreet knock.

She said, 'I have sent Christophine away twice. We wake very early here. The morning is the best time.'

'Come in,' she called and Christophine came in with our coffee on a tray. She was dressed up and looking very imposing. The skirt of her flowered dress trailed after her making a rustling noise as she walked and her yellow silk turban was elaborately tied. Long heavy gold earrings pulled down the lobes of her ears. She wished us good morning smiling and put the tray of coffee, cassava cakes and guava jelly on the round table. I got out of bed and went into the dressing-room. Someone had laid my dressing-gown on the narrow bed. I looked out of the window. The cloudless sky was a paler blue than I'd imagined but as I looked I thought I saw the colour changing to a deeper blue. At noon I knew it would be gold, then brassy in the heat. Now it was fresh and cool and the air itself was blue. At last I turned away from the light and space and went back into the bedroom, which was still in the half dark. Antoinette was leaning back against the pillows with her eyes closed. She opened them and smiled when I came in. It was the black woman hovering over her who said, 'Taste my bull's blood, master.' The coffee she handed me was delicious and she had long-fingered hands, thin and beautiful I suppose.

'Not horse piss like the English madams drink,' she said. 'I know them. Drink drink their yellow horse piss, talk, talk their lying talk.' Her dress trailed and rustled as she walked to the door. There she turned. 'I send the girl to clear up the mess you make with the frangipani, it bring cockroach in the house. Take care not to slip on the flowers, young master.' She slid through the door.

'Her coffee is delicious but her language is horrible and she might hold her dress up. It must get very dirty, yards of it trailing on the floor.'

'When they don't hold their dress up it's for respect,' said Antoinette. 'Or for feast days or going to Mass.'

'And is this a feast day?'

'She wanted it to be a feast day.'

'Whatever the reason it is not a clean habit.'

'It is. You don't understand at all. They don't care about getting a dress dirty because it shows it isn't the only dress they have. Don't you like Christophine?'

'She is a very worthy person no doubt. I can't say I like her language.'

'It doesn't mean anything,' said Antoinette.

'And she looks so lazy.[3] She dawdles about.'

'Again you are mistaken. She seems slow, but every move she makes is right so it's quick in the end.'

I drank another cup of bull's blood. (Bull's blood, I thought. The Young Bull.)

'How did you get that dressing-table up here?'

'I don't know. It's always been here ever since I can remember. A lot of the furniture was stolen, but not that.'

There were two pink roses on the tray, each in a small brown jug. One was full blown and as I touched it the petals dropped.

'Rose elle a vécu,'[4] I said and laughed. 'Is that poem true? Have all beautiful things sad destinies?'

'No, of course not.'

Her little fan was on the table, she took it up laughing, lay back and shut her eyes. 'I think I won't get up this morning.'

'Not get up. Not get up at all?'

'I'll get up when I wish to. I'm very lazy you know. Like Christophine. I often stay in bed all day.' She flourished her fan. 'The bathing pool is quite near. Go before it gets hot, Baptiste will show you. There are two pools, one we call the champagne pool because it has a waterfall, not a big one you understand, but it's good to feel it on your shoulders. Underneath is the nutmeg pool, that's brown and shaded by a big nutmeg tree. It's just big enough to swim in. But be careful. Remember to put your clothes on a rock and before you dress again shake them very well. Look for the red ant, that is the worst. It is very small but bright red so you will be able to see it easily if you look. Be careful,' she said and waved her little fan.

One morning soon after we arrived, the row of tall trees outside my window were covered with small pale flowers too fragile to resist the wind. They fell in a day, and looked like snow on the rough grass—snow with a faint sweet scent. Then they were blown away.

The fine weather lasted longer. It lasted all that week and the next and the next and the next. No sign of a break. My fever weakness left me, so did all misgiving.

I went very early to the bathing pool and stayed there for hours, unwilling to leave the river, the trees shading it, the flowers that opened at night. They were tightly shut, drooping, sheltering from the sun under their thick leaves.

It was a beautiful place—wild, untouched, above all untouched, with

3. This stereotype of black laziness was central to plantocratic ideology.
4. From a poem written in 1599 by François de Malherbe entitled "Consolation à M. du Périer." The poem is an elegy for M. de Périer's daughter: "Et Rose elle a vécu ce que vivent les roses / C'espace d'un matin" (Rose has lived as roses live / for one morning).

an alien, disturbing, secret loveliness. And it kept its secret. I'd find myself thinking, 'What I see is nothing—I want what it *hides*—that is not nothing.'

In the late afternoon when the water was warmer she bathed with me. She'd spend some time throwing pebbles at a flat stone in the middle of the pool. 'I've seen him. He hasn't died or gone to any other river. He's still there. The land crabs are harmless. People *say* they are harmless. I wouldn't like to—'

'Nor would I. Horrible looking creatures.'

She was undecided, uncertain about facts—any fact. When I asked her if the snakes we sometimes saw were poisonous, she said, 'Not those. The *fer de lance* of course, but there are none here,' and added, 'but how can they be sure? Do you think they know?' Then, 'Our snakes are not poisonous. Of course not.'[5]

However, she was certain about the monster crab and one afternoon when I was watching her, hardly able to believe she was the pale silent creature I had married, watching her in her blue chemise, blue with white spots hitched up far above her knees, she stopped laughing, called a warning and threw a large pebble. She threw like a boy, with a sure graceful movement, and I looked down at very long pincer claws, jagged-edged and sharp, vanishing.

'He won't come after you if you keep away from that stone. He lives there. Oh it's another sort of crab. I don't know the name in English. Very big, very old.'

As we were walking home I asked her who had taught her to aim so well. 'Oh, Sandi taught me, a boy you never met.'

Every evening we saw the sun go down from the thatched shelter she called the *ajoupa*,[6] I the summer house. We watched the sky and the distant sea on fire—all colours were in that fire and the huge clouds fringed and shot with flame. But I soon tired of the display. I was waiting for the scent of the flowers by the river—they opened when darkness came and it came quickly. Not night or darkness as I knew it but night with blazing stars, an alien moon—night full of strange noises. Still night, not day.

'The man who owns Consolation Estate is a hermit,' she was saying. 'He never sees anyone—hardly ever speaks, they say.'

'A hermit neighbour suits me. Very well indeed.'

---

5. Although the *Bothrops lanceolatus*, found only in Martinique, is the only poisonous snake there, the name *fer de lance* (referring to the lance-shaped head) gets applied to a larger species of poisonous snake, the *Bothrops atrox*, which is found on a variety of Caribbean islands and in northern South America. Whether poisonous snakes exist on Dominica has long been a matter of scientific debate. In his 1791 description of Dominica, Thomas Atwood wrote that there were no poisonous snakes on the island.

6. A Carib word referring to an Amerindian-type hut with wattle-and-daub walls and a thatched roof.

'There are four hermits in this island,' she said. 'Four real ones. Others pretend but they leave when the rainy season comes. Or else they are drunk all the time. That's when sad things happen.'

'So this place is as lonely as it feels?' I asked her.

'Yes it is lonely. Are you happy here?'

'Who wouldn't be?'

'I love it more than anywhere in the world. As if it were a person. More than a person.'

'But you don't know the world,' I teased her.

'No, only here, and Jamaica of course. Coulibri, Spanish Town. I don't know the other islands at all. Is the world more beautiful, then?'

And how to answer that? 'It's different,' I said.

She told me that for a long time they had not known what was happening at Granbois. 'When Mr Mason came' (she always called her stepfather Mr Mason) 'the forest was swallowing it up.' The overseer drank, the house was dilapidated, all the furniture had been stolen, then Baptiste was discovered. A butler. In St Kitts. But born in this island and willing to come back. 'He's a very good overseer,' she'd say, and I'd agree, keeping my opinion of Baptiste, Christophine and all the others to myself. 'Baptiste says . . . Christophine wants . . .'

She trusted them and I did not. But I could hardly say so. Not yet.

We did not see a great deal of them. The kitchen and the swarming kitchen life were some way off. As for the money which she handed out so carelessly, not counting it, not knowing how much she gave, or the unfamiliar faces that appeared then disappeared, though never without a large meal eaten and a shot of rum I discovered—sisters, cousins, aunts and uncles—if she asked no questions how could I?

The house was swept and dusted very early, usually before I woke. Hilda brought coffee and there were always two roses on the tray. Sometimes she'd smile a sweet childish smile, sometimes she would giggle very loudly and rudely, bang the tray down and run away.

'Stupid little girl,' I'd say.

'No, no. She is shy. The girls here are very shy.'

After breakfast at noon there'd be silence till the evening meal which was served much later than in England. Christophine's whims and fancies, I was sure. Then we were left alone. Sometimes a sidelong look or a sly knowing glance disturbed me, but it was never for long. 'Not now,' I would think. 'Not yet.'

It was often raining when I woke during the night, a light capricious shower, dancing playful rain, or hushed muted, growing louder, more persistent, more powerful, an inexorable sound. But always music, a music I had never heard before.

Then I would look at her for long minutes by candlelight, wonder why she seemed sad asleep, and curse the fever or the caution that had made me so blind, so feeble, so hesitating. I'd remember her effort to escape. *(No, I am sorry, I do not wish to marry you.)* Had she given way to that man Richard's arguments, threats probably, I wouldn't trust him far, or to my half-serious blandishments and promises? In any case she had given way, but coldly, unwillingly, trying to protect herself with silence and a blank face. Poor weapons, and they had not served her well or lasted long. If I have forgotten caution, she has forgotten silence and coldness.

Shall I wake her up and listen to the things she says, whispers, in darkness. Not by day.

'I never wished to live before I knew you. I always thought it would be better if I died. Such a long time to wait before it's over.'

'And did you ever tell anyone this?'

'There was no one to tell, no one to listen. Oh you can't imagine Coulibri.'

'But after Coulibri?'

'After Coulibri it was too late. I did not change.'

All day she'd be like any other girl, smile at herself in her looking-glass *(do you like this scent?)*, try to teach me her songs, for they haunted me.

Adieu foulard, adieu madras,[7] or *Ma belle ka di maman li.* My beautiful girl said to her mother[8] *(No it is not like that. Now listen. It is this way).* She'd be silent, or angry for no reason, and chatter to Christophine in patois.

'Why do you hug and kiss Christophine?' I'd say.

'Why not?'

'I wouldn't hug and kiss them,' I'd say, 'I couldn't.'

At this she'd laugh for a long time and never tell me why she laughed.

But at night how different, even her voice was changed. Always this talk of death. (Is she trying to tell me that is the secret of this place? That there is no other way? She knows. She knows.)

'Why did you make me want to live? Why did you do that to me?'

'Because I wished it. Isn't that enough?'

---

7. The *foulard* is a large silk scarf worn over a dress as part of the national costume of Dominica and Martinique; *madras* is brightly colored, printed plaid or floral material used for headties, handkerchiefs, or skirts. These costumes were so beautiful that the French colonies passed "sumptuary laws" that, among other things, made it illegal for the "gens de couleur," the free women of color, to wear extravagant clothes surpassing those of the white women. Many free people of color left Martinique for Dominica because of the severity of these laws. The song is a popular Creole waltz always sung when ships leave Martinique. The refrain is a final farewell to a lover and to Martinique. At the time Rhys would have heard it the song would have been a nostalgic farewell to the colonial folklore and fashion of the Caribbean.

8. This is one of the Creole songs Rhys recorded on tape (now held at the McFarlin Library, University of Tulsa). The theme is that the beautiful girl asks her mother why pretty flowers die in a day or an instant, and the mother answers that a day and a thousand years are the same to God. Antoinette recalls these words several times during this section.

'Yes, it is enough. But if one day you didn't wish it. What should I do then? Suppose you took this happiness away when I wasn't looking . . .'

'And lose my own? Who'd be so foolish?'

'I am not used to happiness,' she said. 'It makes me afraid.'

'Never be afraid. Or if you are tell no one.'

'I understand. But trying does not help me.'

'What would?' She did not answer that, then one night whispered, 'If I could die. Now, when I am happy.[9] Would you do that? You wouldn't have to kill me. Say die and I will die. You don't believe me? Then try, try, say die and watch me die.'

'Die then! Die!' I watched her die many times. In my way, not in hers.[1] In sunlight, in shadow, by moonlight, by candlelight. In the long afternoons when the house was empty. Only the sun was there to keep us company. We shut him out. And why not? Very soon she was as eager for what's called loving as I was—more lost and drowned afterwards.

She said, 'Here I can do as I like,' not I, and then I said it too. It seemed right in that lonely place. 'Here I can do as I like.'

We seldom met anyone when we left the house. If we did they'd greet us and go on their way.

I grew to like these mountain people, silent, reserved, never servile, never curious (or so I thought), not knowing that their quick sideways looks saw everything they wished to see.

It was at night that I felt danger and would try to forget it and push it away.

'You are safe,' I'd say. She'd liked that—to be told 'you are safe.' Or I'd touch her face gently and touch tears. Tears—nothing! Words—less than nothing. As for the happiness I gave her, that was worse than nothing. I did not love her. I was thirsty for her, but that is not love. I felt very little tenderness for her, she was a stranger to me, a stranger who did not think or feel as I did.

One afternoon the sight of a dress which she'd left lying on her bedroom floor made me breathless and savage with desire. When I was exhausted I turned away from her and slept, still without a word or a caress. I woke and she was kissing me—soft light kisses. 'It is late,' she said and smiled. 'You must let me cover you up—the land breeze can be cold.'

'And you, aren't you cold?'

'Oh I will be ready quickly. I'll wear the dress you like tonight.'

'Yes, do wear it.'

The floor was strewn with garments, hers and mine. She stepped

9. Cf. *Othello* (2.1.189–91): "If it were now to die / 'Twere now to be most happy."
1. Refers to the use of death as a metaphor for sexual orgasm in poetry and colloquial speech.

over them carelessly as she walked to her clothes press. 'I was thinking, I'll have another made exactly like it,' she promised happily. 'Will you be pleased?'

'Very pleased.'

If she was a child she was not a stupid child but an obstinate one. She often questioned me about England and listened attentively to my answers, but I was certain that nothing I said made much difference. Her mind was already made up. Some romantic novel, a stray remark never forgotten, a sketch, a picture, a song, a waltz, some note of music, and her ideas were fixed. About England and about Europe. I could not change them and probably nothing would. Reality might disconcert her, bewilder her, hurt her, but it would not be reality. It would be only a mistake, a misfortune, a wrong path taken, her fixed ideas would never change.

Nothing that I told her influenced her at all.

Die then. Sleep. It is all that I can give you. . . . I wonder if she ever guessed how near she came to dying. In her way, not in mine. It was not a safe game to play—in that place. Desire, Hatred, Life, Death came very close in the darkness. Better not know how close. Better not think, never for a moment. Not close. The same . . . 'You are safe,' I'd say to her and to myself. 'Shut your eyes. Rest.'

Then I'd listen to the rain, a sleepy tune that seemed as if it would go on for ever . . . Rain, for ever raining. Drown me in sleep. And soon.

Next morning there would be very little sign of these showers. If some of the flowers were battered, the others smelt sweeter, the air was bluer and sparkling fresh. Only the clay path outside my window was muddy. Little shallow pools of water glinted in the hot sun, red earth does not dry quickly.

'It came for you this morning early, master,' Amélie said. 'Hilda take it.' She gave me a bulky envelope addressed in careful copperplate. '*By hand. Urgent*' was written in the corner.

'One of our hermit neighbours,' I thought. 'And an enclosure for Antoinette.' Then I saw Baptiste standing near the veranda steps, put the letter in my pocket and forgot it.

I was later than usual that morning but when I was dressed I sat for a long time listening to the waterfall, eyes half closed, drowsy and content. When I put my hand in my pocket for my watch, I touched the envelope and opened it.

Dear Sir. I take up my pen after long thought and meditation but in the end the truth is better than a lie. I have this to say. You have been shamefully deceived by the Mason family. They tell you perhaps that your wife's name is Cosway, the English gentleman Mr Mason being her stepfather only, but they don't tell you what sort of people were these Cosways. Wicked and detestable slave-owners since generations—yes everybody hate them in Jamaica and also in this beautiful island where I hope your stay will be long and pleasant in spite of all, for some not worth sorrow. Wickedness is not the worst. There is madness in that family. Old Cosway die raving like his father before him.

You ask what proof I have and why I mix myself up in your affairs. I will answer you. I am your wife's brother by another lady, half-way house as we say. Her father and mine was a shameless man and of all his illegitimates I am the most unfortunate and poverty stricken.

My momma die when I was quite small and my godmother take care of me. The old mister hand out some money for that though he don't like me. No, that old devil don't like me at all, and when I grow older I see it and I think, Let him wait my day will come. Ask the older people sir about his disgusting goings on, some will remember.

When Madam his wife die the reprobate marry again quick, to a young girl from Martinique—it's too much for him. Dead drunk from morning till night and he die raving and cursing.

Then comes the glorious Emancipation Act and trouble for some of the high and mighties. Nobody would work for the young woman and her two children and that place Coulibri goes quickly to bush as all does out here when nobody toil and labour on the land. She have no money and she have no friends, for French and English like cat and dog in these islands since long time. Shoot, Kill, Everything.[2]

The woman call Christophine also from Martinique stay with her and an old man Godfrey, too silly to know what happen. Some like that. This young Mrs Cosway is worthless and spoilt, she can't lift a hand for herself and soon the madness that is in her, and in all these white Creoles, come out.[3] She shut herself away, laughing and talking to nobody as many can bear witness. As for the little girl, Antoinetta, as soon as she can walk she hide herself if she see anybody.

We all wait to hear the woman jump over a precipice 'fini batt'e' as we say here which mean 'finish to fight'.

But no. She marry again to the rich Englishman Mr Mason, and there is much I could say about that but you won't believe so I shut my

2. Although France and England fought for control over most of the islands, Dominica passed back and forth between the two European powers for the entire second half of the eighteenth century, leading the Caribs to call the island "Waitukubuli," "land of many battles." France controlled Saint-Domingue, Martinique, and Guadeloupe, and Britain controlled Jamaica, Antigua, St. Kitts, and Barbados. Because of its mountainous terrain, Dominica remained in the hands of the Caribs longer than any of the other islands; although Britain and France had agreed to this arrangement in 1748, France broke the treaty and claimed Dominica. In 1763 Britain won the island, but it was recaptured by the French in 1778 and again by the British in 1783. Finally, in 1805 France sold the island to England for £12,000 and handed it over after first burning down the capital, Roseau.

3. Common metropolitan belief about the effect of "the tropics" on European colonists and their descendants.

mouth. They say he love her so much that if he have the world on a plate he give it to her—but no use.

The madness gets worse and she has to be shut away for she try to kill her husband—madness not being all either.

That sir is your wife's mother—that was her father. I leave Jamaica. I don't know what happen to the woman. Some say she is dead, other deny it. But old Mason take a great fancy for the girl Antoinetta and give her half his money when he die.

As for me I wander high and low, not much luck but a little money put by and I get to know of a house for sale in this island near Massacre. It's going very cheap so I buy it. News travel even to this wild place and next thing I hear from Jamaica is that old Mason is dead and that family plan to marry the girl to a young Englishman who know nothing of her. Then it seems to me that it is my Christian duty to warn the gentleman that she is no girl to marry with the bad blood she have from both sides. But they are white, I am coloured. They are rich, I am poor. As I think about these things they do it quick while you still weak with fever at the magistrate's, before you can ask questions. If this is true or not you must know for yourself.

Then you come to this island for your honeymoon and it's certain that the Lord put the thing on my shoulders and that it is I must speak the truth to you. Still I hesitate.

I hear you young and handsome with a kind word for all, black, white, also coloured. But I hear too that the girl is beautiful like her mother was beautiful, and you bewitch with her. She is in your blood and your bones. By night and by day. But you, an honourable man, know well that for marriage more is needed than all this. Which does not last. Old Mason bewitch so with her mother and look what happen to him. Sir I pray I am in time to warn you what to do.

Sir ask yourself how I can make up this story and for what reason. When I leave Jamaica I can read write and cypher[4] a little. The good man in Barbados teach me more, he give me books, he tell me read the Bible every day and I pick up knowledge without effort.[5] He is surprise how quick I am. Still I remain an ignorant man and I do not make up this story. I cannot. It is true.

I sit at my window and the words fly past me like birds—with God's help I catch some.

A week this letter take me. I cannot sleep at night thinking what to say. So quickly now I draw to a close and cease my task.

---

4. Do sums in arithmetic.
5. Called "little England" since it was controlled by Britain for 300 years, Barbados was known for its educational opportunities. Schools were racially segregated, and education for blacks was largely synonymous with religious instruction. The first Anglican bishop of Barbados, William Hart Coleridge, a nephew of the poet Samuel Taylor Coleridge, established a number of new chapels and church schools in the 1830s. The British government supported religious education to counteract the more liberatory teachings of the nonconformist missionaries.

Still you don't believe me? *Then ask that devil of a man Richard Mason three questions and make him answer you. Is your wife's mother shut away, a raging lunatic and worse besides? Dead or alive I do not know.*

Was your wife's brother an idiot from birth, though God mercifully take him early on?

Is your wife herself going the same way as her mother and all knowing it?

Richard Mason is a sly man and he will tell you a lot of nancy stories,[6] *which is what we call lies here, about what happen at Coulibri and this and that. Don't listen. Make him answer—yes or no.*

If he keep his mouth shut ask others for many think it shameful how that family treat you and your relatives.

I beg you sir come to see me for there is more that you should know. But my hand ache, my head ache and my heart is like a stone for the grief I bring you. Money is good but no money can pay for a crazy wife in your bed. Crazy and worse besides.

I lay down my pen with one last request. Come and see me quickly. Your obt servant. Daniel Cosway.

Ask the girl Amélie where I live. She knows, and she knows me. She belongs to this island.

I folded the letter carefully and put it into my pocket. I felt no surprise. It was as if I'd expected it, been waiting for it. For a time, long or short I don't know, I sat listening to the river. At last I stood up, the sun was hot now. I walked stiffly nor could I force myself to think. Then I passed an orchid with long sprays of golden-brown flowers. One of them touched my cheek and I remembered picking some for her one day. 'They are like you,' I told her. Now I stopped, broke a spray off and trampled it into the mud. This brought me to my senses. I leaned against a tree, sweating and trembling. 'Far too hot today,' I said aloud, 'far too hot.' When I came in sight of the house I began to walk silently. No one was about. The kitchen door was shut and the place looked deserted. I went up the steps and along the veranda and when I heard voices stopped behind the door which led into Antoinette's room. I could see it reflected in the looking-glass. She was in bed and the girl Amélie was sweeping.

'Finish quickly,' said Antoinette, 'and go and tell Christophine I want to see her.'

Amélie rested her hands on the broom handle. 'Christophine is going,' she said.

'Going?' repeated Antoinette.

'Yes, going,' said Amélie. 'Christophine don't like this sweet honey-

6. Deriving from West African and Caribbean tales about Anancy, a cunning and greedy spider who can take on different forms and who succeeds not by strength but by trickery.

moon house.' Turning round she saw me and laughed loudly. 'Your husban' he outside the door and he look like he see zombi. Must be he tired of the sweet honeymoon too.'

Antoinette jumped out of bed and slapped her face.

'I hit you back white cockroach, I hit you back,' said Amélie. And she did.

Antoinette gripped her hair. Amélie, whose teeth were bared, seemed to be trying to bite.

'Antoinette, for God's sake,' I said from the doorway.

She swung round, very pale. Amélie buried her face in her hands and pretended to sob, but I could see her watching me through her fingers.

'Go away, child,' I said.

'You call her child,' said Antoinette. 'She is older than the devil himself, and the devil is not more cruel.'

'Send Christophine up,' I said to Amélie.

'Yes master, yes master,' she answered softly, dropping her eyes. But as soon as she was out of the room she began to sing:

> 'The white cockroach she marry
> The white cockroach she marry
> The white cockroach she buy young man
> The white cockroach she marry.'

Antoinette took a few steps forward. She walked unsteadily. I went to help her but she pushed me away, sat on the bed and with clenched teeth pulled at the sheet, then made a clicking sound of annoyance. She took a pair of scissors from the round table, cut through the hem and tore the sheet in half, then each half into strips.

The noise she made prevented me from hearing Christophine come in, but Antoinette heard her.

'You're not leaving?' she said.

'Yes,' said Christophine.

'And what will become of me?' said Antoinette.

'Get up, girl, and dress yourself. Woman must have spunks[7] to live in this wicked world.'

She had changed into a drab cotton dress and taken off her heavy gold ear-rings.

'I see enough trouble,' she said. 'I have right to my rest. I have my house that your mother give me so long ago and I have my garden and my son to work for me. A lazy boy but I make him work. Too besides[8] the young master don't like me, and perhaps I don't like him so much. If I stay here I bring trouble and bone of contention in your house.'

7. Boldness, courage.
8. Moreover.

'If you are not happy here then go,' said Antoinette.

Amélie came into the room with two jugs of hot water. She looked at me sideways and smiled.

Christophine said in a soft voice, 'Amélie. Smile like that once more, just once more, and I mash your face like I mash plantain.[9] You hear me? Answer me, girl.'

'Yes, Christophine,' Amélie said. She looked frightened.

'And too besides I give you bellyache like you never see bellyache. Perhaps you lie a long time with the bellyache I give you. Perhaps you don't get up again with the bellyache I give you. So keep yourself quiet and decent. You hear me?'

'Yes, Christophine,' Amélie said and crept out of the room.

'She worthless and good for nothing,' said Christophine with contempt. 'She creep and crawl like centipede.'

She kissed Antoinette on the cheek. Then she looked at me, shook her head, and muttered in patois before she went out.

'Did you hear what that girl was singing?' Antoinette said.

'I don't always understand what they say or sing.' Or anything else.

'It was a song about a white cockroach. That's me. That's what they call all of us who were here before their own people in Africa sold them to the slave traders.[1] And I've heard English women call us white niggers. So between you I often wonder who I am and where is my country and where do I belong and why was I ever born at all. Will you go now please. I must dress like Christophine said.'

After I had waited half an hour I knocked at her door. There was no answer so I asked Baptiste to bring me something to eat. He was sitting under the Seville orange tree at the end of the veranda. He served the food with such a mournful expression that I thought these people are very vulnerable. How old was I when I learned to hide what I felt? A very small boy. Six, five, even earlier. It was necessary, I was told, and that view I have always accepted. If these mountains challenge me, or Baptiste's face, or Antoinette's eyes, they are mistaken, melodramatic, unreal (England must be quite unreal and like a dream she said).

The rum punch I had drunk was very strong and after the meal was over I had a great wish to sleep. And why not? This is the time when everyone sleeps. I imagined the dogs the cats the cocks and hens all sleeping, even the water in the river running more slowly.

I woke up, thought at once of Antoinette and opened the door into her room, but she was sleeping too. Her back was towards me and she

9. A starchy banana, cooked like a vegetable.
1. When African societies did acquire or sell slaves, they were usually recent prisoners of war, those not considered part of the society. African slavery was a popular white apology for and defense of the enslavement of blacks by whites in the New World.

was quite still. I looked out of the window. The silence was disturbing, absolute. I would have welcomed the sound of a dog barking, a man sawing wood. Nothing. Silence. Heat. It was five minutes to three.

I went out following the path I could see from my window. It must have rained heavily during the night for the red clay was very muddy. I passed a sparse plantation of coffee trees, then straggly guava bushes. As I walked I remembered my father's face and his thin lips, my brother's round conceited eyes. They knew. And Richard the fool, he knew too. And the girl with her blank smiling face. They all knew.

I began to walk very quickly, then stopped because the light was different. A green light. I had reached the forest and you cannot mistake the forest. It is hostile. The path was overgrown but it was possible to follow it. I went on without looking at the tall trees on either side. Once I stepped over a fallen log swarming with white ants. How can one discover truth I thought and that thought led me nowhere. No one would tell me the truth. Not my father nor Richard Mason, certainly not the girl I had married. I stood still, so sure I was being watched that I looked over my shoulder. Nothing but the trees and the green light under the trees. A track was just visible and I went on, glancing from side to side and sometimes quickly behind me. This was why I stubbed my foot on a stone and nearly fell. The stone I had tripped on was not a boulder but part of a paved road. There had been a paved road through this forest. The track led to a large clear space. Here were the ruins of a stone house and round the ruins rose trees that had grown to an incredible height. At the back of the ruins a wild orange tree covered with fruit, the leaves a dark green. A beautiful place. And calm—so calm that it seemed foolish to think or plan. What had I to think about and how could I plan? Under the orange tree I noticed little bunches of flowers tied with grass.[2]

I don't know how long it was before I began to feel chilly. The light had changed and the shadows were long. I had better get back before dark, I thought. Then I saw a little girl carrying a large basket on her head. I met her eyes and to my astonishment she screamed loudly, threw up her arms and ran. The basket fell off, I called after her, but she screamed again and ran faster. She sobbed as she ran, a small frightened sound. Then she disappeared. I must be within a few minutes of the path I thought, but after I had walked for what seemed a long time I found that the undergrowth and creepers caught at my legs and the trees closed over my head. I decided to go back to the clearing and start again, with the same result. It was getting dark. It was useless to tell myself that I was not far from the house. I was lost and afraid among these enemy trees, so certain of danger that when I heard

2. A Vodou offering.

footsteps and a shout I did not answer. The footsteps and the voice came nearer. Then I shouted back. I did not recognize Baptiste at first. He was wearing blue cotton trousers pulled up above his knees and a broad ornamented belt round his slim waist. His machete was in his hand and the light caught the razor-sharp blue-white edge. He did not smile when he saw me.

'We look for you a long time,' he said.

'I got lost.'

He grunted in answer and led the way, walking in front of me very quickly and cutting off any branch or creeper that stopped us with an easy swing of his machete.

I said, 'There was a road here once, where did it lead to?'

'No road,' he said.

'But I saw it. A *pavé* road like the French made in the islands.'

'No road.'

'Who lived in that house?'

'They say a priest. Père Lilièvre. He lived here a long time ago.'[3]

'A child passed,' I said. 'She seemed very frightened when she saw me. Is there something wrong about the place?' He shrugged his shoulders.

'Is there a ghost, a zombi there?' I persisted.

'Don't know nothing about all that foolishness.'

'There was a road here sometime.'

'No road,' he repeated obstinately.

It was nearly dark when we were back on the red clay path. He walked more slowly, turned and smiled at me. It was as if he'd put his service mask on the savage reproachful face I had seen.

'You don't like the woods at night?'

He did not answer, but pointed to a light and said, 'It's a long time I've been looking for you. Miss Antoinette frightened you come to harm.'

When we reached the house I felt very weary.

'You look like you catch fever,' he said.

3. A reference to the Parisian Dominican priest Père Jean-Baptiste Labat who arrived in colonial Martinique in 1693 and visited Dominica several times. His book about French Caribbean society, *Nouveau Voyage aux Isles de l'Ameríque*, was published in Paris in 1722. He was particularly appalled by black spiritual practices and recounts having an obeahman viciously beaten and tortured. Labat believed slavery to be a legitimate means of redeeming slaves from what he maintained were dangerous superstitions incited by the devil. In his 1890 book *Two Years in the French West Indies*, Lafcadio Hearn documents various legends that developed about Père Labat. Based, perhaps, on Labat's defense of slavery and his cruelty, one of the legends incorrectly attributes to him the introduction of slavery and holds that his spirit, sometimes visible in remote forested places, wanders the islands in penance for his crime. He is supposed to haunt especially the Morne d'Orange in Martinique, and stories of his ghostly presence are used to frighten children into good behavior. Hearn writes of Père Labat that, ironically, "his very name is seldom uttered but in connection with superstitions,—has been, in fact, preserved among the blacks by the power of superstition alone, by the belief in zombis and goblins" (Lafcadio Hearn, *Two Years in the French West Indies* [New York: Harper & Bros, 1890], pp. 151–74).

'I've had that already.'

'No limit to times you catch fever.'

There was no one on the veranda and no sound from the house. We both stood in the road looking up, then he said, 'I send the girl to you, master.'

Hilda brought me a large bowl of soup and some fruit. I tried the door into Antoinette's room. It was bolted and there was no light. Hilda giggled. A nervous giggle.

I told her that I did not want anything to eat, to bring me the decanter of rum and a glass. I drank, then took up the book I had been reading, *The Glittering Coronet of Isles*[4] it was called, and I turned to the chapter 'Obeah':

'*A zombi is a dead person who seems to be alive or a living person who is dead. A zombi can also be the spirit of a place, usually malignant but sometimes to be propitiated with sacrifices or offerings of flowers and fruit.*' I thought at once of the bunches of flowers at the priest's ruined house. '*"They cry out in the wind that is their voice, they rage in the sea that is their anger."*

'*So I was told, but I have noticed that negroes as a rule refuse to discuss the black magic in which so many believe. Voodoo as it is called in Haiti—Obeah in some of the islands, another name in South America. They confuse matters by telling lies if pressed. The white people, sometimes credulous, pretend to dismiss the whole thing as nonsense. Cases of sudden or mysterious death are attributed to a poison known to the negroes which cannot be traced. It is further complicated by . . .*'[5]

I did not look up though I saw him at the window but rode on without thinking till I came to the rocks.[6] People here call them Mounes Mors (the Dead Ones). Preston shied at them, they say horses always do. Then he stumbled badly, so I dismounted and walked along with the bridle over my arm. It was getting hot and I was tired when I reached

---

4. This fictional title might have been suggested to Rhys by the many uses of "glittering" in *Jane Eyre*, including Mr. Rochester's question, "Jane, have you a glittering ornament round your neck?" (*Jane Eyre*, ch. 38).

5. The zombi is a specifically Caribbean figure created by the magic of Vodou. Vodou itself is a creolized, syncretic religion, a combination of several West African religions transported to Saint-Domingue with the slaves, adapted to the new social and political situation of slavery, and overlaid with Christian symbols introduced by the English, French, and Spanish slaveholders. It is currently the religion and worldview of the greater part of the peasants and urban proletariat of the Republic of Haiti as well as of members of the Haitian elite. Ethnobiologists provide a non-magical interpretation of zombiism as the result of poisoning by tetrodotoxin, derived from various species of the puffer fish, which causes a catatonic state resembling death. Given an antidote and kept in isolation, the victim becomes a zombi—disoriented, amnesiac, one of the living dead.

6. The following section is narrated by Antoinette.

the path to Christophine's two-roomed house, the roof shingled, not thatched. She was sitting on a box under her mango tree, smoking a white clay pipe and she called out, 'It's you, Antoinette? Why you come up here so early?'

'I just wanted to see you,' I said.

She helped me loosen Preston's girth and led him to a stream near by. He drank as if he were very thirsty, then shook himself and snorted. Water flew out of his nostrils. We left him cropping grass and went back to the mango tree. She sat on her box and pushed another towards me, but I knelt close to her touching a thin silver bangle that she always wore.

'You smell the same,' I said.

'You come all this long way to tell me that?' she said. Her clothes smelled of clean cotton, starched and ironed. I had seen her so often standing knee deep in the river at Coulibri, her long skirt hitched up, washing her dresses and her white shifts, then beating them against the stones. Sometimes there would be other women all bringing their washing down on the stones again and again, a gay busy noise. At last they would spread the wet clothes in the sun, wipe their foreheads, start laughing and talking. She smelled too, of their smell, so warm and comforting to me (but he does not like it). The sky was dark blue through the dark green mango leaves, and I thought, 'This is my place and this is where I belong and this is where I wish to stay.' Then I thought, 'What a beautiful tree, but it is too high up here for mangoes and it may never bear fruit,' and I thought of lying alone in my bed with the soft silk cotton mattress and fine sheets, listening. At last I said, 'Christophine, he does not love me, I think he hates me. He always sleeps in his dressing-room now and the servants know. If I get angry he is scornful and silent, sometimes he does not speak to me for hours and I cannot endure it any more, I cannot. What shall I do? He was not like that at first,' I said.

Pink and red hibiscus grew in front of her door, she lit her pipe and did not answer.

'Answer me,' I said. She puffed out a cloud of smoke.

'You ask me a hard thing, I tell you a hard thing, pack up and go.'

'Go, go where? To some strange place where I shall never see him? No, I will not, then everyone, not only the servants, will laugh at me.'

'It's not you they laugh at if you go, they laugh at him.'

'I will not do that.'

'Why you ask me, if when I answer you say no? Why you come up here if when I tell you the truth, you say no?'

'But there must be something else I can do.'

She looked gloomy. 'When man don't love you, more you try, more he hate you, man like that. If you love them they treat you bad, if you don't love them they after you night and day bothering your soul case out.[7] I hear about you and your husband,' she said.

'But I cannot go. He is my husband after all.'

She spat over her shoulder. 'All women, all colours, nothing but fools. Three children I have. One living in this world, each one a different father, but no husband, I thank my God. I keep my money. I don't give it to no worthless man.'

'When must I go, where must I go?'

'But look me trouble,[8] a rich white girl like you and more foolish than the rest. A man don't treat you good, pick up your skirt and walk out. Do it and he come after you.'

'He will not come after me. And you must understand I am not rich now, I have no money of my own at all, everything I had belongs to him.'

'What you tell me there?' she said sharply.

'That is English law.'[9]

'Law! The Mason boy fix it, that boy worse than Satan and he burn in Hell one of these fine nights. Listen to me now and I advise you what to do. Tell your husband you feeling sick, you want to visit your cousin in Martinique. Ask him pretty for some of your own money, the man not bad-hearted, he give it. When you get away, stay away. Ask more. He give again and well satisfy. In the end he come to find out what you do, how you get on without him, and if he see you fat and happy he want you back. Men like that. Better not stay in that old house. Go from that house, I tell you.'

'You think I must leave him?'

'You ask me so I answer.'

'Yes,' I said. 'After all I could, but why should I go to Martinique? I wish to see England, I might be able to borrow money for that. Not from him but I know how I might get it. I must travel far, if I go.'

I have been too unhappy, I thought, it cannot last, being so unhappy, it would kill you. I will be a different person when I live in England and different things will happen to me. . . . England, rosy pink in the geography book map, but on the page opposite the words are closely crowded, heavy looking. Exports, coal, iron, wool. Then Imports and Character of Inhabitants. Names, Essex, Chelmsford on the Chelmer. The Yorkshire and Lincolnshire wolds. Wolds? Does that mean hills?

7. Wearing you out, making you work too hard; "soul case": the body.
8. Expression of alarm.
9. Until the Married Woman's Property Act of 1870, a wife's personal property before marriage became her husband's absolutely, unless settled in trust for her. The husband could assign or dispose of it at his pleasure, whether he and his wife lived together or not. Any income that descended to her as an heiress and any money she earned belonged absolutely to her husband. John Stuart Mill described this law in *The Subjection of Women* (1869): "[The wife] can acquire no property but for him; the instant it becomes hers, even if by inheritance, it becomes *ipso facto* his. In this respect the wife's position under the common law of England is worse than that of slaves in the laws of many countries."

How high? Half the height of ours, or not even that? Cool green leaves
in the short cool summer. Summer. There are fields of corn like sugar-
cane fields, but gold colour and not so tall. After summer the trees are
bare, then winter and snow. White feathers falling? Torn pieces of
paper falling? They say frost makes flower patterns on the window
panes. I must know more than I know already. For I know that house
where I will be cold and not belonging, the bed I shall lie in has red
curtains and I have slept there many times before, long ago. How long
ago? In that bed I will dream the end of my dream. But my dream had
nothing to do with England and I must not think like this, I must
remember about chandeliers and dancing, about swans and roses and
snow. And snow.

   'England,' said Christophine, who was watching me. 'You think there
is such a place?'

   'How can you ask that? You know there is.'

   'I never see the damn place, how I know?'

   'You do not believe that there is a country called England?'

   She blinked and answered quickly, 'I don't say I don't *believe*, I say
I don't *know*, I know what I see with my eyes and I never see it.[1] Besides
I ask myself is this place like they tell us? Some say one thing, some
different, I hear it cold to freeze your bones and they thief your money,
clever like the devil. You have money in your pocket, you look again
and bam! No money. Why you want to go to this cold thief place? If
there is this place at all, I never see it, that is one thing sure.'

   I stared at her, thinking, 'but how can she know the best thing for
me to do, this ignorant, obstinate old negro woman, who is not certain
if there is such a place as England?' She knocked out her pipe and
stared back at me, her eyes had no expression at all.

   'Christophine,' I said, 'I may do as you advise. But not yet.' (Now, I
thought, I must say what I came to say.) 'You knew what I wanted as
soon as you saw me, and you certainly know now. Well, don't you?' I
heard my voice getting high and thin.

   'Hush up,' she said. 'If the man don't love you, I can't make him
love you.'

   'Yes you can, I know you can. That is what I wish and that is why
I came here. You can make people love or hate. Or . . . or die,' I
said.

   She threw back her head and laughed loudly. (But she never laughs
loudly and why is she laughing at all?)

   'So you believe in that tim-tim story[2] about obeah, you hear when

1. Rhys refers to a quote she particularly liked by Somerset Maugham, whom she knew from
   his novels set in the Caribbean: " 'We *believe* the earth is round; we *know* it is flat.' Quite so.
   That applies to a lot of other things. We believe what we have been told, the theory. What
   we know, we know" (*SP*, p. 144).
2. A tall tale, an unbelievable story; from the cry by a storyteller announcing to the audience
   the beginning of the folk tale.

you so high? All that foolishness and folly. Too besides, that is not for
béké.[3] Bad, bad trouble come when *béké* meddle with that.'

'You must,' I said. 'You must.'

'Hush up. Jo-jo my son coming to see me, if he catch you crying,
he tell everybody.'

'I will be quiet, I will not cry. But Christophine, if he, my husband,
could come to me one night. Once more, I would make him love me.'

'No *doudou*. No.'

'Yes, Christophine.'

'You talk foolishness. Even if I can make him come to your bed, I
cannot make him love you. Afterward he hate you.'

'No. And what do I care if he does? He hates me now. I hear him
every night walking up and down the veranda. Up and down. When
he passes my door he says, "Good-night, Bertha."[4] He never calls me
Antoinette now. He has found out it was my mother's name. "I hope
you will sleep well, Bertha"—it cannot be worse,' I said. 'That one night
he came I might sleep afterwards. I sleep so badly now. And I dream.'

'No, I don't meddle with that for you.'

Then I beat my fist on a stone, forcing myself to speak calmly.

'Going away to Martinique or England or anywhere else, that is the
lie. He would never give me any money to go away and he would be
furious if I asked him. There would be a scandal if I left him and he
hates scandal. Even if I got away (and how?) he would force me back.
So would Richard. So would everybody else. Running away from him,
from this island, is the lie. What reason could I give for going and who
would believe me?'

When she bent her head she looked old and I thought, 'Oh Christophine, do not grow old. You are the only friend I have, do not go
away from me into being old.'

'Your husband certainly love money,' she said. 'That is no lie. Money
have pretty face for everybody, but for that man money pretty like pretty
self, he can't see nothing else.'

'Help me then.'

'Listen *doudou ché*. Plenty people fasten bad words on you and on
your mother. I know it. I know who is talking and what they say. The
man not a bad man, even if he love money, but he hear so many stories
he don't know what to believe. That is why he keep away. I put no
trust in none of those people round you. Not here, not in Jamaica.'

'Not Aunt Cora?'

'Your aunty old woman now, she turn her face to the wall.'

'*How do you know?*' I said. For that is what happened.

---

3. A white person.
4. In *Jane Eyre*, Mrs. Rochester's name before marriage is Bertha Antoinetta Mason.

When I passed her room, I heard her quarrelling with Richard and I knew it was about my marriage. 'It's disgraceful,' she said. 'It's shameful. You are handing over everything the child owns to a perfect stranger. Your father would never have allowed it. She should be protected, legally. A settlement can be arranged and it should be arranged. That was his intention.'

'You are talking about an honourable gentleman, not a rascal,' Richard said. 'I am not in a position to make conditions, as you know very well. She is damn lucky to get him, all things considered. Why should I insist on a lawyer's settlement when I trust him? I would trust him with my life,' he went on in an affected voice.

'You are trusting him with her life, not yours,' she said.

He told her for God's sake shut up you old fool and banged the door when he left. So angry that he did not notice me standing in the passage. She was sitting up in bed when I went into her room. 'Halfwit that the boy is, or pretends to be. I do not like what I have seen of this honourable gentleman. Stiff. Hard as a board and stupid as a foot, in my opinion, except where his own interests are concerned.'

She was very pale and shaking all over, so I gave her the smelling salts on the dressing-table. They were in a red glass bottle with a gilt top. She put the bottle to her nose but her hand dropped as though she were too tired to hold it steady. Then she turned away from the window, the sky, the looking-glass, the pretty things on the dressing-table. The red and gilt bottle fell to the floor. She turned her face to the wall. 'The Lord has forsaken us,' she said, and shut her eyes. She did not speak again, and after a while I thought she was asleep. She was too ill to come to my wedding and I went to say good-bye, I was excited and happy thinking now it is my honeymoon. I kissed her and she gave me a little silk bag. 'My rings. Two are valuable. Don't show it to him. Hide it away. Promise me.'

I promised, but when I opened it, one of the rings was plain gold. I thought I might sell another yesterday but who will buy what I have to sell here? . . .

Christophine was saying, 'Your aunty too old and sick, and that Mason boy worthless. Have spunks and do battle for yourself. Speak to your husband calm and cool, tell him about your mother and all what happened at Coulibri and why she get sick and what they do to her. Don't bawl at the man and don't make crazy faces. Don't cry either. Crying no good with him. Speak nice and make him understand.'

'I have tried,' I said, 'but he does not believe me. It is too late for that now' (it is always too late for truth, I thought). 'I will try again if you will do what I ask. Oh Christophine, I am so afraid,' I said, 'I do not know why, but so afraid. All the time. Help me.'

She said something I did not hear. Then she took a sharp stick and drew lines and circles on the earth under the tree, then rubbed them out with her foot.

'If you talk to him first I do what you ask me.'

'Now?'

'Yes,' she said. 'Now look at me. Look in my eyes.'

I was giddy when I stood up, and she went into the house muttering and came out with a cup of coffee.

'Good shot of white rum in that,' she said. 'Your face like dead woman and your eyes red like *soucriant*.[5] Keep yourself quiet—look, Jo-jo coming, he talk to everybody about what he hear. Nothing but leaky calabash that boy.'

When I had drunk the coffee I began to laugh. 'I have been so unhappy for nothing, nothing,' I said.

Her son was carrying a large basket on his head. I watched his strong brown legs swinging along the path so easily. He seemed surprised and inquisitive when he saw me, but he asked politely in patois, was I well, was the master in good health?

'Yes, Jo-jo, thank you, we are both well.'

Christophine helped him with the basket, then she brought out the bottle of white rum and poured out half a tumblerful. He swallowed it quickly. Then she filled the glass with water and he drank that like they do.

She said in English, 'The mistress is going, her horse at the back there. Saddle him up.'

I followed her into the house. There was a wooden table in the outer room, a bench and two broken-down chairs. Her bedroom was large and dark. She still had her bright patchwork counterpane, the palm leaf from Palm Sunday[6] and the prayer for a happy death. But after I noticed a heap of chicken feathers in one corner, I did not look round any more.

'So already you frightened eh?' And when I saw her expression I took my purse from my pocket and threw it on the bed.

'You don't have to give me money. I do this foolishness because you beg me—not for money.'

'Is it foolishness?' I said, whispering and she laughed again, but softly.

'If *béké* say it foolishness, then it foolishness. *Béké* clever like the devil. More clever than God. Ain't so? Now listen and I will tell you what to do.'

5. Legendary blood-sucking creature, usually female, who travels by night as a ball of fire but looks like an ordinary person by day. "Souciants were always women . . . who came at night and sucked your blood. During the day they looked like ordinary women but you could tell them by their red eyes" (SP, p. 23). In *Jane Eyre*, Jane associates Bertha with "the foul German spectre—the Vampyre" (ch. 25).
6. The Sunday before Easter; it commemorates with palms Christ's triumphal entry into Jerusalem. Christophine does not find Catholic symbology or belief incompatible with beliefs of African origin.

When we came out into the sunlight, Jo-jo was holding Preston near a big stone. I stood on it and mounted.

'Good-bye, Christophine; good-bye, Jo-jo.'

'Good-bye, mistress.'

'You will come and see me very soon, Christophine?'

'Yes, I will come.'

I looked back at the end of the path. She was talking to Jo-jo and he seemed curious and amused. Nearby a cock crew and I thought, 'That is for betrayal, but who is the traitor?' She did not want to do this. I forced her with my ugly money. And what does anyone know about traitors, or why Judas did what he did?[7]

I can remember every second of that morning, if I shut my eyes I can see the deep blue colour of the sky and the mango leaves, the pink and red hibiscus, the yellow handkerchief she wore round her head, tied in the Martinique fashion with the sharp points in front, but now I see everything still, fixed for ever like the colours in a stained-glass window. Only the clouds move. It was wrapped in a leaf, what she had given me, and I felt it cool and smooth against my skin.

'The mistress pay a visit,' Baptiste told me when he brought my coffee that morning.[8] 'She will come back tonight or tomorrow. She make up her mind in a hurry and she has gone.'

In the afternoon Amélie brought me a second letter.

Why you don't answer. You don't believe me? Then ask someone else—everybody in Spanish Town know. Why you think they bring you to this place? You want me to come to your house and bawl out your business before everybody? You come to me or I come—

At this point I stopped reading. The child Hilda came into the room and I asked her, 'Is Amélie here?'

'Yes, master.'

'Tell her I wish to speak to her.'

'Yes, master.'

She put her hand over her mouth as if to stifle laughter, but her eyes, which were the blackest I had ever seen, so black that it was impossible to distinguish the pupils from the iris, were alarmed and bewildered.

I sat on the veranda with my back to the sea and it was as if I had done it all my life. I could not imagine different weather or a different sky. I knew the shape of the mountains as well as I knew the shape

---

7. Judas Iscariot, one of Jesus' twelve disciples, betrayed Jesus to the authorities. In the Gospel of St. Matthew, Judas is given thirty pieces of silver and identifies Jesus by kissing him.
8. Antoinette's husband resumes the narration for the remainder of Part Two.

of the two brown jugs filled with white sweet-scented flowers on the
wooden table. I knew that the girl would be wearing a white dress.
Brown and white she would be, her curls, her white girl's hair she called
it, half covered with a red handkerchief, her feet bare. There would be
the sky and the mountains, the flowers and the girl and the feeling that
all this was a nightmare, the faint consoling hope that I might wake
up.

She leaned lightly against the veranda post, indifferently graceful,
just respectful enough, and waited.

'Was this letter given to you?' I asked.

'No, master. Hilda take it.'

'And is this man who writes a friend of yours?'

'Not my friend,' she said.

'But he knows you—or says he does.'

'Oh yes, I know Daniel.'

'Very well then. Will you tell him that his letters annoy me, and that
he'd better not write again for his own sake. If he brings a letter give it
back to him. Understand?'

'Yes, master. I understand.'

Still leaning against the post she smiled at me, and I felt that at any
moment her smile would become loud laughter. It was to stop this that
I went on, 'Why does he write to me?'

She answered innocently, 'He don't tell you that? He write you two
letters and he don't say why he is writing? If you don't know then I
don't know.'

'But you know him?' I said. 'Is his name Cosway?'

'Some people say yes, some people say no. That's what he calls
himself.'

She added thoughtfully that Daniel was a very superior man, always
reading the Bible and that he lived like white people. I tried to find
out what she meant by this, and she explained that he had a house like
white people, with one room only for sitting in. That he had two pictures on the wall of his father and his mother.

'White people?'

'Oh no, coloured.'

'But he told me in his first letter that his father was a white man.'

She shrugged her shoulders. 'All that too long ago for me.' It was
easy to see her contempt for long ago. 'I tell him what you say, master.'
Then she added, 'Why you don't go and see him? It is much better.
Daniel is a bad man and he will come here and make trouble for you.
It's better he don't come. They say one time he was a preacher in
Barbados, he talk like a preacher, and he have a brother in Jamaica in
Spanish Town, Mr Alexander. Very wealthy man. He own three rum
shops and two dry goods stores.' She flicked a look at me as sharp as a
knife. 'I hear one time that Miss Antoinette and his son Mr Sandi get

married, but that all foolishness. Miss Antoinette a white girl with a lot
of money, she won't marry with a coloured man even though he don't
look like a coloured man. You ask Miss Antoinette, she tell you.'

Like Hilda she put her hand over her mouth as though she could
not stop herself from laughing and walked away.

Then turned and said in a very low voice, 'I am sorry for you.'

'What did you say?'

'I don't say nothing, master.'

A large table covered with a red fringed cloth made the small room
seem hotter; the only window was shut.

'I put your chair near the door,' Daniel said, 'a breeze come in from
underneath.' But there was no breeze, not a breath of air, this place
was lower down the mountain almost at sea-level.

'When I hear you coming I take a good shot of rum, and then I take
a glass of water to cool me down, but it don't cool me down, it run
out of my eyes in tears and lamentations. Why don't you give me an
answer when I write to you the first time?' He went on talking, his eyes
fixed on a framed text hanging on the dirty white wall, 'Vengeance is
Mine'.[9]

'You take too long, Lord,' he told it. 'I hurry you up a bit.' Then he
wiped his thin yellow face and blew his nose on a corner of the
tablecloth.

'They call me Daniel,' he said, still not looking at me, 'but my name
is Esau.[1] All I get is curses and get-outs from that damn devil my father.
My father old Cosway, with his white marble tablet in the English
church at Spanish Town for all to see.[2] It have a crest on it and a motto
in Latin and words in big black letters. I never know such lies. I hope
that stone tie round his neck and drag him down to Hell in the end.
"Pious", they write up. "Beloved by all". Not a word about the people
he buy and sell like cattle. "Merciful to the weak", they write up.
Mercy! The man have a heart like stone. Sometimes when he get sick
of a woman which is quickly, he free her like he free my mother, even
he give her a hut and a bit of land for herself (a garden some call that),
but it is no mercy, it's for wicked pride he do it. I never put my eyes

9. In Paul's epistle to Romans (12:17–21), Paul counsels, "never pay back evil with evil . . . as
scripture says 'Vengeance is Mine—I will pay them back, the Lord promises' " (cf. Deuter-
onomy 32:35).
1. Esau is the biblical first-born son of Isaac and Rebecca who is cheated out of his birthright
and paternal blessing by his younger twin brother, Jacob. For the most part, the biblical
literature accepts Jacob's deceitful actions and portrays Esau as a godless and jealous person
rejected by God because of wicked deeds and an evil disposition. There are two Daniels in
the Bible. The first is David's second son, born between Amnon and Absolom. The second
is the prophet of apocalyptic visions who interpreted dreams and mysterious signs by divine
revelation. An addition to the Book of Daniel recounts Daniel clearing Susanna of spurious
charges of adultery.
2. Rhys's great-grandfather, the slave-owner James Potter Lockhart, was similarly commemorated
with a marble plaque in the Anglican church in Dominica.

on a man haughty and proud like that—he walk like he own the earth. "I don't give a damn," he says. Let him wait. . . . I can still see that tablet before my eyes because I go to look at it often. I know by heart all the lies they tell—no one to stand up and say, Why you write lies in the church? . . . I tell you this so you can know what sort of people you mix up with. The heart know its own bitterness but to keep it lock up all the time, that is hard. I remember it like yesterday the morning he put a curse on me. Sixteen years old I was and anxious. I start very early. I walk all the way to Coulibri—five six hours it take. He don't refuse to see me; he receive me very cool and calm and first thing he tell me is I'm always pestering him for money. This because sometimes I ask help to buy a pair of shoes and such. Not to go barefoot like a nigger. Which I am not. He look at me like I was dirt and I get angry too. "I have my rights after all,"[3] I tell him and you know what he do? He laugh in my face. When he finished laughing he call me what's-your-name. "I can't remember all their names—it's too much to expect of me," he says, talking to himself. Very old he look in the bright sunshine that morning. "It's you yourself call me Daniel," I tell him. "I'm no slave like my mother was."

' "Your mother was a sly-boots[4] if ever there was one," he says, "and I'm not a fool. However the woman's dead and that's enough. But if there's one drop of my blood in your spindly carcass I'll eat my hat." By this time my own blood at boiling point, I tell you, so I bawl back at him, "Eat it then. Eat it. You haven't much time. Not much time either to kiss and love your new wife. She too young for you." "Great God!" he said and his face go red and then a kind of grey colour. He try to get up but he falls back in his chair. He have a big silver inkstand on his desk, he throw it at my head and he curse me, but I duck and the inkstand hit the door. I have to laugh but I go off quick. He send me some money—not a word, only the money. It's the last time I see him.'

Daniel breathed deeply and wiped his face again and offered me some rum. When I thanked him and shook my head he poured himself half a glassful and swallowed it.

'All that long time ago,' he said.

'Why did you wish to see me, Daniel?'

The last drink seemed to have sobered him. He looked at me directly and spoke more naturally.

'I insist because I have this to say. When you ask if what I tell you is true, you will ask though you don't like me, I see that; but you know well my letter was no lie. Take care who you talk to. Many people like

---

3. By 1813 there was legislation that allowed free people of color to inherit unlimited property; there was, however, no obligation for a white father to will any part of his estate to illegitimate children from interracial relations.
4. A person (usually a woman) who is cunning and tricky especially in an engaging, diverting way.

to say things behind your back, to your face they get frightened, or they don't want to mix up. The magistrate now, he know a lot, but his wife very friendly with the Mason family and she stop him if she can. Then there is my half brother Alexander, coloured like me but not unlucky like me, he will want to tell you all sorts of lies. He was the old man's favourite and he prosper right from the start. Yes, Alexander is a rich man now but he keep quiet about it. Because he prosper he is two-faced, he won't speak against white people. There is that woman up at your house, Christophine. She is the worst. She have to leave Jamaica because she go to jail: you know that?'

'Why was she sent to jail? What did she do?'

His eyes slid away from mine. 'I tell you I leave Spanish Town, I don't know all that happen. It's something very bad. She is obeah woman and they catch her.[5] I don't believe in all that devil business but many believe. Christophine is a bad woman and she will lie to you worse than your wife. Your own wife she talks sweet talk and she lies.'

The black and gilt clock on a shelf struck four.

I must go. I must get away from his yellow sweating face and his hateful little room. I sat still, numb, staring at him.

'You like my clock?' said Daniel. 'I work hard to buy it. But it's to please myself. I don't have to please no woman. Buy me this and buy me that—demons incarnate in my opinion. Alexander now, he can't keep away from them, and in the end he marry a very fair-coloured girl, very respectable family. His son Sandi is like a white man, but more handsome than any white man, and received by many white people they say. Your wife know Sandi since long time. Ask her and she tell you. But not everything I think.' He laughed. 'Oh no, not everything. I see them when they think nobody see them. I see her when she . . . You going eh?' He darted to the doorway.

'No you don't go before I tell you the last thing. You want me to shut my mouth about what I know. She start with Sandi. They fool you well about that girl. She look you straight in the eye and talk sweet talk—and it's lies she tell you. Lies. Her mother was so. They say she worse than her mother, and she hardly more than a child. Must be you deaf you don't hear people laughing when you marry her. Don't waste your anger on me, sir. It's not I fool you, it's I wish to open your eyes.'

5. As healers and spiritual leaders, practitioners of obeah wielded a great deal of influence in slave communities and received worried attention from white legislators, especially in Jamaica after the slave rebellion of 1760, which was said to have been fomented by obeah men and women. The penalties for the practice of obeah included execution or transportation. As Matthew Gregory "Monk" Lewis wrote in 1834, "The good old practice of burning has fallen into disrepute; so [the obeah worker] was sentenced to be transported, and was shipped off the island, to the great satisfaction of persons of all colours." Similarly, in the United States by 1748 the colonial legislature prohibited all slaves from practicing medicine for fear of their access to poisons and of their power to inspire insurrection. The 1791 Haitian War of Independence, the only successful slave revolt in the Americas, reputedly began with a Vodou ceremony.

. . . A tall fine English gentleman like you, you don't want to touch a little yellow rat like me eh? Besides I understand well. You believe me, but you want to do everything quiet like the English can. All right. But if I keep my mouth shut it seems to me you owe me something. What is five hundred pounds to you? To me it's my life.'

Now disgust was rising in me like sickness. Disgust and rage.

'All right,' he yelled, and moved away from the door. 'Go then . . . get out. Now it's me to say it. Get out. Get out. And if I don't have the money I want you will see what I can do.

'Give my love to your wife—my sister,' he called after me venomously. 'You are not the first to kiss her pretty face. Pretty face, soft skin, pretty colour—not yellow like me. But my sister just the same . . .'

At the end of the path out of sight and sound of the house I stopped. The world was given up to heat and to flies, the light was dazzling after his little dark room. A black and white goat tethered near by was staring at me and for what seemed minutes I stared back into its slanting yellow-green eyes. Then I walked to the tree where I'd left my horse and rode away as quickly as I could.

The telescope was pushed to one side of the table making room for a decanter half full of rum and two glasses on a tarnished silver tray. I listened to the ceaseless night noises outside, and watched the procession of small moths and beetles fly into the candle flames, then poured out a drink of rum and swallowed. At once the night noises drew away, became distant, bearable, even pleasant.

'Will you listen to me for God's sake,' Antoinette said. She had said this before and I had not answered, now I told her, 'Of course. I'd be the brute you doubtless think me if I did not do that.'

'Why do you hate me?' she said.

'I do not hate you, I am most distressed about you, I am distraught,' I said. But this was untrue, I was not distraught, I was calm, it was the first time I had felt calm or self-possessed for many a long day.

She was wearing the white dress I had admired, but it had slipped untidily over one shoulder and seemed too large for her. I watched her holding her left wrist with her right hand, an annoying habit.

'Then why do you never come near me?' she said. 'Or kiss me, or talk to me. Why do you think I can bear it, what reason have you for treating me like that? Have you any reason?'

'Yes,' I said, 'I have a reason,' and added very softly, 'My God.'

'You are always calling on God,' she said. 'Do you believe in God?'

'Of course, of course I believe in the power and wisdom of my creator.'

She raised her eyebrows and the corners of her mouth turned down in a questioning mocking way. For a moment she looked very much like Amélie. Perhaps they are related, I thought. It's possible, it's even probable in this damned place.

'And you,' I said. 'Do you believe in God?'

'It doesn't matter,' she answered calmly, 'what I believe or you believe, because we can do nothing about it, we are like these.' She flicked a dead moth off the table. 'But I asked you a question, you remember. Will you answer that?'

I drank again and my brain was cold and clear.

'Very well, but question for question. Is your mother alive?'

'No, she is dead, she died.'

'When?'

'Not long ago.'

'Then why did you tell me that she died when you were a child?'

'Because they told me to say so and because it is true. She did die when I was a child. There are always two deaths, the real one and the one people know about.'

'Two at least,' I said, 'for the fortunate.' We were silent for a moment, then I went on, 'I had a letter from a man who calls himself Daniel Cosway.'

'He has no right to that name,' she said quickly. 'His real name, if he has one, is Daniel Boyd.[6] He hates all white people, but he hates me the most. He tells lies about us and he is sure that you will believe him and not listen to the other side.'

'Is there another side?' I said.

'There is always the other side, always.'

'After his second letter, which was threatening, I thought it best to go and see him.'

'You saw him,' she said. 'I know what he told you. That my mother was mad and an infamous woman and that my little brother who died was born a cretin,[7] an idiot, and that I am a mad girl too. That is what he told you, isn't it?'

'Yes, that was his story, and is any of it true?' I said, cold and calm.

One of the candles flared up and I saw the hollows under her eyes, her drooping mouth, her thin, strained face.

'We won't talk about it now,' I said. 'Rest tonight.'

'But we must talk about it.' Her voice was high and shrill.

'Only if you promise to be reasonable.'

But this is not the place or the time, I thought, not in this long dark veranda with the candles burning low and the watching, listening night outside. 'Not tonight,' I said again. 'Some other time.'

'I might never be able to tell you in any other place or at any other

6. See note 2, p. 12.
7. Someone characterized by a congenital condition that stunts physical and mental development.

time. No other time, now. You frightened?' she said, imitating a negro's voice, singing and insolent.

Then I saw her shiver and remembered that she had been wearing a yellow silk shawl. I got up (my brain so clear and cold, my body so weighted and heavy). The shawl was on a chair in the next room, there were candles on the sideboard and I brought them on to the veranda, lit two, and put the shawl around her shoulders. 'But why not tell me tomorrow, in the daylight?'

'You have no right,' she said fiercely. 'You have no right to ask questions about my mother and then refuse to listen to my answer.'

'Of course I will listen, of course we can talk now, if that's what you wish.' But the feeling of something unknown and hostile was very strong. 'I feel very much a stranger here,' I said. 'I feel that this place is my enemy and on your side.'

'You are quite mistaken,' she said. 'It is not for you and not for me. It has nothing to do with either of us. That is why you are afraid of it, because it is something else. I found that out long ago when I was a child. I loved it because I had nothing else to love, but it is as indifferent as this God you call on so often.'[8]

'We can talk here or anywhere else,' I said, 'just as you wish.'

The decanter of rum was nearly empty so I went back into the dining-room, and brought out another bottle of rum. She had eaten nothing and refused wine, now she poured herself a drink, touched it with her lips then put it down again.

'You want to know about my mother, I will tell you about her, the truth, not lies.' Then she was silent for so long that I said gently, 'I know that after your father died, she was very lonely and unhappy.'

'And very poor,' she said. 'Don't forget that. For five years. Isn't it quick to say. And isn't it long to live. And lonely. She was so lonely that she grew away from other people. That happens. It happened to me too but it was easier for me because I hardly remembered anything else. For her it was strange and frightening. And then she was so lovely. I used to think that every time she looked in the glass she must have hoped and pretended. I pretended too. Different things of course. You can pretend for a long time, but one day it all falls away and you are alone. We were alone in the most beautiful place in the world, it is not possible that there can be anywhere else so beautiful as Coulibri. The sea was not far off but we never heard it, we always heard the river. No sea. It was an old-time house and once there was an avenue

8. Travel writer Alec Waugh called Dominica "one of the most beautiful islands in the world and one of the unluckiest." As Rhys wrote about her father's small estate: "It was there . . . that I began to feel I loved the land and to know I would never forget it. There I would go for long walks alone. It's strange growing up in a very beautiful place and seeing that it is beautiful. It was alive, I was sure of it. . . . There was something austere, sad, lost, all these things. I wanted to identify myself with it, to lose myself in it. (But it turned its head away, indifferent, and that broke my heart)" (*SP*, p. 66).

of royal palms but a lot of them had fallen and others had been cut down and the ones that were left looked lost. Lost trees. Then they poisoned her horse and she could not ride about any more. She worked in the garden even when the sun was very hot and they'd say "You go in now, mistress." '

'And who were they?'

'Christophine was with us, and Godfrey the old gardener stayed, and a boy, I forget his name. Oh yes,' she laughed. 'His name was Disastrous because his godmother thought it such a pretty word. The parson said, "I cannot christen this child Disastrous, he must have another name," so his name was Disastrous Thomas, we called him Sass. It was Christophine who bought our food from the village and persuaded some girls to help her sweep and wash clothes. We would have died, my mother always said, if she had not stayed with us. Many died in those days, both white and black, especially the older people, but no one speaks of those days now. They are forgotten, except the lies. Lies are never forgotten, they go on and they grow.'

'And you,' I said. 'What about you?'

'I was never sad in the morning,' she said, 'and every day was a fresh day for me. I remember the taste of milk and bread and the sound of the grandfather clock ticking slowly and the first time I had my hair tied with string because there was no ribbon left and no money to buy any. All the flowers in the world were in our garden and sometimes when I was thirsty I licked raindrops from the Jasmine leaves after a shower. If I could make you see it, because they destroyed it and it is only here now.' She struck her forehead. 'One of the best things was a curved flight of shallow steps that went down from the *glacis* to the mounting stone, the handrail was ornamented iron.'

'Wrought iron,' I said.

'Yes, wrought iron, and at the end of the last step it was curved like a question mark and when I put my hand on it, the iron was warm and I was comforted.'

'But you said you were always happy.'

'No, I said I was always happy in the morning, not always in the afternoon and never after sunset, for after sunset the house was haunted, some places are. Then there was that day when she saw I was growing up like a white nigger and she was ashamed of me, it was after that day that everything changed. Yes, it was my fault, it was my fault that she started to plan and work in a frenzy, in a fever to change our lives. Then people came to see us again and though I still hated them and was afraid of their cool, teasing eyes, I learned to hide it.'

'No,' I said.

'Why no?'

'You have never learned to hide it,' I said.

'I learned to try,' said Antoinette. Not very well, I thought.

'And there was that night when they destroyed it.' She lay back in the chair, very pale. I poured some rum out and offered it to her, but she pushed the glass away so roughly that it spilled over her dress. 'There is nothing left now. They trampled on it. It was a sacred place. It was sacred to the sun!' I began to wonder how much of all this was true, how much imagined, distorted. Certainly many of the old estate houses were burned. You saw ruins all over the place.

As if she'd guessed my thoughts she went on calmly, 'But I was telling you about my mother. Afterwards I had fever. I was at Aunt Cora's house in Spanish Town. I heard screams and then someone laughing very loud. Next morning Aunt Cora told me that my mother was ill and had gone to the country. This did not seem strange to me for she was part of Coulibri, and if Coulibri had been destroyed and gone out of my life, it seemed natural that she should go too. I was ill for a long time. My head was bandaged because someone had thrown a stone at me. Aunt Cora told me that it was healing up and that it wouldn't spoil me on my wedding day. But I think it did spoil me for my wedding day and all the other days and nights.'

I said, 'Antoinette, your nights are not spoiled, or your days, put the sad things away. Don't think about them and nothing will be spoiled, I promise you.'

But my heart was heavy as lead.

'Pierre died,' she went on as if she had not heard me, 'and my mother hated Mr Mason. She would not let him go near her or touch her. She said she would kill him, she tried to, I think. So he bought her a house and hired a coloured man and woman to look after her. For a while he was sad but he often left Jamaica and spent a lot of time in Trinidad. He almost forgot her.'

'And you forgot her too,' I could not help saying.

'I am not a forgetting person,' said Antoinette. 'But she—she didn't want me. She pushed me away and cried when I went to see her. They told me I made her worse. People talked about her, they would not leave her alone, they would be talking about her and stop if they saw me. One day I made up my mind to go to her, by myself. Before I reached her house I heard her crying. I thought I will kill anyone who is hurting my mother. I dismounted and ran quickly on to the veranda where I could look into the room. I remember the dress she was wearing—an evening dress cut very low, and she was barefooted. There was a fat black man with a glass of rum in his hand. He said, "Drink it and you will forget." She drank it without stopping. He poured her some more and she took the glass and laughed and threw it over her shoulder. It smashed to pieces. "Clean it up," the man said, "or she'll walk in it."

' "If she walk in it a damn good thing," the woman said. "Perhaps she keep quiet then." However she brought a pan and brush and swept up the broken glass. All this I saw. My mother did not look at them. She walked up and down and said, "But this is a very pleasant surprise, Mr Luttrell. Godfrey, take Mr Luttrell's horse." Then she seemed to grow tired and sat down in the rocking-chair. I saw the man lift her up out of the chair and kiss her. I saw his mouth fasten on hers and she went all soft and limp in his arms and he laughed. The woman laughed too, but she was angry. When I saw that I ran away. Christophine was waiting for me when I came back crying. "What you want to go up there for?" she said, and I said, "You shut up devil, damned black devil from Hell." Christophine said, "Aie Aie Aie! Look me trouble, look me cross!" '

After a long time I heard her say as if she were talking to herself, 'I have said all I want to say. I have tried to make you understand. But nothing has changed.' She laughed.

'Don't laugh like that, Bertha.'

'My name is not Bertha; why do you call me Bertha?'

'Because it is a name I'm particularly fond of. I think of you as Bertha.'

'It doesn't matter,' she said.

I said, 'When you went off this morning where did you go?'

'I went to see Christophine,' she said. 'I will tell you anything you wish to know, but in a few words because words are no use, I know that now.'

'Why did you go to see her?'

'I went to ask her to do something for me.'

'And did she do it?'

'Yes.' Another long pause.

'You wanted to ask her advice, was that it?'

She did not answer.

'What did she say?'

'She said that I ought to go away—to leave you.'

'Oh did she?' I said, surprised.

'Yes, that was her advice.'

'I want to do the best for both of us,' I said. 'So much of what you tell me is strange, different from what I was led to expect. Don't you feel that perhaps Christophine is right? That if you went away from this place or I went away—exactly as you wish of course—for a time, it might be the wisest thing we could do?' Then I said sharply, 'Bertha, are you asleep, are you ill, why don't you answer me?' I got up, went over to her chair and took her cold hands in mine. 'We've been sitting here long enough, it is very late.'

'You go,' she said. 'I wish to stay here in the dark . . . where I belong,' she added.

'Oh nonsense,' I said. I put my arms round her to help her up, I kissed her, but she drew away.

'Your mouth is colder than my hands,' she said. I tried to laugh. In the bedroom, I closed the shutters. 'Sleep now, we will talk things over tomorrow.'

'Yes,' she said, 'of course, but will you come in and say goodnight to me?'

'Certainly I will, my dear Bertha.'

'Not Bertha tonight,' she said.

'Of course, on this of all nights, you must be Bertha.'

'As you wish,' she said.

As I stepped into her room I noticed the white powder strewn on the floor. That was the first thing I asked her—about the powder. I asked what it was. She said it was to keep cockroaches away.

'Haven't you noticed that there are no cockroaches in this house and no centipedes. If you knew how horrible these things can be.' She had lit all the candles and the room was full of shadows. There were six on the dressing-table and three on the table near her bed. The light changed her. I had never seen her look so gay or so beautiful. She poured wine into two glasses and handed me one but I swear it was before I drank that I longed to bury my face in her hair as I used to do. I said, 'We are letting ghosts trouble us. Why shouldn't we be happy?' She said, 'Christophine knows about ghosts too, but that is not what she calls them.' She need not have done what she did to me. I will always swear that, she need not have done it. When she handed me the glass she was smiling. I remember saying in a voice that was not like my own that it was too light. I remember putting out the candles on the table near the bed and that is all I remember. All I will remember of the night.

I woke in the dark after dreaming that I was buried alive, and when I was awake the feeling of suffocation persisted.[9] Something was lying across my mouth; hair with a sweet heavy smell. I threw it off but still I could not breathe. I shut my eyes and lay without moving for a few seconds. When I opened them I saw the candles burnt down on that abominable dressing-table, then I knew where I was. The door on to the veranda was open and the breeze was so cold that I knew it must be very early in the morning, before dawn. I was cold too, deathly cold and sick and in pain. I got out of bed without looking at her, staggered

---

9. Christophine has prescribed traditional conjure remedies such as a hex of powder, candles in multiples of three, and a wine and herb potion. In his study of zombiism, ethnobiologist Wade Davis remarks that frequently the difference between a medicine, a poison, and a narcotic is merely a matter of dosage, the prepared powder being either spread on the ground or ingested. Symptoms of poisoning include dizziness, respiratory difficulty, nausea, vomiting, lowered blood pressure, and paralysis (Wade Davis, *Passage of Darkness: The Ethnobiology of the Haitian Zombie* [Chapel Hill: University of North Carolina Press, 1988]). A zombi is created by a sorcerer who by the use of certain potions makes the victim's body appear to be dead; after being buried alive and later secretly disinterred, the victim is given an antidote to revitalize the physical functions of the body.

into my dressing-room and saw myself in the glass. I turned away at once. I could not vomit. I only retched painfully.

I thought, I have been poisoned. But it was a dull thought, like a child spelling out the letters of a word which he cannot read, and which if he could would have no meaning or context. I was too giddy to stand and fell backwards on to the bed, looking at the blanket which was of a peculiar shade of yellow. After looking at it for some time I was able to go over to the window and vomit. It seemed like hours before this stopped. I would lean up against the wall and wipe my face, then the retching and sickness would start again. When it was over I lay on the bed too weak to move.

I have never made a greater effort in my life than I made then. I longed to lie there and sleep but forced myself up. I was weak and giddy but no longer sick or in pain. I put on my dressing-gown and splashed water on my face, then I opened the door into her room.

The cold light was on her and I looked at the sad droop of her lips, the frown between her thick eyebrows, deep as if it had been cut with a knife. As I looked she moved and flung her arm out. I thought coldly, yes, very beautiful, the thin wrist, the sweet smell of the forearm, the rounded elbow, the curve of her shoulder into her upper arm. All present, all correct. As I watched, hating, her face grew smooth and very young again, she even seemed to smile. A trick of the light perhaps. What else?

She may wake at any moment, I told myself. I must be quick. Her torn shift was on the floor, I drew the sheet over her gently as if I covered a dead girl. One of the glasses was empty, she had drained hers. There was some wine left in the other which was on the dressing-table. I dipped my finger into it and tasted it. It was bitter. I didn't look at her again, but holding the glass went on to the veranda. Hilda was there with a broom in her hand. I put my finger to my lips and she looked at me with huge eyes, then imitated me, putting her own finger to her lips.

As soon as I had dressed and got out of the house I began to run.

I do not remember that day clearly, where I ran or how I fell or wept or lay exhausted. But I found myself at last near the ruined house and the wild orange tree. Here with my head in my arms I must have slept and when I woke it was getting late and the wind was chilly. I got up and found my way back to the path which led to the house. I knew how to avoid every creeper, and I never stumbled once. I went to my dressing-room and if I passed anyone I did not see them and if they spoke I did not hear them.

There was a tray on the table with a jug of water, a glass and some brown fish cakes. I drank almost all the water, for I was very thirsty, but I did not touch the food. I sat on the bed waiting, for I knew Amélie would come, and I knew what she would say: 'I am sorry for you.'

She came soundlessly on bare feet. 'I get you something to eat,' she said. She brought cold chicken, bread, fruit and a bottle of wine, and I drank a glass without speaking, then another. She cut some of the food up and sat beside me and fed me as if I were a child. Her arm behind my head was warm but the outside when I touched it was cool, almost cold. I looked into her lovely meaningless face, sat up and pushed the plate away. Then she said, 'I am sorry for you.'

'You've told me so before, Amélie. Is that the only song you know?'

There was a spark of gaiety in her eyes, but when I laughed she put her hand over my mouth apprehensively. I pulled her down beside me and we were both laughing. That is what I remember most about that encounter. She was so gay, so natural and something of this gaiety she must have given to me, for I had not one moment of remorse. Nor was I anxious to know what was happening behind the thin partition which divided us from my wife's bedroom.

In the morning, of course, I felt differently.

Another complication. Impossible. And her skin was darker, her lips thicker than I had thought.

She was sleeping very soundly and quietly but there was awareness in her eyes when she opened them, and after a moment suppressed laughter. I felt satisfied and peaceful, but not gay as she did, no, by God, not gay. I had no wish to touch her and she knew it, for she got up at once and began to dress.

'A very graceful dress,' I said and she showed me the many ways it could be worn, trailing on the floor, lifted to show a lace petticoat, or hitched up far above the knee.

I told her that I was leaving the island soon but that before I left I wanted to give her a present. It was a large present but she took it with no thanks and no expression on her face. When I asked her what she meant to do she said, 'It's long time I know what I want to do and I know I don't get it here.'

'You are beautiful enough to get anything you want,' I said.

'Yes,' she agreed simply. 'But not here.'

She wanted, it seemed, to join her sister who was a dressmaker in Demerara, but she would not stay in Demerara, she said. She wanted to go to Rio. There were rich men in Rio.[1]

'And when will you start all this?' I said, amused.

'I start now.' She would catch one of the fishing boats at Massacre and get into town.

---

1. Demerara is the "El Dorado" of the early days of discovery; this coastal area of Guyana was officially incorporated into the British Empire at the beginning of the nineteenth century and in 1823 was the site of the greatest slave uprising in the New World, swiftly and brutally repressed. Despite the excellent port at Rio de Janeiro, which certainly attracted wealthy men in business, Rio would have been a risky choice because Brazil maintained slavery until 1888 and the safety of free persons of color was never secure.

I laughed and teased her. She was running away from the old woman Christophine, I said.

She was unsmiling when she answered, 'I have malice to no one but I don't stay here.'

I asked her how she would get to Massacre. 'I don't want no horse or mule,' she said. 'My legs strong enough to carry me.'

As she was going I could not resist saying, half longing, half triumphant, 'Well, Amélie, are you still sorry for me?'

'Yes,' she said, 'I am sorry for you. But I find it in my heart to be sorry for her too.'

She shut the door gently. I lay and listened for the sound I knew I should hear, the horse's hoofs as my wife left the house.

I turned over and slept till Baptiste woke me with coffee. His face was gloomy.

'The cook is leaving,' he announced.

'Why?'

He shrugged his shoulders and spread his hands open.

I got up, looked out of the window and saw her stride out of the kitchen, a strapping woman. She couldn't speak English, or said she couldn't. I forgot this when I said, 'I must talk to her. What is the huge bundle on her head?'

'Her mattress,' said Baptiste. 'She will come back for the rest. No good to talk to her. She won't stay in this house.'

I laughed.

'Are you leaving too?'

'No,' said Baptiste. 'I am overseer here.'

I noticed that he did not call me 'sir' or 'master.'

'And the little girl, Hilda?'

'Hilda will do as I tell her. Hilda will stay.'

'Capital,' I said. 'Then why are you looking so anxious? Your mistress will be back soon.'

He shrugged again and muttered, but whether he was talking about my morals or the extra work he would have to do I couldn't tell, for he muttered in patois.

I told him to sling one of the veranda hammocks under the cedar trees and there I spent the rest of that day.

Baptiste provided meals, but he seldom smiled and never spoke except to answer a question. My wife did not return. Yet I was not lonely or unhappy. Sun, sleep and the cool water of the river were enough. I wrote a cautious letter to Mr Fraser on the third day.

I told him that I was considering a book about obeah and had remembered his story of the case he had come across. Had he any idea of the whereabouts of the woman now? Was she still in Jamaica?

This letter was sent down by the twice weekly messenger and he must have answered at once for I had his reply in a few days:

I have often thought of your wife and yourself. And was on the point of writing to you. Indeed I have not forgotten the case. The woman in question was called Josephine or Christophine Dubois, some such name and she had been one of the Cosway servants. After she came out of jail she disappeared, but it was common knowledge that old Mr Mason befriended her. I heard that she owned or was given a small house and a piece of land near Granbois. She is intelligent in her way and can express herself well, but I did not like the look of her at all, and consider her a most dangerous person. My wife insisted that she had gone back to Martinique her native island, and was very upset that I had mentioned the matter even in such a roundabout fashion. I happen to know now that she has not returned to Martinique, so I have written very discreetly to Hill, the white inspector of police in your town. If she lives near you and gets up to any of her nonsense let him know at once. He'll send a couple of policemen up to your place and she won't get off lightly this time. I'll make sure of that. . . .

So much for you, Josephine or Christophine, I thought. So much for you, Pheena.[2]

It was that half-hour after the sunset, the blue half-hour I called it to myself. The wind drops, the light is very beautiful, the mountains sharp, every leaf on every tree is clear and distinct. I was sitting in the hammock, watching, when Antoinette rode up. She passed me without looking at me, dismounted and went into the house. I heard her bedroom door slam and her handbell ring violently. Baptiste came running along the veranda. I got out of the hammock and went to the sitting-room. He had opened the chest and taken out a bottle of rum. Some of this he poured into a decanter which he put on a tray with a glass.

'Who is that for?' I said. He didn't answer.

'No road?' I said and laughed.

'I don't want to know nothing about all this,' he said.

'Baptiste!' Antoinette called in a high voice.

'Yes, mistress.' He looked straight at me and carried the tray out.

As for the old woman, I saw her shadow before I saw her. She too passed me without turning her head. Nor did she go into Antoinette's room or look towards it. She walked along the veranda, down the steps

2. As opposed to Josephine, a name associated with Napoleon Bonaparte, the name Christophine is associated with Henri Christophe, who led a victorious black army against Napoleon and established Haiti in 1804, the first independent black-governed nation in the Caribbean. A christophine is also a local vegetable. Dominican writer Phyllis Shand Allfrey had a daughter named Josephine, whom Rhys knew, who was called Phina.

the other side, and went into the kitchen. In that short time the dark had come and Hilda came in to light the candles. When I spoke to her she gave me an alarmed look and ran away. I opened the chest and looked at the rows of bottles inside. Here was the rum that kills you in a hundred years, the brandy, the red and white wine smuggled, I suppose, from St Pierre, Martinique—the Paris of the West Indies. It was rum I chose to drink. Yes, it was mild in the mouth, I waited a second for the explosion of heat and light in my chest, the strength and warmth running through my body. Then I tried the door into Antoinette's room. It yielded very slightly. She must have pushed some piece of furniture against it, that round table probably. I pushed again and it opened enough for me to see her. She was lying on the bed on her back. Her eyes were closed and she breathed heavily. She had pulled the sheet up to her chin. On a chair beside the bed there was the empty decanter, a glass with some rum left in it and a small brass handbell.

I shut the door and sat down with my elbows on the table for I thought I knew what would happen and what I must do. I found the room oppressively hot, so I blew out most of the candles and waited in the half darkness. Then I went on to the veranda to watch the door of the kitchen where a light was showing.

Soon the little girl came out followed by Baptiste. At the same time the handbell in the bedroom rang. They both went into the sitting-room and I followed. Hilda lit all the candles with a frightened roll of the eyes in my direction. The handbell went on ringing.

'Mix me a good strong one, Baptiste. Just what I feel like.'

He took a step away from me and said, 'Miss Antoinette—'

'Baptiste, where are you?' Antoinette called. 'Why don't you come?'

'I come as quick as I can,' Baptiste said. But as he reached for the bottle I took it away from him.

Hilda ran out of the room. Baptiste and I stared at each other. I thought that his large protuberant eyes and his expression of utter bewilderment were comical.

Antoinette shrieked from the bedroom, 'Baptiste! Christophine! Pheena, Pheena!'

'Que komesse!'[3] Baptiste said. 'I get Christophine.'

He ran out almost as fast as the little girl had done.

The door of Antoinette's room opened. When I saw her I was too shocked to speak. Her hair hung uncombed and dull into her eyes which were inflamed and staring, her face was very flushed and looked swollen. Her feet were bare. However when she spoke her voice was low, almost inaudible.

3. What a scandal, what confusion!

'I rang the bell because I was thirsty. Didn't anybody hear?'

Before I could stop her she darted to the table and seized the bottle of rum.

'Don't drink any more,' I said.

'And what right have you to tell me what I'm to do? Christophine!' she called again, but her voice broke.

'Christophine is an evil old woman and you know it as well as I do,' I said. 'She won't stay here very much longer.'

'She won't stay here very much longer,' she mimicked me, 'and nor will you, nor will you. I thought you liked the black people so much,' she said, still in that mincing voice, 'but that's just a lie like everything else. You like the light brown girls better, don't you? You abused the planters and made up stories about them, but you do the same thing. You send the girl away quicker, and with no money or less money, and that's all the difference.'

'Slavery was not a matter of liking or disliking,' I said, trying to speak calmly. 'It was a question of justice.'

'Justice,' she said. 'I've heard that word. It's a cold word. I tried it out,' she said, still speaking in a low voice. 'I wrote it down. I wrote it down several times and always it looked like a damn cold lie to me. There is no justice.' She drank some more rum and went on, 'My mother whom you all talk about, what justice did she have? My mother sitting in the rocking-chair speaking about dead horses and dead grooms and a black devil kissing her sad mouth. Like you kissed mine,' she said.

The room was now unbearably hot. 'I'll open the window and let a little air in,' I said.

'It will let the night in too,' she said, 'and the moon and the scent of those flowers you dislike so much.'

When I turned from the window she was drinking again.

'Bertha,' I said.

'Bertha is not my name. You are trying to make me into someone else, calling me by another name. I know, that's obeah too.'[4]

Tears streamed from her eyes.

'If my father, my real father, was alive you wouldn't come back here in a hurry after he'd finished with you. If he was alive. Do you know what you've done to me? It's not the girl, not the girl. But I loved this place and you have made it into a place I hate. I used to think that if everything else went out of my life I would still have this, and now you have spoilt it. It's just somewhere else where I have been unhappy, and all the other things are nothing to what has happened here. I hate it

---

4. Part of the ritual of creating a zombi is to baptize the victim with a new name. In traditional African societies, names are so important that a change of name is powerful enough to transform a person's life. Also significant here is Antoinette's changed surname, part of the ritual of Anglo-American marriage.

now like I hate you and before I die I will show you how much I hate you.'

Then to my astonishment she stopped crying and said, 'Is she so much prettier than I am? Don't you love me at all?'

'No, I do not,' I said (at the same time remembering Amélie saying, 'Do you like my hair? Isn't it prettier than hers?'). 'Not at this moment,' I said.

She laughed at that. A crazy laugh.

'You see. That's how you are. A stone. But it serves me right because didn't Aunt Cora say to me don't marry him. Not if he were stuffed with diamonds. And a lot of other things she told me. Are you talking about England, I said, and what about Grandpappy passing his glass over the water decanter and the tears running down his face for all the friends dead and gone, whom he would never see again. That was nothing to do with England that I ever heard, she said. On the contrary:

> A Benky foot and a Benky leg
> For Charlie over the water.
> Charlie, Charlie,'[5]

she sang in a hoarse voice. And lifted the bottle to drink again.

I said, and my voice was not very calm, 'No.'

I managed to hold her wrist with one hand and the rum with the other, but when I felt her teeth in my arm I dropped the bottle. The smell filled the room. But I was angry now and she saw it. She smashed another bottle against the wall and stood with the broken glass in her hand and murder in her eyes.

'Just you touch me once. You'll soon see if I'm a dam' coward like you are.'

Then she cursed me comprehensively, my eyes, my mouth, every member of my body, and it was like a dream in the large unfurnished room with the candles flickering and this red-eyed wild-haired stranger who was my wife shouting obscenities at me.[6] It was at this nightmare moment that I heard Christophine's calm voice.

'You hush up and keep yourself quiet. And don't cry. Crying's no good with him. I told you before. Crying's no good.'

Antoinette collapsed on the sofa and went on sobbing. Christophine looked at me and her small eyes were very sad. 'Why you do that eh?

---

5. Passing glasses "over the water" was a Jacobite gesture of support for Stuart king James II and his descendants exiled in France after the Revolution of 1688. After some Jacobites used the gesture at King George III's coronation, finger bowls were abolished from royal banquets until 1905. The Jacobite movement was strong in Scotland, Wales, and Ireland and among the Catholics. In Scottish dialect "benky" means bent. This is one of the hundreds of "Charlie over the water" songs, most popular in the Scottish Highlands, that followed the unsuccessful rebellion of 1745 led by Charles Edward, the Young Pretender, grandson of James II.

6. Jane's description of Bertha in *Jane Eyre*: "It was a discoloured face—it was a savage face. I wish I could forget the roll of the red eyes and the fearful blackened inflammation of the lineaments" (ch. 25).

Why you don't take that worthless good-for-nothing girl somewhere else? But she love money like you love money—must be why you come together. Like goes to like.'

I couldn't bear any more and again I went out of the room and sat on the veranda.

My arm was bleeding and painful and I wrapped my handkerchief round it, but it seemed to me that everything round me was hostile. The telescope drew away and said don't touch me. The trees were threatening and the shadows of the trees moving slowly over the floor menaced me. That green menace. I had felt it ever since I saw this place. There was nothing I knew, nothing to comfort me.

I listened. Christophine was talking softly. My wife was crying. Then a door shut. They had gone into the bedroom. Someone was singing 'Ma belle ka di', or was it the song about one day and a thousand years. But whatever they were singing or saying was dangerous. I must protect myself. I went softly along the dark veranda. I could see Antoinette stretched on the bed quite still. Like a doll. Even when she threatened me with the bottle she had a marionette quality. 'Ti moun,' I heard and 'Doudou ché,' and the end of a head handkerchief made a finger on the wall. 'Do do l'enfant do.'[7] Listening, I began to feel sleepy and cold.

I stumbled back into the big candlelit room which still smelt strongly of rum. In spite of this I opened the chest and got out another bottle. That was what I was thinking when Christophine came in. I was thinking of a last strong drink in my room, fastening both doors, and sleeping.

'I hope you satisfy, I hope you well satisfy,' she said, 'and no good to start your lies with me. I know what you do with that girl as well as you know. Better. Don't think I frightened of you either.'

'So she ran off to tell you I'd ill-treated her, did she? I ought to have guessed that.'

'She don't tell me a thing,' said Christophine. 'Not one single thing. Always the same. Nobody is to have any pride but you. She have more pride than you and she say nothing. I see her standing at my door with that look on her face and I know something bad happen to her. I know I must act quick and I act.'

'You seem to have acted, certainly. And what did you do before you brought her back in her present condition?'

'What did I do! Look! don't you provoke me more than I provoke already. Better not I tell you. You want to know what I do? I say doudou, if you have trouble you are right to come to me. And I kiss her. It's when I kiss her she cry—not before. It's long time she hold it back, I think. So I let her cry. That is the first thing. Let them cry—it eases

7. *Ti moun* means "young one"; *doudou chè* means "darling dear"; *do do l'enfant do* means "sleep, sleep, child, sleep."

the heart. When she can't cry no more I give her a cup of milk—it's lucky I have some. She won't eat, she won't talk. So I say, "Lie down on the bed *doudou* and try to sleep, for me I can sleep on the floor, don't matter for me." She isn't going to sleep natural that's certain, but I can make her sleep. That's what I do. As for what you do—you pay for it one day.

'When they get like that,' she said, 'first they must cry, then they must sleep. Don't talk to me about doctor, I know more than any doctor. I undress Antoinette so she can sleep cool and easy; it's then I see you very rough with her eh?'

At this point she laughed—a hearty merry laugh. 'All that is a little thing—it's nothing. If you see what I see in this place with the machete bright and shining in the corner, you don't have such a long face for such a little thing. You make her love you more if that's what you want. It's not for that she have the look of death on her face. Oh no.

'One night,' she went on, 'I hold on a woman's nose because her husband nearly chop it off with his machete. I hold it on, I send a boy running for the doctor and the doctor come galloping at dead of night to sew up the woman. When he finish he tell me, "Christophine you have a great presence of mind." That's what he tell me. By this time the man crying like a baby. He says, "Doctor I don't mean it. It just happened." "I know, Rupert," the doctor says, "but it mustn't happen again. Why don't you keep the damn machete in the other room?" he says. They have two small rooms only so I say, "No, doctor—it much worse near the bed. They chop each other up in no time at all." The doctor he laugh and laugh. Oh he was a good doctor. When he finished with that woman nose I won't say it look like before but I will say it don't notice much. Rupert that man's name was. Plenty Ruperts here you notice? One is Prince Rupert, and one who makes songs is Rupert the Rine. You see him? He sells his songs down by the bridge there in town. It's in the town I live when I first leave Jamaica. It's a pretty name eh—Rupert—but where they get it from? I think it's from old time they get it.[8]

'That doctor an old-time doctor. These new ones I don't like them. First word in their mouth is police. Police—that's something I don't like.'

'I'm sure you don't,' I said. 'But you haven't told me yet what happened when my wife was with you. Or exactly what you did?'

'*Your wife!*' she said. 'You make me laugh. I don't know all you did

8. Prince Rupert was a Royalist leader in the English Civil War who engaged in battle and privateering in the West Indies in 1652. There is a Rupert's Bay on the west side of Dominica. Explaining her reference in this passage, Rhys wrote, "Rupert the Rine—a negro singer *very* poor. Not like now at all. He claimed that Prince Rupert of the Rhine was an ancestor. Some of that lot *did* arrive in the West Indies (Cromwell's way of killing them off). No Princes Rupert though. There is Prince Rupert's Bay. Or was" (Manuscript held at the British Library, Add. MS. 57857, fol. 119).

but I know some. Everybody know that you marry her for her money and you take it all. And then you want to break her up, because you jealous of her. She is more better than you, she have better blood in her and she don't care for money—it's nothing for her. Oh I see that first time I look at you. You young but already you hard. You fool the girl. You make her think you can't see the sun for looking at her.'

It was like that, I thought. It was like that. But better to say nothing. Then surely they'll both go and it will be my turn to sleep—a long deep sleep, mine will be, and very far away.

'And then,' she went on in her judge's voice, 'you make love to her till she drunk with it, no rum could make her drunk like that, till she can't do without it. It's *she* can't see the sun any more. Only you she see. But all you want is to break her up.'

(Not the way you mean, I thought)

'But she hold out eh? She hold out.'

(Yes, she held out. A pity)

'So you pretend to believe all the lies that damn bastard tell you.'

(That damn bastard tell you)

Now every word she said was echoed, echoed loudly in my head.

'So that you can leave her alone.'

(Leave her alone)

'Not telling her why.'

(Why?)

'No more love, eh?'

(No more love)

'And that,' I said coldly, 'is where you took charge, isn't it? You tried to poison me.'

'Poison you? But look me trouble, the man crazy! She come to me and ask me for something to make you love her again and I tell her no I don't meddle in that for *béké*. I tell her it's foolishness.'

(Foolishness foolishness)

'And even if it's no foolishness, it's too strong for *béké*.'

(Too strong for béké. *Too strong)*

'But she cry and she beg me.'

(She cry and she beg me)

'So I give her something for love.'

(For love)

'But you don't love. All you want is to break her up. And it help you break her up.'

(Break her up)

'She tell me in the middle of all this you start calling her names. Marionette. Some word so.'

'Yes, I remember, I did.'

(Marionette, Antoinette, Marionetta, Antoinetta)

'That word mean doll, eh? Because she don't speak. You want to force her to cry and to speak.'

(Force her to cry and to speak)

'But she won't. So you think up something else. You bring that worthless girl to play with next door and you talk and laugh and love so that she hear everything. You meant her to hear.'

Yes, that didn't just happen. I meant it.

(I lay awake all night long after they were asleep, and as soon as it was light I got up and dressed and saddled Preston. And I came to you. Oh Christophine. O Pheena, Pheena, help me.)

'You haven't yet told me exactly what you did with my—with Antoinette.'

'Yes I tell you. I make her sleep.'

'What? All the time?'

'No, no. I wake her up to sit in the sun, bathe in the cool river. Even if she dropping with sleep. I make good strong soup. I give her milk if I have it, fruit I pick from my own trees. If she don't want to eat I say, "Eat it up for my sake, *doudou*." And she eat it up, then she sleep again.'

'And why did you do all this?'

There was a long silence. Then she said, 'It's better she sleep. She must sleep while I work for her—to make her well again. But I don't speak of all that to you.'

'Unfortunately your cure was not successful. You didn't make her well. You made her worse.'

'Yes I succeed,' she said angrily. 'I succeed. But I get frightened that she sleep too much, too long. She is not *béké* like you, but she is *béké*, and not like us either. There are mornings when she can't wake, or when she wake it's as if she still sleeping. I don't want to give her any more of—of what I give. So,' she went on after another pause, 'I let her have rum instead. I know that won't hurt her. Not much. As soon as she has the rum she starts raving that she must go back to you and I can't quiet her. She says she'll go alone if I don't come but she beg me to come. And I hear well when you tell her that you don't love her—quite calm and cool you tell her so, and undo all the good I do.'

'The good you did! I'm very weary of your nonsense, Christophine. You seem to have made her dead drunk on bad rum and she's a wreck. I scarcely recognized her. Why you did it I can't say—hatred of me I suppose. And as you heard so much perhaps you were listening to all she admitted—boasted about, and to the vile names she called me. Your *doudou* certainly knows some filthy language.'

'I tell you no. I tell you it's nothing. You make her so unhappy she don't know what she is saying. Her father old Mister Cosway swear like half past midnight—she pick it up from him. And once, when she was little she run away to be with the fishermen and the sailors on the bayside. Those men!' She raised her eyes to the ceiling. 'Never would you think they was once innocent babies. She come back copying them. She don't understand what she says.'

'I think she understood every word, and meant what she said too. But you are right, Christophine—it was all a very little thing. It was nothing. No machete here, so no machete damage. No damage at all by this time. I'm sure you took care of that however drunk you made her.'

'You are a damn hard man for a young man.'

'So you say, so you say.'

'I tell her so. I warn her. I say this is not a man who will help you when he sees you break up. Only the best can do that. The best—and sometimes the worst.'

'But you think I'm one of the worst, surely?'

'No,' she said indifferently, 'to me you are not the best, not the worst. You are—' she shrugged '—you will not help her. I tell her so.'

Nearly all the candles were out. She didn't light fresh ones—nor did I. We sat in the dim light. I should stop this useless conversation, I thought, but could only listen, hypnotized, to her dark voice coming from the darkness.

'I know that girl. She will never ask you for love again, she will die first. But I Christophine I beg you. She love you so much. She thirsty for you. Wait, and perhaps you can love her again. A little, like she say. A little. Like you can love.'

I shook my head and went on shaking it mechanically.

'It's lies all that yellow bastard tell you. He is no Cosway either. His mother was a no-good woman and she try to fool the old man but the old man isn't fooled. "One more or less" he says, and laughs. He was wrong. More he do for those people, more they hate him. The hate in that man Daniel—he can't rest with it. If I know you coming here I stop you. But you marry quick, you leave Jamaica quick. No time.'

'She told me that all he said was true. She wasn't lying then.'

'Because you hurt her she want to hurt you back, that's why.'

'And that her mother was mad. Another lie?'

Christophine did not answer me at once. When she did her voice was not so calm.

'They drive her to it. When she lose her son she lose herself for a while and they shut her away. They tell her she is mad, they act like she is mad. Question, question. But no kind word, no friends, and her husban' he go off, he leave her. They won't let me see her. I try, but no. They won't let Antoinette see her. In the end—mad I don't know —she give up, she care for nothing. That man who is in charge of her he take her whenever he want and his woman talk. That man, and others. Then they have her. Ah there is no God.'

'Only your spirits,' I reminded her.

'Only my spirits,' she said steadily. 'In your Bible it say God is a spirit—it don't say no others. Not at all. It grieve me what happen to her mother, and I can't see it happen again. You call her a doll? She don't satisfy you? Try her once more, I think she satisfy you now. If you forsake her they will tear her in pieces—like they did her mother.'

'I will not forsake her,' I said wearily. 'I will do all I can for her.'

'You will love her like you did before?'

(*Give my sister your wife a kiss from me. Love her as I did—oh yes I did. How can I promise that?*) I said nothing.

'It's she won't be satisfy. She is Creole girl, and she have the sun in her. Tell the truth now. She don't come to your house in this place England they tell me about, she don't come to your beautiful house to beg you to marry with her. No, it's you come all the long way to her house—it's you beg her to marry. And she love you and she give you all she have. Now you say you don't love her and you break her up. What you do with her money, eh?' Her voice was still quiet but with a hiss in it when she said 'money.' I thought, of course, that is what all the rigmarole is about. I no longer felt dazed, tired, half hypnotized, but alert and wary, ready to defend myself.

Why, she wanted to know, could I not return half of Antoinette's dowry and leave the island—'leave the West Indies if you don't want her no more.'

I asked the exact sum she had in mind, but she was vague about that.

'You fix it up with lawyers and all those things.'

'And what will happen to her then?'

She, Christophine, would take good care of Antoinette (and the money of course).

'You will both stay here?' I hoped that my voice was as smooth as hers.

No, they would go to Martinique. Then to other places.

'I like to see the world before I die.'

Perhaps because I was so quiet and composed she added maliciously, 'She marry with someone else. She forget about you and live happy.'

A pang of rage and jealousy shot through me then. Oh no, she won't forget. I laughed.

'You laugh at me? Why you laugh at me?'

'Of course I laugh at you—you ridiculous old woman. I don't mean to discuss my affairs with you any longer. Or your mistress. I've listened to all you had to say and I don't believe you. Now, say good-bye to Antoinette, then go. You are to blame for all that has happened here, so don't come back.'

She drew herself up tall and straight and put her hands on her hips.

'Who you to tell me to go? This house belong to Miss Antoinette's mother, now it belong to her. Who you to tell me to go?'

'I assure you that it belongs to me now. You'll go, or I'll get the men to put you out.'

'You think the men here touch me? They not damn fool like you to put their hand on me.'

'Then I will have the police up, I warn you. There must be some law and order even in this God-forsaken island.'

'No police here,' she said. 'No chain gang, no tread machine, no dark jail either.[9] This is free country and I am free woman.'

'Christophine,' I said, 'you lived in Jamaica for years, and you know Mr Fraser, the Spanish Town magistrate, well. I wrote to him about you. Would you like to hear what he answered?' She stared at me. I read the end of Fraser's letter aloud: '*I have written very discreetly to Hill, the white inspector of police in your town. If she lives near you and gets up to any of her nonsense let him know at once. He'll send a couple of policemen up to your place and she won't get off lightly this time. . . .* You gave your mistress the poison that she put into my wine?'

'I tell you already—you talk foolishness.'

'We'll see about that—I kept some of that wine.'

'I tell her so,' she said. 'Always it don't work for *béké*. Always it bring trouble. . . . So you send me away and you keep all her money. And what you do with her?'

'I don't see why I should tell you my plans. I mean to go back to Jamaica to consult the Spanish Town doctors and her brother. I'll follow their advice. That is all I mean to do. She is not well.'

'Her brother!' She spat on the floor. 'Richard Mason is no brother to her. You think you fool me? You want her money but you don't want her. It is in your mind to pretend she is mad. I know it. The doctors say what you tell them to say. That man Richard he say what you want him to say—glad and willing too, I know. She will be like her mother. You do that for money? But you wicked like Satan self!'

I said loudly and wildly, 'And do you think that I wanted all this? I would give my life to undo it. I would give my eyes never to have seen this abominable place.'

She laughed. 'And that's the first damn word of truth you speak. You choose what you give, eh?[1] Then you choose. You meddle in something

9. See also note 7, p. 15. Under the apprenticeship system, recalcitrant workers were sent to plantation dungeons and parish houses of correction. Imported from Britain during this period, the treadmill was designed as a method of hard labor punishment. The device consisted of a hollow cylinder of wood on an iron frame with a series of steps around its circumference. With wrists strapped to a bar above the machine, the prisoner was forced to turn the wheel continually by walking the steps, or "dancing the treadmill." These prisons and methods of torture violated the prison reform ideals then accepted in England (see photograph on p. 116).
1. In *Jane Eyre* Rochester is blinded and maimed by the fire at Thornfield Hall.

and perhaps you don't know what it is.' She began to mutter to herself. Not in patois. I knew the sound of patois now.

She's as mad as the other, I thought, and turned to the window.

The servants were standing in a group under the clove tree. Baptiste, the boy who helped with the horses and the little girl Hilda.

Christophine was right. They didn't intend to get mixed up in this business.

When I looked at her there was a mask on her face and her eyes were undaunted. She was a fighter, I had to admit. Against my will I repeated, 'Do you wish to say good-bye to Antoinette?'

'I give her something to sleep—nothing to hurt her. I don't wake her up to no misery. I leave that for you.'

'You can write to her,' I said stiffly.

'Read and write I don't know. Other things I know.'

She walked away without looking back.

All wish to sleep had left me. I walked up and down the room and felt the blood tingle in my finger-tips. It ran up my arms and reached my heart, which began to beat very fast. I spoke aloud as I walked. I spoke the letter I meant to write.

'I know now that you planned this because you wanted to be rid of me. You had no love at all for me. Nor had my brother. Your plan succeeded because I was young, conceited, foolish, trusting. Above all because I was young. You were able to do this to me . . .'

But I am not young now, I thought, stopped pacing and drank. Indeed this rum is mild as mother's milk or father's blessing.

I could imagine his expression if I sent that letter and he read it.

'*Dear Father,*' I wrote. '*We are leaving this island for Jamaica very shortly. Unforeseen circumstances, at least unforeseen by me, have forced me to make this decision. I am certain that you know or can guess what has happened, and I am certain you will believe that the less you talk to anyone about my affairs, especially my marriage, the better. This is in your interest as well as mine. You will hear from me again. Soon I hope.*'

Then I wrote to the firm of lawyers I had dealt with in Spanish Town. I told them that I wished to rent a furnished house not too near the town, commodious enough to allow for two separate suites of rooms. I also told them to engage a staff of servants whom I was prepared to pay very liberally—so long as they keep their mouths shut, I thought—provided that they are discreet, I wrote. My wife and myself would be in Jamaica in about a week and expected to find everything ready.

All the time I was writing this letter a cock crowed persistently outside. I took the first book I could lay hands on and threw it at him, but he stalked a few yards away and started again.

Baptiste appeared, looking towards Antoinette's silent room.

'Have you got much more of this famous rum?'

'Plenty rum,' he said.

'Is it really a hundred years old?'

He nodded indifferently. A hundred years, a thousand all the same to *le bon Dieu*[2] and Baptiste too.

'What's that damn cock crowing about?'

'Crowing for change of weather.'

Because his eyes were fixed on the bedroom I shouted at him, 'Asleep, *dormi, dormi.*'

He shook his head and went away.

He scowled at me then, I thought. I scowled too as I re-read the letter I had written to the lawyers. However much I paid Jamaican servants I would never buy discretion. I'd be gossiped about, sung about (but they make up songs about everything, everybody. You should hear the one about the Governor's wife).[3] Wherever I went I would be talked about. I drank some more rum and, drinking, I drew a house surrounded by trees. A large house. I divided the third floor into rooms and in one room I drew a standing woman—a child's scribble, a dot for a head, a larger one for the body, a triangle for a skirt, slanting lines for arms and feet. But it was an English house.

English trees. I wondered if I ever should see England again.

Under the oleanders . . . I watched the hidden mountains and the mists drawn over their faces. It's cool today; cool, calm and cloudy as an English summer. But a lovely place in any weather, however far I travel I'll never see a lovelier.

The hurricane months[4] are not so far away, I thought, and saw that tree strike its roots deeper, making ready to fight the wind. Useless. If and when it comes they'll all go. Some of the royal palms stand (she told me). Stripped of their branches, like tall brown pillars, still they stand—defiant. Not for nothing are they called royal. The bamboos take an easier way, they bend to the earth and lie there, creaking, groaning, crying for mercy. The contemptuous wind passes, not caring for these abject things. (*Let them live.*) Howling, shrieking, laughing the wild blast passes.

But all that's some months away. It's an English summer now, so

---

2. The good Lord.
3. Refers, perhaps, to the historical legend of the 1640 Carib kidnapping of the pregnant wife and children of the English governor of Antigua and the wife's subsequent refusal to be rescued.
4. August to October.

cool, so grey. Yet I think of my revenge and hurricanes. Words rush through my head (deeds too). Words. Pity is one of them. It gives me no rest.

Pity like a naked new-born babe striding the blast.[5]

I read that long ago when I was young—I hate poets now and poetry. As I hate music which I loved once. Sing your songs, Rupert the Rine, but I'll not listen, though they tell me you've a sweet voice. . . .

Pity. Is there none for me? Tied to a lunatic for life—a drunken lying lunatic—gone her mother's way.

'*She love you so much, so much. She thirsty for you. Love her a little like she say. It's all that you can love—a little.*'

Sneer to the last, Devil. Do you think that I don't know? She thirsts for *anyone*—not for me . . .

She'll loosen her black hair, and laugh and coax and flatter (a mad girl. She'll not care who she's loving). She'll moan and cry and give herself as no sane woman would—or could. Or *could*. Then lie so still, still as this cloudy day. A lunatic who always knows the time. But never does.

Till she's drunk so deep, played her games so often that the lowest shrug and jeer at her. And I'm to know it—I? No, I've a trick worth two of that.

'*She love you so much, so much. Try her once more.*'

I tell you she loves no one, anyone. I could not touch her. Excepting as the hurricane will touch that tree—and break it. You say I did? No. That was love's fierce play. Now I'll do it.

She'll not laugh in the sun again. She'll not dress up and smile at herself in that damnable looking-glass. So pleased, so satisfied.

Vain, silly creature. Made for loving? Yes, but she'll have no lover, for I don't want her and she'll see no other.

The tree shivers. Shivers and gathers all its strength. And waits.

(There is a cool wind blowing now—a cold wind. Does it carry the babe born to stride the blast of hurricanes?)

She said she loved this place. This is the last she'll see of it. I'll watch for one tear, one human tear. Not that blank hating moonstruck face. I'll listen. . . . If she says good-bye perhaps adieu. *Adieu*—like those old-time songs she sang. Always *adieu* (and all songs say it). If she too says it, or weeps, I'll take her in my arms, my lunatic. She's mad but *mine, mine*. What will I care for gods or devils or for Fate itself. If she smiles or weeps or both. *For me.*

Antoinetta—I can be gentle too. Hide your face. Hide yourself but in my arms. You'll soon see how gentle. My lunatic. My mad girl.

---

5. A line from Macbeth's last doubting monologue (*Macbeth* 1.7.21–22) as he tries to convince himself to betray and murder Duncan, King of Scotland. He carries out the murder.

Here's a cloudy day to help you. No brazen sun.
No sun . . . No sun. The weather's changed.

Baptiste was waiting and the horses saddled. That boy stood by the clove
tree and near him the basket he was to carry. These baskets are light
and waterproof. I'd decided to use one for a few necessary clothes—
most of our belongings were to follow in a day or two. A carriage was
to meet us at Massacre. I'd seen to everything, arranged everything.

She was there in the *ajoupa*; carefully dressed for the journey, I
noticed, but her face blank, no expression at all. Tears? There's not a
tear in her. Well, we will see. Did she remember anything, I wondered,
feel anything? (That blue cloud, that shadow, is Martinique. It's clear
now. . . . Or the names of the mountains. No, not mountain. *Morne*,
she'd say. 'Mountain is an ugly word—for them.' Or the stories about
Jack Spaniards.[6] Long ago. And when she said, 'Look! The Emerald
Drop! That brings good fortune.' Yes, for a moment the sky was
green—a bright green sunset. Strange. But not half so strange as saying
it brought good fortune.)

After all I was prepared for her blank indifference. I knew that my
dreams were dreams. But the sadness I felt looking at the shabby white
house—I wasn't prepared for that. More than ever before it strained
away from the black snake-like forest. Louder and more desperately it
called: Save me from destruction, ruin and desolation. Save me from
the long slow death by ants. But what are you doing here you folly? So
near the forest. Don't you know that this is a dangerous place? And
that the dark forest always wins? Always. If you don't, you soon will,
and I can do nothing to help you.

Baptiste looked very different. Not a trace of the polite domestic. He
wore a very wide-brimmed straw hat, like the fishermen's hats, but the
crown flat, not high and pointed. His wide leather belt was polished,
so was the handle of his sheathed cutlass, and his blue cotton shirt and
trousers were spotless. The hat, I knew, was waterproof. He was ready
for the rain and it was certainly on its way.

I said that I would like to say good-bye to the little girl who
laughed—Hilda. 'Hilda is not here,' he answered in his careful English.
'Hilda has left—yesterday.'

He spoke politely enough, but I could feel his dislike and contempt.
The same contempt as that devil's when she said, 'Taste my bull's
blood.' Meaning that will make you a man. Perhaps. Much I cared for
what they thought of me! As for her, I'd forgotten her for the moment.
So I shall never understand why, suddenly, bewilderingly, I was certain
that everything I had imagined to be truth was false. False. Only the

---

6. *Polistes cinctus*, a common species of wasp in the West Indies, twice as large as a British wasp,
that often builds its "paper houses" in the rafters.

magic and the dream are true—all the rest's a lie. Let it go. Here is the secret. Here.

(But it is lost, that secret, and those who know it cannot tell it.)

Not lost. I had found it in a hidden place and I'd keep it, hold it fast. As I'd hold her.

I looked at her. She was staring out to the distant sea. She was silence itself.

Sing, Antoinetta. I can hear you now.

> *Here the wind says it has been, it has been*
> *And the sea says it must be, it must be*
> *And the sun says it can be, it will be*
> *And the rain . . . ?*

'You must listen to that. Our rain knows all the songs.'

'And all the tears?'

'All, all, all.'

Yes, I will listen to the rain. I will listen to the mountain bird. Oh, a heartstopper is the solitaire's[7] one note—high, sweet, lonely, magic. You hold your breath to listen . . . No . . . Gone. What was I to say to her?

Do not be sad. Or think Adieu. Never Adieu. We will watch the sun set again—many times, and perhaps we'll see the Emerald Drop, the green flash that brings good fortune. And you must laugh and chatter as you used to do—telling me about the battle off the Saints or the picnic at Marie Galante—that famous picnic that turned into a fight. Or the pirates and what they did between voyages. For every voyage might be their last. Sun and sangoree's a heady mixture. Then—the earthquake.[8] Oh yes, people say that God was angry at the things they did, woke from his sleep, one breath and they were gone. He slept again. But they left their treasure, gold and more than gold. Some of it is found—but the finders never tell, because you see they'd only get one-third then: that's the law of treasure. They want it all, so never speak of it. Sometimes precious things, or jewels. There's no end to what they find and sell in secret to some cautious man who weighs and measures, hesitates, asks questions which are not answered, then hands over money in exchange. Everybody knows that gold pieces, treasures, appear in Spanish Town—(here too). In all the islands, from nowhere, from no one knows where. For it is better not to speak of treasure. Better not to tell them.

7. A thrush known for its magnificent ethereal songs. Rhys considered naming the novel *Solitaire*.
8. Marie Gallante and the Saints are small islands between Guadeloupe and Dominica. Refers to the naval battle on April 12, 1782, between England and France off the Saints Islands. After winning the battle, Admiral Lord Rodney was considered a savior of Jamaica and became something of a cult figure, and April 12 became a day of national celebration. Port Royal in Jamaica was almost completely destroyed by an earthquake on June 17, 1692. In 1843 another severe earthquake struck the Windward and Leeward islands causing substantial destruction and death.

Yes, better not to tell them. I won't tell you that I scarcely listened to your stories. I was longing for night and darkness and the time when the moonflowers open.

> Blot out the moon,
> Pull down the stars.
> Love in the dark, for we're for the dark
> So soon, so soon.

Like the swaggering pirates, let's make the most and best and worst of what we have. Give not one-third but everything. All—all—all. Keep nothing back. . . .

No, I would say—I knew what I would say. 'I have made a terrible mistake. Forgive me.'

I said it, looking at her, seeing the hatred in her eyes—and feeling my own hate spring up to meet it. Again the giddy change, the remembering, the sickening swing back to hate. They bought me, *me* with your paltry money. You helped them to do it. You deceived me, betrayed me, and you'll do worse if you get the chance. . . . (*That girl she look you straight in the eye and talk sweet talk—and it's lies she tell you. Lies. Her mother was so. They say she worse than her mother.*)

. . . If I was bound for hell let it be hell. No more false heavens. No more damned magic. You hate me and I hate you. We'll see who hates best. But first, first I will destroy your hatred. Now. My hate is colder, stronger, and you'll have no hate to warm yourself. You will have nothing.

I did it too. I saw the hate go out of her eyes. I forced it out. And with the hate her beauty. She was only a ghost. A ghost in the grey daylight. Nothing left but hopelessness. *Say die and I will die. Say die and watch me die.*

She lifted her eyes. Blank lovely eyes. Mad eyes. A mad girl. I don't know what I would have said or done. In the balance—everything. But at this moment the nameless boy leaned his head against the clove tree and sobbed. Loud heartbreaking sobs. I could have strangled him with pleasure. But I managed to control myself, walk up to them and say coldly, 'What is the matter with him? What is he crying about?' Baptiste did not answer. His sullen face grew a shade more sullen and that was all I got from Baptiste.

She had followed me and she answered. I scarcely recognized her voice. No warmth, no sweetness. The doll had a doll's voice, a breathless but curiously indifferent voice.

'He asked me when we first came if we—if you—would take him with you when we left. He doesn't want any money. Just to be with you. Because—' She stopped and ran her tongue over her lips, 'he loves you very much. So I said you would. Take him. Baptiste has told him that you will not. So he is crying.'

'I certainly will not,' I said angrily. (God! A half-savage boy as well as . . . as well as . . .)

'He knows English,' she said, still indifferently. 'He has tried very hard to learn English.'

'He hasn't learned any English that I can understand,' I said. And looking at her stiff white face my fury grew. 'What right have you to make promises in my name? Or to speak for me at all?'

'No, I had no right, I am sorry. I don't understand you. I know nothing about you, and I cannot speak for you. . . .'

And that was all. I said good-bye to Baptiste. He bowed stiffly, unwillingly and muttered—wishes for a pleasant journey, I suppose. He hoped, I am sure, that he'd never set eyes on me again.

She had mounted and he went over to her. When she stretched her hand out he took it and still holding it spoke to her very earnestly. I did not hear what he said but I thought she would cry then. No, the doll's smile came back—nailed to her face. Even if she had wept like Magdalene[9] it would have made no difference. I was exhausted. All the mad conflicting emotions had gone and left me wearied and empty. Sane.

I was tired of these people. I disliked their laughter and their tears, their flattery and envy, conceit and deceit. And I hated the place.

I hated the mountains and the hills, the rivers and the rain. I hated the sunsets of whatever colour, I hated its beauty and its magic and the secret I would never know. I hated its indifference and the cruelty which was part of its loveliness. Above all I hated her. For she belonged to the magic and the loveliness. She had left me thirsty and all my life would be thirst and longing for what I had lost before I found it.

So we rode away and left it—the hidden place. Not for me and not for her. I'd look after that. She's far along the road now.

Very soon she'll join all the others who know the secret and will not tell it. Or cannot. Or try and fail because they do not know enough. They can be recognized. White faces, dazed eyes, aimless gestures, high-pitched laughter. The way they walk and talk and scream or try to kill (themselves or you) if you laugh back at them. Yes, they've got to be watched. For the time comes when they try to kill, then disappear. But others are waiting to take their places, it's a long, long line. She's one of them. I too can wait—for the day when she is only a memory to be avoided, locked away, and like all memories a legend.[1] Or a lie. . . .

9. A disciple of Jesus who witnessed the crucifixion and found the empty tomb after the resurrection; she announced the meaning of the resurrection to the other disciples. There is a tradition of confusing Mary Magdalene with the woman of Luke 7:36–50 who weeps and bathes Jesus' feet and is forgiven for her sins.
1. Rhys wrote in a letter: "I was going to call the book 'False Legend' then—a bad title. But I'd quite convinced myself that something like that *did* happen, that Charlotte Brontë knew of the story and used it in the plot of *Jane Eyre*" (*LJR*, p. 234).

I remember that as we turned the corner, I thought about Baptiste and wondered if he had another name—I'd never asked. And then that I'd sell the place for what it would fetch. I had meant to give it back to her. Now—what's the use?

That stupid boy followed us, the basket balanced on his head. He used the back of his hand to wipe away his tears. Who would have thought that any boy would cry like that. For nothing. Nothing. . . .

Part Three

'They knew that he was in Jamaica when his father and his brother died,' Grace Poole[1] said. 'He inherited everything, but he was a wealthy man before that. Some people are fortunate, they said, and there were hints about the woman he brought back to England with him. Next day Mrs Eff wanted to see me and she complained about gossip. I don't allow gossip. I told you that when you came. Servants will talk and you can't stop them, I said. And I am not certain that the situation will suit me, madam. First when I answered your advertisement you said that the person I had to look after was not a young girl. I asked if she was an old woman and you said no. Now that I see her I don't know what to think. She sits shivering and she is so thin. If she dies on my hands who will get the blame? Wait, Grace, she said. She was holding a letter. Before you decide will you listen to what the master of the house has to say about this matter. "If Mrs Poole is satisfactory why not give her double, treble the money," she read, and folded the letter away but not before I had seen the words on the next page, "but for God's sake let me hear no more of it." There was a foreign stamp on the envelope. "I don't serve the devil for no money," I said. She said, "If you imagine that when you serve this gentleman you are serving the devil you never made a greater mistake in your life. I knew him as a boy. I knew him as a young man. He was gentle, generous, brave. His stay in the West Indies has changed him out of all knowledge. He has grey in his hair and misery in his eyes. Don't ask me to pity anyone who had a hand in that. I've said enough and too much. I am not prepared to treble your money, Grace, but I am prepared to double it. But there must be no more gossip. If there is I will dismiss you at once. I do not think it will be impossible to fill your place. I'm sure you understand." Yes, I understand, I said.

'Then all the servants were sent away and she engaged a cook, one maid and you, Leah. They were sent away but how could she stop them talking? If you ask me the whole county knows. The rumours I've heard —very far from the truth. But I don't contradict, I know better than to say a word. After all the house is big and safe, a shelter from the world

1. In *Jane Eyre* Grace Poole is Bertha Rochester's guard and nurse at Thornfield Hall. Mrs. Eff and Leah are references to Mrs. Fairfax and Leah, the housekeeper and housemaid of Thornfield Hall.

outside which, say what you like, can be a black and cruel world to a
woman. Maybe that's why I stayed on.'

The thick walls, she thought. Past the lodge gate a long avenue of
trees and inside the house the blazing fires and the crimson and white
rooms. But above all the thick walls, keeping away all the things that
you have fought till you can fight no more. Yes, maybe that's why we all
stay—Mrs Eff and Leah and me. All of us except that girl who lives in
her own darkness. I'll say one thing for her, she hasn't lost her spirit.
She's still fierce. I don't turn my back on her when her eyes have that
look. I know it.

In this room I wake early and lie shivering for it is very cold. At last
Grace Poole, the woman who looks after me, lights a fire with paper
and sticks and lumps of coal. She kneels to blow it with bellows. The
paper shrivels, the sticks crackle and spit, the coal smoulders and glow-
ers. In the end flames shoot up and they are beautiful. I get out of bed
and go close to watch them and to wonder why I have been brought
here. For what reason? There must be a reason. What is it that I must
do? When I first came I thought it would be for a day, two days, a week
perhaps. I thought that when I saw him and spoke to him I would be
wise as serpents, harmless as doves. 'I give you all I have freely,' I would
say, 'and I will not trouble you again if you will let me go.' But he
never came.

The woman Grace sleeps in my room. At night I sometimes see her
sitting at the table counting money. She holds a gold piece in her hand
and smiles. Then she puts it all into a little canvas bag with a drawstring
and hangs the bag round her neck so that it is hidden in her dress. At
first she used to look at me before she did this but I always pretended
to be asleep, now she does not trouble about me. She drinks from a
bottle on the table then she goes to bed, or puts her arms on the table,
her head on her arms, and sleeps. But I lie watching the fire die out.
When she is snoring I get up and I have tasted the drink without colour
in the bottle. The first time I did this I wanted to spit it out but managed
to swallow it. When I got back into bed I could remember more and
think again. I was not so cold.

There is one window high up—you cannot see out of it. My bed had
doors but they have been taken away. There is not much else in the
room. Her bed, a black press, the table in the middle and two black
chairs carved with fruit and flowers. They have high backs and no arms.
The dressing-room is very small, the room next to this one is hung with
tapestry. Looking at the tapestry one day I recognized my mother
dressed in an evening gown but with bare feet. She looked away from
me, over my head just as she used to do. I wouldn't tell Grace this.
Her name oughtn't to be Grace. Names matter, like when he wouldn't

call me Antoinette, and I saw Antoinette drifting out of the window with her scents, her pretty clothes and her looking-glass.

There is no looking-glass here and I don't know what I am like now. I remember watching myself brush my hair and how my eyes looked back at me. The girl I saw was myself yet not quite myself. Long ago when I was a child and very lonely I tried to kiss her. But the glass was between us—hard, cold and misted over with my breath. Now they have taken everything away. What am I doing in this place and who am I?

The door of the tapestry room is kept locked. It leads, I know, into a passage. That is where Grace stands and talks to another woman whom I have never seen. Her name is Leah. I listen but I cannot understand what they say.

So there is still the sound of whispering that I have heard all my life, but these are different voices.

When night comes, and she has had several drinks and sleeps, it is easy to take the keys. I know now where she keeps them. Then I open the door and walk into their world. It is, as I always knew, made of cardboard. I have seen it before somewhere, this cardboard world where everything is coloured brown or dark red or yellow that has no light in it. As I walk along the passages I wish I could see what is behind the cardboard. They tell me I am in England but I don't believe them. We lost our way to England. When? Where? I don't remember, but we lost it. Was it that evening in the cabin when he found me talking to the young man who brought me my food? I put my arms round his neck and asked him to help me. He said, 'I didn't know what to do, sir.' I smashed the glasses and plates against the porthole. I hoped it would break and the sea come in. A woman came and then an older man who cleared up the broken things on the floor. He did not look at me while he was doing it. The third man said drink this and you will sleep. I drank it and I said, 'It isn't like it seems to be.'—'I know. It never is,' he said. And then I slept. When I woke it was a different sea. Colder. It was that night, I think, that we changed course and lost our way to England. This cardboard house where I walk at night is not England.

One morning when I woke I ached all over. Not the cold, another sort of ache. I saw that my wrists were red and swollen. Grace said, 'I suppose you're going to tell me that you don't remember anything about last night.'

'When was last night?' I said.

'Yesterday.'

'I don't remember yesterday.'

'Last night a gentleman came to see you,' she said.

'Which of them was that?'

Because I knew that there were strange people in the house. When

I took the keys and went into the passage I heard them laughing and talking in the distance, like birds, and there were lights on the floor beneath.

Turning a corner I saw a girl coming out of her bedroom. She wore a white dress and she was humming to herself. I flattened myself against the wall for I did not wish her to see me, but she stopped and looked round. She saw nothing but shadows, I took care of that, but she didn't walk to the head of the stairs. She ran. She met another girl and the second girl said, 'Have you seen a ghost?'—'I didn't see anything but I thought I felt something.'—'That is the ghost,' the second one said and they went down the stairs together.

'Which of these people came to see me, Grace Poole?' I said.

He didn't come. Even if I was asleep I would have known. He hasn't come yet. She said, 'It's my belief that you remember much more than you pretend to remember. Why did you behave like that when I had promised you would be quiet and sensible? I'll never try and do you a good turn again. Your brother came to see you.'

'I have no brother.'

'He said he was your brother.'

A long long way my mind reached back.

'Was his name Richard?'

'He didn't tell me what his name was.'

'I know him,' I said, and jumped out of bed. 'It's all here, it's all here, but I hid it from your beastly eyes as I hide everything. But where is it? Where did I hide it? The sole of my shoes? Underneath the mattress? On top of the press? In the pocket of my red dress? Where, where is this letter? It was short because I remembered that Richard did not like long letters. Dear Richard please take me away from this place where I am dying because it is so cold and dark.'

Mrs Poole said, 'It's no use running around and looking now. He's gone and he won't come back—nor would I in his place.'

I said, 'I can't remember what happened. I can't remember.'

'When he came in,' said Grace Poole, 'he didn't recognize you.'

'Will you light the fire,' I said, 'because I'm so cold.'

'This gentleman arrived suddenly and insisted on seeing you and that was all the thanks he got. You rushed at him with a knife and when he got the knife away you bit his arm.[2] You won't see him again. And where did you get that knife? I told them you stole it from me but I'm much too careful. I'm used to your sort. You got no knife from me. You must have bought it that day when I took you out. I told Mrs Eff you ought to be taken out.'

'When we went to England,' I said.

'You fool,' she said, 'this is England.'

---

2. Cf. *Jane Eyre*, ch. 20, and pp. 124–25 of this volume.

'I don't believe it,' I said, 'and I never will believe it.'

(That afternoon we went to England. There was grass and olive-green water and tall trees looking into the water. This, I thought, is England. If I could be here I'd get well again and the sound in my head would stop. Let me stay a little longer, I said, and she sat down under a tree and went to sleep. A little way off there was a cart and horse—a woman was driving it. It was she who sold me the knife. I gave her the locket round my neck for it.)

Grace Poole said, 'So you don't remember that you attacked this gentleman with a knife? I said that you would be quiet. "I must speak to her," he said. Oh he was warned but he wouldn't listen. I was in the room but I didn't hear all he said except "I cannot interfere legally between yourself and your husband." It was when he said "legally" that you flew at him and when he twisted the knife out of your hand you bit him. Do you mean to say that you don't remember any of this?'

I remember now that he did not recognize me. I saw him look at me and his eyes went first to one corner and then to another, not finding what they expected. He looked at me and spoke to me as though I were a stranger. What do you do when something happens to you like that? Why are you laughing at me? 'Have you hidden my red dress too? If I'd been wearing that he'd have known me.'

'Nobody's hidden your dress,' she said. 'It's hanging in the press.'

She looked at me and said, 'I don't believe you know how long you've been here, you poor creature.'

'On the contrary,' I said, 'only I know how long I have been here. Nights and days and days and nights, hundreds of them slipping through my fingers. But that does not matter. Time has no meaning. But something you can touch and hold like my red dress, that has a meaning. Where is it?'

She jerked her head towards the press and the corners of her mouth turned down. As soon as I turned the key I saw it hanging, the colour of fire and sunset. The colour of flamboyant flowers. 'If you are buried under a flamboyant tree,' I said, 'your soul is lifted up when it flowers.[3] Everyone wants that.'

She shook her head but she did not move or touch me.

The scent that came from the dress was very faint at first, then it grew stronger. The smell of vetivert and frangipanni, of cinnamon and dust and lime trees when they are flowering. The smell of the sun and the smell of the rain.

. . . I was wearing a dress of that colour when Sandi came to see me for the last time.

'Will you come with me?' he said. 'No,' I said, 'I cannot.'

---

3. *Delonix regia* is a large tree (40 feet high) with large leaves and flame-red, orange, or yellow petals. Also known as a Flame Tree and Royal Poinciana.

'So this is good-bye?'

Yes, this is good-bye.

'But I can't leave you like this,' he said, 'you are unhappy.'

'You are wasting time,' I said, 'and we have so little.'

Sandi often came to see me when that man was away and when I went out driving I would meet him. I could go out driving then. The servants knew, but none of them told.

Now there was no time left so we kissed each other in that stupid room. Spread fans decorated the walls. We had often kissed before but not like that. That was the life and death kiss and you only know a long time afterwards what it is, the life and death kiss. The white ship whistled three times, once gaily, once calling, once to say good-bye.[4]

I took the red dress down and put it against myself. 'Does it make me look intemperate and unchaste?' I said. That man told me so. He had found out that Sandi had been to the house and that I went to see him. I never knew who told. 'Infamous daughter of an infamous mother,'[5] he said to me.

'Oh put it away,' Grace Poole said, 'come and eat your food. Here's your grey wrapper. Why they can't give you anything better is more than I can understand. They're rich enough.'

But I held the dress in my hand wondering if they had done the last and worst thing. If they had *changed* it when I wasn't looking. If they had changed it and it wasn't my dress at all—but how could they get the scent?

'Well don't stand there shivering,' she said, quite kindly for her.

I let the dress fall on the floor, and looked from the fire to the dress and from the dress to the fire.

I put the grey wrapper round my shoulders, but I told her I wasn't hungry and she didn't try to force me to eat as she sometimes does.

'It's just as well that you don't remember last night,' she said. 'The gentleman fainted and a fine outcry there was up here. Blood all over the place and I was blamed for letting you attack him. And the master is expected in a few days. I'll never try to help you again. You are too far gone to be helped.'

I said, 'If I had been wearing my red dress Richard would have known me.'

'Your red dress,' she said, and laughed.

But I looked at the dress on the floor and it was as if the fire had

---

4. After Judas betrays Jesus with a kiss, Peter denies Jesus three times before the cock crows. (Matthew 26:31–35, 69–75).

5. In *Jane Eyre*, Rochester describes Bertha Mason as "the true daughter of an infamous mother" (see p. 127 of this volume).

spread across the room. It was beautiful and it reminded me of something I must do. I will remember I thought. I will remember quite soon
now.

That was the third time I had my dream, and it ended. I know now
that the flight of steps leads to this room where I lie watching the
woman asleep with her head on her arms. In my dream I waited till
she began to snore, then I got up, took the keys and let myself out with
a candle in my hand. It was easier this time than ever before and I
walked as though I were flying.

All the people who had been staying in the house had gone, for the
bedroom doors were shut, but it seemed to me that someone was following me, someone was chasing me, laughing. Sometimes I looked to
the right or to the left but I never looked behind me for I did not want
to see that ghost of a woman who they say haunts this place. I went
down the staircase. I went further than I had ever been before. There
was someone talking in one of the rooms. I passed it without noise,
slowly.

At last I was in the hall where a lamp was burning. I remember that
when I came. A lamp and the dark staircase and the veil over my face.
They think I don't remember but I do. There was a door to the right.
I opened it and went in. It was a large room with a red carpet and red
curtains. Everything else was white. I sat down on a couch to look at
it and it seemed sad and cold and empty to me, like a church without
an altar. I wished to see it clearly so I lit all the candles, and there were
many. I lit them carefully from the one I was carrying but I couldn't
reach up to the chandelier. I looked round for the altar for with so
many candles and so much red, the room reminded me of a church.
Then I heard a clock ticking and it was made of gold. Gold is the idol
they worship.

Suddenly I felt very miserable in that room, though the couch I was
sitting on was so soft that I sank into it. It seemed to me that I was
going to sleep. But I imagined that I heard a footstep and I thought
what will they say, what will they do if they find me here? I held my
right wrist with my left hand and waited. But it was nothing. I was very
tired after this. Very tired. I wanted to get out of the room but my own
candle had burned down and I took one of the others. Suddenly I was
in Aunt Cora's room. I saw the sunlight coming through the window,
the tree outside and the shadows of the leaves on the floor, but I saw
the wax candles too and I hated them. So I knocked them all down.
Most of them went out but one caught the thin curtains that were
behind the red ones. I laughed when I saw the lovely colour spreading
so fast, but I did not stay to watch it. I went into the hall again with
the tall candle in my hand. It was then that I saw her—the ghost. The

woman with streaming hair.[6] She was surrounded by a gilt frame but I
knew her. I dropped the candle I was carrying and it caught the end
of a tablecloth and I saw flames shoot up. As I ran or perhaps floated
or flew I called help me Christophine help me and looking behind me
I saw that I had been helped. There was a wall of fire protecting me
but it was too hot, it scorched me and I went away from it.

There were more candles on a table and I took one of them and ran
up the first flight of stairs and the second. On the second floor I threw
away the candle. But I did not stay to watch. I ran up the last flight of
stairs and along the passage. I passed the room where they brought me
yesterday or the day before yesterday, I don't remember. Perhaps it was
long ago for I seemed to know the house well. I knew how to get away
from the heat and the shouting, for there was shouting now. When I
was out on the battlements it was cool and I could hardly hear them.
I sat there quietly. I don't know how long I sat. Then I turned round
and saw the sky. It was red and all my life was in it. I saw the grandfather
clock and Aunt Cora's patchwork, all colours, I saw the orchids and
the stephanotis[7] and the jasmine and the tree of life in flames. I saw
the chandelier and the red carpet downstairs and the bamboos and the
tree ferns, the gold ferns and the silver, and the soft green velvet of
the moss on the garden wall. I saw my doll's house and the books and
the picture of the Miller's Daughter. I heard the parrot call as he did
when he saw a stranger, *Qui est là? Qui est là?* and the man who hated
me was calling too, Bertha! Bertha! The wind caught my hair and it
streamed out like wings. It might bear me up, I thought, if I jumped
to those hard stones. But when I looked over the edge I saw the pool
at Coulibri. Tia was there. She beckoned to me and when I hesitated,
she laughed. I heard her say, You frightened? And I heard the man's
voice, Bertha! Bertha! All this I saw and heard in a fraction of a second.
And the sky so red. Someone screamed and I thought, *Why did I
scream?* I called 'Tia!' and jumped and woke.

Grace Poole was sitting at the table but she had heard the scream
too, for she said, 'What was that?' She got up, came over and looked
at me. I lay still, breathing evenly with my eyes shut. 'I must have been
dreaming,' she said. Then she went back, not to the table but to her
bed. I waited a long time after I heard her snore, then I got up, took
the keys and unlocked the door. I was outside holding my candle. Now
at last I know why I was brought here and what I have to do. There
must have been a draught for the flame flickered and I thought it was
out. But I shielded it with my hand and it burned up again to light me
along the dark passage.

6. Cf. *Jane Eyre*, ch. 36, p. 131 of this volume: "She was a big woman, and had long black hair:
   we could see it streaming against the flames as she stood."
7. Climbing vine with sweet-smelling flowers.

BACKGROUNDS

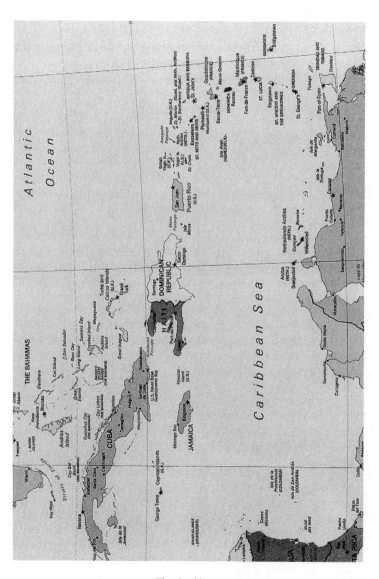

The Caribbean

"A Tread-Mill Scene in Jamaica," c. 1837.
Courtesy of the National Library of Jamaica.

RACHEL L. CARSON

[The Sargasso Sea]†

*   *   *

The mid-ocean regions, bounded by the currents that sweep around the ocean basins, are in general the deserts of the sea. There are few birds and few surface-feeding fishes, and indeed there is little surface plankton to attract them. The life of these regions is largely confined to deep water. The Sargasso Sea is an exception, not matched in the anticyclonic centers of other ocean basins. It is so different from any other place on earth that it may well be considered a definite geographic region. A line drawn from the mouth of Chesapeake Bay to Gibraltar would skirt its northern border; another from Haiti to Dakar would mark its southern boundary. It lies all about Bermuda and extends more than halfway across the Atlantic, its entire area being roughly as large as the United States. The Sargasso, with all its legendary terrors for sailing ships, is a creation of the great currents of the North Atlantic that encircle it and bring into it the millions of tons of floating sargassum weed from which the place derives its name, and all the weird assemblage of animals that live in the weed.

The Sargasso is a place forgotten by the winds, undisturbed by the strong flow of waters that girdle it as with a river. Under the seldom-clouded skies, its waters are warm and heavy with salt. Separated widely from coastal rivers and from polar ice, there is no inflow of fresh water to dilute its saltiness; the only influx is of saline water from the adjacent currents, especially from the Gulf Stream or North Atlantic Current as it crosses from America to Europe. And with the little, inflowing streams of surface water come the plants and animals that for months or years have drifted in the Gulf Stream.

The sargassum weeds are brown algae belonging to several species. Quantities of the weeds live attached to reefs or rocky outcroppings off the coasts of the West Indies and Florida. Many of the plants are torn away by storms, especially during the hurricane season. They are picked up by the Gulf Stream and are drifted northward. With the weeds go, as involuntary passengers, many small fishes, crabs, shrimps, and innumerable larvae of assorted species of marine creatures, whose home had been the coastal banks of sargassum weed.

Curious things happen to the animals that have ridden on the sar-

† From *The Sea Around Us* by Rachel L. Carson. Copyright © 1950, 1951, 1961 by Rachel Carson. Renewed 1979 by Roger Christie. Used by permission of Oxford University Press, Inc.

gassum weed into a new home. Once they lived near the sea's edge, a few feet or a few fathoms below the surface, but never far above a firm bottom. They knew the rhythmic movements of waves and tides. They could leave the shelter of the weeds at will and creep or swim about over the bottom in search of food. Now, in the middle of the ocean, they are in a new world. The bottom lies two or three miles below them. Those who are poor swimmers must cling to the weed, which now represents a life raft, supporting them above the abyss. Over the ages since their ancestors came here, some species have developed special organs of attachment, either for themselves or for their eggs, so that they may not sink into the cold, dark water far below. The flying fish make nests of the weed to contain their eggs, which bear an amazing resemblance to the sargassum floats or 'berries.'

Indeed, many of the little marine beasts of the weedy jungle seem to be playing an elaborate game of disguise in which each is camouflaged to hide it from the others. The Sargasso sea slug — a snail without a shell — has a soft, shapeless brown body spotted with dark-edged circles and fringed with flaps and folds of skin, so that as it creeps over the weed in search of prey it can scarcely be distinguished from the vegetation. One of the fiercest carnivores of the place, the sargassum fish Pterophryne, has copied with utmost fidelity the branching fronds of the weed, its golden berries, its rich brown color, and even the white dots of encrusting worm tubes. All these elaborate bits of mimicry are indications of the fierce internecine wars of the Sargasso jungles, which go on without quarter and without mercy for the weak or the unwary.

In the science of the sea there has been a long-standing controversy about the origin of the drifting weeds of the Sargasso Sea. Some have held that the supply is maintained by weeds recently torn away from coastal beds; others say that the rather limited sargassum fields of the West Indies and Florida cannot possibly supply the immense area of the Sargasso. They believe that we find here a self-perpetuating community of plants that have become adapted to life in the open sea, needing no roots or holdfasts for attachment, and able to propagate vegetatively. Probably there is truth in both ideas. New plants do come in each year in small numbers, and now cover an immense area because of their very long life once they have reached this quiet central region of the Atlantic.

It takes about half a year for the plants torn from West Indian shores to reach the northern border of the Sargasso, perhaps several years for them to be carried into the inner parts of this area. Meanwhile, some have been swept onto the shores of North America by storms, others have been killed by cold during the passage from offshore New England across the Atlantic, where the Gulf Stream comes into contact with waters from the Arctic. For the plants that reach the calm of the Sargasso, there is virtual immortality. A. E. Parr of the American Museum has recently suggested that the individual plants may live, some for decades, others for centuries, according to their species. It might well be that some of the very weeds you would see if you visited the place today were seen by Columbus and his men. Here, in the heart of the Atlantic, the weed drifts endlessly, growing, reproducing vegetatively by a process of fragmentation. Apparently almost the only plants that die are the ones that drift into unfavorable conditions around the edges of the Sargasso or are picked up by outward-moving currents.

Such losses are balanced, or possibly a little more than balanced, by the annual addition of weeds from distant coasts. It must have taken eons of time to accumulate the present enormous quantities of weed, which Parr estimates as about 10 million tons. But this, of course, is distributed over so large an area that most of the Sargasso is open water. The dense fields of weeds waiting to entrap a vessel never existed except in the imaginations of sailors, and the gloomy hulks of vessels doomed to endless drifting in the clinging weed are only the ghosts of things that never were.

CHARLOTTE BRONTË

From Jane Eyre†

[*Jane Eyre and Bertha*]

*   *   *

'I dreamt another dream, sir: that Thornfield Hall was a dreary ruin, the retreat of bats and owls. I thought that of all the stately front nothing remained but a shell-like wall, very high, and very fragile-looking. I wandered, on a moonlight night, through the grass-grown enclosure within: here I stumbled over a marble hearth, and there over a fallen fragment of cornice. Wrapped up in a shawl, I still carried the unknown little child: I might not lay it down anywhere, however tired were my arms — however much its weight impeded my progress, I must retain it. I heard the gallop of a horse at a distance on the road: I was sure it was you; and you were departing for many years, and for a distant country. I climbed the thin wall with frantic, perilous haste, eager to catch one glimpse of you from the top: the stones rolled from under my feet, the ivy branches I grasped gave way, the child clung round my neck in terror, and almost strangled me: at last I gained the summit. I saw you like a speck on a white track, lessening every moment. The blast blew so strong I could not stand. I sat down on the narrow ledge; I hushed the scared infant in my lap: you turned an angle of the road;

† From Charlotte Brontë, *Jane Eyre*, A Norton Critical Edition, Second Edition, edited by Richard J. Dunn (New York: W. W. Norton, 1988).

I bent forward to take a last look; the wall crumbled; I was shaken; the child rolled from my knee, I lost my balance, fell, and woke.'

'Now, Jane, that is all.'

'All the preface, sir; the tale is yet to come. On waking, a gleam dazzled my eyes: I thought—oh, it is daylight! But I was mistaken: it was only candlelight. Sophie, I supposed, had come in. There was a light on the dressing-table, and the door of the closet, where, before going to bed, I had hung my wedding-dress and veil, stood open: I heard a rustling there. I asked, "Sophie, what are you doing?" No one answered; but a form emerged from the closet: it took the light, held it aloft, and surveyed the garments pendent from the portmanteau. "Sophie! Sophie!" I again cried: and still it was silent. I had risen up in bed; I bent forward: first, surprise, then bewilderment, came over me; and then my blood crept cold through my veins. Mr. Rochester, this was not Sophie, it was not Leah, it was not Mrs. Fairfax: It was not— no, I was sure of it, and am still—it was not even that strange woman, Grace Poole.'

'It must have been one of them,' interrupted my master.

'No, sir, I solemnly assure you to the contrary. The shape standing before me had never crossed my eyes within the precincts of Thornfield Hall before; the height, the contour, were new to me.'

'Describe it, Jane.'

'It seemed, sir, a woman, tall and large, with thick and dark hair hanging long down her back. I know not what dress she had on: it was white and straight; but whether gown, sheet, or shroud, I cannot tell.'

'Did you see her face?'

'Not at first. But presently she took my veil from its place; she held it up, gazed at it long, and then she threw it over her own head, and turned to the mirror. At that moment I saw the reflection of the visage and features quite distinctly in the dark oblong glass.'

'And how were they?'

'Fearful and ghastly to me—oh, sir, I never saw a face like it! It was a discoloured face—it was a savage face. I wish I could forget the roll of the red eyes and the fearful blackened inflation of the lineaments.'

'Ghosts are usually pale, Jane.'

'This, sir, was purple: the lips were swelled and dark; the brow furrowed; the black eyebrows widely raised over the bloodshot eyes. Shall I tell you of what it reminded me?'

'You may.'

'Of the foul German spectre—the Vampyre.'

'Ah?—What did it do?'

'Sir, it removed my veil from its gaunt head, rent it in two parts, and flinging both on the floor, trampled on them.'

'Afterwards?'

'It drew aside the window-curtain and looked out: perhaps it saw

dawn approaching, for, taking the candle, it retreated to the door. Just
at my bedside the figure stopped: the fiery eye glared upon me — she
thrust up her candle close to my face, and extinguished it under my
eyes. I was aware her lurid visage flamed over mine, and I lost consciousness: for the second time in my life — only the second time — I
became insensible from terror.'

* * *

[The Ruined Wedding]

* * *

Our place was taken at the communion rails. Hearing a cautious step
behind me, I glanced over my shoulder: one of the strangers — a gentleman, evidently — was advancing up the chancel. The service began.
The explanation of the intent of matrimony was gone through; and
then the clergyman came a step further forward, and, bending slightly
towards Mr. Rochester, went on.

'I require and charge you both (as ye will answer at the dreadful day
of judgment, when the secrets of all hearts shall be disclosed), that if
either of you know any impediment why ye may not lawfully be joined
together in matrimony, ye do now confess it; for be ye well assured that
so many as are coupled together otherwise than God's word doth allow,
are not joined together by God, neither is their matrimony lawful.'

He paused, as the custom is. When is the pause after that sentence
ever broken by reply? Not, perhaps, once in a hundred years. And the
clergyman, who had not lifted his eyes from his book, and had held
his breath but for a moment, was proceeding: his hand was already
stretched towards Mr. Rochester, as his lips unclosed to ask, 'Wilt thou
have this woman for thy wedded wife?' — when a distinct and near voice
said: — 'The marriage cannot go on: I declare the existence of an
impediment.'

The clergyman looked up at the speaker, and stood mute; the clerk
did the same; Mr. Rochester moved slightly, as if an earthquake had
rolled under his feet: taking a firmer footing, and not turning his head
or eyes; he said, 'Proceed.'

Profound silence fell when he had uttered that word, with deep but
low intonation. Presently Mr. Wood said: — 'I cannot proceed without
some investigation into what has been asserted, and evidence of its truth
or falsehood.'

'The ceremony is quite broken off,' subjoined the voice behind us.
'I am in a condition to prove my allegation: an insuperable impediment
to this marriage exists.'

Mr. Rochester heard, but heeded not: he stood stubborn and rigid:
making no movement, but to possess himself of my hand. What a hot
and strong grasp he had! — and how like quarried marble was his pale,

firm, massive front at this moment! How his eye shone, still, watchful, and yet wild beneath!

Mr. Wood seemed at a loss. 'What is the nature of the impediment?' he asked. 'Perhaps it may be got over — explained away?'

'Hardly,' was the answer: 'I have called it insuperable, and I speak advisedly.'

The speaker came forwards, and leaned on the rails. He continued, uttering each word distinctly, calmly, steadily, but not loudly.

'It simply consists in the existence of a previous marriage. Mr. Rochester has a wife now living.'

My nerves vibrated to those low-spoken words as they had never vibrated to thunder — my blood felt their subtle violence as it had never felt frost or fire: but I was collected, and in no danger of swooning. I looked at Mr. Rochester: I made him look at me. His whole face was colourless rock: his eye was both spark and flint. He disavowed nothing: he seemed as if he would defy all things. Without speaking, without smiling, without seeming to recognise in me a human being, he only twined my waist with his arm, and riveted me to his side.

'Who are you?' he asked of the intruder.

'My name is Briggs — a solicitor of —— Street, London.'

'And you would thrust on me a wife?'

'I would remind you of your lady's existence, sir; which the law recognises, if you do not.'

'Favour me with an account of her — with her name, her parentage, her place of abode.'

'Certainly.' Mr. Briggs calmly took a paper from his pocket, and read out in a sort of official, nasal voice: —

'"I affirm and can prove that on the 20th of October, A.D. —— (a date of fifteen years back), Edward Fairfax Rochester, of Thornfield Hall, in the county of ——, and of Ferndean Manor, in ——shire, England, was married to my sister, Bertha Antoinetta Mason, daughter of Jonas Mason, merchant, and of Antoinetta his wife, a Creole — at —— church, Spanish Town, Jamaica. The record of the marriage will be found in the register of that church — a copy of it is now in my possession. Signed, Richard Mason."'

'That — if a genuine document — may prove I have been married, but it does not prove that the woman mentioned therein as my wife is still living.'

'She was living three months ago,' returned the lawyer.

'How do you know?'

'I have a witness to the fact, whose testimony even you, sir, will scarcely controvert.'

'Produce him — or go to hell.'

'I will produce him first — he is on the spot: Mr. Mason, have the goodness to step forward.'

Mr. Rochester, on hearing the name, set his teeth; he experienced, too, a sort of strong convulsive quiver; near to him as I was, I felt the spasmodic movement of fury or despair run through his frame. The second stranger, who had hitherto lingered in the background, now drew near; a pale face looked over the solicitor's shoulder — yes, it was Mason himself. Mr. Rochester turned and glared at him. His eye, as I have often said, was a black eye: it had now a tawny, nay a bloody light in its gloom; and his face flushed — olive cheek and hueless forehead received a glow, as from spreading, ascending heart-fire: and he stirred, lifted his strong arm — he could have struck Mason — dashed him on the church-floor — shocked by ruthless blow the breath from his body — but Mason shrank away, and cried faintly, 'Good God!' Contempt fell cool on Mr. Rochester — his passion died as if a blight had shrivelled it up: he only asked, 'What have *you* to say?'

An inaudible reply escaped Mason's white lips.

'The devil is in it if you cannot answer distinctly. I again demand, what have *you* to say?'

'Sir — sir' — interrupted the clergyman, 'do not forget you are in a sacred place.' Then, addressing Mason, he inquired gently, 'Are you aware, sir, whether or not this gentleman's wife is still living?'

'Courage,' urged the lawyer, — 'speak out.'

'She is now living at Thornfield Hall,' said Mason, in more articulate tones: 'I saw her there last April. I am her brother.'

'At Thornfield Hall!' ejaculated the clergyman. 'Impossible! I am an old resident in this neighbourhood, sir, and I never heard of a Mrs. Rochester at Thornfield Hall.'

I saw a grim smile contort Mr. Rochester's lip, and he muttered: — 'No — by God! I took care that none should hear of it — or of her under that name.' He mused — for ten minutes he held counsel with himself: he formed his resolve, and announced it: — 'Enough — all shall bolt out at once, like a bullet from the barrel. — Wood, close your book, and take off your surplice; John Green (to the clerk) leave the church: there will be no wedding to-day:' the man obeyed.

Mr. Rochester continued, hardily and recklessly: 'Bigamy is an ugly word! — I meant, however, to be a bigamist; but fate has outmanœu-vered me; or Providence has checked me, — perhaps the last. I am little better than a devil at this moment; and, as my pastor there would tell me, deserve no doubt the sternest judgments of God, — even to the quenchless fire and deathless worm. Gentlemen, my plan is broken up! — what this lawyer and his client say is true: I have been married; and the woman to whom I was married lives! You say you never heard of a Mrs. Rochester at the house up yonder, Wood: but I dare say you have many a time inclined your ear to gossip about the mysterious lunatic kept there under watch and ward. Some have whispered to you that she is my bastard half-sister: some, my cast-off mistress; I now in-

form you that she is my wife, whom I married fifteen years ago, —
Bertha Mason by name; sister of this resolute personage, who is now,
with his quivering limbs and white cheeks, showing you what a stout
heart men may bear. Cheer up, Dick! — never fear me! — I'd almost as
soon strike a woman as you. Bertha Mason is mad; and she came of a
mad family; — idiots and maniacs through three generations! Her
mother, the Creole, was both a mad woman and a drunkard! — as I
found out after I had wed the daughter: for they were silent on family
secrets before. Bertha, like a dutiful child, copied her parent in both
points. I had a charming partner — pure, wise, modest: you can fancy
I was a happy man. — I went through rich scenes! Oh! my experience
has been heavenly, if you only knew it! But I owe you no further
explanation. Briggs, Wood, Mason, — I invite you all to come up to the
house and visit Mrs. Poole's patient, and *my wife*! You shall see what
sort of a being I was cheated into espousing, and judge whether or not
I had a right to break the compact, and seek sympathy with something
at least human. This girl,' he continued, looking at me, 'knew no more
than you, Wood, of the disgusting secret: she thought all was fair and
legal; and never dreamt she was going to be entrapped into a feigned
union with a defrauded wretch, already bound to a bad, mad, and
embruted partner! Come, all of you, follow.'

Still holding me fast, he left the church: the three gentlemen came
after. At the front door of the hall we found the carriage.

'Take it back to the coach-house, John,' said Mr. Rochester, coolly;
'it will not be wanted to-day.'

At our entrance Mrs. Fairfax, Adèle, Sophie, Leah, advanced to meet
and greet us.

'To the right about — every soul!' cried the master: 'away with your
congratulations! Who wants them? — Not I! — they are fifteen years too
late!'

He passed on and ascended the stairs, still holding my hand, and
still beckoning the gentlemen to follow him; which they did. We
mounted the first staircase, passed up the gallery, proceeded to the third
storey: the low, black door, opened by Mr. Rochester's master key, admitted us to the tapestried room, with its great bed and its pictorial
cabinet.

'You know this place, Mason,' said our guide; 'she bit and stabbed
you here.'

He lifted the hangings from the wall, uncovering the second door:
this, too, he opened. In a room without a window there burnt a fire,
guarded by a high and strong fender, and a lamp suspended from the
ceiling by a chain. Grace Poole bent over the fire, apparently cooking
something in a saucepan. In the deep shade, at the further end of the
room, a figure ran backwards and forwards. What it was, whether beast
or human being, one could not, at first sight, tell: it grovelled, seem-

ingly, on all fours; it snatched and growled like some strange wild animal: but it was covered with clothing; and a quantity of dark, grizzled
hair, wild as a mane, hid its head and face.

'Good-morrow, Mrs. Poole!' said Mr. Rochester. 'How are you? and
how is your charge to-day?'

'We're tolerable, sir, I thank you,' replied Grace, lifting the boiling
mess carefully on to the hob: 'rather snappish, but not 'rageous.'

A fierce cry seemed to give the lie to her favourable report: the
clothed hyena rose up, and stood tall on its hind feet.

'Ah, sir, she sees you!' exclaimed Grace: 'you'd better not stay.'

'Only a few moments, Grace: you must allow me a few moments.'

'Take care then, sir!—for God's sake, take care!'

The maniac bellowed: she parted her shaggy locks from her visage,
and gazed wildly at her visitors. I recognised well that purple face—
those bloated features. Mrs. Poole advanced.

'Keep out of the way,' said Mr. Rochester, thrusting her aside: 'she
has no knife now, I suppose? and I'm on my guard.'

'One never knows what she has, sir: she is so cunning: it is not in
mortal discretion to fathom her craft.'

'We had better leave her,' whispered Mason.

'Go to the devil!' was his brother-in-law's recommendation.

'Ware!' cried Grace. The three gentlemen retreated simultaneously.
Mr. Rochester flung me behind him: the lunatic sprang and grappled
his throat viciously, and laid her teeth to his cheek: they struggled. She
was a big woman, in stature almost equalling her husband, and cor-
pulent besides: she showed virile force in the contest—more than once
she almost throttled him, athletic as he was. He could have settled her
with a well-planted blow; but he would not strike: he would only wres-
tle. At last he mastered her arms; Grace Poole gave him a cord, and
he pinioned them behind her: with more rope, which was at hand, he
bound her to a chair. The operation was performed amidst the fiercest
yells and the most convulsive plunges. Mr. Rochester then turned to
the spectators: he looked at them with a smile both acrid and desolate.

'That is *my wife*,' said he. 'Such is the sole conjugal embrace I am
ever to know—such are the endearments which are to solace my leisure
hours! And *this* is what I wished to have' (laying his hand on my shoulder): 'this young girl, who stands so grave and quiet at the mouth of
hell, looking collectedly at the gambols of a demon. I wanted her just
as a change after that fierce ragout. Wood and Briggs, look at the difference! Compare these clear eyes with the red balls yonder—this face
with that mask—this form with that bulk; then judge me, priest of
the gospel and man of the law, and remember, with what judgment
ye judge ye shall be judged! Off with you now. I must shut up my
prize.'

*   *   *

[Rochester's Story]

* * *

'I am a fool!' cried Mr. Rochester suddenly. 'I keep telling her I am not married, and do not explain to her why. I forget she knows nothing of the character of that woman, or of the circumstances attending my infernal union with her. Oh, I am certain Jane will agree with me in opinion when she knows all that I know! Just put your hand in mine, Janet, that I may have the evidence of touch as well as sight to prove you are near me — and I will in a few words show you the real state of the case. Can you listen to me?'

'Yes, sir; for hours if you will.'

'I ask only minutes. Jane, did you ever hear or know that I was not the eldest son of my house; that I had once a brother older than I?'

'I remember Mrs. Fairfax told me so once.'

'And did you ever hear that my father was an avaricious grasping man?'

'I have understood something to that effect.'

'Well, Jane, being so, it was his resolution to keep the property together; he could not bear the idea of dividing his estate and leaving me a fair portion: all, he resolved, should go to my brother Rowland. Yet as little could he endure that a son of his should be a poor man. I must be provided for by a wealthy marriage. He sought me a partner betimes. Mr. Mason, a West India planter and merchant, was his old acquaintance. He was certain his possessions were real and vast: he made inquiries. Mr. Mason, he found, had a son and daughter; and he learned from him that he could and would give the latter a fortune of thirty thousand pounds: that sufficed. When I left college I was sent out to Jamaica, to espouse a bride already courted for me. My father said nothing about her money: but he told me Miss Mason was the boast of Spanish Town for her beauty: and this was no lie. I found her a fine woman, in the style of Blanche Ingram; tall, dark, and majestic. Her family wished to secure me, because I was of a good race; and so did she. They showed her to me in parties, splendidly dressed. I seldom saw her alone, and had very little private conversation with her. She flattered me, and lavishly displayed for my pleasure her charms and accomplishments. All the men in her circle seemed to admire her and envy me. I was dazzled, stimulated: my senses were excited; and being ignorant, raw, and inexperienced, I thought I loved her. There is no folly so besotted that the idiotic rivalries of society, the prurience, the rashness, the blindness of youth, will not hurry a man to its commission. Her relatives encouraged me; competitors piqued me; she allured me: a marriage was achieved almost before I knew where I was. Oh, I have no respect for myself when I think of that act! — an agony of inward contempt masters me. I never loved, I never esteemed, I did not even know her. I was not sure of the existence of one virtue in her nature: I had marked neither modesty, nor benevolence, nor candour, nor refinement in her mind or manners — and, I married her: — gross, grovelling, mole-eyed blockhead that I was! With less sin I might have — but let me remember to whom I am speaking.

'My bride's mother I had never seen: I understood she was dead. The honeymoon over, I learned my mistake; she was only mad, and shut up in a lunatic asylum. There was a younger brother, too, a complete dumb idiot. The elder one, whom you have seen (and whom I cannot hate, whilst I abhor all his kindred, because he has some grains of affection in his feeble mind; shown in the continued interest he takes in his wretched sister, and also in a dog-like attachment he once bore me), will probably be in the same state one day. My father, and my brother Rowland, knew all this; but they thought only of the thirty thousand pounds, and joined in the plot against me.

'These were vile discoveries; but, except for the treachery of concealment, I should have made them no subject of reproach to my wife: even when I found her nature wholly alien to mine; her tastes obnoxious to me; her cast of mind common, low, narrow, and singularly incapable of being led to anything higher, expanded to anything larger — when I found that I could not pass a single evening, nor even a single hour of the day, with her in comfort: that kindly conversation could not be sustained between us, because whatever topic I started immediately received from her a turn at once coarse and trite, perverse and imbecile — when I perceived that I should never have a quiet or settled household, because no servant would bear the continued outbreaks of her violent and unreasonable temper, or the vexations of her absurd, contradictory, exacting orders — even then I restrained myself: I eschewed upbraiding, I curtailed remonstrance; I tried to devour my repentance and disgust in secret; I repressed the deep antipathy I felt.

'Jane, I will not trouble you with abominable details: some strong words shall express what I have to say. I lived with that woman upstairs four years, and before that time she had tried me indeed: her character ripened and developed with frightful rapidity; her vices sprang up fast and rank: they were so strong, only cruelty could check them; and I would not use cruelty. What a pigmy intellect she had — and what giant propensities! How fearful were the curses those propensities entailed on me! Bertha Mason, — the true daughter of an infamous mother, — dragged me through all the hideous and degrading agonies which must attend a man bound to a wife at once intemperate and unchaste.

'My brother in the interval was dead; and at the end of the four years my father died too. I was rich enough now — yet poor to hideous indigence: a nature the most gross, impure, depraved, I ever saw, was associated with mine, and called by the law and by society a part of me. And I could not rid myself of it by any legal proceedings: for the doctors now discovered that *my wife* was mad — her excesses had prematurely developed the germs of insanity * * *

'One night I had been awakened by her yells — (since the medical men had pronounced her mad she had of course been shut up) — it was a fiery West Indian night; one of the description that frequently precede the hurricanes of those climates; being unable to sleep in bed, I got up and opened the window. The air was like sulphur-steams — I could find no refreshment anywhere. Mosquitoes came buzzing in and hummed sullenly round the room; the sea, which I could hear from thence, rumbled dull like an earthquake — black clouds were casting up over it; the moon was setting in the waves, broad and red, like a hot cannon-ball — she threw her last bloody glance over a world quivering with the ferment of tempest. I was physically influenced by the atmosphere and scene, and my ears were filled with the curses the maniac still shrieked out; wherein she momentarily mingled my name with such a tone of demon-hate, with such language! — no professed harlot ever had a fouler vocabulary than she: though two rooms off, I heard every word — the thin partitions of the West India house opposing but slight obstruction to her wolfish cries.

' "This life," said I at last, "is hell! this is the air — those are the sounds of the bottomless pit! I have a right to deliver myself from it if I can. The sufferings of this mortal state will leave me with the heavy flesh that now cumbers my soul. Of the fanatic's burning eternity I have no fear; there is not a future state worse than this present one — let me break away, and go home to God!"

'I said this whilst I knelt down at and unlocked a trunk which contained a brace of loaded pistols: I meant to shoot myself. I only entertained the intention for a moment; for not being insane, the crisis of exquisite and unalloyed despair which had originated the wish and design of self-destruction was past in a second.

'A wind fresh from Europe blew over the ocean and rushed through the open casement: the storm broke, streamed, thundered, blazed, and the air grew pure. I then framed and fixed a resolution. While I walked under the dripping orange-trees of my wet garden, and amongst its drenched pomegranates and pine-apples, and while the refulgent dawn of the tropics kindled round me — I reasoned thus, Jane: — and now listen; for it was true Wisdom that consoled me in that hour, and showed me the right path to follow.

'The sweet wind from Europe was still whispering in the refreshed leaves, and the Atlantic was thundering in glorious liberty; my heart, dried up and scorched for a long time, swelled to the tone, and filled with living blood — my being longed for renewal — my soul thirsted for a pure draught. I saw Hope revive — and felt Regeneration possible. From a flowery arch at the bottom of my garden I gazed over the sea — bluer than the sky: the old world was beyond; clear prospects opened thus: —

' "Go," said Hope, "and live again in Europe: there it is not known what a sullied name you bear, nor what a filthy burden is bound to you. You may take the maniac with you to England; confine her with due attendance and precautions at Thornfield: then travel yourself to what clime you will, and form what new tie you like. That woman, who has so abused your long-suffering — so sullied your name; so outraged your honour; so blighted your youth — is not your wife; nor are you her husband. See that she is cared for as her condition demands, and you have done all that God and Humanity require of you. Let her identity, her connection with yourself, be buried in oblivion: you are bound to impart them to no living being. Place her in safety and comfort: shelter her degradation with secrecy, and leave her."

'I acted precisely on this suggestion. My father and brother had not made my marriage known to their acquaintance; because, in the very first letter I wrote to apprise them of the union — having already begun to experience extreme disgust of its consequences; and from the family character and constitution seeing a hideous future opening to me — I added an urgent charge to keep it secret; and very soon the infamous conduct of the wife my father had selected for me was such as to make him blush to own her as his daughter-in-law. Far from desiring to publish the connection, he became as anxious to conceal it as myself.

'To England, then, I conveyed her; a fearful voyage I had with such a monster in the vessel. Glad was I when I at last got her to Thornfield, and saw her safely lodged in that third-storey room, of whose secret inner cabinet she has now for ten years made a wild beast's den — a goblin's cell. I had some trouble in finding an attendant for her: as it was necessary to select one on whose fidelity dependence could be placed; for her ravings would inevitably betray my secret: besides, she had lucid intervals of days — sometimes weeks — which she filled up with abuse of me. At last I hired Grace Poole, from the Grimsby Retreat. She and the surgeon, Carter (who dressed Mason's wounds that night he was stabbed and worried), are the only two I have ever admitted to my confidence. Mrs. Fairfax may indeed have suspected something; but she could have gained no precise knowledge as to facts. Grace has, on the whole, proved a good keeper; though, owing partly to a fault of her own, of which it appears nothing can cure her, and which is incident to her harassing profession, her vigilance has been more than once lulled and baffled. The lunatic is both cunning and malignant; she has never failed to take advantage of her guardian's temporary lapses; once to secrete the knife with which she stabbed her brother, and twice to possess herself of the key of her cell, and issue therefrom in the night-time. On the first of these occasions she perpetrated the attempt to burn me in my bed; on the second she paid that ghastly visit to you. I thank Providence, who watched over you, that she then spent her fury on your wedding apparel; which perhaps brought back vague reminiscences of her own bridal days; but on what might have happened I cannot endure to reflect. * * *

[*Fire at Thornfield Hall*]

* * * The lawn, the grounds [of Thornfield Hall] were trodden and waste: the portal yawned void. The front was, as I had once seen it in a dream, but a shell-like wall, very high and very fragile looking, perforated with paneless windows: no roof, no battlements, no chimneys — all had crashed in.

And there was the silence of death about it: the solitude of a lonesome wild. No wonder that letters addressed to people here had never received an answer: as well despatch epistles to a vault in a church aisle. The grim blackness of the stones told by what fate the Hall had fallen — by conflagration: but how kindled? What story belonged to this disaster? What loss, besides mortar and marble and wood-work, had followed upon it? Had life been wrecked, as well as property? If so, whose? Dreadful question: there was no one here to answer it — not even dumb sign, mute token.

* * *

'Is Mr. Rochester living at Thornfield Hall now?' I asked, knowing, of course, what the answer would be, but yet desirous of deferring the direct question as to where he really was.

'No, ma'am — oh, no! No one is living there. I suppose you are a stranger in these parts, or you would have heard what happened last autumn, — Thornfield Hall is quite a ruin: it was burnt down just about harvest time. A dreadful calamity! such an immense quantity of valuable property destroyed: hardly any of the furniture could be saved. The fire broke out at dead of night, and before the engines arrived from Millcote, the building was one mass of flame. It was a terrible spectacle: I witnessed it myself.'

'At dead of night!' I muttered. Yes, that was ever the hour of fatality at Thornfield. 'Was it known how it originated?' I demanded.

'They guessed, ma'am: they guessed. Indeed, I should say it was ascertained beyond a doubt. You are not perhaps aware,' he continued, edging his chair a little nearer the table, and speaking low, 'that there was a lady, — a — a lunatic, kept in the house?'

'I have heard something of it.'

'She was kept in very close confinement, ma'am; people even for some years was not absolutely certain of her existence. No one saw her: they only knew by rumour that such a person was at the Hall; and who or what she was it was difficult to conjecture. They said Mr. Edward had brought her from abroad; and some believed she had been his mistress. * * *

'This lady, ma'am,' he answered, 'turned out to be Mr. Rochester's wife! * * * it's quite certain that it was her and nobody but her, that set it going. She had a woman to take care of her called Mrs. Poole — an able woman in her line, and very trustworthy, but for one fault — a fault common to a deal of them nurses and matrons — *she kept a private bottle of gin by her*, and now and then took a drop over much. It is excusable, for she had a hard life of it: but still it was dangerous; for when Mrs. Poole was fast asleep, after the gin-and-water, the mad lady, who was as cunning as a witch, would take the keys out of her pocket, let herself out of her chamber, and go roaming about the house, doing any wild mischief that came into her head. They say she had nearly burnt her husband in his bed once: but I don't know about that. However, on this night, she set fire first to the hangings of the room next her own; and then she got down to a lower story, and made her way to the chamber that had been the governess's — (she was like as if she knew somehow how matters had gone on, and had a spite at her) — and she kindled the bed there; but there was nobody sleeping in it fortunately. The governess had run away two months before; and for all Mr. Rochester sought her as if she had been the most precious thing he had in the world, he never could hear a word of her; and he grew savage — quite savage on his disappointment: he never was a wild man, but he got dangerous after he lost her. He would be alone, too. He sent Mrs. Fairfax, the housekeeper, away to her friends at a distance; but he did it handsomely, for he settled an annuity on her for life: and she deserved it — she was a very good woman. Miss Adèle, a ward he had, was put to school. He broke off acquaintance with all the gentry, and shut himself up, like a hermit, at the Hall.'

* * *

'Then Mr. Rochester was at home when the fire broke out?'

'Yes, indeed was he; and he went up to the attics when all was burning above and below, and got the servants out of their beds and helped them down himself — and went back to get his mad wife out of her cell. And then they called out to him that she was on the roof; where she was standing, waving her arms, above the battlements, and shouting out till they could hear her a mile off; I saw her and heard her with my own eyes. She was a big woman, and had long black hair: we could see it streaming against the flames as she stood. I witnessed, and several more witnessed Mr. Rochester ascend through the skylight on to the roof: we heard him call "Bertha!" We saw him approach her; and then, ma'am, she yelled, and gave a spring, and the next minute she lay smashed on the pavement.'

'Dead?'

'Dead? Ay, dead as the stones on which her brains and blood were scattered.'

'Good God!'

'You may well say so, ma'am: it was frightful!'

He shuddered.

'And afterwards?' I urged.

'Well, ma'am, afterwards the house was burnt to the ground: there are only some bits of walls standing now.'

'Were any other lives lost?'

'No — perhaps it would have been better if there had.'

'What do you mean?'

'Poor Mr. Edward!' he ejaculated, 'I little thought ever to have seen it! Some say it was a just judgment on him for keeping his first marriage secret, and wanting to take another wife while he had one living: but I pity him, for my part.'

'You said he was alive?' I exclaimed.

'Yes, yes: he is alive; but many think he had better be dead.'

*   *   *

'He is stone-blind,' he said at last. 'Yes — he is stone-blind — is Mr. Edward.'

I had dreaded worse. I had dreaded he was mad. I summoned strength to ask what had caused this calamity.

'It was all his own courage, and a body may say, his kindness, in a way, ma'am: he wouldn't leave the house till every one else was out before him. As he came down the great staircase at last, after Mrs. Rochester had flung herself from the battlements, there was a great crash — all fell. He was taken out from under the ruins, alive, but sadly hurt: a beam had fallen in such a way as to protect him partly; but one eye was knocked out, and one hand so crushed that Mr. Carter, the surgeon, had to amputate it directly. The other eye inflamed: he lost the sight of that also. He is now helpless, indeed — blind and a cripple.'

*   *   *

JEAN RHYS

Selected Letters†

TO PEGGY KIRKALDY   *October 4th* [1949]
                                        Beckenham

*   *   *

I know Peggy that you don't care for Americans but they have one great virtue, they don't stifle criticism. You can write about the Chain Gang or a canned meat factory or a loony bin and what have you and there's a chance of an audience. But not here! The English clamp

† From *The Letters of Jean Rhys*, selected and edited by Francis Wyndham and Diana Melly (New York: Viking, 1984). Reprinted by permission of Sheil Land Associates Ltd.

down on unpleasant facts and some of the facts they clamp down on are very unpleasant indeed, believe me.

My dear I hope I may write again some day. I have a novel half done and the rest safely in my head. It's about the West Indies about 1780 something.

But this horrible creeping *indifference* stops me — I can't find anything worth while.

* * *

TO MARYVONNE MOERMAN *November 9th [1949]*
Beckenham

* * *

I have had some news which may cheer you up. The enclosed advertisement was in the New Statesman on Friday. I answered it at once — very puzzled.

It turned out to be from a BBC actress called Selma Vaz Dias who wants to broadcast my work. She says she has been looking for me for "years" as the BBC like my stuff.

The preliminary reading is tomorrow.

I am very astonished that the BBC like my work (especially Good Morning) but it seems they thought I was dead — which of course would make a great difference. In fact they were going to follow it up with a broadcast "Quest for Jean Rhys" and I feel rather tactless being still alive!

However I'm cheered up too for if they can make a fuss of me dead surely they can make a *little fuss* though I'm not.

* * *

TO PEGGY KIRKALDY *December 6th [1949]*
Beckenham

* * *

Now I'm really hanging on to my belief in fate — I never wanted to write. I wished to be happy and peaceful and obscure. I was *dragged* into writing by a series of coincidences — Mrs Adam, Ford, Paris[1] — need for money.

1. Mrs George Adam was the wife of *The Times* correspondent in Paris during the early 1920s. Jean, who had met her briefly in London during the war, approached her for help in placing three articles by Jean Lenglet which she had translated from the French. Instead Mrs Adam asked to see work of her own, and Jean showed her a diary she had kept between 1910 and 1919. Mrs Adam rewrote parts of it in the form of a novel called *Susie Tells* and sent the typescript to Ford Madox Ford. He changed the book's title to *Triple Sec* and the author's name (then Ella Lenglet) to Jean Rhys. The book was not published, but Ford encouraged

I tried to stop—again I've been dragged back.

So I must go on now failure or not—lies or no lies.

Please forgive this exalted letter, I know that's a great fault of mine. I get exalted and make people hate me and wish to avoid me. And as I have no money background or friends—well off they are with a juicy morsel to laugh at and lie about.

Well that's the first fault.

The second danger is that my fierce boiling hatred of this dirty mob is going to sink me because I do silly things when I'm enraged.

Well well. Do wish me luck Peggy as I wish you all luck for the New Year and for always.

Jean

P.S. I can't resist quoting something Miss Vaz Dias said: "Dear Miss Rhys—You're so *gentle* and *quiet*—Not at all what I expected!"—I gathered afterwards that she expected a raving and not too clean maniac with straws in gruesome unwashed hair. Maybe I should have played it that way.

Never disappoint your audience.

TO MORCHARD BISHOP   *January 27th* [1953]
                                              Milestone Road

*   *   *

Everyone does seem very pessimistic about the future of writing and art in general. But hasn't it always been a fight? I remember how very bitter most of the English in Paris were about that very subject ages ago.

And—please don't think me impertinent—but I do find that so many people here are not phoney but *unreal*.

I read a letter in the Observer last Sunday from some editor—Peter Green—promising to accept any story up to (of) the standard of "Boule de Suif"[2]. Well I should damned well think he would! And Hemingway's last thing[3]. Why not add Prosper Merimée's "Carmen" for good measure.

Poor Boule de Suif. They won't let her rest—

The thing is I very much doubt whether any story seriously glorifying the prostitute and showing up not one but several British housewives

---

her to go on writing and eventually printed her story "Vienne" in the last issue of *the transatlantic review* (December 1924). By then, Lenglet had been extradited to Holland and Jean and Ford had become lovers. Jean jettisoned *Triple Sec* but later used the original diaries as a basis for *Voyage in the Dark.*

2. Story by Guy de Maupassant.
3. Hemingway's novel *The Old Man and the Sea.*

to say nothing of two nuns! — their meannesses and cant and spite —
would be accepted by the average editor or any editor.

And "La Maison Tellier"[4]? — Well imagine —

Of course I may be quite wrong. I don't know much about it these
days. But I do read a lot and have a very definite impression that
"thought control" is on the way and ought to be resisted. But will it be
resisted?

Why say as Mr Green does "I demand a positive and creative view
of life?" What is that? And why *demand* a view of life. Not his business
surely.

It's all very well to talk about The Old Man and the Sea but what
about "Hills like White Elephants" or "A Way You'll Never Be"[5]. . . .
[. . . . . .]
Would those be up to his "positive and creative" standard?

*   *   *

But I do feel rather deeply about the thought control matter. So
insidious. And suddenly it's there — Not to be resisted any more.

Yours sincerely
Jean Rhys

I have seen two or three people. They tell me I am generally supposed
to be dead. Also that my last book was cribbed from Henry Miller's
Tropic of Cancer.

That makes me fierce, though it is also rather comic. It would take
too long to tell you why.

J.R.

TO FRANCIS WYNDHAM   *March 29th* [1958]
Rocket House

Dear Mr Wyndham,

This is to tell you something about the novel I am trying to write —
provisional title "The First Mrs Rochester". I mean, of course, the mad
woman in "Jane Eyre".

It's difficult for me to explain an unfinished book, this one particularly, and I hope I won't be tedious — or disappointing.

For some time I've been getting down all I remembered about the
West Indies as the West Indies used to be. (Also all I was told, which
is more important). I called this "Creole" but it had no shape or plan
— it wasn't a book at all and I didn't try to force it.

Then when I was in London last year it "clicked in my head" that

4. Story by Maupassant.
5. "Hills Like White Elephants," "A Way You'll Never Be": stories by Hemingway.

I had material for the story of Mr Rochester's first wife. The real story
—as it might have been. I don't know why this happened. I was thinking of something else and had a title for it, hadn't read "Jane Eyre" for
years and nearly forgotten Creole.

However (suddenly) I was very excited about "The First Mrs Rochester" and imagined it could be done quickly.

When I got back to Cornwall I read then re-read "Jane Eyre" and
was rather taken aback. Still, I was all the more determined to write
my book —

It has no connection with any play film or adaptation of "Jane Eyre"
who does not appear at all — once perhaps. Mr Rochester does, of
course, but only as a very young man.

It might be possible to unhitch the whole thing from Charlotte Brontë's novel, but I don't want to do that. It is that particular mad Creole
I want to write about, not any of the other mad Creoles. There were
quite a number it seems, and large dowries did not help them. On the
contrary * * *

I have no title yet. "The First Mrs Rochester" is not right. Nor, of
course is "Creole". That has a different meaning now. I hope I'll get
one soon, for titles mean a lot to me. Almost half the battle. I thought
of "Sargasso Sea" or "Wide Sargasso Sea" but nobody knew what I
meant.

Yours sincerely
Jean Rhys

TO SELMA VAZ DIAS   *April 9th* [1958]
                                                                    Rocket House

* * *

Eventually I got back to being a Creole lunatic in the 1840's. Quite
an effort. Sometimes am almost there, sometimes I think I'll stay
there!! —

Now this is not serious or business like enough. Must try — though
still quivering and shivering with cold, men on ladders and bad wine.

I've read and re-read "Jane Eyre" of course, and I am sure that the
character must be "built up". I wrote you about that. The Creole in
Charlotte Brontë's novel is a lay figure — repulsive which does not matter, and not once alive which does. She's necessary to the plot, but
always she shrieks, howls, laughs horribly, attacks all and sundry — *off
stage*. For me (and for you I hope) she must be right *on stage*. She
must be at least plausible with a past, the *reason* why Mr Rochester
treats her so abominably and feels justified, the *reason* why he thinks
she is mad and why of course she goes mad, even the *reason* why she

tries to set everything on fire, and eventually succeeds. (Personally, I think *that* one is simple. She is cold — and fire is the only warmth she knows in England.)

I do not see how Charlotte Brontë's madwoman could possibly convey all this. It *might* be done but it would not be convincing. At least I doubt it. Another "I" must talk, two others perhaps. Then the Creole's "I" will come to life.

I tried this way and that, even putting her into modern dress. No good.

At last I decided on a possible way showing the start and the Creole speaking. Lastly: Her end — I want it in a way triumphant!

The Creole is of course the important one, the others explain her. I see it and can do it — as a book. About half is done.

Jean

I will not disappoint you. Come with me and you will see. Take a look at Jane Eyre. That unfortunate death of a Creole! I'm fighting mad to write *her* story.

But it's a good book — and so one must be wary and careful. Sober and plausible. At first.

* * *

TO FRANCIS WYNDHAM
Sunday 27th [*September 1959*]
Rocket House

* * *

I did not mean to be impertinent about Charlotte Brontë. I admire her greatly. Emily also. And I envy them both more than I can say.

Sometimes I have wondered if Miss Brontë does not *want* her book tampered with! This is the effect of N Cornwall which is rather a dour place. Superstition? — But so many things have got in my way. Never mind. It will be done.

Yours sincerely
Jean Rhys

TO DIANA ATHILL
Friday August 16th [*1963*]
Cheriton Fitz Paine

* * *

I started, ages ago, with a different idea, another *kind* of idea. The book began with a dream and ended with a dream (though I didn't get the last dream right for a long time). All the rest was to be a long monologue. Antoinette in her prison room remembers, loves, hates, raves, talks to imaginary people, hears imaginary voices answering and overhears meaningless conversations outside. The story, if any, to be implied, *never* told straight.

*   *   *

I remembered the last part of "Voyage in the Dark" written like that — time and place abolished, past and present the same — and I had been almost satisfied. Then everybody said it was "confused and confusing — impossible to understand etc." and I had to cut and rewrite it (I still think I was right, and they were wrong, tho' it was long ago). Still I thought "if they fussed over one part of a book, nobody will get the hang of a whole book written that way at all" or "A mad girl speaking all the time is too much!" And anyway there was a lot left to be done and could I do it? I think I was tired. Anyway after a week or two I decided to write it again as a story, a romance, but keeping the dream feeling and working up to the madness (I hoped). *   *   *

TO FRANCIS WYNDHAM   *March 7th 1964*
                                          Cheriton Fitz Paine

*   *   *

I know that explaining makes the book more conventional — but I tried the other way and could not do it. In the end I had to tell the story straight — more or less — and keep the madness for the last act.

I've never read a long novel about a mad mind or an unusual mind or anybody's mind at all. Yet it is the only thing that matters and so difficult to get over without being dull.

*   *   *

TO FRANCIS WYNDHAM   *April 14th* [1964]
                                          Cheriton Fitz Paine

[. . . . . .]

Dear Mr Windham,
    [. . . . . .]
I am now so taken up with "Sargasso Sea" that I am proud to say that I've got "writer's cramp" — must be the only person in the world who has it — what with typists, tape recorders and so on. Isn't *that* something? I have to write carefully though — to be legible which slows me up (still more).

*   *   *

Now about the book — I was rather down with this and that, so flew to writing poems. This I've always done (aged 12 or 10 when I started).

They are strewn all over the places I've lived in — didn't keep many. I like some of them and can do them quickly.

Well I wrote four. The best, I think, is called "The Old Man's Home" but it's the one I enclose which gave me the clue to my book. (Please remember that what I write helps me — written clearly or not it helps. So don't be bored.) A struggle with my handwriting plus writer's cramp. Still — It is quite true that I've brooded over "Jane Eyre" for years.

The Brontë sisters had of course a touch of genius (or much more) especially Emily. So reading "Jane Eyre" one's swept along regardless. But *I*, reading it later, and often, was vexed at her portrait of the "paper tiger" lunatic, the all wrong creole scenes, and above all by the real cruelty of Mr Rochester. After all, he was a very wealthy man and there were many kinder ways of disposing of (or hiding) an unwanted wife — I heard the true story of one — and the man behaved very differently. (Another clue.)

Even when I knew I *had* to write the book — still it did not click into place — that is one reason (though only one) why I was so long. It didn't click. It wasn't there. However I tried.

Only when I wrote this poem — then it clicked — and all was there and always had been.

The first clue is Obeah which I assure you existed, and still does, in Haiti South America and of course in Africa — under different names. The others — sais pas. It was against the law in the "English" islands. The second clue was when Miss Athill suggested a few weeks of happiness for the unfortunate couple — before he gets disturbing letters. As soon as I wrote that bit I realised that he must have fallen for her — and violently too. The black people have or had a good word for it — "she *magic* with him" or "he *magic* with her". Because you see, that is what it is — magic, intoxication. Not "Love" at all. There is too the magic of the place, which is not all lovely beaches or smiling people — it can be a very disturbing kind of beauty. Many people have felt that and written about it too. So poor Mr R, being in this state gets this letter and is very unhappy indeed.

Now is the time for Obeah. The poor (she too) girl doesn't know *why* he's so suddenly left her in the lurch, so flies off to her nurse (presence explained) for a love drink. From the start it must be made clear that Christophine is "an obeah woman". When her, Antoinette's (rather confused) explanations fall flat, she slips him the love drink. *At once*. That is the only change to be made. It must be *at once*.

In obeah these drinks or sacrifices or whatever have this effect: The god himself enters the person who has drunk. Afterwards he (or she) faints, recovers, and remembers very little of what has happened (they say). I wouldn't know.

Not Mr R. He remembers *everything* including the fact that he has felt a bit uneasy in the early happy days and asked her to tell him what's wrong, promised to believe her, and stand by her, and she's always answered "Nothing is wrong." For, poor child, she is *afraid* to tell him, and cries if he insists.

So he strides into her bedroom, not himself, but angry love and that is what the poem is about.

Even when the love has gone the anger is still there and remains. (No obeah needed for that!) And remains.

Well this is now a long letter. Have you got so far? Continuez —

Mr Rochester tries hard not to be a tyrant. Back in Spanish Town he gives her a certain freedom, *tries* to be kindly if distant.

But now she is angry too. Like a hurricane. Like a Creole. For his second revenge — his affair with her maid (and next door) has hurt more than the first.

She uses her freedom to rush off and have an affair too — first with her pal Sandi — then with others. All coloured or black, which was, in those days, a *terrible* thing for a white girl to do. Not to be forgiven. The men did as they liked. The women — *never*.

So imagine Mr R's delight when he can haul her to England, lock her up in a cold dark room, deprive her of all she's used to — watch her growing mad. And so on — I think the governess and the house party rash. But I suppose he thought her fini by that time. Well, she wasn't —

I think there were several Antoinettes and Mr Rochesters. Indeed I am sure. Mine is *not* Miss Brontë's, though much suggested by "Jane Eyre". She is, to start with, young not old. She is still a girl when she fires the house and jumps to her death. And hates last. Mr R's name ought to be changed. Raworth? A Yorkshire name isn't it? The sound is right. In the poem (if it's that) Mr Rochester (or Raworth) consoles himself or justifies himself by saying that *his* Antoinette runs away after the "Obeah nights" and that the creature who comes back is not the one who ran away. I wish this had been thought of before — for that too is part of Obeah.

A Zombie is a dead person raised up by the Obeah woman, it's usually a woman I think, and a zombie can take the appearance of anyone. Or anything.

But I did not write it that way and I'm glad, for it would have been a bit creepy! And probably, certainly I think, beyond me.

Still, it's a thought — for anyone who writes those sort of stories.

No. Antoinette herself comes back but so changed that perhaps she *was* "lost Antoinette". I insist that she must be lovely, and certainly she was lost. "All in the romantic tradition".

*   *   *

Yes I need a holiday, *short*, but I feel that perhaps I'd better get it straight here. I have solitude and privacy — both not so easy to get and there's rather a good tree to look at. I'm sure the neighbours think I'm potty but after all—they can hardly haul me off to the bin for scribble scribble scribble. Quite noiselessly. I really believe that if I had a typewriter they would, for I work late now. (They don't like books much.)

*   *   *

Obeah Night

A night I seldom remember
   (If it can be helped)
The night I saw Love's dark face
   Was Love's dark face
"And cruel as he is"? I've never known that
   I tried my best you may be certain (whoever asks)
   My human best

If the next morning as I looked at what I'd done
(He was watching us mockingly, used to these games)
If I'd stared back at him
If I'd said
"I was a god myself last night
I've tamed and changed a wild girl"
Or taken my hurt darling in my arms
(Conquered at last. And silent. Mine)

Perhaps Love would have smiled then
   Shown us the way
Across that sea. They say it's strewn with wrecks
   And weed-infested
Few dare it, fewer still escape
But *we*, led by smiling Love
We could have sailed
   Reached a safe harbour
Found a sweet, brief heaven
   Lived our short lives

But I was both sick and sad
   (Night always ends)
She was a stranger
Wearing the mask of pain
Bearing the marks of pain—
I turned away—Traitor
Too sane to face my madness (or despair)
   Far, far too cold and sane

Then Love, relenting
Sent clouds and soft rain
Sent sun, light and shadow
   To show me again
Her young face waiting
Waiting for comfort and a gentler lover?
   (You'll not find him)
A kinder loving? *Love is not kind*
I would not look at her
(Once is enough)
Over my dead love
Over a sleeping girl
I drew a sheet
Cover the stains of tears
Cover the marks of blood
(You can say nothing
That I have not said a thousand times and one
Excepting this—That night was Something Else
I was Angry Love Himself
Blind fierce avenging Love—no other that night)

"It's too strong for Béké"
   The black woman said
Love, hate or jealousy
   Which had she seen?
She knew well—the *Devil*!
—What it could mean

How can I forget you Antoinette
   When the spring is here?
Where did you hide yourself

After that shameless, shameful night?
And why come back? Hating and hated?
Was it Love, Fear, Hoping?
Or (as always) Pain?
(*Did* you come back I wonder
Did I ever see you again?)

No. I'll lock that door
Forget it.—
The motto was "Locked Hearts I open
   I have the heavy key"
Written in black letters
Under a Royal Palm Tree
On a slave owner's gravestone

"Look! And look again, hypocrite" he says
   "Before *you* judge *me*"

I'm no damn slave owner
I have no slave
Didn't she (forgiven) betray me
Once more — and then again
Unrepentant — laughing?
I can soon show her
   Who hates the best
Always she answers me
   I will hate last

Lost, lovely Antoinette
How can I forget you
When the spring comes?
(Spring is cold and furtive here
There's a different rain)
Where did you hide yourself
After the obeah nights?
(*What* did you send instead?
   Hating and hated?)
Where did you go?
I'll never see you now
I'll never know
For you left me — my truest Love
Long ago

Edward Rochester or Raworth
Written in Spring 1842

TO FRANCIS WYNDHAM   *Thursday* [*1964*]
                                    Cheriton Fitz Paine

                    ✳   ✳   ✳

   I realise what I lose by cutting loose from Jane Eyre and Mr
Rochester — Only too well. (Indeed *can* I?) Names? Dates?
   But I believe and firmly too that there was more than one Antoinette.
The West Indies was (were?) rich in those days *for* those days and there
was no "married woman's property Act". The girls (very tiresome no
doubt) would soon once in kind England be *Address Unknown*. So
gossip. So a legend. If Charlotte Brontë took her horrible Bertha from
this legend I have the right to take lost Antoinette. And, how to reconcile the two and fix dates I do not know — yet. But, I will. Another
thing is this: —

I have a very great and deep admiration for the Brontë sisters
(Though Charlotte did preachify sometimes). (And all the rest.) And
often boring perhaps. (Me too!)

How then can I of all people, say she was wrong? Or that her Bertha
is impossible? *Which she is.* Or get cheap publicity from her (often)
splendid book?

*   *   *

My dear Diana,

*   *   *

I came to England between sixteen and seventeen, a very impressionable age and Jane Eyre was one of the books I read then.

Of course Charlotte Brontë makes her own world, of course she
convinces you, and that makes the poor Creole lunatic all the more
dreadful. I remember being quite shocked, and when I re-read it rather
annoyed. "That's only one side — the English side" sort of thing.

(I think too that Charlotte had a "thing" about the West Indies being
rather sinister places — because in another of her books "Villette" she
drowns the hero, Professor Somebody, on the voyage to Guadeloupe,
another very alien place — according to her.)

Perhaps most people had this idea then, and perhaps in a way they
were right. Even now white West Indians can be a bit trying — a bit
very (not only white ones) but not quite so awful surely. They have a
side and a point of view.

Well years and *years* afterwards the idea came to me to write this
book.

I started off quite lightheartedly thinking I could do it easily, but I
soon found out that it was going to be a *devil*, partly because I haven't
much imagination really. I do like a basis of fact. I went on — sometimes
blindly.

Part I was not too hard, but by Part II I'd quite abandoned the idea
of "Jane Eyre".

There were many unfortunate marriages at that time and before
— West Indian planters and merchants were wealthy before sugar
crashed — and their daughters were very good matches.

Some of the owners stayed in England and managed their estates
through agents, but some didn't. Perhaps you know all this.

Well this was the story of one arranged marriage, with the bridegroom young, *unwilling*, rather suspicious and ready to believe the
worst, not liking the semi tropics at all, and the bride poor bride very
romantic, with some French or Spanish blood, perhaps with the seeds

of madness, at any rate hysteria. The most seriously wrong thing with Part II is that I've made the obeah woman, the nurse, too articulate. I thought of cutting it a bit, I will if you like, but after all no one will notice. Besides there's no reason why one particular negro woman shouldn't be articulate enough, especially as she's spent most of her life in a white household.

So I only borrowed the name Antoinette — (I carefully haven't named the man at all) and the idea of her seeming a bit mad — to an Englishman.

Of course with Part III, I'm right back with the plot of Jane Eyre, leaving out Jane! I didn't know how else to end it. I didn't even know how to explain their entirely changed life, England not the West Indies, quite mad instead of a bit strange. I thought the best way out was to do it at once through Grace Poole. It *could* be done by putting it in the third person but perhaps that would lose something. I rather shiver at the idea of doing it *again*, but I will if you tell me that it would gain a lot in clarity. By it I mean Part III.

It wouldn't take long — it's casting about trying this way and that — takes the time. And the worry.

I mean all the action to take place between 1834 and 1845 say. *Quick.* My Antoinette marries very young, and when she is brought to England and shut up isn't much over twenty. Her confinement doesn't last long. She burns the house and kills herself (bravo!) very soon. I think she would become first a legend, then a monster, quickly. Charlotte may or may not have heard the legend but that is guesswork and impertinent because really I don't know. Now I must end this monstrous letter which please read when you're in the mood.

Yrs
Jean

TO DIANA ATHILL   *Wednesday March 9th* [1966]
                                          Cheriton Fitz Paine

*   *   *

I've dreamt several times that I was going to have a baby — then I woke with relief.

Finally I dreamt that I was looking at the baby in a cradle — such a puny weak thing.

So the book must be finished, and that must be what I think about it really. I don't dream about it any more.

*   *   *

Jean

It's so *cold*

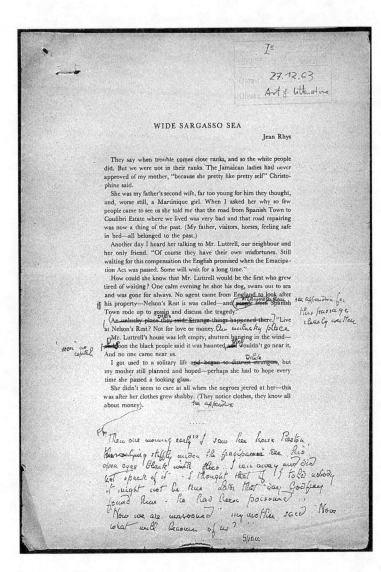

Corrected page proof from Part One of *Wide Sargasso Sea*, published in *Art and Literature* (March 1964).

On page 114

Yet they brought presents of fruit + vegetables + after dark
I often heard low voices from the kitchen.
So I asked questions about Christophine . Was she
very old? Had she always been with us?

On page 118

"They got magistrate, they got fine, they got jail house
+ chain gang. They got tread machine to mash up
people's feet". Mark [M] to crush. Not wash
Tread machine = treadmill   J.R

Alterations about Christophine.
She das (curves) earrings) were of very heavy gold
It was important to say that Christophine had a son
He appears later in the book. Written in proof. Here so far
NB There is too much "frightened" + afraid of Christophine
changed it. Her mother would not be afraid of Christophine
The Black people think she a an obeah woman. I wanted
to hint at this stone. Marked on proof.
I've deleted at the end as the high note is usually
in the middle. I've deleted this because ...   J.R
The number of points has some three last two
corrections are not important - the two marks
in Black. No one would know.

A page of Rhys's additions to the *Art and Literature* publication of *Wide Sargasso Sea*.

147

JEAN RHYS

The Bible Is Modern†

"God said, 'Let there be Light and there was Light.' " There is something short, snappy and utterly modern about this sentence. You have
only got to alter "God said" to "Said God," put a stop in the middle,
and you could almost call it a quotation from the newest, starkest American novel.

The real English of this obviously is "In His great wisdom Jehovah
commanded that the firmament should be illuminated, and it was am-
ply but not excessively illuminated." Or you might say, putting in the
fantastic touch, "Allah, bestriding the universe with the sun in his right
hand and the moon in the left, uttered these words to his chief attendant Gabriel, 'The constellations and the orbs shall march in their
places.' So saying, he flung the sun and the moon into the firmament.
Gabriel, obedient but disapproving, stamped with his foot and there
were the stars. Behold the earth, said Gabriel, and all the angels wept."

Instead of this, you get the stark, modern touch — "Let there be Light,
and there was Light." In this marvellous Book, the Bible — which I am
sure you have yet to discover — there are many such stories expressed
in the modern manner. And, though it is obvious that the significance
of this manner is entirely dependent on an intensity of feeling, let us
remember that we are dealing with primitive people who express themselves in the primitive way. These people are an Oriental people who
have never learned to keep a stiff upper lip.

So buy the Bible. More modern than you know. . . .

You cannot understand it, unless you understand the English social
system. It is a great crime to feel intensely about anything in England,
because if the average Englishman felt intensely about anything, England as it is could not exist; or, certainly, the ruling class in England could not continue to exist.

Thus you get the full force of a very efficient propaganda machine
turned on the average Englishman from the cradle to the grave, warning him that feeling intensely about anything is a quality of the subject
peoples, or that it is old-fashioned, or that it is not done, or something
like that.

The idea that books written in short, simple sentences, depending
for their effectiveness on the intensity of feeling of the author, are inferior books, follows automatically, because the whole solidarity of the
English social system is extraordinary. It is based on the idea that the

---

† Unpublished manuscript from the Jean Rhys Collection, McFarlin Library, University of
Tulsa. Reprinted by permission.

poor Englishman and the middle-class Englishman must not think very much, that they certainly must never feel, and as for expressing their feelings—Never. Or only falsely. When you think of the mentality of the average Englishman, all this is understandable. But then what is difficult for us black people[1] to understand is the ingenious way they set about making money out of "God said 'Let there be Light, and there was Light.'"

JEAN RHYS

From Smile Please†

Books[1]

Before I could read, almost a baby, I imagined that God, this strange thing or person I heard about, was a book. Sometimes it was a large book standing upright and half open and I could see the print inside but it made no sense to me. Other times the book was smaller and inside were sharp flashing things. The smaller book was, I am sure now, my mother's needle-book, and the sharp flashing things were her needles with the sun on them.

I was so slow learning to read that my parents had become worried about me. Then suddenly, with a leap as it were, I could manage quite long words. Soon I could make sense of the fairy stories Irish Granny sent—the red, the blue, the green, the yellow. Then she sent *The Heroes*, *The Adventures of Ulysses*, *Perseus and Andromeda*, I read everything I could get hold of. There was the usual glassed-in bookcase at the end of the sitting-room, but it was never locked, the key was lost, and the only warning was that we must keep it shut, for the books must be protected against insects.

I can still see the volumes of the *Encyclopaedia Britannica* that I never touched, a large Bible and several history books, yellow-backed novels and on the top shelf a rather odd selection of poets, Milton, Byron, then Crabbe, Cowper, Mrs Hemans, also *Robinson Crusoe*, *Treasure Island*, *Gulliver's Travels*, *Pilgrim's Progress*.

My nurse, who was called Meta, didn't like me much anyway, and complete with a book it was too much. One day she found me crouched on the staircase reading a bowdlerised version of the *Arabian Nights* in very small print.

1. While Rhys did not identify herself racially as other than white Creole, her self-identification here as "black" is a political stance meant to position her in opposition to the metropolitan colonizing culture.
† From Jean Rhys, *Smile Please: An Unfinished Autobiography* (London: Andre Deutsch, 1979). Hereafter *SP*. Reprinted by permission of Sheil Land Associates Ltd.
1. *SP*, pp. 27–28.

She said, 'If all you read so much, you know what will happen to you? Your eyes will drop out and they will look at you from the page.'

'If my eyes dropped out I wouldn't see,' I argued.

She said, 'They drop out except the little black points you see with.'

I half believed her and imagined my pupils like heads of black pins and all the rest gone. But I went on reading.

Meta[2]

Now it is time to talk about Meta, my nurse and the terror of my life. She had been there ever since I could remember: a short, stocky woman, very black and always, I thought, in a bad temper. I never saw Meta smile. She always seemed to be brooding over some terrible, unforgettable wrong. * * *

It was Meta who talked so much about zombies, souciants, and loups-garoux. She was the only person I've heard talk about loups-garoux (werewolves) in the West Indies. Souciants were always women she said, who came at night and sucked your blood. During the day they looked like ordinary women but you could tell them by their red eyes. Zombies were black shapeless things. They could get through a locked door and you heard them walking up to your bed. You didn't see them, you felt their hairy hands round your throat. For a long time I never slept except right at the bottom of the bed with the sheet well over my head, listening for zombies. I suppose someone came in and pulled it down or I would have suffocated.

She also taught me to fear cockroaches hysterically. She said that when I was asleep at night they would fly in and bite my mouth and that the bite would never heal. Cockroaches can be about two inches long, they fly and they smell very disagreeable, but it was Meta who taught me to be truly afraid of them. It didn't help that my mother, who tackled centipedes with great spirit, would go out of the room if a cockroach flew in and refuse to come back until it had been caught. Meta also told me that if a centipede was killed all the different bits would be alive and run into corners to become bigger, stronger centipedes. It must be crushed. She said 'mashed up'. To this day I'm not quite sure if I really saw two halves of a centipede walking away from each other, still alive.

Even Meta's stories were tinged with fear and horror. They all ended like this: 'So I went to the wedding and they say to me "What you doing here?" I say, "I come to get something to eat and drink." He give me one kick and I fly over the sea and come here to tell you this story.'

Years later I made great friends with a negro girl called Francine. I've written about her before. Francine's stories were quite different,

2. *SP*, pp. 29–32.

full of jokes and laughter, descriptions of beautiful dresses and good things to eat. But the start was always a ceremony. Francine would say 'Tim-tim'. I had to answer 'Bois sêche,' then she'd say, 'Tablier Madame est derrière dos' (Madam's apron is back to front). She always insisted on this ceremony before starting a story and it wasn't until much later, when I was reading a book about obeah, that I discovered that 'Bois sêche' is one of the gods. I grew very fond of Francine and admired her; when she disappeared without a word to me I was hurt. People did disappear, they went to one of the other islands, but not without saying goodbye. I still think of Francine and now I can imagine other reasons for her complete disappearance from the house and from my life.

*   *   *

[Meta] was forbidden to slap me and she never did but she got her own back by taking me by the shoulders and shaking me violently. Hair flying, while I still had any breath to speak I would yell, 'Black Devil, Black Devil, Black Devil!' I never dreamed of complaining to my mother about all this, and I doubt if it would have been any good if I had, but my relief was enormous when Meta left or was sent away. I can't remember who took her place or if anybody did. But in any case it was too late, the damage had been done. Meta had shown me a world of fear and distrust, and I am still in that world.

My Mother[3]

I once came on a photograph of my mother on horseback which must have been taken before she was married. Young, slim and pretty. I hated it. I don't know whether I was jealous or whether I resented knowing that she had once been very different from the plump, dark and only sometimes comfortable woman I knew. I didn't dare tear it up but I pushed it away to the back of the drawer. What wouldn't I give to have it now? Yet wasn't there a time when I remembered her pretty and young?

That must have been when I was the baby, sleeping in the crib. They were going out somewhere, for she was wearing a low-cut evening dress. She had come to say 'Good night, sleep well.' She smelled so sweet as she leaned over and kissed me.

She loved babies, any babies. Once I heard her say that black babies were prettier than white ones. Was this the reason why I prayed so ardently to be black, and would run to the looking-glass in the morning to see if the miracle had happened? And though it never had, I tried again. Dear God, let me be black.

Even after the new baby was born there must have been an interval before she seemed to find me a nuisance and I grew to dread her.

3. *SP*, pp. 42–43.

Another interval and she was middle-aged and plump and uninterested in me.

Yes, she drifted away from me and when I tried to interest her she was indifferent.

* * *

Black/White[4]

I remember the Riot as if it were yesterday. I must have been about twelve. One night my mother came into the bedroom I shared with my baby sister, woke us up, told us to put on dressing-gown and slippers and to come downstairs. We followed her half asleep. When we got into the sitting-room my father said: 'Why do you want to wake the children up at this time of night? It's ridiculous.'

I heard far away a strange noise like animals howling but I knew it wasn't animals, it was people and the noise came nearer and nearer.

My father said: 'They're perfectly harmless.'

'That's what you think,' my mother said.

I half realised that we had dressed to run away from the ugly noise, but run where? We could run as far as Mr Steadman's house on the bay but long before we got there they'd kill us.

Kill us! This strange idea didn't frighten me but excited me.

They surged past the window, howling, but they didn't throw stones. As the noise grew faint my mother said: 'You can go up to bed again now.'

My father said: 'It was nonsense waking them up.'

My mother didn't answer, she only tightened her mouth in a way that meant 'you think one thing, I think another.'

Upstairs I didn't sleep for a long time. He thinks one thing, she thinks another, Who is right?

This particular riot was aimed at the editor of the local paper. His house was near ours. He had written an article attacking the power of the Catholic priests in Dominica. The crowd was some of the faithful who intended to stone his house, frighten him and prevent him ever writing about religion again.

However, I could not forget the howling sound and there's no doubt that a certain wariness did creep in when I thought about the black people who surrounded me.

The black people whom I knew well were different, individuals whom I liked or disliked. If I hated Meta, I admired the groom, like the housemaid Victoria. She came from one of the 'English Islands', Antigua I think, and was an ardent Methodist. As she washed up she would sing hymns in a low voice (Steal away, steal away, steal away to

4. *SP*, pp. 47–50.

Jesus). She was sad and unsmiling and I was vaguely sorry for her and wished she was happier.

Josephine the cook was a Dominican. A tall, good-looking woman who kept herself very much to herself. I was rather afraid of her and so, I am sure, was my mother who never went to the kitchen. They met in the pantry — neutral ground — and there she'd be given money to go to the market and buy food; fish, vegetables, fruit, sometimes meat. The fishing boats went out then, very early. Fresh bread was delivered by women carrying laden trays on their heads.

Josephine liked to be talked to in patois. Luckily my mother knew patois well. She was, in her way, a good cook. Her fish dishes were delicious, she made good curries, and often gave us crapeaux (frogs), crayfish, or stuffed crab. But I never liked her soup and she refused to make puddings. All the sweets from Floating Island to Christmas pudding were made by my mother.

I once peeped into the kitchen. It was very smoky and Josephine scowled at me. There were several people there that I didn't know so I never ventured again.

But it was the others I was wary of, the others I didn't know. Did they like us as much as all that? Did they like us at all?

The next thing that shook me happened at the convent. I was young and shy and I was sitting next to a girl much older than myself. She was so tall and so pretty, and she spoke in such a confident way that she quite awed me. She had aquiline features, large flashing eyes and a great deal of not too frizzy hair which she wore in a loose, becoming way. She didn't look coloured but I knew at once that she was. This did not prevent me from admiring her and longing to be friendly.

My father was not a prejudiced man or he would never have allowed me to go to the convent, for white girls were very much in the minority. If my mother was prejudiced she never talked about it so I tried, shyly at first, then more boldly, to talk to my beautiful neighbour.

Finally, without speaking, she turned and looked at me. I knew irritation, bad temper, the 'Oh, go away' look; this was different. This was hatred — impersonal, implacable hatred. I recognised it at once and if you think that a child cannot recognise hatred and remember it for life you are most damnably mistaken.

I never tried to be friendly with any of the coloured girls again. I was polite and that was all.

They hate us. We are hated.

Not possible.

Yes it is possible and it is so.

* * *

Side by side with my growing wariness of black people there was envy. I decided that they had a better time than we did, they laughed a lot though they seldom smiled. They were stronger than we were, they could walk a long way without getting tired, carry heavy weights with ease.

Every night someone gave a dance, you could hear the drums. We had few dances. They were more alive, more a part of the place than we were.

The nuns said that Time didn't matter, only Eternity matters. Wouldn't black people have a better chance in Eternity? They were Catholics and I envied their faith, for I was much attracted by what I saw of Catholicism.

*   *   *

Facts of Life[5]

*   *   *

The older I grew the more things there were to worry about. Religion was then as important as politics are now. Would I insist on knowing more about Catholicism or would I stick to the English church? There was the business of black, white, not to say coloured. Had I ever really thought about it? Was my wariness justified? Or was my feeling 'this is not fair, not fair' nearer the truth?

There was also the business about ladies and gentlemen and that was terribly complicated and very important. It takes three generations to make a gentleman I was told, or was it four? And though I didn't quite believe this I counted up the generations I knew anxiously. 'Nature's gentlemen' existed, but apparently no 'Nature's ladies'. That was probably right.

So as soon as I could I lost myself in the immense world of books, and tried to blot out the real world which was so puzzling to me. Even then I had a vague, persistent feeling that I'd always be lost in it, defeated.

However books too were all about the same thing, I discovered, but in a different way. I could accept it in books and from books (fatally) I gradually got most of my ideas and beliefs.

The old Victoria Memorial Library had been pulled down and there was a new Carnegie Library in its place. It was very pleasant, usually empty. Sitting in a rocking-chair on the veranda, lost in what I thought was the real world, no one could have been happier than I was. My one ambition was to plunge into it and forget everything else.

No one ever advised me what to read or forbade me to read something. I even looked at the rare and curious shelf but I don't remember any of it making much impression. I liked books about prostitutes, there were a good many then, and vividly recollect a novel called *The Sands of Pleasure* written by a man named Filson Young. It must have been well written otherwise I would never have remembered it so perfectly

5. *SP*, pp. 62–64.

to this day. It was about an Englishman's love affair with an expensive demi-mondaine in Paris.

I thought a great deal about England, not factually but what I had read about it. I pictured it in the winter, a country covered with snow and ice but also with millions upon millions of fires. Books, especially Dickens's, talked of hunger, starvation and poverty but very rarely of cold. So I concluded that either the English didn't feel the cold, which surely wasn't possible, or that everybody had a fire. Bill Sykes and Nancy, in fact, talked in front of a blazing fire. Cold: I couldn't imagine being cold but hated the word.

I'd fallen in love with other words, 'wisteria' for instance. I realised it was a creeper strong enough for the Wild Irish Girls to climb down from the dormitory window and escape to freedom and life. I was sure it had flowers, what colour? Red, no; blue, no; and not white. Favourite words, and words I loathed.

When years later I paid a short visit to Dominica I went to the library of course. Instead of being empty it was crowded, a long queue before the librarian's desk. At first I thought it was a very touching sight, all the black hands, eagerly stretched out, holding books. Then I noticed how ill the librarian, whom of course I knew, looked. As people filed past her she'd take the book, stamp it and give it back. No one looked at her and no one thanked her. They seemed to think that she was a machine and indeed there was something robotlike about the way she was working. Book after book and with each one she seemed to get more tired, look more ill. I wasn't at all surprised when I heard a few days later that she was dead.

I seem to be brought up willy-nilly against the two sides of the question. Sometimes I ask myself if I am the only one who is; for after all, who knows or cares if there are two sides?

JEAN RHYS

From Black Exercise Book†

I was curious about black people. They stimulated me and I felt akin to them. It added to my sadness that I couldn't help but realise that they didn't really like or trust white people. White cockroaches they called us behind our backs. (Cockroach again.) One could hardly blame them. I would feel sick with shame at some of the stories I heard of the slave days told casually even jokingly. The ferocious punishments the salt kept ready to rub into the wounds etc etc. I became an ardent

† Unpublished manuscript, Rhys Collection, McFarlin Library, University of Tulsa. Reprinted by permission.

socialist and champion of the down-trodden argued insisted of giving my opinion was generally insufferable. Yet all the time knowing that there was another side to it. Sometimes seeing myself as powerful [. . .] for a moment. Sometimes being proud of my great grandfather the estate the good old days the wealth etc. etc. Sometimes I'd look at his picture and think with pride, He was goodlooking anyway — Perhaps he wasn't entirely ignoble. Surely absolute power over a people needn't make a man a brute. Might make him noble in a way. No — no use. My great grandfather and his beautiful Spanish wife. Spanish? I wonder. I thought a lot about them. But the end of my thought was always revolt, a sick revolt, and I longed to be identified once and for all with the other side which of course was impossible. I couldn't change the colour of my skin.

CRITICISM

DEREK WALCOTT

Jean Rhys†

In their faint photographs
mottled with chemicals,
like the left hand of some spinster aunt,
they have drifted to the edge
of verandahs in Whistlerian
white, their jungle turned tea-brown —
even its spiked palms —
their features pale,
to be pencilled in:
bone-collared gentlemen
with spiked moustaches
and their wives embayed in the wickerwork
armchairs, all looking coloured
from the distance of a century
beginning to groan sideways from the axe stroke!

Their bay horses blacken
like spaniels, the front lawn a beige
carpet, brown moonlight and a moon
so sallow, so pharmaceutical
that her face is a feverish child's,
some malarial angel
whose grave still cowers
under a fury of bush,
a mania of wild yams
wrangling to hide her from ancestral churchyards.

And the sigh of that child
is white as an orchid
on a crusted log
in the bush of Dominica,
a V of Chinese white
meant for the beat of a seagull
over a sepia souvenir of Cornwall,
as the white hush between two sentences.

Sundays! Their furnace
of boredom after church.
A maiden aunt canoes through lilies of clouds
in a Carib hammock, to a hymn's metronome,
and the child on the varnished, lion-footed couch
sees the hills dip and straighten with each lurch.
The green-leaved uproar of the century
turns dim as the Atlantic, a rumourous haze
behind the lime trees, breakers
advancing in decorous, pleated lace;
the cement grindstone of the afternoon
turns slowly, sharpening her senses,
the bay below is green as calalu, stewing Sargasso.

In that fierce hush
between Dominican mountains
the child expects a sound
from a butterfly clipping itself to a bush
like a gold earring to a black maid's ear —
one who goes down to the village, visiting,
whose pink dress wilts like a flower between the limes.

There are logs
wrinkled like the hand of an old woman
who wrote with a fine courtesy to that world
when grace was common as malaria,
when the gas lanterns' hiss on the verandah
drew the aunts out like moths
doomed to be pressed in a book, to fall
into the brown oblivion of an album,
embroiderers of silence
for whom the arches of the Thames,
Parliament's needles,
and the petit-point reflections of London Bridge
fade on the hammock cushions from the sun,
where one night
a child stares at the windless candle flame
from the corner of a lion-footed couch
at the erect white light,
her right hand married to *Jane Eyre*,
foreseeing that her own white wedding dress
will be white paper.

1981

MARY LOU EMERY

Modernist Crosscurrents†

* * *

To view Jean Rhys as a woman writer only or to discuss her as a West Indian author or a European modernist exclusively limits our understanding of her work. For in each context, her writing remains outside the main current by virtue of its participation in the other two. I see her novels as textual sites both in between and intersecting these three important currents of twentieth-century cultural history and literature. My interest in the events of her life, therefore, does not lie in building a psychological portrait or even in constructing a unified narrative that ties the events together. Rather, I am interested in her plural and often conflicting outsider identities as West Indian writer, European modernist, and woman writer at the closing of the era of empire, and the ways in which she occupied the spaces in between such identities.

* * *

The pressures of language and literary tradition from three emerging canons — the female, European modernist, and the West Indian — reshape the biographical facts as literary truths in Rhys's novels. The larger social context of these literary movements gives meaning to both the distorting mirror of the text and the truths we may see in it, and a sociocritical perspective can give us the wide focus we need to see the multiple contexts of Rhys's writing. We can distinguish then between an approach that views her characters as psychological types or reflections of Jean Rhys and one that sees connections among the social forces shaping the author and the novels. The first approach draws upon and develops European literary and psychological notions of "character" and "self" and so misses the implications of the Caribbean context of Rhys's writing and her identity as a West Indian writer critical of the colonizing countries' concepts and values even if governed by them. The second approach views the events of Rhys's life as indicators of the conflicting values, ideologies, and social circumstances in which she wrote. It allows us to perceive in the same mirror competing cultural visions and to understand them within a larger gendered colonial system as it declines.

Primary materials are available to tell us about Rhys's life, including her incomplete autobiography *Smile Please* (1979), *The Letters of Jean Rhys* (1984), and the unpublished notebooks that Teresa O'Connor has

† From Mary Lou Emery, *Jean Rhys at "World's End": Novels of Colonial and Sexual Exile* (Austin: University of Texas Press, 1990) 7–20. Copyright © 1990. Reprinted by permission of the University of Texas Press.

incorporated into her recent study.[1] Many of the "facts" are now well
known: her upbringing in Dominica, various jobs in England with trav-
eling theatrical companies followed by a disastrous love affair, a marriage, and a period spent wandering in Europe.

Many critics view her mentorship with Ford Madox Ford in Paris
during the 1920s as the most important influence of her writing career,
and certainly he must have helped her along. Their relation seems all
the more significant since she also became Ford's mistress.[2] However,
I think that such influences as Ford's on Rhys's writing are similar to
those of European modernism on other West Indian writers who found
in it techniques and aesthetic values that they adapted to express the
concerns of an emerging Third World literature. Edward Brathwaite,
Derek Walcott, and Wilson Harris, for example, found formal models
in T. S. Eliot and in Joseph Conrad that helped them to shape the
materials of Caribbean culture, its multiracial societies, folk dialects,
and the historical conflicts of colonialism.[3]

Viewing Rhys as a Third World writer as well as a woman in exile
in Paris helps us to better understand her outsider status there. In her
study *Women of the Left Bank*, Shari Benstock has described Rhys as
"an outsider among outsiders," who never found a community of writers or of women who might nurture and stimulate her talent.[4] Isolated
from women and taken up by men as a protégée or mistress, Rhys
experienced exile differently, by virtue of her colonial background, from
someone like Gertrude Stein and, by virtue of her sex, from someone
like Claude McKay. She married three times and gave birth to two
children, one of whom died three weeks after its birth. She suffered
from illness, poverty, and dependence on alcohol. In these "facts" are
the traces of social forces that denied poor women proper medical and
child care and denied unmarried women livelihoods and respectability.
Our understanding of Rhys's novels depends upon an understanding of
the local nature of such social forces, particularly their ideological and
actual operations in specific places and times, operations I will discuss
later in this chapter and throughout the book.

In 1927, Rhys returned to England, where she eventually settled even
though she said she hated its climate and values. To readers of her
fiction-as-her-life, such contrariness, along with passivity, masochism,
victimage — drifting aimlessly, feeling fated to suffer helplessly — characterize Rhys and her protagonists as if they mirrored one another

1. Teresa O'Connor, *Jean Rhys: The West Indian Novels* (New York and London: New York
   University Press, 1986).
2. For a summary of Rhys's life that includes a description of her relationship with Ford, see
   Thomas F. Staley, *Jean Rhys: A Critical Study* (Austin: University of Texas Press, 1979),
   chap. I.
3. Bruce King, *The New English Literatures: Cultural Nationalism in a Changing World* (New
   York: St. Martin's Press, 1980), chaps. 6 and 7.
4. Shari Benstock, *Women of the Left Bank: Paris, 1900–1940* (Austin: University of Texas Press,
   1986), p. 448.

clearly.[5] While we can find similarities between Rhys, as she and others present her life and psyche, and critics' interpretations of her characters, the texts themselves question the evaluation of psychological and moral character in terms like "helpless," "passive," and "masochistic." The themes of masquerade, along with other narrative elements, challenge such psychological essentialism. What does it mean to describe, diagnose, and judge "character," especially female Caribbean character?

To explore the question further, we should consider the doubled homelessness of Rhys's characters. In North American and European psychology, character begins at home, in interaction with a specific family in a particular culture. Yet the characters in Rhys's early novels lack homes and homelands. Circumstances and their own actions have isolated them from families, husbands, and friends. How dispossessed women constitute and know themselves becomes the question the novels explore. They do so in the in-between spaces, both physical and psychological, inhabited by the homeless.

If all women by virtue of their sexual positioning as Other are marginalized, as many feminists have argued, the female protagonists of Rhys's early novels experience a doubled marginality in their exile from the homes of men who could grant them lives of feminine domesticity and sexual respectability. Bereft of husbands and fathers, the heroines of Rhys's novels contend with the violence of feminized poverty and sexual barter. They do not stay at home; nor do they go home at night. They climb the stairs to a room somewhere on the Left Bank or in Bloomsbury, perhaps alone, perhaps not. They inhabit, for the most part, the streets, cafés, bars, and, if they can afford it, dress shops of European cities where no one knows where they come from or even their names. In this sense they participate in the anonymity of mass culture as they consume its manufactured clothes, movies, and world exhibitions. But their participation is specifically female; they constitute members of the crowds of women that Andreas Huyssen argues threatened the precarious masculine order of modernity.[6] Huyssen refers to the first wave of the feminist movement and the deliberate efforts made by women to enter public life, but in the case of Rhys's characters, we encounter women who entertain no ambitions; they simply find themselves thrust by circumstance outside the protections and constraints of the family. They wander almost aimlessly, living in between the gendered urban spaces of early twentieth-century England and Europe.

While Rhys's novels inscribe specifically female experiences and differ markedly from the works of male modernists in their point of view,

5. Peter Wolfe, in *Jean Rhys* (Boston: Twayne, 1980), states that Rhys disguised herself in her characters, but he sees this disguise as a means of autobiography and does not consider the subversive nature of masquerade.
6. Andreas Huyssen, "Mass Culture as Woman: Modernism's Other," *After the Great Divide* (Bloomington: Indiana University Press, 1986), pp. 44–64.

even among works by women they are, as Benstock says of Rhys herself, marginal. The characters walk the streets of Paris and London without money, friends, or family. Unlike the narrator of Virginia Woolf's essay *Street Haunting*, they never return from their twilight wanderings to "their own doorstep again . . . to feel the old possessions, the old prejudices, fold us round; and the self which has been blown about at so many street corners . . . sheltered and enclosed."[7] We have only to compare Rhys's homeless protagonists to May Sinclair's Mary Olivier or to Woolf's Clarissa Dalloway or even Lily Brisco, with her nearby father and ties to upper-middle-class gentility, to see the differences in class and kinship that isolate them and that prohibit even the illusion of an enclosed and sheltered self.

Without such illusions, it becomes difficult in Rhys's novels to distinguish the mask from the masquerade; the play between these aspects of disguise, rather than a discovery of authentic selfhood, shapes the narrative and characterizations. Lacking authentic selfhood in European terms, Rhys's characters do not appear capable of overcoming difficulties; they seem weak, lacking in courage, and willingly exploited. They continually miss opportunities for epiphany or self-awareness. Perhaps for these reasons, unlike Virginia Woolf or H. D., Rhys has remained a disturbing presence on the edges of current feminist criticism.

If sexual difference is the major screen of interpretation, the characters and their fates (for they always seem "fated") conform to clichés of the feminine rather than expectations for the feminist. Obsessions with makeup, clothes, and men mark the novels, perhaps even stigmatize them. Especially the early novels remain disturbing to feminist readers who sometimes prefer to exclude all but the "West Indian" novels, *Wide Sargasso Sea* and *Voyage in the Dark*, from their discussions.[8] Even so, they do not treat them as West Indian literature. Instead they attribute the novels' merits to their status as exemplary women's texts or to Jean Rhys's superior technique,[9] not recognizing their Caribbean values and aesthetics. Another kind of homelessness, that of colonial exile, brings to the novels this alternate aesthetic.

Through colonial exile, the marginality of Rhys's female characters multiplies. Anna Morgan of *Voyage in the Dark* lives in England in exile from her place of birth on the island of Dominica. However, she never felt truly at home on her native island because of her status as a white Creole woman. Elizabeth Nunez-Harrell has described this status

7. Virginia Woolf, *Street Haunting* (San Francisco: Westgate Press, 1930), p. 35.
8. Both O'Connor (*Jean Rhys*) and Nancy Harrison (*Jean Rhys and the Novel as Women's Text* [Chapel Hill: University of North Carolina Press, 1988]) treat only *Wide Sargasso Sea* and *Voyage in the Dark*.
9. These are the reasons given by Harrison (*Jean Rhys and the Novel as Women's Text*) for her exclusive focus on these two novels. O'Connor does stress the importance of the West Indies as a place in a governing fictional myth. However, her study brings their history to bear as evidence for a psychological thesis concerning Rhys's relation to her mother and the trajectory of Rhys's career.

as that of "an outcast, a sort of freak rejected by both Europe and England, whose blood she shares, and by the black West Indian people, whose culture and home have been hers for two generations or more."[1] In *Wide Sargasso Sea*, the young blacks call Antoinette "white cockroach" and "white nigger," epithets for the Euro-Creole woman who, as Nunez-Harrell points out, bears the brunt of guilt for the history of slavery and the cruelties perpetrated by her ancestors. At the same time, she identifies and is identified with the lowest social castes. Anna longs, then, for a lost home, but one in which she could never feel at ease. Thus, she envies what she perceives as the ease, warmth, and gaiety of black culture and longs also to be black. For these reasons, we can understand why, though the character and the author of the novel are of European descent, Kenneth Ramchand has called it "our first Negritude novel."[2]

In some ways white Creoles experience a double dose of a quintessential aspect of Caribbean experience, the marginality of living in between cultures. Derek Walcott expresses the pain of this division as experienced by black West Indians when he asks in "A Far Cry from Africa": "Where shall I turn, divided to the vein?"[3] Black West Indians must construct their identities as always divided by the history of slave trading; if educated, they have learned to admire English language and culture while detesting British colonial rule. The search for a lost identity through Africa becomes complicated, as it does in Walcott's poem, by the current realities of an Africa which the West Indian has not personally known but made into a metaphor, or, as Louis James puts it, "an area of the mind."[4] Living in between two cultures, belonging to neither completely, characterizes what sociologists have called the "marginal man": "one who is poised in psychological uncertainty between two (or more) social worlds; reflecting in his soul the discords and harmonies, repulsions and attractions of these worlds, one of which is often 'dominant' over the other . . ."[5] James feels that West Indian writers, living between Africa and Europe, find a moment of self-discovery when they reject possession by either. In this simultaneous acknowledgment and rejection, writers find new forms for a West Indian literature unique to its own location, history, and cultural plurality.

But white Creoles are divided precisely within the context of the islands' histories and cultures. They descend from a class that no longer exists and whose history is morally shameful. They feel close to a black

1. Elizabeth Nunez-Harrell, "The Paradoxes of Belonging: The White West Indian Woman in Fiction," *Modern Fiction Studies* 31, no. 2 (Summer 1985): 1–2.
2. Kenneth Ramchand, "An Introduction to the Novel," in *The Lonely Londoners*, by Samuel Selvon (1957, reprint; Essex: Longman Group, Ltd., 1987), p. 3.
3. Derek Walcott, "A Far Cry from Africa," in *The Penguin Book of Caribbean Verse in English*, ed. Paula Burnett, p. 243.
4. Louis James, "Introduction," in *The Islands in Between*, ed. Louis James (London: Oxford University Press, 1968), p. 8.
5. Everett V. Stonequist, *The Marginal Man* (New York: Scribners, 1937), p. 8.

culture that they cannot be part of and that can only resent them, and they may still look to a "mother" country that long ago abandoned them and still considers them inferior. Discussing the colonial motifs in Rhys's novels, Helen Tiffin explains, "The white Creole is, as a double outsider, condemned to self-consciousness, a sense of inescapable difference and even deformity in the two societies by whose judgements she always condemns herself."[6] As Tiffin points out, following African-American and Caribbean writers such as W. E. B. Du Bois and Frantz Fanon, cultural marginality divides the psyche, makes it Other to itself, and permits no unified — even if illusory — sense of self.

Rhys's identity as a white Creole West Indian writer, then, is an unstable one — although that instability may make her all the more a part of the heterogeneity of Caribbean cultures. Among the West Indian writers who command our attention today, such as Derek Walcott, Edward Brathwaite, Samuel Selvon, Earl Lovelace, and Michelle Cliff, to name a few, Rhys remains an odd one out, a Euro-Creole woman who, in fifty-six years, returned to her native Dominica for only one brief visit. Hence, to some readers, only *Voyage in the Dark* of her four early novels seems to be influenced by her West Indian background. Since the other three take place, for the most part, on the continent, they appear to chronicle an almost generic expatriate's down-and-out bohemian life. Yet, as Benstock points out, even among the expatriates, Rhys remained an outsider. The specific and multiple nature of her exile stems from the difference of the place from which she came — not England, not originally anyway, nor an increasingly powerful United States, but a tiny colony wherein her identity was always divided.

Rhys once asked, "Am I an expatriate? Expatriate from where?"[7] Her question repeats the European attitude toward the Caribbean as a "background of nothing" or, at best, an "antique romance," but it also alludes to a background of plural, unconsolidated cultures and a divided national identity of rich potential that the European eye could only perceive as disorganized or simply "nothing."[8] Her question states implicitly the discovery of West Indian writers that identity depends upon place even as it questions the identity of that place. Living as an outcast even among expatriates, Rhys writes novels that reinscribe the colonial divisions of a Caribbean heritage displaced once more.

It is not surprising then that a passage from the novel considered her most European, *Good Morning, Midnight*, is quoted in the introduc-

6. Helen Tiffin, "Mirror and Mask: Colonial Motifs in the Novels of Jean Rhys," *World Literature Written in English* 17 (April 1978): 328.

7. Jean Rhys, "How I Became a Novelist," unpub. ms., Jean Rhys Collection, quoted in Veronica Marie Gregg, "Jean Rhys and Modernism: A Different Voice," *Jean Rhys Review* 1, no. 2 (Spring 1982): 32.

8. V. S. Naipaul uses these phrases to describe what must have been the European attitude toward the Caribbean in the 1920s. Quoted in Gregg, "Jean Rhys and Modernism," pp. 32–33.

tions to two studies of Caribbean literature as expressing "the concerns that pervade West Indian writing."[9] One editor states that when the narrator of the novel remarks, "I have no pride — no name, no face, no country. I don't belong anywhere," she conveys the West Indian "uncertainty of cultural identity" and "sense of estrangement." But it is important to understand the specific difference of this estrangement, that as outsiders among already eccentric texts, Rhys's novels portray an absence rather than loss of identity and the homelessness of one who never had a home.

Because of the always-divided identity of the white Creole, we cannot view Rhys's most well-received and widely read novel as taking either its protagonist or its author "home." *Wide Sargasso Sea* does take place in Jamaica and Dominica, making explicit a colonial background referred to or suggested in the earlier novels. But the setting in itself cannot give the protagonist a home; rather it places her divided identity within the cultural and historical context of its division, enabling a reconceptualization of the very concept of identity. Reading *Wide Sargasso Sea*, we find named the specific historical and social forces of the female homelessness and exile it chronicles. And we come closer to answering the question of what it means to diagnose and judge female Caribbean "character."

Since *Wide Sargasso Sea* comprises a "prequel" to what may be every woman's favorite novel, *Jane Eyre*, it invites rereadings of Brontë's novel and comparisons between the protagonists. *Wide Sargasso Sea* has challenged readers of *Jane Eyre* to reconsider the monstrous figure of the madwoman in the attic so that some feminist critics recognize Rhys's subversion of the good woman/bad woman dichotomy, viewing Jane and Antoinette as parts of the same psyche, and some perceive the parallels Rhys draws between the madwoman and the woman of reason, making them sisters rather than rivals.[1] The deliberate intertextuality of *Wide Sargasso Sea* with *Jane Eyre* sets *Wide Sargasso Sea* apart from Rhys's earlier novels by more than its date of publication and lends it greater interest to most readers. However, while all readers recognize the difference in setting between this novel, placed in nineteenth-century Jamaica and Dominica, and Rhys's earlier novels, set in early

9. Trevor James, *English Literature from the Third World* (Beirut and England: York Press, Longman Group, Ltd., 1986), p. 17. See also Bruce King, "Introduction," in *West Indian Literature*, ed. Bruce King (Hamden, Conn.: Archon Books, 1979), p. 6.
1. See Sandra M. Gilbert and Susan Gubar, *The Madwoman in the Attic: The Woman Writer and the Nineteenth-Century Literary Imagination* (New Haven and London: Yale University Press, 1979), for a post–*Wide Sargasso Sea* discussion of *Jane Eyre* that views Bertha Rochester as symbolic of Jane's repressed rage. Elizabeth Baer traces the parallels between Jane and Antoinette in both novels, arguing that in *Wide Sargasso Sea* Jean Rhys presents them as "sisters" ("The Sisterhood of Jane Eyre and Antoinette Cosway Mason," in *The Voyage In: Fictions of Female Development*, ed. Elizabeth Abel, Marianne Hirsch, and Elizabeth Langland [New Hampshire: University Press of New England, 1983]).

twentieth-century England and Europe, few feminist readers actually approach the novel as Caribbean or Third World literature. This is an odd oversight, due I think to its connection to the earlier English novel but also to the extreme specialization within literary studies. Of all her novels, it is the only one set in the West Indies, and it is the novel that established her reputation among critics of Caribbean literature as a West Indian writer. The novel seems to have found two communities of readers, those who take a feminist approach and those who take a West Indian approach, and the two groups rarely converse with one another.[2]

In *Wide Sargasso Sea*, the madwoman silenced in *Jane Eyre* speaks, and her voice exposes and turns upside down the values, patriarchal and colonialist, upon which the plot and characters of Brontë's novel depend. perhaps one reason this novel attracts feminist critics more strongly than Rhys's earlier novels is that in it a forced and exploitative marriage provides a context missing in the early novels for understanding the uniquely female vulnerability of the protagonist and her specifically feminine defense of beauty, a defense her husband perceives as deceit. Overwhelmed by what he thinks of as her alien beauty and that of the island she loves, Antoinette's husband feels he has been tricked and seeks revenge by appropriating the mechanisms of illusion and beauty on which she depends. Thus, he gives her another name, diagnoses her as mad, and speaks of her as his "marionette." She seems all the more passive and victimized, but clearly driven to enact this quintessential femininity.

Much of European modernist writing by authors such as Joyce, Woolf, Conrad, and Ford explores and reconceptualizes the self, and we can also read Rhys's novels as texts of ironic alienation or portrayals of divided consciousness. But Rhys's characters are not just divided through the unconscious or alienated by what Perry Meisel calls the "myth of the modern," the loss of a natural self: they fragment most importantly through suppressed histories and eclipsed geo-cultural locations. Though European psychological concepts of the privatized and

2. The exceptions usually appear in essays by critics of Third World literature who address the implications of womanhood as presented in Rhys's novels. They tend not to draw on feminist theory or criticism to do so. These include, most notably, Tiffin, "Mirror and Mask"; Elizabeth Nunez-Harrell, "The Paradoxes of Belonging," *Modern Fiction Studies* 31, no. 2 (Summer 1985): 281–293; and Erika Smilowitz, "Childlike Women and Paternal Men: Colonialism in Jean Rhys's Fiction," *Ariel* 17, no. 4 (October 1986): 93–104. Their analyses also tend to make analogous the social hierarchies of colonial and sexual oppression so that the protagonists are seen as all the more victimized. Selma James (*The Ladies and the Mammies* [Bristol, England: Falling Wall Press, 1983]) identifies Rhys as a West Indian writer in sensibility and style. James, nevertheless, bases her discussion of Rhys's work on the comparison with that of Jane Austen. O'Connor's study (*Jean Rhys*) examines the "West Indian" novels within their Caribbean setting, but their location is important to her more for a psychological than a literary, cultural, or historical reading of Jean Rhys's vision. Bev E. L. Brown's essay, "Mansong and Matrix: A Radical Experiment," *Kunapipi* 7, nos. 2 and 3 (1985): 68–80, is exceptional in its analysis of specifically female Creole patterns in Rhys's writing.

autonomous self may be available, both within the text and "outside" it to readers, they do not adequately explain protagonists whose psyches find expression and meaning through interdependence with their social-historical context, a context "foreign" to Europeans.

Read as Caribbean fiction that also turns on (in both senses of revolving on and turning against) a classic "woman's novel," *Wide Sargasso Sea* requires a feminist reading that takes into account more than sexual difference and that recognizes the formal ruptures of convention that cultural difference may introduce to modernism. In this way, treating *Wide Sargasso Sea* as Caribbean fiction directs our readings of Rhys's earlier "continental" novels. The numerous allusions in these early novels to cultures and places other than the European are more than incidental or autobiographical. They place alongside the narratives made possible by European modernism a difference of place and identity that alters the structure of even modernist narrative conventions. * * *

The alterations of conventional narrative that we find in Rhys's early novels may appear as silences, inactions, or even formal flaws; however, they record a double displacement, colonial and sexual, that the conventional narrative and even European modernist narratives, with their presumption of a self to be displaced, divided, or lost, cannot adequately express. Rhys's narrative strategies and the masquerade that in her novels *is* character, expose the limits of novelistic convention and give us glimpses of other possibilities. Once we take masquerade seriously to question "character" in all of its meanings as literary convention, individual personality, and moral integrity, other qualities of the fiction move into focus.

An early passage in *Wide Sargasso Sea* narrates the child Antoinette's ability to mentally visit a place "somewhere else" where she becomes "something else. Not myself any longer." The protagonists in all of Rhys's novels struggle to inhabit a mental or imaginative world view that comes from "somewhere else" and counters negative judgments of their characters which they are always in danger of internalizing. The notion of "elsewhere" figures in feminists such as Luce Irigaray's theories of women's divided position within masculine discourse,[3] but it also derives from the creative turnabout of Carnival, the magic of obeah, the lore of the zombie, and the Arawak concept of *zemi*. Sandra Drake explains this concept in her study of Wilson Harris's fiction: "For the Arawak, the *zemi* existed not only in itself, as it could be experienced in the physical world as a stone or a shell, but it also contained and generated other possibilities of itself. These might be other shapes,

3. Luce Irigaray writes, "It is therefore useless to trap women into giving an exact definition of what they mean, to make them repeat (themselves) so the meaning will be clear. They are already elsewhere than in this discursive machinery where you claim to take them by surprise." See Luce Irigaray, "This Sex Which Is Not One," trans. Claudia Reeder, in *New French Feminisms*, ed. Elaine Marks and Isabelle de Courtivron, p. 103.

other forms, other existences in parallel universes of possibility."[4] All of
Rhys's novels offer glimpses of possibilities conjured by the *zemi*.
Through dreams and what Mikhail Bakhtin has called "internal dia-
logization," the narratives dispel the hegemony of prevailing ideologies,
including that of the consolidated and privatized self, and counter them
with "other shapes," "other forms" that have their sources in West Indian history and culture.

In the ways that Rhys's writing subverts the European concept of
character, it closely resembles that of Third World modernists such as
Wilson Harris.[5] A Caribbean writer from Guyana, Harris has commented on the traditional realist convention of character "consolidation" which he rejects in favor of the idea of "fulfillment." In his novels,
dreamlike narratives trace fulfillments of the person in which dichoto-
mies of past and present, inner and outer, individual and collective blur
as identities double and multiply in a palimpsest of history and plurality
of cultures. It is no accident that Harris's *Palace of the Peacock* and
Rhys's *Wide Sargasso Sea* both appeared in the 1960s and share similar
textual qualities.

The 1960s mark a culmination of a West Indian literary naissance
that began tentatively in the 1930s and became established in the 1950s.
Reading *Wide Sargasso Sea* alongside Rhys's earlier novels suggests connections between European modernism of the 1920s and 1930s and
the birth and development of West Indian literature from the 1930s
through the present. Both the European and Third World modernist
movements in which Rhys played an outsider role took, or are taking,
place within a context of social conflict and change that we have come
to describe as modernization. The conditions of modernization in
Third World countries, such as the adoption of new technologies, have
joined with the forces of nationalism and revolution at varying moments
from the 1930s until the present, creating the context for the emergence
of new literatures in Africa, India, and other former colonies, including
those of the Caribbean.[6] In the 1920s and 1930s, these movements

---

4. Sandra Drake, *Wilson Harris and the Modern Tradition: A New Architecture of the World*
   (New York: Greenwood Press, 1986), p. 175.
5. Drake identifies Third World modernism in her book on Wilson Harris (ibid.). I am aware
   of the problems in using the term "Third World"; it can become, as Régis Dwebray has
   charged, a dumping ground or "shapeless sack" that obscures whole peoples and continents
   and the differences among them. I use it here to call attention to emerging literatures that
   are ignored or marginalized in English departments and also to set up a view of Jean Rhys's
   writing as working in between problematic categories such as "British," "English," and "Third
   World." For a history of the term "Third World," see Barbara Harlow, *Resistance Literature*
   (New York and London: Methuen, 1987), pp. 5–6.
6. Perry Anderson identifies the social, political, and economic conditions of literary modernism
   in "Modernity and Revolution," in *Marxism and the Interpretation of Culture*, ed. Cary Nelson
   and Lawrence Grossberg (Urbana and Chicago: University of Illinois Press, 1988). He describes a triad of factors—persisting dominance by the aristocratic land-owning classes; emergence of novel and key technologies; and the imaginative proximity of social revolution—as
   present in Europe in the late nineteenth and early twentieth centuries and in "developing"
   Third World countries in the 1960s and 1970s.

overlapped with movements for social change in Europe. As Rhys wandered the streets of Montparnasse during her visits to the continent, labor strikes, political riots, and factionalist bombs exploded in Paris. And during her visit to the West Indies in 1936, unemployment marches and movements for racial pride and national independence were shaking the Caribbean. Though she found the life of a tourist in Dominica a bit dull, Rhys's personal papers indicate that she was aware of the agitation among black people of the islands for better working and living conditions and for cultural pride.[7] Not coincidentally, she began writing *Good Morning, Midnight* with its threatening Parisian setting punctuated by allusions to Martinique, West Africa, masquerade, and masks while on her stay in the Caribbean.[8] Because of Rhys's upbringing in a plural and divided colonial culture, she could give modernism a distinctly different cast, reshaping what she learned from people like Ford in light of her uniquely eccentric experience and within a larger context of social and literary change.

The movements of negritude in Africa and the Caribbean and the transition of many former colonies to self-governing independent states gave rise to the new literatures in English which are at once connected to the traditions of English literature and also break radically from them. New literary journals emerged in the 1930s in Trinidad, Barbados, British Guiana, and Jamaica that provided an audience to native writers. In 1949 Hogarth Press published Edgar Mittelholzer's novel *A Morning at the Office*. Also in the 1940s a BBC program called *Caribbean Voices* introduced Caribbean writers to the English public, of which Rhys, then living in London, was a member.[9]

Rhys kept in touch with the struggles of her native island for self-governance through a friendship with her sister Dominican Phyllis Shand Allfrey. Allfrey was politically active in the effort to form the short-lived West Indian Federation and thus partly responsible for the developing sense of community among West Indian countries. She regularly sent Rhys issues of the *Dominican Herald*, which she and her husband edited, and later their opposition paper the *Star*, both of which chronicled the struggles of the island for independence. Through Allfrey, Rhys remained informed about a new West Indies and a West

7. Rhys's personal feelings about the history of slavery were quite mixed, for she wished to believe that her slave-owning grandfather might not have been a cruel man; yet she also identified closely with the blacks and their sufferings. See the Black Exercise Book, Jean Rhys Collection; and O'Connor, *Jean Rhys*, especially chap. 1. Writing about the struggles for independence, however, Rhys stated that it served the white people of the West Indies right to be no longer on top (Black Exercise Book).

8. Staley, *Jean Rhys*, p. 16; and O'Connor, *Jean Rhys*, p. 70.

9. Rhonda Cobham, "The Background," in *West Indian Literature*, ed. Bruce King; Bruce King, "Introduction," in ibid.; and Trevor James, "The Caribbean," in *English Literature from the Third World*.

Indian literature marked by pride in its heterogeneous cultural past.[1] Writers such as Edward Brathwaite, Derek Walcott, and Wilson Harris were finding poetic and fictional forms through which to express a plurality of Caribbean histories and voices: Arawak, Carib, Maroon, black African, Creole. Following her marginalized participation in European modernism, Jean Rhys enriched this chorus of voices in *Wide Sargasso Sea* with that of a white Creole woman in a specific historical moment of dispossession. The tracing in her early "continental novels" of colonial difference is retraced and replaced in the explicitly West Indian novel of the 1960s.

Edward Brathwaite has asserted that the term "West Indian" refers to "someone of African descent" who shares "a common history of slavery."[2] Through writings by Caribbean women, the term gains an expanded, though no less precise, meaning. Simone Schwarz-Bart, a novelist from Guadeloupe, connects the historical period of slavery to which Brathwaite refers to the dynamics of sexual slavery. In her novel *The Bridge of Beyond*, the character Telumee descends from slaves but does not fully understand "the curse of being a master, the curse of being a slave" that the blacks of Guadeloupe "carry in [their] veins" until she emerges, with the help of a community of women, from the spell of an abusive sexual relationship. Only then can she go "beyond" her inheritance of slavery to discover a new magic and power.[3] The protagonist of *Wide Sargasso Sea*, Antoinette (Bertha) Cosway Mason (Rochester), undergoes sexual and class enslavement as a white Creole woman that positions her, too, within multiplicitous West Indian histories of possession and dispossession. Even her names, acquired through her mother's marriages, her own, and reference to an earlier English novel record the layering of identities within the history and literature of colonialism. The interconnecting dynamics of sexual and colonial slavery in *Wide Sargasso Sea* cast a new light on the early novels and their seemingly passive and masochistic "victims." We can see in them instead a quest for identity that is also a quest for "elsewhere" as an alternate history and community. Reviewing Rhys's novels in this light, it soon becomes difficult to maintain the categories dividing British or even English, European, and Commonwealth, Third World, or West Indian literatures. Rhys's writing lies somewhere be-

---

1. Elaine Campbell, "Introduction," in *The Orchid House*, by Phyllis Shand Allfrey (London: Virago Press, 1982); and "From Dominica to Devonshire, A Momento of Jean Rhys," *Kunapipi* 1, no. 2 (1979): 13; Nunez-Harrell, "The Paradox of Belonging." In a letter dated December 6, 1960, Rhys describes her attempts to write "patois" and says that she has not read "any of the 'West Indian' people" Jean Rhys, *The Letters of Jean Rhys*, edited by Francis Wyndham and Diana Melly [New York: Viking, 1984] p. 197). She may not have read them but she clearly knew about them and shared their project of representing in literature the folk dialects of the Caribbean.
2. Edward Brathwaite, quoted in Campbell, "Introduction," p. xv.
3. Simone Schwarz-Bart, *The Bridge of Beyond*, trans. Barbara Bray (1972, reprint. London and Kingston: Heinemann Educational Books, Ltd. 1982).

tween them and thus enables us to see again the social conflicts and
histories that the categories and their oppositions sometimes obscure.

MICHAEL THORPE

"The Other Side": *Wide Sargasso Sea* and *Jane Eyre*†

The crucial question *Wide Sargasso Sea*, as a work of art, might seem
to pose is whether it can stand and be judged alone, or whether in the
view expressed by Walter Allen it is only "a triumph of atmosphere
[which] does not exist in its own right, as Mr. Rochester is almost as
shadowy as Charlotte Brontë's Bertha Mason."[1] Jean Rhys's own comment, "She seemed such a poor ghost, I thought I'd like to write her
life,"[2] might seem to lend support to Allen's generalization, suggesting
as it does that Rhys expended her whole creative effort upon an act of
moral restitution to the stereotyped lunatic Creole heiress in Rochester's
attic. Certainly, Rhys's Antoinette (Bertha), who tells Edward (Rochester) "There is always the other side, always" (p. 106) [77][3], is given a
passionate voice to make "the other side" felt. Yet hers is still only one
side and, though it might be argued of her creator's earlier novels between the wars that Rhys was more concerned to do fictional justice
rather to her women than their men, *Wide Sargasso Sea* stands out as
her most balanced novel in its even-handed treatment of the sexes. Her
inward presentation, in the second part of the novel, of Rochester's
viewpoint—complex but not "shadowy"—is unmatched in her earlier
work, and its strength is enhanced by our contrasting recollections of
Jane Eyre.

It is not Rhys's manner to spell out her characters' viewpoints, or to
eke them out with detailed authorial commentary on background or
theme. For her, as for Hardy, a novel is "an impression, not an argument."[4] Though I have seen people ignorant of *Jane Eyre* respond to
this novel as a self-sufficient work, it would be foolish to deny that many
average readers come to it with some recollection of *Jane Eyre* and that
Rhys relied in a general way on their doing so. Still, she did not assume
that her reader's remembrance would be anything but dim and perhaps
composed of stereotypes: Rochester recalled as a passionate, Byronically
moody man, his life blighted by the secret existence of the mad wife
in the attic, she being little more than a figment of the "gothic"

† From *ARIEL, A Review of International English Literature*, 8:3 (July 1977). Copyright © 1977
  The Board of Governors and The University of Calgary. Reprinted by permission. Page references to this Norton Critical Edition are given in brackets after Thorpe's original citations.
1. *New York Times Book Review*, 18 June 1967, 5.
2. Interview, *The Guardian*, 8th August 1968.
3. References to *Wide Sargasso Sea* (Harmondsworth: Penguin, 1968), by page number.
4. Preface, Thomas Hardy, *Tess of the d'Urbervilles*.

imagination—though the compassionate Charlotte Brontë asks that we pity her, there is no effort to understand. Only in the brief Part Three, the climactic passage set at Thornfield, is some specific knowledge of *Jane Eyre* assumed. This part is introduced by Grace Poole, the woman readers of *Jane Eyre* may remember as looking after the confined heiress. Consistent with her approach, Rhys gives more credibly human substance even to this minor character, Bertha's sullen jailor being presented as another woman as victim, sinking low that she may sink no lower:

> After all the house is big and safe, a shelter from the world outside which, say what you like, can be a black and cruel world to a woman. (p. 146) [105–06]

This passage implicitly echoes that which closes Part One, and the security Antoinette feels in the cold "refuge" of her convent is contrasted with "outside" (pp. 47, 50) [34, 36]: the mad woman and her jailor are, unwittingly, sisters beneath the skin.

Again in Part Three, it is perhaps unlikely that even readers of *Jane Eyre* will recognize that the passage in which Antoinette, holding her red dress against herself, asks if it makes her "look intemperate and unchaste" as "that man" said, calling her "infamous daughter of an infamous mother" (p. 152) [110], closely echoes Rochester's words in his self-exculpatory account to Jane of his relations with his first wife (Ch. XXVII).[5] This is not only an unusually explicit attempt to humanize our understanding of Bertha, but also that of Rochester, for his words are transferred in Rhys's novel to "that man", Antoinette's stepfather Mr. Mason in his virulent disapproval of her relationship with her half-caste cousin, Sandi. The remainder of Part Three allows us to see Antoinette's incendiarism, not as a maniac's melodramatic finale, but as the inevitable tragic sequel to what we have learnt, not only of her embittered relationship with Edward, but also of her early life and trials.

An unexpected consequence of re-reading *Jane Eyre* in search of links with *Wide Sargasso Sea* is finding Brontë's novel a more "dated" work, marred by stereotyping and crude imaginings at points where a vaulting imagination such as Emily possessed was needed. I do not refer to the crude "gothic" of Bertha's characterisation, which has been often enough deplored since the novel appeared, but to the coarse assumptions about madness, mingled with the racial prejudice inherent in the insistent suggestion that "the fiery West Indian" place of Bertha's upbringing (Ch. XXVII) and her Creole blood are the essence of her lunacy: "Her mother, the Creole, was both a mad woman and a drunkard" (Ch. XXVI). Later she is "my Indian Messalina"

5. *Jane Eyre* references by chapter number.

(Ch. XXVII), a byword for debauchery, while Rochester's own con-fessed peccadilloes go under the milder name of "dissipation". Of course, the blackening of the dehumanized creature from the West Indian past readily serves Brontë's purpose of winning sympathy for the deceived and deluded Rochester from both Jane and those of the Vic-torian audience prone to racial prejudice.[6]

Radical though she undoubtedly was in her frank portrayal of passion in this novel, Charlotte Brontë observed certain righteous limits, which she spelt out to a correspondent — not without misgivings:

> It is true that profound pity ought to be the only sentiment elicited by the view of such degradation [as Bertha's], and equally true is it that I have not sufficiently dwelt on that feeling: I have erred in making *horror* too predominant. Mrs. Rochester, indeed, lived a sinful life before she was insane, but sin is itself a species of insanity — the truly good behold and compassionate it as such.[7]

Evidently Brontë herself felt that she had not sufficiently realized Ber-tha's humanity: it was easier to make a mere figure of a character who was, unlike Rochester and Jane, wholly imagined as a means to an end. *Jane Eyre* itself is contradictory on the issues the letter touches upon: in his account Rochester complains that Bertha's descent from "idiots and maniacs through three generations" was concealed from him, but also that her "gross, impure, depraved" vices "prematurely developed the germs of insanity" (Ch. XXVII). Thus, Bertha must be both con-genitally insane and yet depraved *before* that madness shows itself — a shaky diagnosis but convenient or else it would have been possible to pity her, as indeed before she knows all Jane once beseeches him to do. Essentially, of course, our pity is needed for Rochester.

In getting *behind* Bertha's insanity, eschewing the catch-all dismissive generalization — "sin is itself a species of insanity" — Rhys joins those modern writers, novelists especially, who have sought to win their read-ers' understanding and compassion for those whose mental state is of-ten, and for deeply complex reasons, just the wrong side of a thin dividing line from "normality". This concern was foreshadowed in her earlier novels, especially *Good Morning, Midnight* (1939). There her heroine, Sasha, is one of Rhys's "weak", to whom the whole world is alien and menacing; her passions are a clinging to security, her fears of others' cruelty "imagination" to the strong. A passage in which one of her lovers, Serge, relates an encounter with a drunk "half-negro — a mulatto" woman who lives caged with her "monsieur" in the attic of his Paris boarding house prefigures the plight of Antoinette, everywhere an exile:

6. Christine Bolt, *Victorian Attitudes to Race* (London: Routledge, 1971), *passim*.
7. Letter to W. S. Williams, 4th January, 1848: Clement Shorter, ed., *The Brontës: Life and Letters*, Vol. 1 (London: Hodder & Stoughton, 1908).

> She told me she hadn't been out, except after dark, for two years.
> When she said this I had an extraordinary sensation, as if I were
> looking down into a pit. It was the expression in her eyes. I said:
> "But this monsieur you are living with. What about him?" "Oh,
> he is very Angliche, he says I imagine everything."[8]

This brief episode holds the seeds of the Edward/Antoinette relationship, as Rhys was to treat it twenty-five years later, in what was to be
her most fairly and fully realized analysis of that fatal want of imaginative and emotional understanding repeatedly presented in her earlier
work as "very Angliche". If it may be argued that she shows some bias
in that work, in *Wide Sargasso Sea* she rises above any temptation to
blacken Rochester in his turn. Clearly, she set herself, not only to humanize the West Indian exotic, but also to portray subtly and sympa-
thetically its effect upon Edward (an aspect I shall develop later). She
does not for her purposes need Jane Eyre, not merely because this is
the story of Edward and Antoinette, but because in a bold departure
she draws implicit parallels, not only between Antoinette and Jane, so
underlining their common plight as women, but also draws out hidden
affinities between Antoinette and Edward, affinities which are the substance of their tragedy.

The development of Rhys's narrative, where it centres upon Antoinette, bears striking resemblances to Brontë's portrayal of the younger
Jane. Both heroines grow up fatherless and emotionally threatened by
those who take charge of them; they live much within themselves and
in their imaginations, made fearful by emotional and physical insecu-
rity. Jane is an orphan: Antoinette virtually one, losing her father in
childhood and seeing her mother marry again, infatuated, only to become insane after the burning of their estate by the emancipated negroes (in the disturbances of the late 1830's). The real life of both, as
children, is driven inward by maltreatment or indifference. Life is the
nightmare, only in dreams and fantasy do they find relief. In fact, Jane's
experience is such that she might have recognized much in Bertha's
suffering at Thornfield Hall: her agonies in the red-room, where her
aunt confines her, correspond to Bertha's incarceration, while her temptation to a superstitious doubt of her own reality, as when she peers in
the looking glass (Ch. II), is counterpointed in Rhys's novel by the
looking-glass motif linked with Antoinette, who constantly needs one to
be reassured of her identity. Another implicit link between Jane and
Antoinette is in the oppressed Jane's search for escape in the "charm"
of exotic far places conjured up for her by *Gulliver's Travels* — but her
imagination more often torments than consoles her, inflamed by her
daily struggles for survival. Those around her set her down as "a mad
cat" subject to "tantrums"; before she goes to Lowood she is, like Ber-

---

8. *Good Morning, Midnight* (Harmondsworth: Penguin, 1969), pp. 79–80.

tha, virtually confined, and treated as a wild, unstable being. It is hardly surprising that the pictures she paints at school, which she later shows Rochester, recall her fevered imaginings: one, of the "woman's shape to the bust . . . the eyes shone dark and wild; the hair streamed shadowy" (Ch. XIII), might have been an unconscious presentiment of Bertha as she is later shown, but Brontë certainly points no such link.

Re-reading Chapters I to X of *Jane Eyre* one cannot help but notice how much in them corresponds to Antoinette's essential experience as a solitary, unloved child in Part One of *Wide Sargasso Sea*. Both heroines seek imaginative escape, know terrors beyond the common, endure the encroachment of menace that threatens the very soul, and reach out for a seemingly impossible happiness. Jane's Lowood, the school that "excludes every glimpse of prospect" (Ch. V) is nevertheless, like Antoinette's convent, a "refuge" (p. 47) [34] from a harsher world without. But here a crucial difference arises. Jane finds support and inspiration in the example of the saintly Helen: Antoinette can only envy the so well-adjusted de Plana sisters, especially Hélène (p. 45) [33]. Antoinette can only learn from her how ill fitted she is to enter life beyond the convent, where she acquires no shield against reality; she will always carry on the surface the ineradicable marks of her harsh early experience. Jane, however, goes forth armed with the saving talisman of Helen's Christian example which keeps her proof at the centre against later misfortune and temptation. The significance of this, which crystallizes clearly when Jane rebuffs Rochester's plea for love after he has confessed his "horrible life" with the words "trust in God and yourself. Believe in Heaven. Hope to meet again there" (Ch. XXVII), may easily be overlooked by modern commentators seeking to define Jane as a free spirit.[9] Jane's severe morality reflects her creator's views — "sin is a species of insanity." Brontë's moral forcing, despite her casting of Jane as a seeker after liberty and self-determination, is reductive and constricting — nowhere is this more clearly shown than in the novel's dehumanizing of Bertha, the hapless creature for whom her own experience might have taught her more than a perfunctory plea for pity, soon set aside by Rochester (Ch. XXVII). Of course, Jane is a child of her author's imagination and of her time: I do not claim that Brontë could have been expected to write the greater, more complex novel potential in the parallel experiences of the early Jane and the imprisoned wife. This, in part, is what Rhys has done, writing clear of the racial prejudices that must have limited Brontë's reach and creating in the affinities between her Antoinette and Brontë's Jane a subtle, implicit comment on the shortcomings of *Jane Eyre*.

9. Cf. Dennis Porter, "Of Heroines and Victims: Jean Rhys and *Jane Eyre*," *The Massachusetts Review*, 17, No. 3 (Autumn 1976), 540–551, *passim*; Porter stresses Jane's "strength of character" and "self-esteem" by contrast with Antoinette as passive victim, disabled by her colonial experience and circumstance. He overlooks the religious aspect, vital to Brontë as to her heroine.

Helen Burns, Jane's moral exemplar, tells Jane that she cannot believe God's creatures will "be suffered to degenerate from man to fiend"
and holds "another creed . . . [which] makes Eternity a rest—a mighty
home, not a terror and an abyss" (Ch. VI). Helen's creed is instinctive
and positive, a sure stay for Jane and a vanquisher of goblins. Antoinette
in her convent would hold to a similar faith, if she could, as taught by
the nun who "knew about Heaven and the attributes of the blessed, of
which the least is transcendent beauty . . . I could hardly wait for all
this ecstasy and once I prayed for a long time to be dead" (p. 48) [34].
But to despair is mortal sin, there is also Hell: what has become of the
soul of her mother who in her madness has died both of the "two
deaths" (p. 106) [77]? Part One ends with Antoinette trembling on the
brink of "*outside*" (p. 50) [36]; dreading the "security" of the arranged
marriage her dubiously solicitous step-father, Mr. Mason, has arranged
for her, she dreams of Hell and the menacing male figure who draws
her into darkness. She goes forth to meet her fate in Edward (Rochester)
unsupported by other-worldly sanctions. All seems prepared for a treatment of Edward that will redress Brontë's bias against Bertha, but instead Part Two, which takes us at once into his consciousness, makes
possible a sympathetic insight into him also.

In Brontë's novel, when Jane returns to Rochester after his blinding
in the fire Bertha caused, he recognizes her voice and thinks it a "sweet
delusion"; but Jane assures him, "your mind, sir, is too strong for delusion, your health too sound for frenzy" (Ch. XXXVII). We can readily
believe this, despite Rochester's trials with Bertha and his losing Jane:
his account of his marriage and Bertha's "mad" blood comes from one
whose reason is always proof against the West Indian "hell"—despite
the passing temptation to despair and suicide from which "A wind fresh
from Europe" cleanses him (Ch. XXVII). For Rochester's highly coloured and, finally, self-exculpatory account of his hapless marriage Rhys
substitutes in her Part Two a more complex, inward account, counterpointing it in many aspects against our prior insight into Antoinette's
warped life. She thus achieves a poignant depiction of a mutual incomprehension that rests, in fact, on a closer identity of personal experience
than Edward or Antoinette ever imagine. As he rides with her toward
Granbois, their honeymoon house, Edward broods upon his invidious
position and composes the first of his mental letters of reproach to his
father in England:

> I have a modest competence now. I will never be a disgrace to
> you or to my dear brother, the son you love. No begging letters,
> no mean requests. None of the furtive shabby manoeuvres of a
> younger son. I have sold my soul or you have sold it, and after all
> is it such a bad bargain? The girl is thought to be beautiful, she
> is beautiful. . . . (p. 59) [41]

Edward's dubious bought "security" counterpoints Antoinette's (who is bought, who sold? . . . "The white cockroach she buy young man" sings the half-caste Amélie in his and Antoinette's hearing p. 83 [60]), his inferior position in his family, his exile from what is familiar, the fever he is plunged into on his arrival in Jamaica, these all leave him groping for some sure ground for self; he is sceptical of life's promises and, like Antoinette, of "happiness": "As for my confused impressions they will never be written. There are blanks in my mind that cannot be filled up" (p. 64) [45] — Edward's words, not Antoinette's. Edward, too, is young; and Rhys has built upon Rochester's expressed resentment, in *Jane Eyre*, of his "avaricious" father: "When I left college I was sent out to Jamaica to espouse a bride already courted for me" (Ch. XXVII). In her portrayal Edward (a milder name than the formidable "Rochester") is an uncertain, perhaps emotionally crippled young man.[1]

Rhys's counterpointing of Antoinette and Edward is deliberate and hardly to be missed. Their shared desire for "peace" (pp. 58, 66) [41, 47] is disabling, for each demands it of the other, neither can accept the unfamiliar as "real" (p. 67) [47]. Their potential mutual dependence is aborted by a deeply shared vulnerability, which Antoinette exposes and Edward conceals: "I thought these people are very vulnerable. How old was I when I learned to hide what I felt? A very small boy. Six, five, even earlier. It was necessary, I was told, and that view I have always accepted" (p. 85) [61]. This is an "English" flaw, clearly, but Edward is not incapable of feeling; only in him a genuine emotional susceptibility, distrusted and constricted by a willed morality, has gone dangerously awry. Rhys brings this out in various ways, of which one becomes a persistent thematic contrast — Edward's and Antoinette's conflicting responses to the place, Granbois, and its surroundings.[2] At first Edward goes often to Antoinette's bathing pool, finding there "an alien, disturbing, secret loveliness. And it kept its secret. I'd find myself thinking, 'What I see is nothing — I want what it *hides* — that is not nothing' " (p. 73) [52]. His early hopes and promises, to Antoinette, of "happiness" in this inauspicious marriage are as fragile as his sense of his own reality — and little less so than hers. The passion they share at first, sharing the sun, is sure to recoil upon her. It would have taken less than Daniel Cosway's malicious gossip about her mother's madness

---

1. Here again I must differ with Dennis Porter, who roundly states "Rochester's failure to care enough for the feelings and the fate of his vulnerable child-bride is represented by Jean Rhys as a paradigm of male cruelty towards women" (*op. cit.*, 543): "child-bride" is hardly apt, not only because Antoinette Cosway is 18, but Edward himself is "young" — he reflects bitterly "a short youth mine was" [p. 50]. Porter reduces the novel's complexity, seeing it simplistically as reflecting Rhys's semi-autobiographical concern with women's victimage in a male-dominated world. His paper rests upon the fashionable poles of male chauvinism and women's liberation between which the weak Antoinette falls.

2. Cf. Kenneth Ramchand's perceptive brief discussion, stressing the "highly subjective landscape," *The West Indian Novel and Its Background* (London: Faber, 1970), pp. 230–36.

and her own past relationship with her half-caste cousin, Sandi (of which her step-father so violently disapproved) to harden Edward's habit of repressed feeling into cold alienation. The warmer Antoinette, who "have the sun in her" (p. 130) [95] confronts him too late with her truth. She recalls Coulibri and the garden where she had been "happy": this nakedly remembered past merges into the alien place which is "my enemy and on your side" (p. 107) [78]. In vain she tells him, "It is not for you and not for me. It has nothing to do with either of us. That is why you are afraid of it, because it is something else" (p. 107) [78]. Her risky recognition of non-meaning (there is no moral scheme — contrived by "people", whom she has learnt to fear) conflicts with that rigid invocation of "the power and wisdom of my creator" (p. 105) [76] which Rhys's Edward fearfully stands upon, shunning the freedom of facing the world's "dark forest" (p. 137) [100] — which surely involves passionate relationship — existentially.

Could Edward have acknowledged with Antoinette that dangerous freedom and have helped her face it, he might have grasped the elusive "secret". Antoinette gives him passion, a self-abandon in desire he cannot trust: Daniel Cosway's accusations,[3] Antoinette's foolishly countering use of the love potion certainly deepen their alienation, but are not essential. Their shared tragedy is that Edward has never learnt to give, nor Antoinette to receive securely. The "secret" is denied by their deep, shared incapacity for relationship and love. At the moment of departure Edward is "suddenly, bewilderingly . . . certain that everything I had imagined to be truth was false. False. Only the magic and the dream are true — all the rest's a lie. Let it go. Here is the secret. Here" (p. 138) [100–01]. The place holds the "secret"; it is Antoinette's, spiritually her only stay: in carrying her away to England he vents his frustration, rationalized as revenge for her suspected betrayal, not only upon her but upon himself. He acts with the calculating cruelty of the sensitive, not the brutal. His romantic desires for a marriage of self and place — more possible for him, as for Antoinette, than a relationship with people, for he despises her "savage" people, as she had learnt from her step-father's example to fear his — ends with "nothing" (p. 142) [104].

At the beginning of Part Three Grace Poole remembers "Mrs. Eff" (Mrs. Fairfax in *Jane Eyre*) reproving her for her unwillingness to accept

---

3. Daniel Cosway, not Daniel *Mason* (the name of Antoinette's step-father), as Porter mistakenly calls him, *op. cit.*, p. 544: Daniel claims to be Antoinette's half-brother, her father's illegitimate son by a black woman, and plays in his accusations upon that repugnance toward the darker races and the issue of miscegenation which was as natural to an Englishman of Edward's time as breathing. While it is true that Edward betrays Antoinette with the half-caste servant, Amelie, only to realize in the morning that "her skin was darker, her lips thicker than I had thought" [p. 84], this is no simple case of "male cruelty towards women" (see note 9 above). Edward is reacting from his conviction that Antoinette, who had given him a love-potion in a foolish effort to secure him, had tried to poison him; perhaps, too, he is bitterly imitating the affair with her half-caste cousin, Sandi, that Daniel Cosway has broadly hinted at.

Edward's proposition that she look after his mad wife with this plea for sympathy: "I knew him as a boy. I knew him as a young man. He was gentle, generous, brave. His stay in the West Indies has changed him out of all knowledge. He has grey in his hair and misery in his eyes. Don't ask me to pity anyone who had a hand in that" (p. 145) [105]. Another side, of course, and a partial one, but by this time Rhys has allowed Edward claims upon our pity; we have seen him steel himself against pity (p. 135) [98], fearful of his own disintegration, and thus violate his own soul in destroying Antoinette's. His future does not concern Jean Rhys (though he could have none in the Brontëan manner), but his relationship with Antoinette has been developed into a many-sided and complete study of tragic incompatibilities retrieved from Charlotte Brontë's workshop floor.

KENNETH RAMCHAND

[The Place of Jean Rhys and *Wide Sargasso Sea*]†

Had rationalisation been necessary, the case for including Jean Rhys's *Wide Sargasso Sea* in a course on West Indian literature would be that this novel challenges us to think a little more carefully about two questions: What makes a novel a West Indian novel? and what do we mean when we say that a writer is a West Indian writer? A safe enough generalisation to begin with is that those literary works are West Indian which describe a social world that is recognisably West Indian, in a West Indian landscape; and which are written by people who were born or who grew up in the West Indies. Where the disruption of intimacy between an author and his native world has not been acute, or where the separation between them has not been absolute and prolonged, our generalisation works satisfactorily. But the case of Miss Rhys, the author of *Wide Sargasso Sea*, is a tempting one.

Francis Wyndham begins his Introduction to this novel with the information that Jean Rhys, daughter of a Welsh doctor and a White West Indian mother spent her childhood in Dominica before going to England at the age of sixteen. Memories from a West Indian childhood float about in her earliest writing; and in *Voyage in the Dark* (1934), it is the memory of another life now lost, and another place still felt in the blood which benumbs the heroine and unfits her for existence in the England to which she has been brought: 'hundreds thousands of white people white people rushing along and dark houses all alike frowning down one after the other all alike all stuck together — the

† From Kenneth Ramchand, *An Introduction to the Study of West Indian Literature* (Middlesex: Thomas Nelson and Sons Ltd., 1976) 91–107. Reprinted by permission of the publisher. Page references are to this Norton Critical Edition.

streets like smooth shut-in ravines and the dark houses frowning down — oh I'm not going to like this place I'm not going to like this place I'm not going to like this place.' What strikes Mr Wyndham more strongly about these earlier works of Miss Rhys, however, is their modern urban background and the present plight of their underdog heroines. Accordingly, when he comes to *Wide Sargasso Sea* he can acknowledge that the setting is now the West Indies but he sees the landscape, conjured up 'with haunting perfection', as yet another nightmare for a beleaguered Rhys heroine, and he links the novel closely to the preceding ones by recognising Antoinette Cosway as 'a logical development of Marya, Julia, Anna and Sasha who were also alienated, menaced, at odds with life.'

A West Indian commentator, Wally Look Lai, is ready to concede that Miss Rhys's other works are European, and that in them the author is more a European than a West Indian writer; but for him there is a radical discontinuity when we come to *Wide Sargasso Sea*. It is a West Indian novel, in which the West Indian setting is crucial; 'It is not that it provides a mere background to the theme of rejected womanhood, but rather that the theme of rejected womanhood is utilised symbolically in order to make an artistic statement about West Indian society, and about an aspect of the West Indian experience.' Implicit in Look Lai's contention, and in the method he adopts to support it, is the principle that in trying to judge whether a writer is a West Indian author we must rely on the tale, and allow that to be the source of our most relevant impressions about the teller; if we come to the conclusion that a certain work is West Indian, then it follows that the writer, as author of that particular work is a West Indian writer. Look Lai's discussion is about the novel itself, and not Miss Rhys's colour, class or nationality, because in difficult cases we are driven to fundamentals: we know a writer is a West Indian writer if the work is West Indian. But this leaves us with our original question, 'What makes a novel a West Indian novel?'

To this question, it is tempting to reply that we just know. For to affirm that a work is West Indian is to suggest that a West Indian reader may be more responsive to landscape and setting, more alive to social and political levels, and more caught up in, sometimes, indeed, more caught out by the work's 'buzz of implication' than he would be if reading a non–West Indian work. In *Wide Sargasso Sea* Jean Rhys employs a variety of devices — detailed descriptions of place and weather; casual references to the colour of the sky and degrees of light, heat or shade; allusions to the scents and tints of flowers; and sometimes, as in the following example, observations of a native's behaviour — all of which bring to the reader's senses a landscape felt and recognised by a West Indian as his own.

We rode on again, silent in the slanting afternoon sun, the wall of trees on one side, a drop on the other. Now the sea was a serene blue, deep and dark. We came to a little river. 'This is the boundary of Granbois.' She smiled at me. It was the first time I had seen her smile simply and naturally. Or perhaps it was the first time I had felt simple and natural with her. A bamboo spout jutted from the cliff, the water coming from it was silver blue. She dismounted quickly, picked a large shamrock-shaped leaf to make a cup and drank. Then she picked another leaf, folded it and brought it to me. 'Taste. This is mountain water.' [42]

Like Wilson Harris and Derek Walcott, Miss Rhys is concerned as much to evoke the landscape as to explore its impact upon human consciousness. The different stages in the changing relationship between English husband and White West Indian wife are marked by the husband's changing and confused attitudes to the landscape; and the difference in temperament between Antoinette and her husband is measured out for us in his reading of the natural world which he identifies with his wife:

'You have no right,' she said fiercely. 'You have no right to ask questions about my mother and then refuse to listen to my answer.'
    'Of course I will listen, of course we can talk now, if that's what you wish.' But the feeling of something unknown and hostile was very strong. 'I feel very much a stranger here,' I said. 'I feel that this place is my enemy and on your side.'
    'You are quite mistaken,' she said. 'It is not for you and not for me. It has nothing to do with either of us. That is why you are afraid of it, because it is something else. I found that out long ago when I was a child.' [78]

As with landscape, so with social background. Jean Rhys's intelligent memory of the West Indian linguistic situation enables her to invent varieties of language to suit respectively, her characters from England; her dialect and French-patois speaking Negro characters; her White West Indian whose language ranges between these two; and the would-be grandiloquent mulatto Daniel Cosway:

Dear Sir,
I take up my pen after long thought and meditation but in the end the truth is better than a lie. I have this to say. You have been shamefully deceived by the Mason family. They tell you perhaps that your wife's name is Cosway, the English gentleman Mr Mason being her stepfather only, but they don't tell you what sort of people were these Cosways. Wicked and detestable slave-owners since generations — yes everybody hate them in Jamaica and also in this beautiful island where I hope your stay will be long and pleasant

in spite of all, for some not worth sorrow. Wickedness is not the
worst. There is madness in that family. Old Cosway die raving like
his father before him. [56–57]

The language in *Wide Sargasso Sea* has an authentic ring to the
West Indian's ear, and evokes, in a way no didactic account can, the
whole social spectrum in the West Indies. A West Indian reader, moreover, armed with a knowledge of West Indian history, and burdened
with attitudes and feelings rooted in the peculiar orderings of the plantation system, recognises the accuracy of the 'factual' data, and responds
to nuances in the situation that could easily be missed by a non–West
Indian reader. This kind of difference between readers of the novel
exists for the fictional characters too. It is brought out with deliberate
obviousness in Part I of the work, where Jean Rhys prepares us for the
mutual incomprehension of Antoinette and her husband by pre-figuring
it in the lack of understanding between the girl's mother and her new
husband from England, Mr Mason. Antoinette's mother senses danger
in the stirrings among the Black population and wants to go away, but
Mr Mason's complacency and his prejudices will not be touched by
the fear and understanding of the slave-owner's daughter:

> 'You have lived alone far too long Annette. You imagine enmity
> which doesn't exist. Always one extreme or the other. Didn't you
> fly at me like a little wild cat when I said nigger. Not nigger, nor
> even negro. Black people I must say.'
> 'You don't like, or even recognise, the good in them,' she said,
> 'and you won't believe in the other side.'
> 'They're too damn lazy to be dangerous,' said Mr Mason. 'I
> know that.'
> 'They are more alive than you are, lazy or not, and they can be
> dangerous and cruel for reasons you wouldn't understand.'
> 'No, I don't understand,' Mr Mason always said. 'I don't under-
> stand at all.' [19–20]

Jean Rhys makes Antoinette's husband different from Mr Mason in
that the former is conscious of the cultural difference between himself
and his West Indian wife: 'I felt very little tenderness for her, she was
a stranger to me, a stranger who did not think or feel as I did' [55]. He
is constantly on his guard with the Blacks: 'She trusted them and I did
not. But I could hardly say so. Not yet' [53]; and he is appalled at
Antoinette's intimacy with them: ' "Why do you hug and kiss Christophine?" I'd say' [54]. The failure of the two social worlds to come to
terms with each other is implied in the failure of the relationship between Antoinette and her husband; and the main elements in this failure are revealed to be the Englishman's inability to accept the White
West Indian's attachment to the landscape of her birth; and his unwillingness to take as natural her closeness in sensibility to the world

of the Blacks, to which Christophine and Antoinette's childhood friend Tia belong, and which is the life-breath of the novel: 'We had eaten the same food, slept side by side, bathed in the same river. As I ran, I thought, I will live with Tia and I will be like her. Not to leave Coulibri. Not to go. Not' [27].

We jump suddenly from the account of Antoinette's childhood in Part I into the relationship that has come about through an arranged marriage between the girl and a young Englishman come out resentfully at his father's behest to the West Indies to make his own fortune. The change in subject matter is accompanied by a change in perspective that is startling and dramatic. Much of Part II is presented from the point of view of the alien husband: 'Everything is too much, I felt as I rode wearily after her. Too much blue, too much purple, too much green. The flowers too red, the mountains too high, the hills too near. And the woman is a stranger' [41]. The difference in background and sensibility is immediately felt by the reader but emerging even more importantly from this entry into the husband's consciousness is our sense of the struggle of a certain kind of mind to break free and expose its buried emotions and yearnings:

> My fever weakness left me, so did all misgiving. I went very early to the bathing pool and stayed there for hours, unwilling to leave the river, the trees shading it, the flowers that opened at night. They were tightly shut, drooping, sheltering from the sun under their thick leaves. It was a beautiful place — wild, untouched, above all untouched, with an alien, disturbing, secret loveliness. And it kept its secret. I'd find myself thinking, 'What I see is nothing — I want what it *hides* — that is not nothing.' [52]

Long before we arrive at anything as definite as the formulation of a theme, the West Indian-ness of *Wide Sargasso Sea* imposes itself upon a responsive reader. But it is difficult to speak about this kind of alertness to a novel's background noises let alone demonstrate it, so it is just as well that we can fall back, in argument, upon a position implicit in Look Lai's discussion: the *theme* of *Wide Sargasso Sea* is West Indian, and it is this that makes the novel a West Indian novel.

One is inclined, then, to agree with Look Lai that in *Wide Sargasso Sea* there is an exploration of 'the encounter between two whole worlds', but with reservations. The last two quotations from *Wide Sargasso Sea* were intended to suggest that any critical approach focusing exclusively on Antoinette must suffer the limitation of being little more than half-satisfactory. For Miss Rhys allows us to explore not just 'the White West Indian's relation to England, the nature and consequences of his involvement with the world from which his ancestors came', but also, and with just as great relevance to an understanding of our colonial situation, the Englishman/coloniser's psychic relationship to the

West Indies. If *Wide Sargasso Sea* has a West Indian theme, its originality arises from the author's peculiar ability to examine 'the encounter
between two whole worlds' from both points of view — that of Antoinette, and that of her husband.

Yet to say that a novel is West Indian is not to deny its accessibility
to a non–West Indian, nor indeed to deny the validity of a non–West
Indian's reading. The differences in emphasis between Francis Wyndham and Wally Look Lai can be accommodated as arising from different cultural/national perspectives, and as another illustration of the
many-sidedness or objectivity of a work of art, making it possible for it
to mean different things to people from different countries, just as it
can mean different things to the same person at different times.

It is interesting in this context to look at the stark differences in interpretation of *Wide Sargasso Sea* between Look Lai, and a fellow West Indian, Edward Brathwaite. Look Lai's explication of the theme of the
White West Indian's relation to England is at the same time an appeal to
his fellow West Indians to take a less tribal view and to see the experience
of White West Indians as an aspect of the West Indian experience. Brathwaite concedes that Jean Rhys's concern was as Look Lai finds it in the
novel, and notes with sadness that 'what really interests Look Lai about
Sargasso Sea is not the deep subtle hopeless black/white "West Indian"
relationships'; he dismisses the novel as 'a fictional statement that ignores
vast areas of social and historical formation', and then seems to quarrel
with the art of fiction itself. He asserts that Tia the African girl and Antoinette, the White Creole, could not have been friends in real life and
therefore could not be in the novel: 'Tia was not and never could have
been her friend. No matter what Jean Rhys might have made Antoinette
think, Tia was historically separated from her by the impassable boundary of colour distinction.' Brathwaite's account of the wrongness of *Wide
Sargasso Sea* is completed and explained by the proclamation of a kind of
'fact' that should have been less binding to a writer who as poet/historian
is often projected as being concerned with ignored and forgotten possibilities for colonised and coloniser in West Indian life:

> Now he was sure
> he heard soft voices mocking in the leaves.
> What did this journey mean, this
>
> new world mean: dis-
> covery? Or a return to terrors
> he had sailed from, known before?
>
> I watched him pause.[1]

---

1. Edward Kamau Brathwaite, *Rights of Passage* (London and New York: Oxford University
   Press, 1967).

Surely, the poet who could imagine such a possibility of self-discovery for the first coloniser has fallen short of his own intuition when he declares that 'White creoles in the English and French West Indies have separated themselves by too wide a gulf and have contributed too little culturally, as a group, to give credence to the notion that they can, given the present structure, meaningfully identify or be identified with the spiritual world on this side of the Sargasso Sea.'

A literary work doesn't only say things *through* the elements (people, places, things, etc.) out of which it has been made; it speaks, and it does so in unexpected ways, to native readers *about* those elements. As the native critic's interpretation of social reality may differ from the presentations of his author or from the interpretations of other critics, the work may become contentious in its country of origin, and native readers may appear to outsiders to be battling over shadowy substances around certain texts and authors. Sometimes, indeed, the commentator may entirely lose sight of what it is that the particular literary work is trying to do or say because of the burden of his own wishes and theories. The extreme example referred to above helps us to see how easy it is to slip away from the literary work when we seek, however legitimately, to extract its social significance; and it calls to our notice the danger of prescription that exists whenever we attempt to base definitions upon social and political content. Even as Brathwaite attempts to persuade us that *Wide Sargasso Sea* is whitewash, however, we can venture to add to our un-theoretical understanding of what makes a West Indian novel West Indian this generalisation relating to social content: a West Indian novel challenges West Indians to understand the world and their social relations better, and with such authenticity that the challenge cannot be ignored even if we want to set it aside.

In arguing for *Wide Sargasso Sea* as a West Indian novel, Look Lai advances its socio-cultural theme as something that 'transcends the purely personal nature' of the encounter between Antoinette and her husband. The general proposition about the relative merits of socio-cultural and personal themes that seems to lie behind this remark is, to say the least, a questionable one. Although, moreover, we recognise the importance of the socio-cultural theme, and in spite of the distancing from the author that is implied in the fabrication of *Wide Sargasso Sea* (historical setting, fictional characters based upon historical types, detailed landscape, narrating characters), we find a lyric intensity in the work which suggests the existence of something much more personal to the author and to the reader imbedded in the fiction.   *   *   *

WILSON HARRIS

Carnival of Psyche: Jean Rhys's *Wide Sargasso Sea*†

Myth, as I use it in this context, implies a force in the universe that is untamed and untamable, but which subsists on paradox. Myth teaches us that sovereign gods and sovereign institutions are partial, partial in the sense that they are biased, but when they begin to penetrate their biases, they also begin to transform their fear of the other, of others, of other parts, in a larger complex of wholeness. In this medium of transformation, the unconscious psyche is in dialogue — in rich marvellous dialogue — with the conscious mind. And out of this arises the living ongoing momentum of the imaginative arts.

Now, the basic thrust of what I have to say has to do with myths that have secreted themselves in certain works of the imagination — I shall confine myself on this occasion to Jean Rhys's *Wide Sargasso Sea* — and of which the writers themselves are or were unaware. But before moving into that territory I think I should make a distinction. It is this: the imaginative artist who makes *deliberate* use of myth may in no way be inferior to the writer or painter or sculptor or composer in whose work one may find an *intuitive* body (or intuitive bodies) of myth.

Writers as varied as James Joyce, St John Perse, Miguel Asturias, David Jones, T. S. Eliot, Camara Laye, Ralph Ellison, Djuna Barnes, D. H. Lawrence, Pablo Neruda, Kathleen Raine — to give outstanding examples — have employed myth with deliberation, but in order to ask new questions, so to speak, of untamable reality. Yet even here — however self-conscious the equilibrium between artist and myth — unconscious variables secrete themselves in the live tapestry of word and image whose enigmatic manifestation lies in the future.

I find myself in agreement with critics and historians of the arts — such as Anton Ehrenzweig, Herbert Read, William James — who point to variables of unconscious motivation in the arts of which generations become differently aware, consciously and partially aware, with the passage of time. Compositions of music, painting, fiction of a certain kind, sculpture, poetry, will address us differently with the passage of time because of unconscious variables of myth that leave apparent gaps, angularities, turbulences, opacities, in the live tapestry in which they function. Those gaps come to be curiously filled, opacities dazzle or lighten, angularities and turbulences become rich and intriguing, as if the life of works of art mutates in depth with changed perceptions and responses of later decades and generations.

† From *Kunapipi* 2.2 (1980): 142–50. Reprinted by permission. Page references to this Norton Critical Edition are given in brackets after Harris's original citations.

Thus even the self-conscious usage of myth by individual imaginations involves a descent into unconscious variables whose manifestation affects the future. * * *

What is intriguing about *intuitive* usage of myth is that the artist may not perceive in his or her own work an activity or concentration which is other than daylight consciousness and which runs into the apparently unconscious past.

Wide Sargasso Sea varies the rainbow arc between cultures in profoundly intuitive spirit. To appreciate that variation we need to recall the bridge between sky and earth that is implicit in the rainbow arc from Central to South America in Quetzalcoatl (snake and bird) and Yurokon (Quetzalcoatl's Carib cousin). Then we need to revise that arc or bridge into a rather different compression of features. The food-bearing tree of the world, in Arawak and Macusi legends, reaches to heaven across forgotten ages, but suddenly we become aware of it as creation myth rooted in catastrophe.[1] The tree is fired by the Caribs at a time of war when the Arawaks seek refuge in its branches. The fire rages and drives the Arawaks up into space until they are themselves burnt and converted into sparks which continue to rise into the sky to become the Pleiades.

Let us note, firstly, the fire-motif in the creation myth, secondly, the ground of war and catastrophe in which the foodbearing tree is rooted, thirdly, the constellation of the Arawaks in 'the sky of fiction' (if I may so put it). All these features are *intuitively* woven into the tapestry of *Wide Sargasso Sea*. There is the persistent fire-motif that runs through the entire fabric of the novel. There are the legacies of slavery and catastrophe in the soil of the Caribbean which leave such deep scars on Antoinette and her relations. There is the re-dress of mad Bertha into the new burning constellation of Antoinette in the sky of fiction. Antoinette turns round and sees 'the sky — the tree of life in flames'. 'It was red and all my life was in it' (p. 155)[2] [112].

Mad Bertha of *Jane Eyre* is symbolically, if not literally, widowed by a husband to all intents and purposes dead and vanished. His presence is the presence of ornament and Jean Rhys straitjackets his 'death' into 'stone' (p. 94) [65] in Antoinette's confession to her black Haitian[3] nurse Christophine, as events begin to move towards their separation — Christophine is soon to be banished from Rochester's West Indian household as an evil witch or obeah woman — Antoinette is soon to live the 'lie'

1. Quetzalcoatl is The Feathered Serpent, one of the major deities of the ancient Mexican pantheon. In Toltec mythology Quetzalcoatl symbolized the evening and morning stars and came in Aztec times to symbolize death and resurrection. One body of myths describes him immolating himself on a pyre, emerging as the planet Venus. The Macusi were aboriginal people of the Guianas, South America [*Editor*].
2. Jean Rhys, *Wide Sargasso Sea*, first published 1966. All page references are to the Penguin edition and given in the text.
3. Christophine is from Martinique [*Editor*].

of a voyage from the West Indies and the setting up of home in England
where she is deemed mad by Rochester and locked away in Thornfield
Hall. Antoinette tells Christophine — as she pleads with her to mix a
love potion to bring Rochester back to her bed — 'I hear him every night
walking up and down the veranda. Up and down. When he passes my
door he says, "Goodnight, Bertha." He never calls me Antoinette now.
And I dream . . . *Then I beat my fist on a stone* . . . Going away to
Martinique or England or anywhere else, that is the lie' (pp. 93–4 [65],
italics mine).

The stone-masked Rochester is an ambiguous yet shrewd alteration
by Jean Rhys of the stature — the almost Gothic stature — of Charlotte
Brontë's creation. Carnival stone or death-in-life mask expressly mourns
a hunger for the dance of life endangered in hunter and hunted, seen
and perceived with such intensity by Antoinette *alone in all the world*,
so to speak, that she begins to redeem the solitary plague of madness
in herself which — in Jean Rhys's ambiguous novel — is nothing but the
magic of faith in the subsistence of fiery love to redeem the terrors of
the dance when the dance is conscripted into feud and war. The fire-
of-the-war-dance-motif in the foodbearing tree casts its shadow of anguish and pain into Antoinette's plea to Christophine for a desperate
love-potion to bring the enemy (yet lover) in Rochester to heel.

Rochester's stone-mask appears to remain pitiless but it is now *psy-
chically* affected by the creature he hunts into madness, the creature to
whom he 'dies' after the honeymoon rape she endures. His symbolic
conquest of her, yet 'death', his Anglo-Saxon stoicism, is now all at
once altered by her uncompromising madness and perception of *his*
needs in *hers*. Nothing — neither duty nor respectability nor the obser-
vance of codes of behaviour so formidably constructed into moral imperative in *Jane Eyre* — possess quite the tone of necessity — that runs
deeper than appearance and logic — with which Jean Rhys imbues Antoinette, and in so doing makes her madness essentially human, and
Rochester's hardhearted sanity a psychical debt to her inimitable passion that borders on precarious divinity. Hard-hearted sanity it is in him
because it remains unconscious of the debt he owes to her that is
infinitely greater than the rich dowry, in money terms, she brings to
him.

* * *

I have spoken of Rochester's indebtedness to Antoinette but she too
is indebted to shadowy, almost nameless, myths within the inarticulate
heterogeneity of the Caribbean. May I pause for a moment to explain,
in some degree, what I mean by 'inarticulate'. There is no short-cut
into the evolution of new or original novel-form susceptible to, im-
mersed in, the heterogeneity of the modern world. If we genuinely
accept the view of variables of unconsciousness a handful of eminent
thinkers has advanced, it will assist us, I think, to realize that the evo-

lution of complex imagery secretes such variables of or from necessity, and that that secretion may sustain a wealth of beauty when it is perceived in its 'true' light by different eyes in other places or by other generations. That is the price of originality. Mere academic lip-service to creativity is useless whatever its militancy or piety or apparent clarity. Jean Rhys's significance, in 'inarticulate' Caribbean complex, lies in the immaterial, subtly visible, pressure to alter the rock-fast nineteenth-century convention Rochester symbolizes. *Wide Sargasso Sea* is written in nineteenth-century realist convention and as a consequence the subtle, ambiguous, poignant, disruptions of homogeneous cultural model may be misunderstood or misconceived as the logic of pathos, as a psychology of pathos, whereas their significance, as dialogue with untamable creation myth, is much more profound in their potential bearing on the evolution or original Caribbean or South American novel form.

We have already looked at the Arawak/Macusi foodbearing tree in which is secreted both physical need or hunger and a hunger for creation or renewed visions of creation. We need also to remember Jean Rhys's Anglo-Saxon yet Caribbean antecedents (she was born of a Welsh father and a white *creole* mother in the West Indies). Her imaginative insights are 'white' and 'black' in tone in their appeal to the catholicity of West Indians in whom are combined primitive religions —such as Haitian vodun myth (or obeah)—and fertile Christianity. Obeah is a pejorative term but it reflects significantly a state of mind or embarrassment in both black and white West Indians, a conviction of necessary magic, necessary hell-fire or purgatory through which to re-enter 'lost' origins, 'lost' heavens, 'lost' divinity.

It is Christophine, in particular, Antoinette's Haitian nurse, who symbolizes the forbidden obeah strain in Jean Rhys's imagination. It is she (Christophine) who mixes the love-potion for Rochester which Antoinette cries for, when Rochester finds himself torn by rumours of madness in her family and steels himself (or relapses into his ingrained Protestant rationality and fear of heretical ecstasy) to 'widow' or abandon her like a dead man, however formally alive, as he paces the verandah.

In strict Catholic context (in contradistinction to alchemy and catholicity of origins) we need to glance at the convent in which Antoinette spent an impressionable period after her home was set on fire by angry ex-slaves, a fire that precipitated a massive nervous breakdown in her mother Annette (also known as Bertha) and occasioned the death of Pierre, the youngest member of the family. It is here, in the convent, that we begin to perceive the depth of subversion or ecstatic hunger which begins to envelop Antoinette, to prepare her, so to speak, to become the bride of a spiritual obeah bull. (It may be intuitive design but no accident, I believe, that during the physical and doomed hon-

eymoon between rock-fast Rochester and subversive Antoinette, before
he abandons her and widows her on the marriage-bed, he is given a
cup of 'bull's blood' by Christophine (p. 71) [50] as a token of his
conversion yet retreat into 'stone' or 'relic' of ecstasy. Thus one of the
portents of *psychical* alteration or stone-mask or death-mask is the obeah
bull Rochester unconsciously wears or consumes. All this is so subtly
woven into the tapestry of the fiction, it is never explicit, never stated,
but lurks, so to speak, between the images in the alchemy of the word.)

It is in the convent that Antoinette is drawn into contemplation of
the elusive life of precarious divinity in 'relics' (p. 45) [32] as if in
anticipation of the 'relic' of 'stone' Rochester wears after his symbolic
death, a relic that undergoes *immaterial* re-animation in the 'sky of
fiction' above 'the tree of life in flames' (p. 155) [112].

The 'tree of life' appears in the convent and bears 'a rose from the
garden of my Spouse' (p. 45) [32]. It is a rose saturated with indebtedness to the black soil of dreams in which Antoinette seeks 'to hold
up (her) dress, it trails in the dirt, my beautiful dress' (p. 50) [36]. The
dream continues:

> We are no longer in the forest but in an enclosed garden—I stum-
> ble over my dress and cannot get up. I touch a tree and my arms
> hold on to it. 'Here, here.' But I think I will not go any further.
> The tree sways and jerks as if it is trying to throw me off. Still I
> cling and the seconds pass and each one is a thousand years. 'Here,
> in here', a strange voice said, and the tree stopped swaying and
> jerking. (p. 50) [36]

Antoinette's indebtedness to 'rose of my Spouse' and to 'soil of
dreams' is a preparation for a dialogue with the 'other' in the garden,
the strange dark terrifying voice she never forgets within her and without her. It is a voice that celebrates and mourns her coming betrothal
and marriage. For it is less Rochester and more symbolically herself
who drinks 'the cup of bull's blood' which Christophine gives to her
insensible bridegroom. It is a voice that pushes her beyond the walls
of convent or school in which she shelters. In the darkness of that voice
the nuns in the school have 'cheerful faces' she resents (p. 50) [00].
They do not understand her magical 'spouse'. They do not perceive a
richer catholicity beneath the formal Catholic education they dispense.
Their religion—however evocative in its relics—has become respectable ritual, undemanding ornament, as undemanding or frozen in pos-
ture as the Greek or Roman goddess of the milky way from whose
breasts the white fluid spurts across the sky into the calloused mouth
of a consumer age.

Whereas the 'bull's blood' of art and religion is imagistic confession
of cross-cultural labyrinth in which the transformation of apparently
incorrigible bias in all mankind tests and challenges the imagination

beyond ideal formula. It is the stigma of complex earthiness and exile from convention. It is raised with anguish into the stars. The incompatibility of consumer callouses and bull's blood holds out madness (if one is enmeshed in a religion of sensuality and mindless academic spirituality) or alternatively it holds out a genuine spiritual sensation that one needs to lose one's ritual soul to find life, and that this means prayer of such depth it is directed to god, however masked by innumerable or magical relics; Antoinette's madness is no less than a hidden surrender of life, a loss of soul to find soul, disrupted ritual callous, disrupted voice of convention in order to find (or begin to find) the voice in the foodbearing tree from the 'spouse' of otherness.

These considerations are never explicitly stated in *Wide Sargasso Sea*. Their authenticity lies, I find, in a measure of confused force and anguish that drives her to say to one of the nuns before she leaves the convent: 'I dreamed I was in Hell.' The nun replies: 'That dream is evil. Put it from your mind — never think of it again' (p. 51) [36].

But she was to dream and think of it again and again. And the nun's incomprehension is woven into Bertha's shroud and damnation. It was Jean Rhys's passion to illumine by fire Antoinette's essential humanity and precarious divinity.

* * *

SANDRA DRAKE

Race and Caribbean Culture as Thematics of Liberation in Jean Rhys' *Wide Sargasso Sea*†

"A zombi is a dead person who seems to be alive or a living person who is dead. A zombi can also be the spirit of a place. . . ." (*WSS*, 107)[1] [64].

". . . I have noticed that negroes as a rule refuse to discuss the black magic in which so many believe. Voodoo as it is called in Haiti — obeah in some of the islands, another name in South America." (*WSS*, 107) [64].

"Is there a ghost, a zombi there?" I persisted.
"Don't know nothing about all that foolishness."
— Rochester queries the Black servant Baptiste, *WSS*, 106 [63].

† From "All That Foolishness / That All Foolishness: Race and Caribbean Culture as Thematics of Liberation in Jean Rhys' *Wide Sargasso Sea*," *Critica* 2, no. 2 (Fall 1990): 97–112. Reprinted by permission. Page references to this Norton Critical Edition are given in brackets after Drake's original citations.
1. All quotations are from the edition published in 1966 by W. W. Norton & Co., Inc., New York.

"I hear one time that Miss Antoinette and his son Mr Sandi get married, but that
all foolishness. Miss Antoinette . . . won't marry with a coloured man. . . ."
— the Black servant Amélie to Rochester, WSS, 121 [73].

Jean Rhys's highly acclaimed novel *Wide Sargasso Sea* is recognized
as a brilliant psychological portrayal. It is also a historical novel, whose
central issue is textualized in the portrait of Antoinette Cosway. That
issue is the abolition of European plantation slavery and the transition — or failed transition — to some other set of social relations that
would constitute a viable Caribbean identity. Since the Voyages of European conquest, European hegemony in the Americas has been practically structured and symbolically cast in terms of the European
patriarchal family. Black human beings were bought and sold; women
were legally at the economic mercy of their male relatives, and Native
Americans (Amerindians) — when not exterminated — were violently
subjugated. Indigenous American, Black slave, woman, colonial, and
child were considered by the colonizer, to differing degrees, to be by
nature dependent and inferior. The relationship of all these groups to
the colonizer is at stake in *Wide Sargasso Sea*.

                            *   *   *

The novel stands on its own. It could have been written without the
relationship of intertextual referentiality of *Jane Eyre*. But this level of
literary intertextual referentiality invokes and is paralleled by the extra-
textual referentiality to Europe's historical narrative. In that narrative,
the Caribbean since the Voyages of European Conquest is construed,
and thus constructed, in the terms of a dominant literary and historical
discourse that takes Europe as origin and reference point. So too does
Wide Sargasso Sea have a European origin-reference point: *Jane Eyre*.
It is in this regard deliberately derivative, an imitation, a copy. Its very
existence derives from the English classical literary canon. It is a novelistic colony. Rhys chose this fact as its starting point. Depending on
whether that is also its conclusion, *Wide Sargasso Sea* narrates a pa-
thetic personal defeat, or an ironic triumph — literally speaking, a triumph of cultural irony.
    The satisfactory resolution of Antoinette Cosway's crisis of identity
can come only with a satisfactory resolution of her relationship to the
part of the Caribbean that is not derived from Europe — in this novel,
especially the Black Caribbean. This relationship is embodied in her
relation to three characters: Christophine, Tia, and Sandi Cosway. Antoinette, who is Caribbean, colonial, and female, is reduced in the
course of the novel to economic and psychological helplessness by European colonialism and patriarchy. History and culture, inscribed as
narrative, plot structure, and symbolism, make the story ultimately one
of triumph, accomplished in the terms of the Afro-Caribbean belief
system. Accomplished with the assistance sought, given, and fully ac-

cepted at last. Given by Christophine, former slave, obeah-worker, model of female independence, arisen from almost unbelievable oppression. Maternal protector and ancestor-figure in the profound African sense. This reading is sustained by the centrally Afro-Caribbean structure of the novel, by the quintessentially Afro-Caribbean figure of the zombi, and by the Africa-derived beliefs about the relations between the living and the dead that the concept of the zombi—the living-dead—incorporates. The Caribbean in *Wide Sargasso Sea* is not exotic backdrop but the central character of the book, embodied in Antoinette Cosway, zombi, "the spirit of a place" (WSS, 107) [64]. Battled for in the dramatic heart of the novel, Part Two, where Christophine and Rochester wage their contest, and Sandi Cosway makes his final plea. Christophine on the ground of the emergent free Black Jamaican peasantry, Sandi Cosway on the ground of the emergent free Jamaican bourgeoisie—but still Black too: Sandi's father, Mr. Alexander,

> "Very wealthy man. He own three rum shops and two dry goods stores. . . . I hear one time that Miss Antoinette and his son Mr Sandi get married, but that all foolishness. Miss Antoinette a white girl with a lot of money, she won't marry with a coloured man even though he don't look like a coloured man." (WSS, 121) [73]

The struggle for Antoinette's survival—for the survival of the Caribbean—against European patriarchy and empire, the struggle for a voice to reinscribe a past history and construct a future out of genuine indigenous cultural materials—to become something other than a copy—is the struggle Christophine and Sandi fight and apparently lose to Rochester at the end of part Two. I argue in this article that it is fought and won, in flame, at the end of Part Three. * * *

Only superficially chronological, *Wide Sargasso Sea*'s true organizational harmony occurs on the level of Antoinette's psyche. And its true action is not the dramatic series of chronologically related events, but the working out of the answer to two questions (and one dream, dreamed three times): "Qui est là?" and "You frightened?" In Part Three, dream and question converge, for the question "You frightened?" is asked and answered in the dream: the answer to "Qui est là?" gives the answer to "You frightened?" In the first occurrence of the dream, Antoinette is immobilized with fear. In the second occurrence, she submits to fate. In the third occurrence, she asks for, receives, and accepts assistance, takes action, and personal and cultural liberation is achieved.

* * *

The centerpiece of the section and of the book is this violently sexual affair. Buried deep within Part Two, however, counterpoised to it, is the affair of love and friendship between Antoinette and Sandi Cosway. Such a relationship is shameful, often tabu in the slave and post-slave

Americas, hardly spoken of. Some critics and commentators seem even
to have missed it. "You ask Miss Antoinette, she tell you" (WSS, 121)
[73]. Rochester never does ask; Antoinette never tells. "Your wife know
Sandi since long time. Ask her and she tell you. But not everything I
think" (WSS, 125) [75]. Rumor, from hostile witnesses. Confirmed —
as distortion — by Antoinette when she is able to speak, at last, in Part
Three. Sandi's name is mentioned only once by Antoinette in Part Two,
and not in the context of sex at all, but of friendship: as, at the end,
she remembers it in the context of love. Counterpoised to her relationship with Rochester in every way. "I did not love her," Rochester says.
"I was thirsty for her, but that is not love" (WSS, 93) [55]. Egalitarian
and not hierarchical, the relationship with Sandi, remarkably undiffer-
entiated by gender-prescribed behavior; playful, happy and assured.
Rochester narrates about Antoinette:

> . . . one afternoon when I was watching her, hardly able to believe
> she was the pale silent creature I had married . . . her blue chemise
> . . . hitched up far above her knees, she stopped laughing, called
> a warning and threw a large pebble [at a crab under water in a
> pool]. She threw like a boy, with a sure graceful movement. . . .
> As we were walking home I asked her who had taught her to throw
> so well. "Oh, Sandi taught me, a boy you never met." (WSS, 88)
> [52]

In the patriarchy, unencumbering garments and sure aim are attributes of boys. In Sandi's company, though, Antoinette has been able to
develop them. And certainly there is something between Antoinette and
Sandi. Before her marriage, and apparently renewed during the time
in Jamaica when she and Rochester, definitively estranged, await their
sailing to England. But a relationship only acknowledged by Antoinette
in her "narratorial consciousness" years later, in her imprisonment at
Thornfield Hall, when she looks at her red dress, so closely connected
with fire and with her own Caribbean identity, and recounts:

> . . . I was wearing a dress of that color when Sandi came to see
> me for the last time.
>   "Will you come with me?" he said. "No," I said, "I cannot."
>   "So this is good-bye?"
>   "Yes, this is good-bye."
>   "But I can't leave you like this," he said, "you are so un-
> happy. . . ."
>   We had often kissed before but not like that. That was the life
> and death kiss and you only know a long time afterwards what it
> is, the life and death kiss. The *white* ship whistled three times.
> . . . (WSS, 185–86 [109–10]; emphasis mine.)

Red for the Caribbean, white for white England, Antoinette, Christophine, Sandi, the Caribbean: they come together as Antoinette sees
the firecolored dress, like the one she wore with Sandi, run across the
floor of her English prison like flame. Very soon, she will dream ("quite
soon now I will remember . . ."), foresee it run up and out a candle
to bring down Thornfield Hall, rise up as a wall of flame between her
and "that man who hated me" (that is, Rochester; WSS, 189 [112]),
see it stand as a wall cast down to protect her by Christophine when
Antoinette calls to her for help and accepts it fully, at last, when it is
given.

   * * * In Part Two Antoinette, in despair over her emotional aban-
donment by Rochester, seeks Christophine's help. Antoinette is the
narrator.

> "But I cannot go. He is my husband after all."
> She [Christophine] spat over her shoulder. "All women, all col-
> ours, nothing but fools. . . . [I have] no husband, I thank my God.
> I keep my money. I don't give it to no worthless man."
> "When must I go, where must I go?"
> "But look me trouble, a rich white girl like you and you more
> foolish than the rest. A man don't treat you good, pick up your
> skirt and walk out. . . ."
> ". . . you must understand I am not rich now, I have no money
> of my own at all, everything I had belongs to him."
> "What you tell me there?" she said sharply.
> "That is English law." (WSS, 109–10) [66]

This declaration establishes Christophine as a model of female in-
dependence-and self-reliance for Antoinette, who responds to her situation in the most basic terms of female subjugation in the patriarchy:
"He is my husband after all" (WSS, 109) [66]. Christophine recognizes
the economic basis of women's independence in society; and having
lived most of her life as a slave — under British law — she perhaps has
an especially good vantage point for developing skepticism about that
legal system. This remarkable passage asserts several things: a similarity
of women's oppression by men across color lines, the psychological
mechanism being their dependence upon romantic acceptance by
men, the practical mechanism being financial dependence upon them.
Implicitly, it suggests the advantages of not being "a rich white girl"
but a former slave woman for understanding the undesirability of dependence and submission and ties together the equation in the novel
between the colonial state, the female state, and the state of the slave
of either sex — in a conversation that also emphasizes the differences in
the two women's situation.

But Antoinette rejects Christophine's shrewd psychological assess-

ment of Rochester and her sober advice on how to extricate herself. "I
stared at her, thinking, 'but how can she know the best thing for me
to do, this ignorant, obstinate old negro woman, who is not certain if
there is such a place as England?' " (WSS, 112) [67]. What Antoinette
wants is an obeah charm to make Rochester love her. Yet when Christophine yields to her distress and agrees, Antoinette shies from this step.
Even while taking it, she tries to distance herself from it, with money.
Christophine comments on her fear, with scorn and hurt at being paid:

> "So already *you frightened eh?*" And when I saw her expression
> I took my purse . . . and threw it on the bed.
> "You don't have to give me money. I do this foolishness because
> you beg me — not for money."
> "Is it foolishness?" I said, whispering and she laughed again, but
> softly.
> "If *béké* say it foolishness, then it foolishness. *Béké* clever like
> the devil. More clever than God. Ain't so?"[2] (WSS, 117 [70–71];
> emphasis mine in line one.)

Antoinette recalls her departure from Christophine after she has ob-
tained the charm: "Nearby a cock crew and I thought, 'That is for
betrayal, but who is the traitor?' She did not want to do this" (WSS,
118) [71]. The deepest answer, in terms of the structure of the novel,
is that Antoinette — here, as in the scene with Sandi — has betrayed
herself.

Blacks may be afraid of obeah, and they may pay the obeah worker,
but this fear and this payment, unlike Antoinette's, is not a denial that
they belong to the culture. Worst, Antoinette wants to use the spell to
complete her assimilation to England and to whiteness. She is afraid
of Afro-Caribbean obeah, but she agrees to what she herself identifies
as "obeah too" — Rochester stealing her name: "My name is not Bertha," she says to Rochester. "Why do you call me Bertha?" (WSS, 135)
[81]. "Bertha is not my name. You are trying to make me into someone
else, calling me by another name. I know, that's obeah too" (WSS, 147)
[88]. But on page 135 [81] she says, "It doesn't matter." Not until she
is nearly ready to triumph does she say, "Names matter, like when he
wouldn't call me Antoinette and I saw Antoinette drifting out the window . . ." (WSS, 180) [106–07]. Here, again, the situation of women
under the patriarchy, and of Blacks, is compared. The slaves lost their
African names, and often took surnames of their owners. Women, in
the British patriarchy, take the surnames of their husbands. Rochester
goes a step farther and seeks to remove Antoinette's given name too. If

2. *Béké* is a word found in various forms throughout the Americas; it is used by Blacks to refer
to Whites. Sometimes it is "Backra." In Toni Morrison's novel *Song of Solomon* (1977) we
find a verse handed down in Virginia since slavery: "Solomon, don't leave me here / Buckra's
arms to yoke me . . ."

she had married Sandi Cosway, she would not have lost either of her names, for she and he carry the same family name.

Christophine says to Antoinette at the point that is perhaps the younger woman's emotional nadir, " 'Get up, girl, and dress yourself. Woman must have spunks to live in this wicked world' " (WSS, 101) [60]. She thus enjoins "dress" upon her as an activity that is like girding on armor — part of a fight for life in a world especially hostile to women. Years later, in her prison in Thornfield Hall, Antoinette acts on her words when she demands of her keeper Grace Poole:

> "Have you hidden my red dress . . . ? If I'd been wearing that he'd have known me."
> "Nobody's hidden your dress," she said. "It's hanging in the press." (WSS, 185) [109]

And a bit farther on:

> ". . . I held the dress in my hand wondering if they had done the last and worst thing. If they had *changed* it when I wasn't looking, if they had changed it and it wasn't my dress at all — but how could they get the scent?" (WSS, 186) [110]

She has finally claimed the red dress of her Caribbean identity. And it is this dress that becomes not noun/object/passivity, but agent of liberating activity, in an Afro-Caribbean idiom:

> I . . . looked from the fire to the dress [that is lying on the floor] and from the dress to the fire. . . . It was as if the fire had spread across the room. It was beautiful and it reminded me of something I must do. I will remember I thought. I will remember quite soon now. (WSS, 186–87) [110–11]

What she must do, and will remember quite soon, is to put to the torch Thornfield Hall, the symbol, in the heart of empire, of that alliance she has made with Rochester, and symbol of her denial of the Caribbean. She does this in her symbolic capacity of zombi.

Like many Caribbean beliefs, the zombi is of African origin. A number of African societies thought that *bokors* — "sorcerers" who turned great powers to evil ends — could reduce persons to automatons and force them to do the *bokor's* will, including work for him. A number of Caribbean scholars have been intrigued with the question of why this belief should have attained much greater importance in the Caribbean than in Africa, coming to its fullest development in Saint Domingue, later Haiti. Laroche and Depestre suggest that it was because it was so well suited to represent the condition of plantation slavery in the Americas.

The zombi's state is symbolic of alienation on the social as well as the individual level:

The zombi is, in reality, the legendary, mythic symbol of . . . a spiritual as well as physical alienation; of the dispossession of the self through the reduction of the self [to a mere source of labour]. . . . They [Haitian writers] see in [the zombi] the image of a fearful destiny which they must combat; a destiny which is at once collective and individual.[3]

Rhys indicates explicitly the importance of the zombi figure in her novel, and makes an equation between "ghosts" and "zombis" that points up Antoinette in that role. " 'Is there a ghost, a zombi here?' " Rochester asks Baptiste (WSS, 106) [63]. And, finally, there is the "ghost" reputed to haunt Thornfield Hall, a rumor about the imprisoned Antoinette—a "ghost" Antoinette thinks she sees when she catches sight of herself in a mirror. But Rhys does more than equate. The action of the novel and the interpretation of its ending require an understanding of the complex nature of the zombi, whose state is "a symbolic one . . . at the centre of a network of symbols concerned with life and death" (E&T, 56).

The zombi's state is understood as a kind of sleep. In Wide Sargasso Sea, England, personified in Rochester, is responsible for Antoinette Cosways's course from increasing reduction to the condition of zombi, to apparent death (insanity) shortly to be followed by real, self-inflicted death (the disposal of the no-longer useful colony) provided for by the ending of Jane Eyre — but, as I argue, really to the waking, revenge, and life which in Haitian belief signal the zombi's freeing itself from its master.

*   *   *

Antoinette's "real" death is not a demented suicide in the flames of Thornfield Hall. That projected death is really only the one "everyone knows about"—through reading Jane Eyre, the European colonizer's writing of history, and of Antoinette's history. Her "real" death is her subjugation by Rochester—by the colonizer—the long slow process of her reduction to the zombi state chronicled in the novel.

But there is more to the Afro-Caribbean belief in the zombi. Related to it is an attitude toward death that is African in origin and fundamentally at variance with European belief. The African attitude, characteristically, is that the living and the dead may almost be said to form one community. The spirit-world of the ancestors continues to function as part of the living community. Throughout the Americas, including the United States, it was well known that many Africans captured as slaves were often willing to commit suicide or to take terrible risks in rebellions because they believed that after death their souls would re-

3. Maximilien Laroche, *Exile and Tradition* (Dalhousie, Can.: Dalhousie University Press, 1968), p. 56. Hereafter referred to as *E&T*.

turn to the ancestral lands in Africa. The belief has been poignantly expressed in the poem by the great Haitian writer Jacques Roumain: "The slow road to Guinea [a term frequently used by Africans in the Americas to mean "Africa"] Death will take you there." But in this belief system death is not an end or even a disengagement from life: it is more a change of state. And the dead ancestors are more powerful than the living. They are revered as the source of strength for both individual and community. Hence the importance, at the end of the novel, of this sentence in Antoinette's narration of the third occurrence of her dream: "I called help me Christophine help me and looking behind me I saw that I had been helped" (WSS, 189) [112].

Mirrors, repetitions, and reversals. In Part Two, narrated by Rochester at the honeymoon house, a passage occurs that is reversed, and narrated by Antoinette in part Three, to form the novel's conclusion. In Part Two we find:

> I thought I knew what would happen and what I must do. I found the room oppressively hot, so I blew out most of the candles and waited in the half darkness. (WSS, 145) [87]

Significantly, this passage occurs immediately before Christophine and Antoinette, very close, go into the bedroom together and shut the door. Rochester feels them close off against him. He hears them speaking, and singing, in patois, and thinks: "But whatever they were singing or saying was dangerous. I must protect myself" (WSS, 150) [90].

Rochester fears that Christophine will intervene on Antoinette's behalf when Antoinette appeals to her for help. She does so in the honeymoon house and, much later, in the corridors and on the battlements of Thornfield Hall. After the scene in the honeymoon house, Rochester concludes that he must separate Antoinette from Christophine, from the Black Caribbean.

The concluding passage of the novel, narrated by Antoinette, reads as follows:

> Now at last I know why I was brought here and what I have to do. There must have been a draught for the flame flickered and I thought it was out. But I shielded it with my hand and it burned up again to light me along the dark passage. (WSS, 190) [112]

Never, since she threw a stone as Sandi taught her, has Antoinette spoken with such authority and assurance. More than Rochester: he *thinks* he knows; she *knows*. A moment before, like Rochester in the passage quoted above, Antoinette too—a *béké*—is uneasy and threatened by fire and heat. The quotation in which she calls on Christophine for help continues:

I called help me Christophine help me and looking behind me I saw that *I had been helped. There was a wall of fire protecting me* but it was too hot, it scorched me and I went away from it. . . . (WSS, 189 [112]; emphasis mine.)

Antoinette has progressed from fearing the power of the Afro-Caribbean and moving away from its protection, to becoming not only mistress and user of the flame, but *its* protector: "I shielded it with my hand and it burned up again to light me along the dark passage."

The reversal — stylistically inscribed — is a textualization of the theme of the zombi, a literary acting-out of a belief about its nature. For Laroche writes that the zombi is the incarnation of the only "truly feared death," but that its fate "is reversible and thus transitory" (*E&T*). Furthermore, "Salt is the agent which renews the awareness of life, the antidote to the spell which brought on the state of zombification. *It is similar to divine fire* . . ." (*E&T*, 56; emphasis mine).

Antoinette calls on Christophine for protection: she uses the answering fire but backs away from its power. This behavior repeats her request for Christophine's help on the honeymoon island and her simultaneous using of it and distancing herself from it. But there are two significant differences between the episodes. The second time, she does not interpose the British "idol" ("Gold is the idol they worship" WSS, 188 [111]). And, the second time, she is asking for protection from Rochester, not for assistance in drawing closer to him.

And, as the novel's conclusion indicates, Antoinette becomes keeper, mistress, and protector of the divine flame that brings freedom — becomes a fit "daughter" of Christophine.

She is able to accomplish this by finally answering the two questions personal and social history have set her as her life work: "Qui est là?" and "You afraid?" They are asked, and answered, in the course of the third occurrence of her dream. It constitutes an awakening to the realities of colonialism, cast in the terms of the zombi. As Depestre puts it: "The history of colonisation is the process of man's general zombification. It is also the quest for a revitalizing salt capable of restoring to man the use of his imagination and his culture" (*E&T*, 56). If zombis taste salt, ". . . the fog enveloping their minds is immediately dispelled and they become suddenly aware of their enslavement" (*E&T*, 51). This discovery arouses in them an immense anger and an uncontrollable desire for revenge. As Rochester reads in part Two, zombis "cry out in the wind that is their voice, they rage in the sea that is their anger" (WSS, 107) [64].

Again, the text transmutes cultural belief into individualized experience and thought with marvellous skill.

'Nobody's hidden your dress,' she [Grace Poole] said. . . . As soon as I turned the key [to the press] I saw it hanging, the colour of fire and sunset. The colour of flamboyant flowers. 'If you are buried under a flamboyant tree,' I said, 'your soul is lifted up when it flowers. Everyone wants that.'

She shook her head but she did not move or touch me.

The scent that came from the dress was very faint at first, then it grew stronger. The smell of vetivert and frangipanni, of cinnamon and dust and lime tress when they are flowering. The smell of the sun and the smell of the rain.[4] (WSS, 185 [109])

Frangipanni, vetivert, cinnamon and lemon are the Caribbean salts which awake the zombi from its slumber. The red dress which Antoinette fears "they" have taken from her — that act which she calls "the last and worst thing," to change its smell — steal the freeing salts which confirm her identity — she sees transmute itself, to flame; and she identifies it, in the comment quoted, with the flamboyant tree. Antoinette converts Thornfield Hall itself into a flamboyant (flaming) tree; her own soul rises up as it "blooms."

The zombi, awakened, takes revenge in flame. But in burning Antoinette-zombi, she also frees Antoinette for her real life — her reverse trip back across the wide Sargasso Sea — "the slow road to Guinea, Death will take you there." In Roumain's classic novel of Haitian peasant life, *Masters of the Dew*, one of the characters declares, to general community agreement: "Life is life. . . . life is an eternal return. It is said that the dead come back to Guinea and that death itself is only another name for life" (quoted in *E&T*, 56–57).

Antoinette's third and final dream is the locus of her awakening. She is able to accomplish this by finally answering the two questions set her by her personal and historical situation: "Qui est là?" and "You frightened?" It is accomplished, stylistically, by yet another repetition and reversal — mirror-imaging — of a scene from Part One: the burning of Coulibri.

Then, not so far off, I saw Tia and her mother and I ran to her, for she was all that was left of my life as it had been. We had eaten the same food, slept side by side, bathed in the same river. As I ran, I thought, I will live with Tia and I will be like her. Not to leave Coulibri. Not to go. Not. When I was close I saw the jagged stone in her hand but I did not see her throw it. I did not feel it either, only something wet, running down my face. I looked at her and I saw her face crumple up as she began to cry. We stared at each other, blood on my face, tears on hers. It was as if I saw myself. Like in a looking-glass. (WSS, 45) [27]

This is a remarkable scene on several counts. Though a situation of genuine social tension, it has also been prepared for in an almost pa-

4. For a discussion of the Amerindian element in Rhys's use of the legend of the flamboyant tree, see Wilson Harris's *Explorations: A Selection of Talks and Articles, 1966–1981*, edited with an introduction by Hena Maes-Jelinek (Mundelstrup, Den.: Dangaroo Press, 1981).

rodic manner: Mason has commented that the drums have been beating. " 'The natives are restless.' " Yet, Antoinette bolts *towards* "the natives," not away from them. She correctly intuits that that is the direction not just of her past but of her future. Yet in one of the most painful scenes of the book, apparently of brutal rejection of white by black, it is made clear that the little girls are equally hurt. Physical, emotional: one bleeds, one weeps. And that apparent rejection has been prepared for, too, in the earlier fight at the pool, where Antoinette has rejected Tia before Tia rejects her, and in racial terms, by calling her a "nigger." Yet it could hardly be made clearer that Antoinette and Tia are — not simply in a relation of ego and alter-ego — but the same person. Even the names are variants of each other. "It was as if I saw myself. Like in a looking-glass." And the scene of resolution, in Part Three, is a mirror-reversal of this sharp division and separation by race, class, and wealth, and conflates the fight at the pool and the scene with the stone in a final scene of reconciliation.

In her dream, Antoinette stands on the battlements of Thornfield Hall:

> I heard the parrot call as he did when he saw a stranger, Qui est là? Qui est là? and the man who hated me was calling too, Bertha! Bertha! The wind caught my hair and it streamed out like wings. It might bear me up, I thought, if I jumped to those hard stones. But when I looked over the edge I saw the pool at Coulibri. Tia was there. She beckoned to me and when I hesitated, she laughed. I heard her say, You frightened? And I heard the man's voice, Bertha! Bertha! All this I saw and heard in a fraction of a second. And the sky so red. Someone screamed and I thought, *Why did I scream?* I called 'Tia!' and jumped and woke. (WSS, 190) [112]

This is the penultimate paragraph of the book, followed by the passage already quoted where Antoinette declares that she knows what she must do, takes a candle, shields the flame, and slips out of her attic prison.

The two questions are here brought together *in the dream*. Antoinette asks them of Tia — that is of herself for it is her dream — and answers them in an action where she jumps into her deepest self and *wakes* — the term for a zombi coming out of a trance. She then possesses herself of the divine fire, of vengeance and self-reclamation.

Because, in Afro-Caribbean belief, the zombi state is transitory and reversible; because, in the words of Roumain, the Haitian novelist and poet, "life comes round again," because "death is only another name for life," Antoinette's life and death, in the context of Afro-Caribbean belief, acquire a far different significance from that accorded them from a Western perspective only. And this is why she is *not* dead at the end of *Wide Sargasso Sea*. The novel's end is not the "end" of "Bertha Mason" — Rochester's creation — in *Jane Eyre*.

In achieving this clarity of decision and action, the novel reads as victory over death itself by changing the cultural and belief system from a European to an Afro-Caribbean one. Antoinette, in accepting Christophine's wall of flame, Depestre's "revitalizing salt" capable of restoring human imagination and culture, takes her place in an American tradition — and an Afro-American tradition, in the wider sense.

Haiti's history and Afro-Caribbean culture hold unique symbolic value for the Caribbean as they did for Afro-American slaves in the U.S. Haiti was the only country in the Americas where slaves successfully revolted against their European masters. They burned the plantations, as Coulibri is burned, as Antoinette burns Thornfield Hall, organized and then sustained themselves through a revolution and a terrible war that lasted twelve years. They held the forces of Napoleon himself at bay, and established the second independent nation in the hemisphere. And throughout this long ordeal, they organized and sustained themselves in terms of an African idiom, reinterpreted according to the American condition:

> We know that the Haitian War of Independence began with a voodoo ceremony: the oath of Bois-Caïman sworn by slaves who were determined to gain their freedom or die, and who pledged therefore to fight the colonisers to the death. . . . (Depestre, in *E&T*, 54.)

As long as she herself rejects the root culture of her native America, which at its substratum — its "bottom line" — is so deeply African in origin — as long as she remains oriented to Europe — Antoinette Cosway is at Europe's mercy. In Rochester's terms she is "Antoinette-marionette"; in the Afro-Caribbean idiom, she is a zombi. But when she accepts Christophine, and her protective, purging, and empowering gift of fire, and answers Tia's "You afraid?" by merging with her, by acknowledging Tia as at the heart of her own identity, Antoinette gains the strength of that Afro-Caribbean idiom, as the Haitians drew strength from the Vaudoûn oath at Bois-Caïman. Her finally victorious struggle against European-colonial imposition of the zombi state — her ultimate regaining of an identity stolen by cultural imperialism — becomes, in Laroche's terms, an American myth in an African-derived idiom; her final realization and action become an American battle against a European colonialism.

* * *

The point is not whether zombis are "real" or not. Any more than the point is whether the Christian beliefs referred to in the novel are "true." The point is that, ever since Europe colonized the Americas,

militarily defeated Africa, and heavily populated the Americas with African slaves, African beliefs have been derided as foolishness. And the
idea of equal relations between people of Caucasian and of African
descent has been derided as foolishness. Today, 150 years after Antoinette Cosway thought to embroider her name, the date and her American location — Spanish Town, Jamaica, 1839 — in "thread of fire,"
probably every society in the Americas is still afflicted by these crippling
attitudes, and faces as a result profound social and cultural problems.
And, today, U.S. society and "high culture" and the U.S. educational
system at every level is so impoverished by this attitude towards African
and Afro-American culture that it has deprived itself of the knowledge
it needs to understand its own indigenous culture and history — and its
own literature.

With that deft mirror-imaging, reversal and variation on word and
phrase so characteristic of the novel's style, Rhys relates the attitudes of
the European-dominated Americas to both persons and cultural beliefs
of African origin:

> "Is there a ghost, a zombi there?" I persisted.
> "Don't know nothing about *all that foolishness.*"
> — Rochester queries the Black servant Baptiste,
> WSS, 106 [63].

> "I hear one time that Miss Antoinette and his son Mr Sandi get
> married, but *that all foolishness.* Miss Antoinette a white girl . . .
> she won't marry with a coloured man. . . .
> — The Black servant Amélie to Rochester, WSS, 121 [73].

> "Is it foolishness?" I said, whispering.
> — Antoinette to Christophine, WSS, 117 [70].

Rhys's novel also assures — and warns — us that we will never understand either her novel or the deeply African, American culture from
which it springs, until we hear the fine irony in Christophine's words
of response to Antoinette's question. Christophine, illiterate old Black
obeah woman/conjure woman. Former slave:

> "If *béké* say it foolishness, then it foolishness. *Béké* clever like the
> devil. More clever than God. Ain't so?"

LEE ERWIN

[History and Narrative in *Wide Sargasso Sea*] †

The dramatic appearance of Jean Rhys's *Wide Sargasso Sea* in 1966, after a quarter-century of silence and obscurity for its author, has tended to occult the less romantic facts of the book's two-decade-long gestation. That the novel had been partly written by 1945 is significant, however. The years between the mid-forties and the mid-sixties having encompassed much of the break-up of the British Empire, and *Wide Sargasso Sea* alone of all of Rhys's novels engaging fully (though at a certain historical remove) with her background in the British West Indies, we might look for a difference in the way the subject of a narrative written at one time or another reads itself into history by means of that narrative. Elizabeth Nunez-Harrell has suggested that *Wide Sargasso Sea* might be a "response to the nationalistic mood [in the West Indies] of the late '50's and '60's," which could have led Rhys to wish "to assume her place in West Indian literature" (287). Yet the novel seems rather to inhabit a limbo *between* nationalisms; it exists as a response to the loss, rather than the recovery, of a "place-to-be-from," enacting a struggle over identity which is a peculiarly modern rereading of West Indian history.

The historical circumstances that set the novel in motion are the Emancipation Act that in 1833 decreed the eventual freedom of the slaves in all of the British colonies and the racial conflicts and social and economic turmoil that surrounded it. As Gayatri Spivak has argued, Rhys takes the risks of writing from the point of view of "the wrong side" in the novel's colonial setting, writing not only from the point of view of Antoinette, the white slave-owner's daughter, but from that of a white Englishman as well ("Production"). Yet, in my view, the greater risk Rhys takes is to suggest an identification between Antoinette (Rhys's revision of Bertha Mason in *Jane Eyre*) in her firing of Thornfield Hall and the ex-slaves who set fire to her family's estate. Besides drawing a parallel between the two events, the novel suggests that it is Christophine's obeah that guides the outcome. Before "Rochester" leaves the West Indies, he is driven by his long last talk with Christophine to cry, "I would give my eyes never to have seen this abominable place." Christophine replies, "You choose what you give, eh? Then you choose. You meddle in something and perhaps you don't know what it is" (557) [96]. Thus, when Antoinette dreams her dream for the third and last

† From " 'Like in a Looking Glass': History and Narrative in *Wide Sargasso Sea*," *Novel: A Forum on Fiction* 22.2 (Winter 1989): 143–58. Copyright NOVEL Corp. © 1989. Reprinted with permission. Page references to this Norton Critical Edition are given in brackets after Erwin's original references.

time, in Thornfield Hall, she cries out to Christophine for help and
sees that she has "been helped" by "a wall of fire" — and we know from
Jane Eyre that Rochester loses exactly what he "chose" to lose. Laid
out in this way, *Wide Sargasso Sea* may seem an exercise in bad faith,
appealing only to any vestige of bourgeois feminism still able to accept
an easy equation between "woman" and "nigger"; yet it is precisely the
problematizing of that equation, and that because it is an aim of the
narrative, that I will suggest drives the novel.

If we lay out the racial issues the novel addresses as they are manifested in its two major narratives, Antoinette's and Rochester's, settler
woman and metropolitan man, it begins to appear that whereas Antoinette sees her own displaced, deracinated condition in terms of historically specific shifts in class and economic power, the Rochester figure
refuses these categories and instead interprets racial difference in moral
and sexual terms, specifically in terms of miscegenation and "contamination." Thus, Antoinette's discourse constantly suggests an interchangeability of racial positions, manifested most obviously in the play
on such terms as "white nigger" and "black Englishman": in a crucial
scene, when in a moment of childhood conflict Antoinette calls her
black playmate Tia a "cheating nigger," Tia's response is,

> "She hear we all poor like beggar. . . . Plenty white people in
> Jamaica. Real white people, they got gold money. They didn't look
> at us, nobody see them come near us. Old time white people
> nothing but white nigger now, and black nigger better than white
> nigger." (470) [14]

Thus, too, the burning of the restored estate house after Antoinette's
mother's remarriage suggests that what might be called racial hatred is
class-specific in origin:[1] "The black people did not hate us as much
when we were poor. We were white but we had not escaped and soon
we would be dead for we had no money left. What was there to hate?"
(476) [20]

The fantasmatic dimension of this notion of interchangeability becomes clear, however, when, as the house burns, Antoinette sees Tia
in the crowd and runs toward her thinking, "I will live with Tia and
. . . be like her":

> When I was close I saw the jagged stone in her hand but I did
> not see her throw it. I did not feel it either, only something wet,
> running down my face. I looked at her and I saw her face crumple
> up as she began to cry. We stared at each other, blood on my face,

---

1. The play on such terms as "white nigger" and "black Englishman" may be read as evidence
of the assignment of "racial" attributes to class positions during slavery days (thus "nigger"
[class designation] must be "black" and "Englishman" "white"), and of the disruptive re-
shuffling of those attributions after Emancipation.

tears on hers. It was as if I saw myself. Like in a looking-glass. (483) [27]

Having been subjected both to her mother's attempts to *make* her "white" and to the metropolitan view that the effort is a failure, Antoinette will try to be black, not an anomalous "white nigger." But the violence with which her wish is met closes off that position as well.

*   *   *

The play between racial terms in Antoinette's narrative, each replacing and suppressing the other by turns, has implications for the novel's temporal structure as well. The linear time of history, which would inevitably recall the history of slavery to consciousness and thus restore the racial differentiation Antoinette's narrative seeks to disrupt, must be foreclosed. Thus her two narratives are defined by only two temporal points: ". . . now and at the hour of our death . . . that is all we have" (491) [34]. Such a foreclosure is most obvious in the chronology of Antoinette's early life: if she is nearly seventeen in 1839, as the date in an embroidery suggests, she would have been born in 1822 or 1823, well before the Emancipation Act, which did not go into effect for another year after its enactment in 1833 and even then decreed from four to six years' further service for slaves (now "apprentices") before they were to be "full free." Any memory of slavery and, for that matter, any memory of her father — avatar of that history — whose death must also have been very recent ("Emancipation troubles killed old Cosway?") is excised from Antoinette's narrative. This excision is duplicated in her mother's speech: "Why do you pester and bother me about all these things that happened long ago?" (468) [12]. The subsequent traversal of that gap by Christophine's references to the old times, then ("New ones worse than old ones — more cunning, that's all"), only marks out what is not there and makes plain the impossibility of any appeal to the past against an equally feared future. It is a past only existing in the narrative in parenthesis: "(My father, visitors, horses, feeling safe in bed — all belonged to the past)" (465) [9].

Antoinette's embroidering the year of her time in the convent thus suggests an attempt to *fix* time, a time which, since the arrival of the "new Luttrells," has been set in motion again: "I woke next morning knowing that nothing would be the same. It would change and go on changing" (472) [16]. The new people's laughter at Antoinette wearing Tia's dress and the subsequent frenzy of activity that it sets in motion in her mother, culminating in the remarriage, suggest that, as in Rhys's *Voyage in the Dark* (1934), racial differentiation is the motor of time. Antoinette's entry into time will be marked out by her being made, like her nearly eponymous predecessor Anna, "not like a nigger."

The novel's figure for its own narrative is Antoinette's dream, with its twice-deferred (but foregone) conclusion ("Not here, not yet") and its dreaded but inevitable forward propulsion. The dream in a sense suggests a subsuming of the "Rochester" narrative under Antoinette's, her narrative enunciating a trajectory in the dreams that it will be the task of the Rochester narrative to fulfill. A notable feature of Rochester's narrative, especially in contradistinction to Antoinette's, however, is precisely its fascination with and search for the "past." His first words ("So it was all over . . . Everything finished, for better or for worse") already suggest a backwards trajectory for his narrative; the difference between his and Antoinette's is encapsulated in their first recorded conversation:

> I looked at the sad leaning cocoanut palms, the fishing boats drawn up on the shingly beach, the uneven row of whitewashed huts, and asked the name of the village.
> "Massacre."
> "And who was massacred here? Slaves?"
> "Oh no." She sounded shocked. "Not slaves. Something must have happened a long time ago. Nobody remembers now." (495) [38]

The shift to Rochester's voice upon their marriage suggests that Antoinette's own narrative is now ended, having reached its proper nineteenth-century conclusion ("for better or for worse"), and that his desire now drives the narrative. In these first moments, this shift also associates his pursuit of the "truth" of the past with naming and with desire, in a revision of the Gothic that puts the male into a threatening and alien environment (if not house, the house at Granbois being a pathetically fragile excuse for a Gothic manse) to seek out its secret. "What I see is nothing—I want what it *hides*—that is not nothing" (509) [52].

* * *

Thus, too, the £30,000 Rochester gains in the West Indies only calls up its missing or shadowed origins, the missing name that alone could transform mere money ("They bought me, *me* with your paltry money") into "man's estate," motivating the search for the "truth" of the past that drives Rochester's narrative. In fact, Rhys has made free with the Brontë text at exactly this point, with the effect of separating Antoinette's money from her *own* father's name and attaching it only to the name of her stepfather. The whole Cosway lineage is "layered" onto a background that in *Jane Eyre* only includes the Masons, of whom "Bertha" is a biological daughter and "Richard" a son. The addition of the Cosway figure does two things in *Wide Sargasso Sea*: first, because Antoinette's mother is not even "old Cosway's" first wife, but the wife of his late years, their marriage and thus Antoinette's and her brother's origins are already coded as "sexual excess," which in fact killed the old man off; second, because Antoinette's mother then herself remarries, the name of the father, of Antoinette's father, that is, is lost. Thus, the problem of Rochester's search is that, unlike the English Name-of-the-Father, which is notable for its exclusive provenance, being assumable in its full privileges only by the first-born son, this name is nowhere and everywhere, disseminated all over the islands and yet vanishing again under scrutiny.

*   *   *

The only defense against such "contamination" is the law, which alone can fix origins (Stephen Dedalus's "legal fiction") and control the otherwise uncontrollable; Rochester's narrative seems to enact a constant punning on Christophine's phrase the "Letter of the Law" (471) [15], as he turns repeatedly to the scribal to fix his position vis-à-vis the father and the past. Thus, for example, the newly married Rochester imagines a letter to his father expressive of his rage at that father's rejection and manipulation of him, but then actually pens a quite different letter that is correct and lifeless in the extreme, expressive only of a submission to patriarchal authority. The scene of the letter's writing, moreover, is the "little England" in the house at Granbois that acts as a patriarchal parody of the beleaguered heroine's room at the center of the Gothic castle:

> It seemed crowded after the emptiness of the rest of the house. There was a carpet, the only one I had seen, a press made of some beautiful wood I did not recognize. Under the open window a small writing desk with paper, pens, and ink. "A refuge" I was thinking when someone said, "This was Mr Mason's room, sir, but he did not come here often. He did not like [Granbois]." Baptiste, standing in the doorway to the veranda, had a blanket over his arm. . . .
> "It can be cold here at night," he said. Then went away. But the feeling of security had left me. I looked around suspiciously. The door into her room could be bolted, a stout wooden bar pushed across the other. This was the last room in the house. . . . There was a crude bookshelf made of three shingles strung together over the desk and I looked at the books, Byron's poems, novels of Sir Walter Scott, *Confessions of an Opium Eater*, some shabby brown volumes, and on the last shelf, *Life and Letters of* . . . the rest was eaten away.[2] (501) [44]

Perhaps, then, the role of Daniel Cosway/Boyd in the narrative is almost literally a battle over the letter. He enters the narrative, of course, by *means* of a letter, perhaps explaining further why Rochester gives his accusations such immediate credence * * * Daniel [does not] ultimately offer any clearer "road" to the truth of the past; although his use of the name Cosway and his ability to "read write and cypher a little" (516) [58] give him access to Rochester, the past he describes

---

2. Another figure of the lost patronymic, as Spivak (1986) suggests.

reveals rather his exclusion from the patronymic than his place in its inscription. Not only does the portrait of his father that he has hanging on his wall reveal a more properly imaginary doubling in the image of, not Cosway, but a "coloured" father, but his recital also reveals his exclusion from the symbolic order, inscribed, literally, on Cosway's tomb:

> "My father old Cosway, with his white marble tablet in the English church at Spanish Town. . . . It have a crest on it and a motto in Latin and words in big black letters. I never know such lies. . . . 'Pious,' they write up. 'Beloved by all.' Not a word about the people he buy and sell like cattle." (532) [73]

Thus the Name-of-the-Father, graven in stone and in the English church, closes off the history of slavery days as thoroughly as does Antoinette's narrative, its refusal to inscribe the history of the Daniels and *their* origins being figured in old Cosway's silencing Daniel by hurling an inkstand at him (533) [74].

The "trouble," finally, in which Rochester's narrative finds itself, then, is that, as in his visit to Daniel, his attempts to fix any "authorized" history are repeatedly lost again in the slipperiness of "mere" orality; just as Père Lilièvre's house, another stone monument, is obeah-ized, and its history transmuted into a little black girl's scream, so the authority of the book Rochester takes up upon his return to Granbois slides away into the bafflement it expresses at the "lies," "nonsense," and finally "poison" ("which cannot be traced") of obeah itself. In the same way, then, Rochester's narrative itself immediately gives way again to Antoinette's, which recounts her visit to Christophine to ask for exactly that obeah potion/poison, which will make Rochester love her again upon swallowing it.

His reaction, however, both to the "poison" and to her words is momentarily to *lose* his literacy — "I thought, I have been poisoned. But it was a dull thought, like a child spelling out letters of a word which he cannot read" — but then to vomit, rejecting both Antoinette's story and the racially tainted sexuality the potion and their resultant love-making represent to him. Afterwards, he retraces without difficulty the path from the ruined house back to Granbois ("I never stumbled once"), suggesting a restoration of scribal history; in fact, practically the next thing he does is to write the letter that will set in motion the final triumph of the law:

> I wrote a cautious letter to Mr Fraser on the third day.
> I told him that I was considering a book about obeah and had remembered his story of the case he had come across. Had he any idea of the whereabouts of the woman now? Was she still in Jamaica? (545) [85–86]

Yet first Rochester must perform another purification; his making love to Amélie suggests a final attempt to displace the contamination he has taken from Antoinette back onto her across the "thin partition" dividing them from her bedroom, where he knows she is lying and hearing all. No wonder then that afterwards he finds Amélie's skin "darker, her lips thicker than [he] had thought," and that he has "no wish to touch her" (544) [84].

Amélie's subsequent exit from the novel anticipates the more significant departure of Christophine herself, who is both the locus of a powerful orality and the purveyor of its materialization as what is poison to "*béké*"; it is Rochester's effort to bring that "poison" into the provenance of the law ("I kept some of that wine") that finally drives Christophine out of the novel. Rochester's letter to Mr. Fraser has, in fact, called up what might literally be termed the "Letter of the Law" that his narrative has sought[.]

*   *   *

The aim of the "Rochester" narrative (if not of the Rochester *character*), realizing its earlier projections ("Not yet"), thus becomes clear. In *Jane Eyre*, Rochester's father must be dead in order for Rochester to return to England and thus for Antoinette/Bertha to be locked away, that is, to come to occupy "Jane's space." In *Wide Sargasso Sea*, the causality is reversed, and Antoinette must be put away (as Freud says what is repressed is *left to itself*) in order for the father to die, for Rochester to assume that father's position and his own patrimony. The renunciation demanded in such an assumption of the Name-of-the-Father is evident most of all in the final few pages of Rochester's narrative, in which Antoinette's *voice* (her "chatter") reemerges more often, and more seductively, than anywhere else in part 2, and in which she is implicitly metaphorized as the "treasure" about which it is "better not to tell."

The subsequent return of Antoinette's voice as narrator ironizes the novelistic conventions of *Wide Sargasso Sea*'s generic forebears: that is, the "ending" of part 1, namely marriage, didn't work out, to say the least, and so the "second moment" of Antoinette's narrative will enact the *other* endings that Rachel Blau DuPlessis has argued close nineteenth-century narratives about women, that is, madness and/or death. The "two moments" of Antoinette's narrative, moreover, standing on either side of the "copula" represented by Rochester's narrative, here seem to constitute an algebra that, translated into a sentence, would read "Marriage *equals* madness and death." Indeed, Antoinette's dread at the approach of a suitor at the close of part 1 and the subsequent nightmare that anticipates her sexual initiation (if we call upon Freud, although it is hardly necessary, to tell us what those steps mean) have already suggested that part 3 is not an alternative, or contingent, ending, but the realization of a trajectory that the narrative has promised to fulfill from very early on.

The forward propulsion of the narrative, however, is simultaneously pulled in the other direction, since, once she is within the third-floor room at Thornfield Hall, Antoinette's whole effort seems to be to *re-member* an imperative somehow already dictated in the past:

> But I looked at the dress on the floor and it was as if the fire had spread across the room. It was beautiful and it reminded me of something I must do. I will remember I thought. I will remember quite soon now. (572) [110–11]

Thus the anticipation that structures part 3 is anticipation inverted, in a sense, in that it is an anticipation of a memory.

*   *   *

In a sense, the conclusion may be read as exemplary of the limitations imposed by the individualism of the genre within which Rhys is working; hence its reduction of the collective violence of a group of freed blacks (in response, in part, to a plan to import "coolie," Indian, labor, as the planters did in the years following Emancipation) to the leap of a lone madwoman with a candle. Yet, even in this last, most reduced field of action, the narrative implicates others in Antoinette's plight; the taciturn Grace Poole from *Jane Eyre* is here given a voice as well, and her brief conversation with Leah suggests that she and others too are locked up, though not by direct force as is her "mad" charge (for whom Grace's first action, significantly, is to light a fire):

> *After all the house is big and safe, a shelter from the world outside which, say what you like, can be a black and cruel world to a woman . . .*
>   *The thick walls, she thought . . . keeping away all the things that you have fought till you can fight no more. Yes, maybe that's why we all stay — Mrs Eff and Leah and me.* (566–67 [106]; italics in original)

Nor is Antoinette alone, it seems, in dreaming her last dream:

> Someone screamed and I thought, *Why did I scream?* I called "Tia!" and jumped and woke.
>   Grace Poole was sitting at the table but she had heard the scream too. . . . [She] came over and looked at me. I lay still. . . . "I must have been dreaming," she said. (574) [112]

But to break the novel down into its constituent narratives is to leave unanswered the question of how those narratives are implicated with each other and thus what the aims of the novel as a whole might be.

I have suggested that Antoinette's narrative realizes itself in the Rochester narrative, subsuming it, in a sense, a point that seems at first to
be irreconcilable with the multiplicity of voices I have claimed speak
in the novel; yet the aims of Antoinette's narrative are in fact realizable
not within that narrative alone but *only* within the novel as a whole,
which, far from making the second narrative simply a kind of ventril-
oquist's dummy for a single voice, instead works by occupying both
points of view. This is not to suggest a reconciliation or synthesis of the
two views; on the contrary, it is to argue that the impossible desire
evident in Antoinette's narrative, that is, to occupy a racial position not
open to her, can only realize itself in the gaze of the Other, in an
attempt to perform the impossible feat of seeing herself from the place
from which she is seen.

That "Antoinette," as a textual point of view herself, cannot realize
such an aim is evident in the still-uncontrollable dualism suggested in
her final leap — any attempt to realize the fantasy of a merging of
"Antoinette" with "Tia," or blackness, can only annihilate that which
wishes to occupy the other place. Only the gaze of England, acting as
a third term to stabilize the transitivism of the other two, to turn that
transitivism into an identification, can effect such a "merging." An early
West Indian critic of the novel has made a similar point:

> Telling the story of their brief marriage from Rochester's point of
> view also enables Jean Rhys to make the crucial point about An-
> toinette, and the white West Indian: their fundamental closeness
> to the Negroes in feeling and sensibility, despite the barrier which
> history has erected between them. This is a fact to which both
> races in the society are blind, but which is very noticeable to the
> observer who stands outside of the history which divides them.
> (Look Lai 47)

Thus, whereas the first English gaze to which Antoinette is subjected,
through its perception of incongruity in a "white" girl wearing a "black"
girl's dress, sets the process of racial differentiation in motion, Rochester's gaze, contaminated as it is by his own desire, dissolves the bar
between the two terms and enables their at least partial merging by
investing them with common features, at times invisible * * * at times
visible:

> [Antoinette] raised her eyebrows and the corners of her mouth
> turned down in a questioning mocking way. For a moment she
> looked very much like Amélie. Perhaps they are related, I thought.
> It's possible, it's even probable in this damned place. (535) [77]

*   *   *

Wide Sargasso Sea, then, with its "double vision," both "writes a life"
for the "poor ghost" Rhys saw in *Jane Eyre* (Vreeland 235) and places

that life under English eyes, in an attempt to construct an identity for
it impossible in the colonial setting itself. Such a double focus also
marks out the particularly modern genesis of the novel, despite its historical setting; *Wide Sargasso Sea* seems born of a historical moment
when the older nationalism of the largely absentee English settlers of
the early nineteenth century, who would have looked unquestioningly
to England for their cultural identity, has given way, in the century
between emancipation and the time of Rhys's beginning the novel, to
the "identity crisis" of the white former colonial at the end of empire.
Perhaps by 1966 Rhys did wish to take her place in an emerging West
Indian literature — but the novel itself is structured around precisely the
absence of the unquestioned national identity that grounds Jane Eyre's
struggles in the "healthy heart of England." Instead, *Wide Sargasso Sea*
finally textualizes the historical dimensions of the "Rhys woman's"
alienation.

WORKS CITED

DuPlessis, Rachel Blau. *Writing Beyond the Ending: Narrative Strate-
gies of Twentieth-Century Women Writers.* Bloomington: Indiana
University Press, 1985.
Look Lai, Wally. "The Road to Thornfield Hall: An Analysis of Jean
Rhys' *Wide Sargasso Sea.*" In *New Beacon Reviews: Collection One,*
edited by John La Rose, 38–52. London: New Beacon Books, 1968.
Nunez-Harrell, Elizabeth. "The Paradoxes of Belonging: The White
West Indian Woman in Fiction." *Modern Fiction Studies* 31 (Sum-
mer 1985): 281–93.
Rhys, Jean. Typescript of *Wide Sargasso Sea.* 1965–66. Item I.A.21 in
the Jean Rhys Collection of the McFarlin Library, University of
Tulsa.
———. *Wide Sargasso Sea.* 1966. In *Complete Novels,* 463–574.
Spivak, Gayatri Chakravorty. "The Production of Colonial Discourse:
A Marxist-Feminist Reading." Course presented as part of the Con-
ference on Marxism and the Interpretation of Culture. University of
Illinois at Urbana-Champaign, 1983.
Vreeland, Elizabeth. Interview. "Jean Rhys: The Art of Fiction LXIV."
Paris Review 21 (Fall 1979): 218–37.

CAROLINE RODY

Burning Down the House: The Revisionary Paradigm
of Jean Rhys's *Wide Sargasso Sea*†

"Whether I have any *right* to do it is a question which I'll face later."
— Jean Rhys, *Letters*

* * *

In imagining a life story for a neglected, marginal character in a
famous book, one must, indeed, attempt a "convincing" supplement or
simulacrum[1] but Rhys's performance of the life of Bertha Mason goes
beyond verisimilitude to demonstrate dramatic and suggestive revisionary uses of intertextuality. Regardless of whether one knows in advance
whose life *Wide Sargasso Sea* is meant to represent, one closes the book
with an eerie feeling about the way Rhys has written a text directly
"into" literary history — an effect intensified by the way the novel's three
sections move the reader progressively "into" contact with Brontë's text.
Rhys seems to have stirred the literary universe into animation, to have
summoned up and then actually changed literary history.[2] We can no
longer think of our cherished heroine Jane Eyre in the same way, having glimpsed her once as Rhys's mad Bertha glimpses her: a pale girl
humming to herself as she walks warily through the house of a man
who, unbeknownst to her, has already destroyed the life of the woman
who watches her pass. And of course, we can never think of Bertha
Mason in the same way, having read of her lonely youth and spurned
love, and remembering most of all the way she stands at the end of
Rhys's narrative, doomed but triumphant, torch in hand, about to fall
once again to the death literature originally gave her — but not just yet.
Forever resisting the self-sacrificial closure of her plot in *Jane Eyre*,
forever forestalling the closure of Rhys's narrative, Antoinette/Bertha in
her last lines advances in furious opposition to her pre-scripted fate,
leaving her potential act, and her end, to our memories of literary
history.

Experiencing this transformation of our interior canon, readers cannot help but be conscious that it is all due to the act of another reader,
like ourselves — one Jean Rhys, who felt an injustice in English literary

† From *Famous Last Words: Changes in Gender and Narrative Closure*, edited by Alison Booth
(Charlottesville: University of Virginia Press, 1993) 300–25. Reprinted with permission of the
University Press of Virginia. Page numbers to this Norton Critical Edition are given in brackets
after Rody's original citations.
1. Some other experiments in the genre include John Gardner's *Grendel*, Tom Stoppard's *Ro-
sencrantz and Guildenstern Are Dead*, and Robert Browning's "Caliban upon Setebos."
2. This essay proposes that Rhys dramatizes the changing of literary history more aggressively
and self-consciously than occurs in the normative processes of literary inheritance and influence theorized by T. S. Eliot in "Tradition and the Individual Talent," or by Harold Bloom
in *The Anxiety of Influence* (New York: Oxford Univ. Press, 1973) and elsewhere.

history and took it upon herself to rewrite it. The implicit will to action of a self-authorizing reader underlies this revisionary text, but becomes most pronounced in the final section, when the sad Creole girl Antoinette is transported to England and becomes the madwoman Bertha, stalking Rochester's Thornfield Hall, plotting and taking her revenge. In this ending Rhys's recuperated and transformed Antoinette/Bertha seems to rebel against her own previous writtenness, to declare the right to tell her "true" story. Her ending plays out the end of Bertha's *Jane Eyre* plot twice: Antoinette/Bertha first dreams of burning down the house, then awakens to interpret her dream's message and set forth, at the very last, intending to carry out its incendiary act. This neatly recapitulates the process by which a person reads a text, interprets it in her own terms, and sets out to rewrite it. Antoinette/Bertha thus embodies in her defiant ending the triumphant revisionist act of Rhys the reader turned writer.

Because of this complex of suggestion at the close of a revisionary novel, I want to claim the rebellious heroine Antoinette/Bertha as our greatest figure for the resisting female reader[3] — a prophetic figure for Rhys to create in 1966, just before so many female readers began to reject their marginalized relationships to writing and, inspired by a visionary impulse, to reenter the big house of English literature with a flame. Not to burn it down, as in Bertha's old, self-immolating plot, but rather, as Rhys's heroine puts it in her last words, "to light me along the dark passage"[4] — to help with some difficult rereading ahead.

With the rereaderly heroine Antoinette/Bertha as its avatar, *Wide Sargasso Sea* "enters and reimagines Brontë's text," in Ellen Friedman's words, "glossing and subverting, reversing and transforming it."[5] Reading and resisting a nineteenth-century novel, Rhys's text manifests early instances of the feminist, postcolonial, and postmodern sensibilities that have come to characterize late twentieth-century experimental fiction, and fusing these revisionary aesthetics, offers in its final section a revisionary paradigm for literary inheritance itself.

I

* * *

Changing the name of Brontë's "Bertha Antoinetta Mason," Rhys creates the defining emblem of her revision, a renaming that makes the original seem to conceal several lies. Bertha, the name of the notorious she-monster of English literary history, in Rhys's text becomes a name imposed arbitrarily by Rochester on his wife to distance her from the

3. See Judith Fetterley, *The Resisting Reader: A Feminist Approach to American Fiction* (Bloomington: Indiana Univ. Press, 1978).
4. Jean Rhys, *Wide Sargasso Sea* (1966; rpt. New York: Norton, 1982), p. 190 [112]. Subsequent quotations from this edition will hereafter be cited parenthetically by page number.
5. Friedman, "Breaking the Master Narrative," p. 117.

name of her mother Annette (Antoinetta in Brontë), whom he believes to be an insane alcoholic. By moving the lovelier name (in its more accurately French form) from second to first position, Rhys at once accuses Rochester of committing an elemental injustice and makes her text seem to correct it: the erasure of the name of the mother from that of the heroine.[6]

Strikingly, Rochester remains completely nameless throughout. Called only "the man," "he," "husband," and "the man who hated me," this speaker is given no body — no physical description whatsoever. Thus "castrating" the formidable lord of Brontë's English manor, Rhys rewrites him as an anonymous, lost voice in a place where the very existence of his fatherland is questioned.[7] That this revision devalues and "suppresses the name of the father"[8] is also evident in the diminishment of "Mason" to the name of mere step-relatives of Antoinette's, and the invention of a patronym, Cosway, which too is devalued, insofar as it becomes the recurrent sign for the island's shameful slaveholding history. Discrediting the father, Rhys recuperates the mother, who, mentioned in *Jane Eyre* only to suggest a genetic source of Bertha's madness, is shown here to have been *driven* mad, like Antoinette, and under similar circumstances of loss, violence, and exploitation in marriage. While the loss of her mother affiliates Antoinette with orphaned Jane Eyre, unlike Jane, Rhys's heroine remembers her mother well, and remembers too the pain of losing her. By reimagining Brontë's monster in the island of her birth, Rhys recuperates for Antoinette/Bertha's plot "a space of privileged contact with the maternal" for which Jane Eyre might have longed.[9]

Thus, while Rhys's revision refuses and transforms patriarchal elements of *Jane Eyre*, its elaboration of the mother-daughter romance

6. See Deborah Kelly Kloepfer, *The Unspeakable Mother: Forbidden Discourse in Jean Rhys and H.D.* (Ithaca, N.Y.: Cornell Univ. Press, 1989), p. 145. Ronnie Scharfman notes that *Antoinette* is "a combination of Annette and 'toi': a hidden built-in bond between mother and daughter" (see "Mirroring and Mothering in Simone Schwarz-Bart's *Pluie et vent sur Telumée Miracle* and Jean Rhys's *Wide Sargasso Sea*," *Yale French Studies* 62 [1981]: 103).

7. Chantal Delourme contrasts this "castrated," nameless man with the "nom-roc," "nom-forteresse," that dominates *Jane Eyre* (see "La Mémoire fécondée. Réflexions sur l'intertextualité: *Jane Eyre*, *Wide Sargasso Sea*," *Études anglaises: Grande-Bretagne, États-Unis* 42, no. 3 [1989]: 262; translations of Delourme are mine).

   Christophine doubts the existence of England because she has never seen it herself (p. 111) [67]. It should be noted that Rhys's depiction of Rochester is not entirely unsympathetic; for example, she carefully delineates his legal victimization as a second son under the law of primogeniture.

8. Molly Hite, *The Other Side of the Story* (Ithaca, N.Y.: Cornell Univ. Press, 1989), p. 40. See also Gayatri Chakravorty Spivak, "Three Women's Texts and a Critique of Imperialism," in *"Race," Writing, and Difference*, ed. Henry Louis Gates, Jr. (Chicago: Univ. of Chicago Press, 1986), p. 271.

9. Kloepfer links Antoinette's madness to Rochester's "denial of her language, her name, and her matrilineage" (*The Unspeakable Mother*, pp. 145–46). But by privileging the maternal, Kloepfer adds, Rhys's rewriting "forces the son to experience . . . [female] psychological and linguistic space" (p. 158). Similarly, Nancy Harrison reads in *Wide Sargasso Sea* the construction of a distinctively female fictional space she calls a "woman's text" (see Harrison, *Jean Rhys and the Novel as Woman's Text* [Chapel Hill: Univ. of North Carolina Press, 1988], p. 6).

inscribes a cherished "daughterly" intertextual relationship with Bron-të's text.[1] A novel born of a "fundamental conversation" between female authors, *Wide Sargasso Sea* privileges dialogue between female characters, and carefully parallels the structure of its mother text, taking Antoinette through a series of haunting dreams parallel to Jane's.[2] Nancy Harrison contends that Rhys "pick[s] up the strand of the dream-text of Brontë's novels as the structural principle of her own," inscribing a "sharing-of-the-text" with *Jane Eyre.* The dreams can be seen to weave a female countertext around the "masculine text" of Rochester's plot "from dreamer to dreamer, woman to woman," blending intimate "conversation" with aggressive revision.[3] We shall return to the implications of this female "relational" style of revision.

* * *

III

The first two parts of Rhys's feminist, postcolonial revision of *Jane Eyre* construct a revised female subjectivity that, in order to undo falsehoods and tell a "true" story, revives the mother and foregrounds female relationships across racial boundaries, representing its identity as relational and interracial while registering the continual experience of division and loss. The brief final section, in which Rhys's text "explodes into Brontë's novel,"[4] and the heroine stalks Rochester's house, sets *en abyme* a representation of the text's revision as a whole, and concentrates the revisionary agendas implicit in the first two parts in the act of a furious woman with a torch.

* * *

We may wonder what stopped Rhys from changing the fate Brontë originally gave to Bertha Mason. While she was rewriting, why not cook up an escape from the house, a return to the islands, or at least a moment of articulate defiance to Rochester or of warning to Jane?

---

1. Delourme, "La Mémoire fécondée," p. 260. Among the details of plot and setting Rhys repeats from *Jane Eyre,* Delourme cites in particular the echo of its phrases: "infamous daughter of an infamous mother" is Rhys's modification of Rochester's epithet for Bertha, "true daughter of an infamous mother."

2. Harrison, *Jean Rhys and the Novel,* p. 143. Elizabeth Baer writes that of all Antoinette and Jane's shared plot elements — lost mothers, nurturance by women servants, narratives of painful progress through five named houses, and so on — the most important is their bond as "visionaries" (p. 135). Both heroines' dreams are "submerged text[s]" that recast the romance plot in nightmare form and "nudge the consciousness" of the dreamers (pp. 137–38). Antoinette's final moment of triumph comes, Baer notes, when she "heeds the dream text" in waking life (p. 147). See Baer, "The Sisterhood of Jane Eyre and Antoinette Cosway," in *The Voyage In: Fictions of Female Development,* ed. Elizabeth Abel, Marianne Hirsch, and Elizabeth Langland (Hanover, N.H.: Univ. Press of New England, 1983), pp. 131–48.
   The interpretation of dreams is a major preoccupation of Rhys critics; see also Friedman, "Breaking the Master Narrative," pp. 124–27; Kloepfer, *The Unspeakable Mother,* pp. 154–58; and Mary Lou Emery, *Jean Rhys at "World's End": Novels of Colonial and Sexual Exile* (Austin: Univ. of Texas Press, 1990), pp. 53–59.

3. Harrison, *Jean Rhys and the Novel,* pp. 130–33.

4. Friedman, "Breaking the Master Narrative," p. 118.

Rhys's acceptance of Bertha's martyrdom seems an acknowledgment of the tragic nature of literary history—which is, after all, history. Bowing to the authority of Brontë's plot even while subjecting it to a radical retelling, Rhys frames her intertextual intervention in the irreversible, historic realm in which readers read. But, as Friedman writes, the very illustration that "her precursor has restricted her to a predetermined narrative," is liberating;[5] when the reader turns to part 3 and finds that Antoinette has become imprisoned, doomed Bertha in Brontë's house, Rhys makes vivid the oppressions involved in the inheritance of a tradition, and justifies aggressive rewriting. At the same time, she makes the canonical text seem always to have contained the germ of this rebellion, and all literary history, by extension, seem to contain potential transformation, awaiting the right rereader.

So although the text that opens a space for Antoinette/Bertha in literary history does not save her from her plot's trajectory downward to madness and death, the novel's trajectory is upward, toward liberation. In effect, the novel achieves what Antoinette/Bertha does not, for though they both burn down houses (or demonstrate the will to burn them down) only the novel actually "survives" to stand in a cleared space of freedom, as it were, out on the roof of the house. Resisting the moment of Bertha's original ending, instead giving the force of an ending to the moment *before* the burning, Rhys's unclosed end leaves Bertha's death to the moments after the reader closes her novel and muses in her intertextual memory. In this way, Rhys forces history—that is, Charlotte Brontë—to bear the responsibility of killing Bertha Mason, as Delourme puts it. When *Jane Eyre* "returns to the surface to write the end of the text born of it,"[6] Brontë is, as it were, forced to consummate Rhys's heroine's desire for revenge, but also to reduce it to a functional subplot once again, and to reextinguish a life we have come to value.

IV

How do we understand the implications raised by this rewriting for a model of contemporary literary inheritance? In its challenge to the boundaries of the text, Rhys's revision evidences an aesthetic that would not have been recognized in 1966 as the postmodern. A text about the rewriting of a text, *Wide Sargasso Sea* inscribes a characteristically heightened postmodern consciousness of the time line of literary history: self-consciously belated but daringly, playfully irreverent about textuality in general—as when the madwoman mocks Brontë's book: "This cardboard house where I walk at night is not England" (p. 181) [107].

5. Friedman, "Breaking the Master Narrative," p. 123.
6. Delourme, "La Mémoire fécondée," p. 263.

The postmodern aspects of this rewriting are evident in its subversion of the authority of authorship, its inscription of the adventure of the reader, and its delight in the empowering possibilities of shared knowledge of a literary tradition. Rhys's re-presentation of *Jane Eyre* offers special "readerly" pleasures: we realize "we have seen those passageways and rooms in fiction before";[7] we come upon odd hints that Antoinette "remembers" her impending fate (p. 111) [67]; and we see "the husband" make a quite amazing sketch, childlike and seemingly innocent, of a house and a woman on its third floor (p. 163) [98], and know it is the bare prototype of an atrocity that will blossom into the imaginative profusion of Charlotte Brontë's novel. Treating text as history and history as text, Rhys writes one of the earliest postmodern metatexts. Her heroine Antoinette/Bertha can be seen as a postmodern as well as a feminist and postcolonial rewriter, for she rebels not only against oppressive political structures and literary plots, but against the incarcerating cardboard house itself—characterization, the very condition of writtenness—and exposes, along with the oppressive conditions of patriarchal, colonial existence, the hierarchical enforcements inherent in language.

But if *Wide Sargasso Sea* is a deconstructing daughter, revising *Jane Eyre* so that "the mother-text is maimed and . . . disarmed,"[8] recent criticism reveals a curious and contradictory aspect of the revision. The term *mother text* is sometimes used by critics to refer, as above, to *Jane Eyre*, and at other times to indicate *Wide Sargasso Sea*, as when Mona Fayad writes that "it is the recognition of . . . [Bertha Mason's] effacement that prompts Jean Rhys to produce a 'mother text' for *Jane Eyre*."[9] That Rhys can be seen to produce a mother text for Brontë, so that both texts are "mothers," points to the truly radical aspects of this revisionary act: though written later, it is not a sequel but a "post-dated prequel."[1] Rhys undertakes to tell the story anterior to that of *Jane Eyre*, to write "The first Mrs. Rochester," thus robbing the older text of its position of origin. As Delourme notes, this usurping act transforms the quest for origins into "a fantasy of auto-engenderment": "Just as the mother is born from the daughter, *Jane Eyre* is issued from *Wide Sargasso Sea* and rewrites it." Rhys thus activates intertextuality, in Delourme's terms, as an oscillation between the two texts, "a modality of co-presence," or in Friedman's terms, as an "audacious grafting"[2]—the adjoining of a new trunk to an old branch; which is the mother of the life that then blossoms?

7. Emery, *Jean Rhys at "World's End,"* p. 37.
8. Friedman, "Breaking the Master Narrative," p. 119.
9. Mona Fayad, "Unquiet Ghosts: The Struggle for Representation in Jean Rhys's *Wide Sargasso Sea*," *Modern Fiction Studies* 34, no. 3 (1988): 442.
1. Baer, "The Sisterhood," p. 132.
2. Delourme, "La Mémoire fécondée," pp. 265, 258, 268; Friedman, "Breaking the Master Narrative," p. 118.

This genre of revision differs notably from an "anxiety of influence," the agonistic struggle of an ephebe for individuation from his literary precursor, in the theory of Harold Bloom. A closer analogue is the "female affiliation complex" theorized by Gilbert and Gubar, in which twentieth-century women writers actively seek affiliation with literary foremothers they admire, even while demonstrating anxiety about their influence.[3] Rhys described her mood during the early stages of the writing as "fighting mad," but she also approached her precursor with hesitation and respect, writing in an early letter, "I think of calling it *The first Mrs. Rochester* with profound apologies to Charlotte Brontë and a deep curtsey too." Later, when the work became vexed and stalled, she reflected: "I did not mean to be impertinent about Charlotte Brontë. I admire her greatly. Emily also. And I envy them both more than I can say. Sometimes I have wondered if Miss Brontë does not *want* her book tampered with!"[4]

Though Rhys clearly aimed at a certain independence, announcing in a 1962 letter that her Antoinette "is not *Jane Eyre*'s lunatic at all," she also decided, early in the project that, though "it might be possible to unhitch the whole thing from Charlotte Brontë's novel . . . I don't want to do that."[5] The project to write "not *Jane Eyre*'s lunatic" into a text that yet stays "hitched" to *Jane Eyre* is a "misreading" that, (p)revising Bloom, desires a complex kind of individuation, one that embodies the imaginative fusion of daughter-writer to mother. As the text approaches its ending and the reader reenters Brontë's house, verbal repetitions and structural connections with *Jane Eyre* create an increasing "enlacement of texts," and can be read as "so many denials of separation, of rupture from the body of the other."[6] In the model of influence suggested by Rhys's revision, the daughter's struggle preserves its matrix, the mother text it both ruptures and reengenders.

But critics do not universally acclaim this privileging of relatedness. An article by Michael Thorpe begins, "The crucial question *Wide Sargasso Sea*, as a work of art, might seem to pose is whether it can stand and be judged alone." Thorpe cites the 1966 *New York Times* review in which Walter Allen concludes that the text does not "exist in its own right," for it depends upon *Jane Eyre* "to complement it, to supply its full meaning." Thorpe disagrees with Allen, as does another critic, Arnold E. Davidson, who argues vehemently for the text's wholeness, citing as precedents the famous literary borrowings of Shakespeare,

3. See Gilbert and Gubar, *No Man's Land: The Place of the Woman Writer in the Twentieth Century*, vol. 1: *The War of the Words* (New Haven: Yale Univ. Press, 1988), p. 168–71. Friedman ("Breaking the Master Narrative," p. 117) mentions that Rhys's revision differs from Bloom's model, but does not develop a theory of Rhysian revision.
4. Jean Rhys, *Letters, 1931–1966*, ed. Francis Wyndham and Diana Melly (London: André Deutsch, 1984); Jean Rhys to Selma Vas Diaz, 9 April 1958, p. 157; JR to Peggy Kirkaldy, 9 March 1949, p. 50; JR to Francis Wyndham, 27 September 1959, p. 175.
5. Jean Rhys to Francis Wyndham, 22 August 1962, p. 214, and 29 March 1958, p. 153.
6. Delourme, "La Mémoire fécondée," pp. 264–65.

Joyce, and others.[7] None of these critics considers the possibility that a work might be whole — and "strong," in Bloom's terms — precisely *because* of the way it remains overtly connected to another, that we might approve a style of revision other than that which accords with what is generally termed the male model of individuation. In striking contrast to these three male critics, none of the dozen or more female critics I have read finds it necessary to consider the "crucial" question of the autonomy of Rhys's text; most are interested, rather, in the nature of its attachment to *Jane Eyre*. The suggestively grim and awesome imperative that a text "stand and be judged alone" is alien to the model of inheritance implicit in *Wide Sargasso Sea*, which privileges relationships — to a mother first and, I shall argue, to daughters to come.

V

How oddly perfect it is, one feels upon turning the page to Rhys's part 3, that the narrator who first locates us in Brontë's Thornfield Hall is Grace Poole. Rhys's unfailing readerly/writerly intelligence locates in Grace the very emblem in *Jane Eyre* of erased, unnarrated female existence. A mystery to Jane, she is the servant Rochester uses to cover for his cackling wife, with whom she shares the attic abode.[8] Though she rarely speaks in Brontë's novel, Grace's voice here provides the most "overt signal of the origin" of Rhys's text and "bridges" the two.[9] Speaking to another female servant from *Jane Eyre*, and then to herself, Grace explains why she works for Rochester.

> The house is big and safe, a shelter from the world outside which, say what you like, can be a black and cruel world to a woman. Maybe that's why I stayed on. . . . above all the thick walls, keeping away all the things you have fought till you can fight no more. Yes, maybe that's why we all stay — Mrs. Eff and Leah and me. All of us except that girl who lives in her own darkness. I'll say one thing for her, she hasn't lost her spirit. She's still fierce. I don't turn my back on her when her eyes have that look. I know it. (p. 178) [105–06]

7. Michael Thorpe, "The Other Side: *Wide Sargasso Sea* and *Jane Eyre*," in *Critical Perspectives on Jean Rhys*, ed. Pierrette M. Frickey (Washington, D.C.: Three Continents, 1990), p. 178; Walter Allen, "Bertha the Doomed," *New York Times Book Review*, 18 June 1967, p. 5; Arnold E. Davidson, *Jean Rhys* (New York: Frederick Ungar, 1985), pp. 16–17.
8. In a chapter entitled "Jane Eyre's Fall from Grace" Susan Fraiman reads the figure of Grace Poole as emblematic of a potentially emancipatory counterplot of homosocial bonding among servants and other working-class women in *Jane Eyre*. Fraiman notes that Jane believes for much of the novel — as do her readers — that the frightening noises coming from the attic of Rochester's house are made by a drunken English servant woman. The composite "madwoman" Bertha-Grace can thus be seen to signify both a "native" and a working-class woman's rage. (See Fraiman, *Unbecoming Women: British Women Writers and the Novel of Development* [New York: Columbia Univ. Press, 1993], pp. 88–120).
9. Harrison, *Jean Rhys and the Novel*, p. 133.

Rhys's imaginative leap to a Grace Poole "knowing" of and sympathetic to Bertha follows the logic of female "conversation" and identification-in-otherness that underlies the whole revisionary enterprise. As she tells her story to a female auditor, Grace reveals to the surprised reader that, indeed, she too has a story, and in the clear parallels drawn between her life and Antoinette's — and Mrs. Eff's and Leah's — Grace here seems a candidate for heroine of her own novel, to be written perhaps by a future reader-turned-writer who, following Rhys, might identify with a marginal personage of literary history, and take it upon herself to do some rewriting.

Infinite potential recuperation of women's stories is suggested here and all made possible, the reader realizes, by the emergence into activism of a woman reader. It is thus a dramatically energized, radically participatory literary universe that Rhys's work seems to open for us — for us female readers and writers, primarily, because most of the players here are female (Jean Rhys, Charlotte Brontë, Bertha, Jane, Grace, etc.). One closes the book with the sense that all sorts of possibilities exist, which might now tremble into being, that if Bertha Mason Rochester's story can be told with such poignant, searing strength, there is no limit to the number of other characters whose lives might reveal themselves, similarly surprising and compelling, to our reading eyes; Christophine and her knowledge of "other things" seems a foremost possibility.

* * *

MONA FAYAD

Unquiet Ghosts: The Struggle for Representation in Jean Rhys's Wide Sargasso Sea†

"We can assume that any theory of the subject has been appropriated by the masculine. . . . When she submits to [such a] theory, woman fails to realize that she is renouncing the specificity of her own relationship to the imaginary. Subjecting herself to objectivization in discourse — by being 'female' " (Irigaray 133). In these words Luce Irigaray aptly summarizes one of the basic problems that Jean Rhys attempts to grapple with in her best-known novel, Wide Sargasso Sea. The tale of Antoinette, as indicated by the critics, is the tale of a schizophrenic, a Creole whose search for identity leads to madness, or, as some would advocate, the story of a woman too weak to resist the

† From Modern Fiction Studies 34.3 (Autumn 1988): 437–52. Reprinted by permission of The Johns Hopkins University Press. Page references to this Norton Critical Edition are given in brackets after Fayad's original citations.

onslaught of a strong male such as Rochester, and whose response is escape through madness. Yet such interpretations fail to take into account an important element of the text: its structure. A basic question remains. Why would a writer such as Jean Rhys, dedicated to portraying a female point of view, choose to write more than half the novel from a male perspective?

In addressing this issue, it is important to bear in mind that *Wide Sargasso Sea* is a rewrite of Charlotte Brontë's *Jane Eyre*. Rhys's statement as to the origin of the novel has been much quoted: "She seemed such a poor ghost, I thought I'd like to write her a life" (O'Conner 144). Arnold Davidson interprets Rhys's words as a reminder, a warning: "We need to be reminded how much the story that is there supercedes and suppresses other possible stories in that first one" (43). A story, *any* story, carries within it the possibility of repression, the exorcising of such "ghosts" that would otherwise "haunt" the narrative and intervene with it. In Brontë's text, the well-being of Jane depends on the death of Bertha. In the *hi*story of patriarchy, the well-being of man depends on the reduction of woman to a ghost, a Woolfian "Angel in the House."

Wide Sargasso Sea is an analysis of how such a process has been accomplished, outlining "the processes whereby the Great Mother Goddess becomes sister to the god, wife of the god, mother of the god, becomes Mary the Virgin mother, becomes lady to be worshipped, becomes, finally, prostitute and temptress to be reviled with hatred" (Nebeker 144) and constitutes, as a novel, a means of fighting the silences that pervade woman's history, the "unnatural" silences to which Tillie Olsen devotes her book: "the unnatural thwarting of what struggles to come into being, but cannot" (6). *Wide Sargasso Sea*, then, is a story of the "struggle to come into being" of Antoinette Cosway, the thwarting of that process, and her stubborn insistence on "speaking herself" no matter what the cost may be.

From the beginning, the possibility of establishing a narrative with woman as subject immediately appears tenuous. The text does not begin with an assertion of an "I" that differentiates itself from the other. Instead, that self is presented as objectified by society. "They say," begins the text, a judgmental "they" whose voice, although "they" are women, immediately sets both mother and child *outside* society because they do not confirm to its narrow standards. Yet at the same time the words that give us our first view of Antoinette and her mother tighten around them, classifying them and fixating them so that it is to these words that Antoinette immediately turns to describe her situation. Even at this early stage, Antoinette has begun to relinquish that control which is her only hope for the establishment of an autonomous self independent of social expectations. The lack of differentiation is further aggravated by Antoinette's emotional dependence on the mother, who, significantly, rarely speaks to Antoinette and whose two frames of reference are marked immediately as patriarchal: the mirror, which is, as Sandra M. Gilbert and Susan Gubar point out, the "voice" of male approval (38) and the case of "succession," which the mother freely bestows on the son in acknowledgment of a patriarchal line as opposed to an emphasis on the daughter that would indicate a matriarchal bond. By presenting us initially with Antoinette as a child, Rhys immediately launches us into the basic problems of the self-representation of a female in a patriarchal society.

The novel starts with innocence, the supposed innocence of the beginnings in paradise. But, unlike the controlled beauty of the Edenic setting, overseen by a watchful patriarch, the garden at Coulibri already bears the seeds of corruption, representing a duality that is the "secret" that Rochester is to be so afraid of. The "tree of life" has "gone wild"; there is "a smell of dead flowers"; the orchids are threatening, "snaky looking" or "like an octopus with long thin tentacles bare of leaves hanging from a twisted root" (Rhys 19 [11]). For, as Mary Daly points out, there is no state of innocence for woman in the patriarchal "Hall of Mirrors" (*Beyond God* 195): "The term innocence is derived from the Latin *in*, meaning not, and *nocere*, meaning hurt, injure. We do not begin in innocence. We begin life in patriarchy, from the very beginning, in an injured state" (*Gyn/Ecology* 413). It is thus significant that, when told that the garden had not been wild before and had been cared for, Antoinette finds that she cannot remember the garden any other way than in its present "chaos."

*   *   *

Closely linked with the Edenic symbol is the myth of the fall. Whereas Daly posits that woman is born into patriarchy and is therefore already fallen, Kristeva presents the notion of the fall through the distinction of the semiotic from the symbolic and bases the fall on language itself. The semiotic world is that anterior to naming, or, in other words, the prelapsarian world before the female's fall into patriarchy:

> All converge on the problematic of space, which innumerable religions of matriarchal (re)appearance attribute to "woman" and which Plato . . . designated as the aporia of the *chora*, matrix space nourishing, unnamable, anterior to the One, to God, and consequently, defying metaphysics. (Kristeva 34)

According to this definition, the semiotic is based on a *spatial* dimension of existence, which creates out of the world a location that replaces the matrix space. Thus the fall displaces this space in order to enter the realm of the symbolic, the patriarchal realm "where the phallus functions . . . as the guarantee of sense(s), the 'figure,' the 'form,' the ultimate signifier" (Irigaray 44). In the symbolic realm it is language that defines reality. Because language is by its very nature phallocratic, the reality of woman must necessarily be defined only by her relationship to the phallus, to the One.

Within the safety of the semiotic, language becomes as much a threat as those other intrusions on female space. The first conflict between Antoinette and language comes upon her discovery of her mother's dead horse. Having already recognized the power of language to shape and control reality in a final way, she seeks to obliterate the unpleasant situation by refusing to speak of it: "For I thought if I told no one it might not be true." Similarly, she does not ask her mother what would happen if Christophine left. When a black girl calls her a "white cockroach," she is terrified and creeps away to hide against the wall, a premonition of her own reshaping through language.

Thus Antoinette seeks alternative ways of self-representation. Because the infant's first and foremost means of identification is through the mother, "the child's first mirror" (see Chodorow), Antoinette tries to wipe away the traces of patriarchy from her mother's face: "A frown came between her black eyebrows, deep — it might have been cut with a knife. I hated this frown and once I touched her forehead trying to smooth it" (8) [11]. The mother cannot reflect Antoinette. She has established her alliances clearly. It is Pierre's face that the mother mirrors and not Antoinette's, despite the male's handicap, while Antoinette is made to feel somehow inadequate, lacking. The mother's identification with the male is all the more ironic in that, as a male, he is incapable of speech, and he will never grow to be an adult, so that he becomes little more than a parody of maleness. Moreover, the mother seeks constantly the approval of a real mirror that is to decide her future and hopes of reintegration into society through marriage. The mirror aptly summarizes Antoinette's problem of representation. If her mother is her mirror, then she must seek to define her mother in order to define herself. But her mother eludes definition because there is no criterion other than the patriarchal by which to define her. Antoinette is thus forced to spend her life searching for that mother who will provide her with her own reflection.

But Antoinette's real loss of innocence comes at the moment of her insertion into language. Until that moment the bond between her and Tia had been primarily outside the symbolic, represented by the pool that is their meeting place, and where they face each other naked with no barrier between them. But now, angered by Tia's deviousness, Antoinette resorts to cultural stereotypes to assert her power over Tia.[1]

> "I did do it," I said when I could speak, but she shook her head.
> I hadn't done it good and besides pennies didn't buy much. Why
> did I look at her like that?

1. "Sexist society maintains its grasp over the psyche by keeping it divided against itself. Through stereotyping it harnesses the power of human becoming" (Daly, *Beyond God* 128).

"Keep them then, you cheating nigger," I said, for I was tired, and the water I swallowed made me feel sick. "I can get more if I want to."

"That's not what she hear," she said. . . . "Old time white people nothing but white nigger now, and black nigger better than white nigger." (24) [14]

The word becomes reality. Having set up the barrier of racial hatred between herself and her friend, Antoinette loses Tia permanently by labeling her as other. With that she also loses her close contact with nature because she never returns to the pool. To reinforce this, Rhys times this entrance into patriarchy with the entrance of Mason. Immediately upon returning home Antoinette finds the visitors and "things were never the same" (27) [16]

At first, Antoinette resists this new and concrete onslaught. She maintains a sense of autonomy through labeling Mason "white pappy" and thus retains her link to the black world of her childhood. But the disjunction has begun. With the entrance of Mason, her dreams begin, becoming her new mode of representation. Irigaray explains in *Speculum* the function of dreams as an alternate way of self-expression:

> Dreams . . . recast the roles history has laid down for "subject" and "object." Mutism that says without speech, inertia that moves without motion, or else with the motions of another language, another script. Dream pictography, dream pornography, phonography, and pornography which compensate for the present *paralysis* of the sleeper. (138)

It is clear that Antoinette feels an external paralysis coming on. Yet her dream does not provide an alternative but a confirmation of her situation. In the dream she is literally paralyzed, for "though [she] struggled and screamed [she] could not move" (27) [15–16] There is no "other" language yet, only a rejection of an unnamed fear through throwing off her bedsheet, a physical act that will later be beyond her.[2] It is significant, moreover, that the mother silences her and chides her for disturbing Paul.[3]

Her second dream again identifies her as victim, but here the association with the male is unmistakable. She has fallen into the trap. Hindered by her long dress and thin slippers, the ideal of femininity, she cannot escape the threat of the male. Moreover, it is the male in the dream who speaks to shape reality, for her timid speech consists of questions whereas his words are the commands by which he controls her.

Nevertheless, she struggles to retain some degree of "authority" over

2. Compare this scene where she throws off the sheet to that where Rochester covers her with the sheet (139) [83].
3. Antoinette's younger brother is called Pierre [*Editor*].

the narrative. But although she succeeds in remaining the key speaker/
creator of her narrative in the first section of the novel, her account is
at the very least problematic, reflecting, as Ronnie Scharfmann points
out, "the dysfunction of a system which inhibits Rhys' heroine from
distinguishing whether she is telling her own story or her mother's"
(88). This confusion of identity grows stronger as the novel develops,
culminating in the concluding episode where the mother/daughter
identification is finally broken. Yet as a child whose fixation on her
mother indicates her as yet undeveloped sexuality, she is allowed some
freedom of self-representation, however limited. Upon her initiation
into sexuality, however, this privilege is curtailed, and Antoinette's narrative disappears for one hundred and seven pages, except for the brief
moment in which Antoinette consults Christophine. Henceforth the
narrative comes to be, as Scharfmann analyzes it, permeated by "voices
from the past," voices hauntingly insisting that they bear the "true story"
(103). As her mother had ceased to become a subject and therefore
was subjected to the inventions of others, she, too, grows increasingly
silent. Unable to assert her existence as subject, she is turned into a
ghost "seen" by others but unable to see herself. Her silence is completed by her incarceration between the walls of Thornfield where only
her "goblin" laughter and "savage" screams are audible to Jane Eyre
and where her existence is so erased that Jane mistakes her for Grace
Poole.[4] It is the recognition of this effacement that prompts Jean Rhys
to produce a "mother text" for *Jane Eyre*, which reproduces a woman
whose words have been reduced to nothing more than subhuman
sounds.

At one point it seems that the monastery may provide a model of
selfhood for Antoinette, for at first sight it seems, as Teresa O'Conner
points out, to be "presented as a female cloister embodying love, peace,
and harmony. It is a rarefied and idealized environment where racial
and class differences disappear and it stands in marked contrast to the
male world outside" (177). This is because, O'Conner goes on to explain, "Rhys' ideal mothers — the nuns and the black obeah women —
are never attached to a man; they are outside sexuality and outside the
continual triangles that occur and reoccur in Rhys' work" (178).

The nun's situation can hardly be compared to the obeah's. The role
that the nun/virgin has played in patriarchal society cannot be called
equivalent to that played by the obeah/witch. Rather, the world of the
monastery provides a counter-model for Antoinette, who is constantly
aware that, although this world is "safe," it is false. Antoinette realizes
consistently the shortcomings of this other option for her life. The con-

---

4. Jane describes Bertha's scream as "a savage, a sharp, a shrilly sound' a "fearful shriek," and
   later listens to "a snarling, snatching sound" which she assumes is Poole's: "A shout of laughter
   greeted [Rochester's] entrance; noisy at first, and terminating in Grace Poole's own goblin ha!
   ha!" (Brontë 233).

trast of inside and outside is a constant reminder that although the walls of the cloister, like the walls of Coulibri, form a female space which is enclosing and protective, these same walls can turn against woman by turning into a prison. For Antoinette, cultivating the "female" virtues of modesty and chastity, even the act of washing, become a perverted contrast to her past practice. Where she had once bathed nakedly and openly in the pool in Coulibri, Antoinette must now wash in "the big stone bath where we splashed about wearing gray cotton chemises which reached to our ankles. The smell of soap as you cautiously soaped yourself under the chemise, a trick to be learned, dressing with modesty, another trick" (57) [34].

Similarly, the girls are allowed no looking glass. Again, given the role of the looking glass for Antoinette's mother, this at first appears as a virtue. But the denial of self-reflection for the young adolescents indicates subsuming everything for a higher "good," the sacrificing of the self rather than the developing of it. We are back to the angel of the house once again: self-denying, living for others with no regard for herself. Rhys reinforces this attitude with the intrusion of the Bishop, who patriarchally dictates what is "proper" for the women in the monastery (59) [35].

With the second section we are invited directly into patriarchy and away from Antoinette's struggle to "write" herself. The male narrator is unnamed in the text, significantly so both because he is his own "subject" and thus free from objectification by naming and also because by not being named he becomes omnipotent, the god-like creator of Bertha's narrative text. His version of the tale (by his definition, *the only* version of the tale) is a familiar one, following as it does the history of patriarchy. The "sanity" that he advocates is the sanity of the "norm," or phallocentric order, and any infringement on that "sanity" provokes an immediate attempt to destroy the source of that infringement.

From the beginning Rochester feels himself outside the protection of this order. Threatened by the "wild" nature of the place and by the reminder that white man is not sole master of this miniature world, he seeks to embody his fear in a form that he can deal with. Thus he immediately associates the island with woman, remarking of Amélie: "A lovely little *creature* but sly, spiteful, malignant perhaps, like much else in this place" (65 [38], emphasis mine). The use of the word "creature" already sets the tone for his complete dehumanization of Antoinette, whom he very soon compares to Amélie. The inexplicable feeling of menace he feels towards the island increases minute by minute. The falling rain causes "a feeling of discomfort and melancholy" (67) [39], and "the sea crept steathily forwards and backwards" (66) [38]. Rochester's basic hostility is increased by the fact that he recognizes in the place a matriarchal tendency. His attempt to smile at a naked boy results in the boy crying and thus initiates the cycle that is to end this section with the "nameless boy" crying inconsolably. In response, a woman calls to the child protectively. His second contact, that with the porters, also points to motherhood. When the Young Bull and Rochester mockingly question Emile about his age, he refers them to his mother: "My mother she know, but she dead" (68) [40]. These two incidents provide the model for the rest. Suddenly removed from a totally male-centered society into one in which women play a dominant role, his whole identity comes into question. Inserted into a "mythical" time/place that belongs primarily to woman, his need to control immediately surfaces, and because he equates the island with woman, the proof of his control must come in being able to control the women around him, especially the woman who seems the key to the whole situation, Antoinette.

> He must challenge her for power. . . . Identify with the law-giving father, with his proper names, his desires for making capital, in every sense of the word, to the exercise of his pleasures, with the exception of his pleasure in trading women — fetishized objects, merchandize of whose value he stands surety — with his peers. (Irigaray 140)

Hence the constant refrain in his head as he mentally addresses his father: "Dear father. . . ."

* * * His constant terror of assimilation into the maternal body/island/Antoinette drives him instead to emphasize them as other, completely separate and unidentifiable: "I felt little tenderness for her, she was a stranger to me, a stranger who did not think or feel as I did" (93) [55].

Yet it is not enough for him simply to label Antoinette as other. Before Rochester can begin to exercise his power to ward off the threat of assimilation, he must first rationalize to the reader (for his narrative is clearly aimed at an audience) his rejection of the apparently innocent young woman whom he has married. To do so involves the creation of a series of roles which Rochester attributes to Antoinette but which in fact effectively echoes the gamut of male projections of woman throughout history.

He starts with the basics. Swiftly, writing out a familiar scenario, he starts his projections by creating an Eve. Bound by his Victorian attitude towards sex, he presents in Antoinette a temptation that he, at best, feels ambivalent towards, as seen almost immediately upon their arrival in Granbois:

> Two wreaths of frangipani lay on the bed. "Am I expected to wear one of these? And when?" I crowned myself in one of the wreaths and made a face in the glass. "I hardly think it suits my handsome face, do you?"
> "You look like a king, an emperor."

"God forbid," I said and took the wreath off. It fell on the floor and as I went towards the window I stepped on it. The room was full of the scent of crushed flowers. (74) [43]

Antoinette has not offered him an apple. Yet his gesture is clear enough. Tempted by the sensuality inherent in the flowers and the visions of power it invokes in him, he sees in Antoinette's words the threat of the fall and proudly casts away temptation. By trampling the flowers, he tramples the sensuality that invades him in the island as a whole. Yet the flowers are not simply temptation but temptation in the form of woman. He makes this equation clear later in the section:

I passed an orchid with long sprays of golden-brown flowers. One of them touched my cheek and I remembered picking some for her one day. "They are like you," I told her. Now I stopped, broke a spray off, and trampled it into the mud. This brought me to my senses. (99) [59]

It is the revulsion about sex which, as Gilbert and Gubar have discussed in detail, is behind many male-authored texts, where the women become "emblems of filthy materiality, committed only to their own private ends . . . accidents of nature, deformities meant to repel, but in their very freakishness they possess unhealthy energies, powerful and dangerous" (29). Hence it is very easy for Antoinette to make the transition from temptress to whore in Rochester's narrative. The letter he receives from Daniel Cosway provides the best excuse to lay the burden of his guilt on her. The contrast between his early projections of her and the later ones is evident. From the girl with the sad eyes she becomes the woman with the wild eyes who "thirsts for *anyone*, not for me. . . . She'll moan and cry and give herself as no sane woman would, or could" (165) [99]. Thus not only does she appear sexually promiscuous, even, as one critic sees her, a nymphomaniac, but she is guilty of the worst of all taboos — incest, for Rochester is only too willing to believe Daniel Cosway's insinuations. Thus the guilt of the oedipal son/mother relationship is displaced and projected "safely" onto the whore whose indiscriminate sexuality echoes the indiscriminate sexuality of her mother, whose story Rochester does not want to hear.

Any projection of woman as temptress/whore must be accompanied by suggestions of witchcraft, for the fact that the male has abandoned his "sanity" must be accounted for. By assigning both Antoinette and Christophine the role of witch, he thus can account for their initial power over him. Daly aptly sums up the importance of this projection for man:

The role of witch . . . was often ascribed to social deviants whose power was fearful. All women are deviants from the male norm of society (a point emphasized by the "misbegotten male" theory of

Aristotle and Aquinas, the "penis-envy" dogma of the Freudians, and other psychological theories such as the "inner space" doctrine of Erikson and the "anima" theory of Jung). However, those singled out as witches were frequently characterized by the fact that they had or were believed to have power arising from a particular kind of knowledge, as in the case of the "wise women" who knew the curative powers of herbs and whom people went to for counsel and help. Defined as evil they became the scapegoats of society, and in this process, the dominant ethos was reinforced. (*Beyond God* 64)

For Rochester both Antoinette and Christophine appear to have some kind of secret knowledge that he cannot have; they seem to have some insight into the ways of the island that eludes and tantalizes him: "It was a beautiful place — wild, untouched, above all untouched, with an alien, disturbing, secret loveliness. And it kept its secret" (87) [51–52]. Although Antoinette does not know "facts," it is she, nevertheless, who knows the dangers of the place, a result of her close contact with nature during her childhood, and for which nothing in his past has prepared him. His calm, cold knowledge of the daylight proves totally useless in providing access to the "secret" he imagines exists. Antoinette thus assumes an eerie quality which frightens him: "But at night how different, even her voice was changed. Always this talk of death. (Is she trying to tell me that is the secret of this place? That there is no other way? She knows. She knows.)" (92) [54]. Not only does Rochester resort to the archetypal association of woman with night in his portrayal of Antoinette as witch, but he also focuses on her story about the rats and the full moon, which in itself seems to cast a spell on him because he is immediately deprived of speech: "I wanted to say something reassuring but the scent of the river flowers was overpoweringly strong. I felt giddy" (83) [49]. Knowledge becomes a powerful weapon that the witch uses to enslave her victim. Rochester's narrative, however, not content with ascribing to Antoinette some supernatural/unnatural qualities, pounces on the "poison" episode, a superb example of Daly's male "sin" of reversal, as the best proof of how dangerous and destructive that power can be. It provides him with yet one more reason why Antoinette must be controlled and bridled. And by containing it, the power can somehow become his:

> Suddenly, bewilderingly, I was certain that everything I had imagined to be truth was false. False. Only the magic and dream are true — all the rest's a lie. Let it go. Here is the secret. Here. (But it is lost, that secret, and those who know it cannot tell it). Not lost. I had found it in a hidden place and I'd keep it, hold it fast. As I'd hold her. (168) [100–01]

Nevertheless, it is clear that Antoinette alone cannot be the source of all this knowledge. Thus, as he finds in Antoinette's mother the "source" of her sexual promiscuity, he finds in Christophine the "source" of her evil magic. Right from their first encounter, Christophine emerges as stronger than he, a towering figure whom Rochester perceives as a "phallic mother" who "castrates" him, first through her gaze and then through her words: "We stared at each other for quite a minute. I looked away first and she smiled to herself" (73) [43]. Her second encounter is presented by Rochester as even more clearly threatening to him. She hands him coffee, calling it "bull's blood." Immediately upon her departure he objects insistently to her speech: "Her language is horrible," and yet again: "I can't say I like her language." Later he reveals the true source of his anxiety; he interprets the incident as a mockery of his manhood: "The same contempt as that devil's when she said, 'Taste my bull's blood.' Meaning that will make you a man" (167) [100]. He is therefore satisfied to discover that he has some legal power over her which he can exercise to put her into jail. By threatening her, he is able to break the "pact" that she has with Antoinette and, therefore, to weaken the power of both women. But it is only by emphasizing her role as obeah and by insisting on the poisonous nature of the potion she has given Antoinette to use "against" him that he can acquire this legal tool.

Henceforth Rochester learns to control his narrative. He has come to recognize the dangers analyzed by Gilbert and Gubar in *Madwoman* of "the monster-woman, threatening to replace her angelic sister" in a text that the author seeks to master completely because the "monster-woman," who is here Antoinette,

> embodies intransigent female autonomy and thus represents both the author's power to allay "his" anxieties by calling their source bad names (witch, bitch, fiend, monster) and, simultaneously, the mysterious power of the character who refuses to stay in her textually ordained "place" and thus generates a story that "gets away" from its author. (34)

The final product of this master-narrative then becomes the sum total of all the different representations in one — a crazed figure deprived of maternal power because of her "debauchery" while denied sexual gratification because of her failed witchcraft. As these conflicting elements battle and thus negate one another, external control becomes easy. She is outside and beyond language, and thus she has no place within it. She can only be represented by another, and that other is Rochester, who, from within the order, becomes master of her desires. And he, having removed all physical traces of her by keeping her out of sight, can deny her existence as her mother's existence was denied to Antoi-

nette. She becomes a ghost, dead/undead, the zombie that Rochester
had been afraid would be *his* fate. And by that, she assures the possibility of his continued existence.

Thus appears his final creation, the "Marionette Antoinette." Having
effectively killed her ("I drew the sheet over her gently as if I covered
a dead girl," 139 [83]), he brings her back again to life but now in
another form: "Antoinette stretched on the bed quite still. Like a doll.
Even when she threatened me with the bottle she had a marionette
quality" (149–151) [90]. He strips her of the possibility of speech by
rendering her words meaningless, for once the words are discredited
they lose all possibility of exerting any influence over reality. This she
recognizes: "I will tell you everything you wish to know, but in a few
words because words are no use. I know that now" (135) [81]. She has
become an "hysteric" and, as such, loses her place in discourse, the
fate of all hysterics, according to Irigaray:

> Hysteria, at least the hysteria that is the privileged lot of the "fe-
> male," *now has nothing to say*. What she "suffers," what she "lusts
> for," even what she "takes pleasure in," all take place on another
> stage, in relation to already codified representation. (140)

She thus becomes "silence itself" (168) [101], "the doll with a doll's
voice" (171) [102], the static "standing woman" of Rochester's drawing:
"a dot for a head, a larger one for the body, a triangle for a skirt, slanting
lines for arms and feet" (163) [98]. His supreme moment comes when
he deprives her even of her beauty:

> I did it too. I saw the hate go out of her eyes. I forced it out. And
> with the hate her beauty. She was only a ghost. A ghost in the
> grey daylight. Nothing left but hopelessness. Say die and I will die.
> Say die and watch me die. (170) [102]

There is no danger now of the narrative escaping. He is the author
completely, moving the character like a puppet on strings. Or so he
thinks.

With the third section we return to a female narrative, this time a
reduced narrative whose very brevity indicates the role a person like
Grace Poole has in society around her. She is a skillful portrayal of
what Daly has called the "male-woman," the token torturer who "often
unwittingly pleases her masters by selling out her own kind. She increases their pleasure by performing the acts which are less than gen-
tlemanly, thus obscuring their role" (*Gyn/Ecology* 335). In Grace's case
male approval takes on the form of money, in return for which she
undertakes to conceal Rochester's secret, to eradicate Antoinette from
the world of Rochester's society, so that he may in time victimize another unsuspecting young woman, Jane Eyre herself. Yet the price she
pays for approval is tremendous. Locked up in a cold prison in which

she herself is jailor, she is reduced to drink and, like Antoinette, to silence: "I know better than to say a word," she says, having learned that only in silence can she find safety: "After all, the house is big and safe, a shelter from the world outside which, say what you like, can be black and cruel to a woman." She is like the nuns, having built around herself "thick walls, keeping away all the things that you have fought till you can fight no longer" (178) [106].

Of the two women in the last section, Antoinette remains, in spite of her problems, the more perceptive of her situation. The walls, far from providing protection, are "cardboard" walls, illusions set up by man to incarcerate woman. As O'Conner points out, "the British interior in *Sargasso Sea* is the most claustrophobic of all Rhys' rooms, unrelieved by glimpses of the outside world except for one brief sojourn arranged by Grace Poole. There is no place for growth, no place for natural expansion" (195). The room in Thornfield completes a series of spaces in Antoinette's life, beginning with the maternal space of Coulibri that seems bound only by the sea and gradually narrowing through her contact with patriarchy until she is finally reduced to a windowless room.

About this, Antoinette remains lucid. And she is not slow to grasp her few moments of freedom to obtain a knife with which to accomplish her revenge. Once again, although with difficulty, she reappropriates the narrative, determined, despite everything, to continue her struggle. This action Grace Poole recognizes, with a mixture of awe and pity, for the resigned Grace has long since discounted rebellion as a form of action: "I'll say one thing for her, she hasn't lost her spirit. She's still fierce. I don't turn my back on her when her eyes have that look. I know it" (179) [106].

Slowly, with hesitation, Antoinette seeks to find for herself a mode of representation. Torn between two irreconcilable images, those projected by society and by her own self-image, she escapes her prison to search for herself outside its confines. The Antoinette floating out of the window is the Antoinette represented in language, whereas the physical entity of Antoinette is denied existence completely to such an extent that her "brother" Richard does not (or refuses to) recognize her. * * * Recognizing in her representation in patriarchy a cruel joke, she flees it, escaping the ghost that is her projection: "It seemed that someone was following me, someone was chasing me, laughing" (187) [111].

It is in her refusal to recognize that ghost as herself that her strength lies. But it is also her weakness. For in order to finally assert her own representation she must confront those "other" selves that have been allocated to her by society. In the hallways, she hears once again "the sound of whispering I have heard all my life, but these are different voices" (181) [107], voices that speak of a ghost who haunts the house:

"The second girl said, 'Have you seen a ghost?' — 'I didn't see anything but I thought I felt something.' 'That is the ghost,' the second said and they went down the stairs together" (182) [108].

Pursued by the dead/undead mother who often represents the problematics of femininity, Antoinette is afraid to look behind her. Yet when she finally does confront her in the mirror, she recognizes her immediately: "The woman with streaming hair. She was surrounded by a gilt frame but I knew her" (189) [112]. The fire that she triggers off sets up a "wall" that protects her so that she becomes, in Elizabeth Abel's words, "separated from the 'ghost' in the mirror by a fire that is the product of her own action and is linked by color to her former self" (174).

Thus Antoinette finally writes herself, as she has always wanted to do ("I will write my name in fire red," 54 [32], she says of her needlework), with fire, traditionally linked with woman:

> Fire is source and symbol of energy, of gynergy. It is because women are known to be energy sources that patriarchal males seek to possess and consume us. This is done less dramatically in day-by-day draining of energy in the slow and steady extinguishing of woman's fire. (Daly, *Gyn/Ecology* 319)

In her action she reappropriates fire from patriarchy, reversing the witch-burning syndrome. On a practical level, she "hits (Rochester) where it will hurt him most, in his quintessential Englishness," by robbing him of Thornfield, his English heritage (Davidson 39). On another level, she proves that the "sanity" of institutionalized patriarchy is self-destructive, for repression and suppression will burn it up from within. The denial of the life principle can only lead, literally, to death. Fire cannot be contained. Sooner or later it must escape its controls to burn everything around it. The symbolic nature of the fire is one of the subtler points of differentiation from Brontë's text that is easily overlooked; but as Davidson indicates "we can note how calculatingly Rhys places her protagonist's death. At the end of the novel, it is yet to come, it is there just beyond the last sentences, which is another way of continuing the text even though it is ostensibly concluded" (40–41).

Thus Rhys breaks the barriers of language by producing an open text that cannot be closed on the death of a woman. "And jumped and *woke*" (190 [112], emphasis mine) is significant and a herald of a beginning, not of an end. We "know" only from the previous text, *Jane Eyre*, what the conclusion should be, but the other text pretends also to "know" many things that are called into question in *Wide Sargasso Sea*. We have only to remember Rhys's anger at Brontë's depiction of Bertha to recognize how much this second text seeks to escape the restrictions imposed upon it by Brontë's novel. * * *

Antoinette jumps out of language, out of the book, into the world of the author. Like Virginia Woolf before her, Rhys has taken up the inkpot and flung it at the "Angel in the House." Or, as Gilbert and Gubar phrase it,

> Before woman can write, declared Virginia Woolf, we must "kill" the "angel in the house." In other words, women must kill the aesthetic ideal through which they themselves have been "killed" into art. And similarly, all women writers must kill the angel's necessary opposite and double, the "monster" in the house, whose Medusa-face also kills feminine creativity. (17)

Thus the conclusion comes to represent the rekindling of Antoinette's energies — and of our energies as women, having left behind the pale ghosts of patriarchal order and refused the incarceration of the male house. Antoinette is not a passive, apathetic girl as she has been made out to be. Nor is she some poor demented creature from whom we can detach ourselves. For, after all, her madness is only a tale told by a "sane" male whose motivations are at best dubious. She is a representative of our constant, long struggle against suppression in a society that still persists in perceiving woman as object and not as subject and continues to tell its tale of woman without her sound and fury, signifying nothing.

WORKS CITED

Abel, Elizabeth. "Women and Schizophrenia in the Fiction of Jean Rhys." *Contemporary Literature* 20 (1979): 155–177.

Brontë, Charlotte, *Jane Eyre*. 1847. New York: Washington Square, 1962.

Chodorow, Nancy, *The Reproduction of Mothering: Psychoanalysis and the Sociology of Gender*. Berkeley: U of California P, 1979.

Daly, Mary. *Beyond God the Father*. Boston: Beacon, 1973.

———. *Gyn/Ecology: A Metaethics of Radical Feminism*. Boston: Beacon, 1978.

Davidson, Arnold E. *Jean Rhys*. New York: Ungar, 1985.

Gilbert, Sandra M., and Susan Gubar. *The Madwoman in the Attic: The Women Writer and the Nineteenth Century Literary Imagination*. New Haven: Yale UP, 1979.

Irigaray, Luce. *Speculum of the Other Woman*. Trans. Gillian C. Gill. Ithaca: Cornell UP, 1985.

Kristeva, Julia. "Woman's Time." *Feminist Theory: A Critique of Ideology*. Eds. Nannerl O. Keohane, et. al. Chicago: U of Chicago P, 1982. 31–54.

Moore, Judith. "Jean Rhys, Sanity and Strength." *Rocky Mountain Review* 141 (1987): 8–20.

Nebeker, Helen. *Jean Rhys, Woman in Passage: A Critical Study*. Montreal: Eden, 1981.

O'Conner, Teresa F. *Jean Rhys: The West Indian Novels*. New York: New York UP, 1986.

Olsen, Tillie. *Silences*. New York: Delacorte/Seymour Lawrence, 1978.

Rhys, Jean. *Wide Sargasso Sea*. New York: Popular, 1966.

Scharfmann, Ronnie. "Mirrors and Mothering in Simone Schwarz-Bart's *Pluie et vent sur Telumee Miracle* and Jean Rhys' *Wide Sargasso Sea*." *Yale French Studies* 62 (1981): 88–106.

GAYATRI CHAKRAVORTY SPIVAK

[*Wide Sargasso Sea* and a Critique of Imperialism]†

It should not be possible to read nineteenth-century British literature without remembering that imperialism, understood as England's social mission, was a crucial part of the cultural representation of England to the English. The role of literature in the production of cultural representation should not be ignored. These two obvious "facts" continue to be disregarded in the reading of nineteenth-century British literature. This itself attests to the continuing success of the imperialist project, displaced and dispersed into more modern forms.

If these "facts" were remembered, not only in the study of British literature but in the study of the literatures of the European colonizing cultures of the great age of imperialism, we would produce a narrative, in literary history, of the "worlding" of what is now called "the Third World." To consider the Third World as distant cultures, exploited but with rich intact literary heritages waiting to be recovered, interpreted, and curricularized in English translation fosters the emergence of "the Third World" as a signifier that allows us to forget that "worlding," even as it expands the empire of the literary discipline.[1]

It seems particularly unfortunate when the emergent perspective of feminist criticism reproduces the axioms of imperialism. A basically isolationist admiration for the literature of the female subject in Europe and Anglo-America establishes the high feminist norm. It is supported and operated by an information-retrieval approach to "Third World" literature which often employs a deliberately "nontheoretical" methodology with self-conscious rectitude.

---

† From "Three Women's Texts and a Critique of Imperialism," *Critical Inquiry* 12.1 (Autumn 1985): 243–61. Copyright © 1985 by Gayatri Chakravorty Spivak. Reprinted by permission of the author. Page references to this Norton Critical Edition are given in brackets after Spivak's original citations.

1. My notion of the "worlding of a world" upon what must be assumed to be uninscribed earth is a vulgarization of Martin Heidegger's idea; see "The Origin of the Work of Art," *Poetry, Language, Thought*, trans. Albert Hofstadter (New York, 1977), pp. 17–87.

In this essay, I will attempt to examine the operation of the "world-ing" of what is today "the Third World" by what has become a cult text of feminism: *Jane Eyre*.[2] I plot the novel's reach and grasp, and locate its structural motors. I read *Wide Sargasso Sea* as *Jane Eyre*'s reinscription * * *

Sympathetic U.S. feminists have remarked that I do not do justice to Jane Eyre's subjectivity. A word of explanation is perhaps in order. The broad strokes of my presuppositions are that what is at stake, for feminist individualism in the age of imperialism, is precisely the making of human beings, the constitution and "interpellation" of the subject not only as individual but as "individualist."[3] This stake is represented on two registers: childbearing and soul making. The first is domestic-society-through-sexual-reproduction cathected as "companionate love"; the second is the imperialist project cathected as civil-society-through-social-mission. As the female individualist, not-quite/not-male, articulates herself in shifting relationship to what is at stake, the "native female" as such (*within* discourse, *as* a signifier) is excluded from any share in this emerging norm.[4] If we read this account from an isola-tionist perspective in a "metropolitan" context, we see nothing there but the psychobiography of the militant female subject. In a reading such as mine, in contrast, the effort is to wrench oneself away from the mesmerizing focus of the "subject-constitution" of the female individualist.

* * *

When Jean Rhys, born on the Caribbean island of Dominica, read *Jane Eyre* as a child, she was moved by Bertha Mason: "I thought I'd try to write her a life."[5] *Wide Sargasso Sea*, the slim novel published in 1965, at the end of Rhys' long career, is that "life."

I have suggested that Bertha's function in *Jane Eyre* is to render indeterminate the boundary between human and animal and thereby to weaken her entitlement under the spirit if not the letter of the Law.

2. See Charlotte Brontë, *Jane Eyre* (New York, 1960); all further references to this work, abbre-viated *JE*, will be included in the text.
3. As always, I take my formula from Louis Althusser, "Ideology an Ideological State Apparatuses (Notes towards an Investigation)," *"Lenin and Philosophy" and Other Essays*, trans. Ben Brew-ster (New York, 1971), pp. 127–86. For an acute differentiation between the individual and individualism, see V. N. Vološinov, *Marxism and the Philosophy of Language*, trans. Ladislav Matejka and I. R. Titunik, Studies in Language, vol. 1 (New York, 1973), pp. 93–94 and 152–53. For a "straight" analysis of the roots and ramifications of English "individualism," see C. B. MacPherson, *The Political Theory of Possessive Individualism: Hobbes to Locke* (Oxford, 1962). I am grateful to Jonathan Rée for bringing this book to my attention and for giving a careful reading of all but the very end of the present essay.
4. I am constructing an analogy with Homi Bhabha's powerful notion of "not-quite/not-white" in his "Of Mimicry and Man: The Ambiguity of Colonial Discourse," *October* 28 (Spring 1984): 132. I should also add that I use the word "native" here in reaction to the term "Third World Woman." It cannot, of course, apply with equal historical justice to both the West Indian and the Indian contexts nor to contexts of imperialism by transportation.
5. Jean Rhys, in an interview with Elizabeth Vreeland, quoted in Nancy R. Harrison, *Jean Rhys and The Novel as Women's Text* (Chapel Hill: The University of North Carolina Press, 1988). This is an excellent, detailed study of Rhys.

When Rhys rewrites the scene in *Jane Eyre* where Jane hears "a snarl-ing, snatching sound, almost like a dog quarrelling" and then encoun-ters a bleeding Richard Mason (*JE*, p. 210), she keeps Bertha's humanity, indeed her sanity as critic of imperialism, intact. Grace Poole, another character originally in *Jane Eyre*, describes the incident to Bertha in *Wide Sargasso Sea*: "So you don't remember that you attacked this gentleman with a knife? . . . I didn't hear all he said except 'I cannot interfere legally between yourself and your husband'. It was when he said 'legally' that you flew at him' " (*WSS*, p. 150 [109]). In Rhys' retelling, it is the dissimulation that Bertha discerns in the word "legally"—not an innate bestiality—that prompts her violent *re*action.

In the figure of Antoinette, whom in *Wide Sargasso Sea* Rochester violently renames Bertha, Rhys suggests that so intimate a thing as per-sonal and human identity might be determined by the politics of im-perialism. Antoinette, as a white Creole child growing up at the time of emancipation in Jamaica, is caught between the English imperialist and the black native. In recounting Antoinette's development, Rhys reinscribes some thematics of Narcissus.

There are, noticeably, many images of mirroring in the text. I will quote one from the first section. In this passage, Tia is the little black servant girl who is Antoinette's close companion: "We had eaten the same food, slept side by side, bathed in the same river. As I ran, I thought, I will live with Tia and I will be like her. . . . When I was close I saw the jagged stone in her hand but I did not see her throw it. . . . We stared at each other, blood on my face, tears on hers. It was as if I saw myself. Like in a looking glass" (*WSS*, p. 38 [27]).

A progressive sequence of dreams reinforces this mirror imagery. In its second occurrence, the dream is partially set in a *hortus conclusus*, or "enclosed garden"—Rhys uses the phrase (*WSS*, p. 50 [36])—a Romance rewriting of the Narcissus topos as the place of encounter with Love.[6] In the enclosed garden, Antoinette encounters not Love but a strange threatening voice that says merely "in here," inviting her into a prison which masquerades as the legalization of love (*WSS*, p. 50 [36]).

In Ovid's *Metamorphoses*, Narcissus' madness is disclosed when he recognizes his Other as his self: "Iste ego sum."[7] Rhys makes Antoinette see her *self* as her Other, Brontë's Bertha. In the last section of *Wide Sargasso Sea*, Antoinette acts out *Jane Eyre*'s conclusion and recognizes herself as the so-called ghost in Thornfield Hall: "I went into the hall again with the tall candle in my hand. It was then that I saw her—the ghost. The woman with streaming hair. She was surrounded by a gilt

6. See Louise Vinge, *The Narcissus Theme in Western European Literature Up to the Early Nineteenth Century*, trans. Robert Dewsnap et al. (Lund, 1967), chap. 5.
7. For a detailed study of this text, see John Brenkman, "Narcissus in the Text," *Georgia Review* 30 (Summer 1976): 293–327. [*Iste ego sum*: That I am (*Editor*).]

frame but I knew her" (WSS, p. 154 [111–12]). The gilt frame encloses a mirror: as Narcissus' pool reflects the selfed Other, so this "pool" reflects the Othered self. Here the dream sequence ends, with an invocation of none other than Tia, the Other that could not be selfed, because the fracture of imperialism rather than the Ovidian pool intervened. (I will return to this difficult point.) "That was the third time I had my dream, and it ended. . . . I called 'Tia' and jumped and woke" (WSS, p. 155 [112]). It is now, at the very end of the book, that Antoinette/Bertha can say: "Now at last I know why I was brought here and what I have to do" (WSS, pp. 155–56 [112]). We can read this as her having been brought into the England of Brontë's novel: "This cardboard house" — a book between cardboard covers — "where I walk at night is not England" (WSS, p. 148 [107]). In this fictive England, she must play out her role, act out the transformation of her "self" into that fictive Other, set fire to the house and kill herself, so that Jane Eyre can become the feminist individualist heroine of British fiction. I must read this as an allegory of the general epistemic violence of imperialism, the construction of a self-immolating colonial subject for the glorification of the social mission of the colonizer. At least Rhys sees to it that the woman from the colonies is not sacrificed as an insane animal for her sister's consolidation.

Critics have remarked that Wide Sargasso Sea treats the Rochester character with understanding and sympathy.[8] Indeed, he narrates the entire middle section of the book. Rhys makes it clear that he is a victim of the patriarchal inheritance law of entailment rather than of a father's natural preference for the firstborn: in Wide Sargasso Sea, Rochester's situation is clearly that of a younger son dispatched to the colonies to buy an heiress. If in the case of Antoinette and her identity, Rhys utilizes the thematics of Narcissus, in the case of Rochester and his patrimony, she touches on the thematics of Oedipus.[9] (In this she has her finger on our "historical moment." If, in the nineteenth century, subject-constitution is represented as childbearing and soul making, in the twentieth century psychoanalysis allows the West to plot the itinerary of the subject from Narcissus [the "imaginary"] to Oedipus [the "symbolic"]. This subject, however, is the normative male subject. In Rhys' reinscription of these themes, divided between the female and the male protagonist, feminism and a critique of imperialism become complicit.)

In place of the "wind from Europe" scene, Rhys substitutes the sce-

8. See, e.g., Thomas F. Staley, Jean Rhys: A Critical Study (Austin, Tex. 1979), pp. 108–16; it is interesting to note Staley's masculist discomfort with this and his consequent dissatisfaction with Rhys' novel.

9. Narcissus and Oedipus are figures from Greek mythology. Narcissus falls in love with his own reflection in a pool of water; unable to touch the object of his desire, he dies of unfulfilled longing. Oedipus unwittingly kills his father and marries his mother. Sigmund Freud used the Oedipus myth to describe a son's feelings of love toward his mother and jealousy and hatred toward his father [Editor].

nario of a suppressed letter to a father, a letter which would be the "correct" explanation of the tragedy of the book.[1] "I thought about the letter which should have been written to England a week ago. Dear Father . . ." (WSS, p. 57 [39]). This is the first instance: the letter not written. Shortly afterward:

> Dear Father. The thirty thousand pounds have been paid to me without question or condition. No provision made for her (that must be seen to). . . . I will never be a disgrace to you or to my dear brother the son you love. No begging letters, no mean requests. None of the furtive shabby manoeuvres of a younger son. I have sold my soul or you have sold it, and after all is it such a bad bargain? The girl is thought to be beautiful, she is beautiful. And yet . . . (WSS, p. 59) [41]

This is the second instance: the letter not sent. The formal letter is uninteresting; I will quote only a part of it:

> Dear Father, we have arrived from Jamaica after an uncomfortable few days. This little estate in the Windward Islands is part of the family property and Antoinette is much attached to it. . . . All is well and has gone according to your plans and wishes. I dealt of course with Richard Mason. . . . He seemed to become attached to me and trusted me completely. This place is very beautiful but my illness has left me too exhausted to appreciate it fully. I will write again in a few days' time. (WSS, p. 63) [44–45]

And so on.

Rhys' version of the Oedipal exchange is ironic, not a closed circle. We cannot know if the letter actually reaches its destination. "I wondered how they got their letters posted," the Rochester figure muses. "I folded mine and put it into a drawer of the desk. . . . There are blanks in my mind that cannot be filled up" (WSS, p. 64 [45]). It is as if the text presses us to note the analogy between letter and mind.

Rhys denies to Brontë's Rochester the one thing that is supposed to be secured in the Oedipal relay: the Name of the Father, or the patronymic. In *Wide Sargasso Sea*, the character corresponding to Rochester has no name. His writing of the final version of the letter to his father is supervised, in fact, by an image of the *loss* of the patronymic: "There was a crude bookshelf made of three shingles strung together over the desk and I looked at the books, Byron's poems, novels by Sir Walter Scott, *Confessions of an Opium Eater* . . . and on the last shelf, *Life and Letters of* . . . The rest was eaten away" (WSS, p. 63 [44]).

Wide Sargasso Sea marks with uncanny clarity the limits of its own discourse in Christophine, Antoinette's black nurse. We may perhaps

---

1. I have tried to relate castration and suppressed letters in my "The Letter As Cutting Edge," in *Literature and Psychoanalysis; The Question of Reading: Otherwise*, ed. Shoshana Felman (New Haven, Conn., 1981), pp. 208–26.

surmise the distance between *Jane Eyre* and *Wide Sargasso Sea* by remarking that Christophine's unfinished story is the tangent to the latter narrative, as St. John Rivers' story is to the former. Christophine is not a native of Jamaica; she is from Martinique. Taxonomically, she belongs to the category of the good servant rather than that of the pure native. But within these borders, Rhys creates a powerfully suggestive figure.

Christophine is the first interpreter and named speaking subject in the text. "The Jamaican ladies had never approved of my mother, 'because she pretty like pretty self' Christophine said," we read in the book's opening paragraph (WSS, p. 15 [9]). I have taught this book five times, once in France, once to students who had worked on the book with the well-known Caribbean novelist Wilson Harris, and once at a prestigious institute where the majority of the students were faculty from other universities. It is part of the political argument I am making that all these students blithely stepped over this paragraph without asking or knowing what Christophine's patois, so-called incorrect English, might mean.

Christophine is, of course, a commodified person. " 'She was your father's wedding present to me' " explains Antoinette's mother, " 'one of his presents' " (WSS, p. 18 [12]). Yet Rhys assigns her some crucial functions in the text. It is Christophine who judges that black ritual practices are culture-specific and cannot be used by whites as cheap remedies for social evils, such as Rochester's lack of love for Antoinette. Most important, it is Christophine alone whom Rhys allows to offer a hard analysis of Rochester's actions, to challenge him in a face-to-face encounter. The entire extended passage is worthy of comment. I quote a brief extract:

> "She is Creole girl, and she have the sun in her. Tell the truth now. She don't come to your house in this place England they tell me about, she don't come to your beautiful house to beg you to marry with her. No, it's you come all the long way to her house — it's you beg her to marry. And she love you and she give you all she have. Now you say you don't love her and you break her up. What you do with her money, eh?" [And then Rochester, the white man, comments silently to himself] Her voice was still quiet but with a hiss in it when she said "money." (WSS, p. 130) [95]

Her analysis is powerful enough for the white man to be afraid: "I no longer felt dazed, tired, half hypnotized, but alert and wary, ready to defend myself" (WSS, p. 130 [95]).

Rhys does not, however, romanticize individual heroics on the part of the oppressed. When the Man refers to the forces of Law and Order, Christophine recognizes their power. This exposure of civil inequality is emphasized by the fact that, just before the Man's successful threat, Christophine had invoked the emancipation of slaves in Jamaica by proclaiming: "No chain gang, no tread machine, no dark jail either. This is free country and I am free woman" (WSS, p. 131 [96]).

As I mentioned above, Christophine is tangential to this narrative. She cannot be contained by a novel which rewrites a canonical English text within the European novelistic tradition in the interest of the white Creole rather than the native. No perspective *critical* of imperialism can turn the Other into a self, because the project of imperialism has always already historically refracted what might have been the absolutely Other into a domesticated Other that consolidates the imperialist self.[2] * * *

Of course, we cannot know Jean Rhys' feelings in the matter. We can, however, look at the scene of Christophine's inscription in the text. Immediately after the exchange between her and the Man, well before the conclusion, she is simply driven out of the story, with neither narrative nor characterological explanation or justice. " 'Read and write I don't know. Other things I know.' She walked away without looking back" (WSS, p. 133 [97]).

Indeed, if Rhys rewrites the mad woman's attack on the Man by underlining of the misuse of "legality," she cannot deal with the passage that corresponds to St. John Rivers' own justification of his martyrdom, for it has been displaced into the current idiom of modernization and development. Attempts to construct the "Third World Woman" as a signifier remind us that the hegemonic definition of literature is itself caught within the history of imperialism. A full literary reinscription cannot easily flourish in the imperialist fracture or discontinuity, covered over by an alien legal system masquerading as Law as such, an alien ideology established as only Truth, and a set of human sciences busy establishing the "native" as self-consolidating Other.

* * *

I must myself close with an idea that I cannot establish within the limits of this essay. Earlier I contended that *Wide Sargasso Sea* is necessarily bound by the reach of the European novel. I suggested that, in contradistinction, to reopen the epistemic fracture of imperialism without succumbing to a nostalgia for lost origins, the critic must turn to the archives of imperialist governance. I have not turned to those archives in these pages. In my current work, by way of a modest and inexpert "reading" of "archives," I try to extend, outside of the reach of the European novelistic tradition, the most powerful suggestion in *Wide Sargasso Sea:* that *Jane Eyre* can be read as the orchestration and staging of the self-immolation of Bertha Mason as "good wife." The power of that suggestion remains unclear if we remain insufficiently

2. This is the main argument of my "Can the Subaltern Speak?"

knowledgeable about the history of the legal manipulation of widow-sacrifice in the entitlement of the British government in India. I would hope that an informed critique of imperialism, granted some attention from readers in the First World, will at least expand the frontiers of the politics of reading.

BENITA PARRY

[Two Native Voices in *Wide Sargasso Sea*]†

* * *

[Gayatri Chakravorty] Spivak argues that because the construction of an English cultural identity was inseparable from othering the native as its object, the articulation of the female subject within the emerging norm of feminist individualism during the age of imperialism, necessarily excluded the native female, who was positioned on the boundary between human and animal as the object of imperialism's social-mission or soul-making.[1] In applying this interactive process to her reading of WSS,[2] Spivak assigns to Antoinette/Bertha, daughter of slave-owners and heiress to a post-emancipation fortune, the role of the native female sacrificed in the cause of the subject-constitution of the European female individualist. Although Spivak does acknowledge that WSS is 'a novel which rewrites a canonical English text within the European novelistic tradition in the interest of the white Creole rather than the native' (*TWT*, 253), and situates Antoinette/Bertha as caught between the English imperialist and the black Jamaican, her discussion does not pursue the text's representations of a Creole culture that is dependent on both yet singular, or its enunciation of a specific settler discourse, distinct from the texts of imperialism. The dislocations of the Creole position are repeatedly spoken by Antoinette, the 'Rochester' figure and Christophine; the nexus of intimacy and hatred between white settler and black servant is written into the text in the mirror imagery of Antoinette and Tia, a trope which for Spivak functions to invoke the other that could not be selved:

> We had eaten the same food, slept side by side, bathed in the same river. As I ran, I thought, I will live with Tia and I will be like her. . . . When I was close I saw the jagged stone in her hand but I did not see her throw it. . . . I looked at her and I saw her

† From "Problems in Current Theories of Colonial Discourse," *The Oxford Literary Review* 9.1–2 (1987): 27–58: Reprinted by permission of the publisher. Page references to this Norton Critical Edition are given in brackets after Parry's original citations.
1. Gayatri Chakravorty Spivak, 'Three Women's Texts and a Critique of Imperialism', *Critical Inquiry* 12:1, abbreviated as *TWT*.
2. Jean Rhys, *Wide Sargasso Sea* (1966) (Harmondsworth: Penguin, 1968), abbreviated as WSS.

face crumble as she began to cry. We stared at each other, blood
on my face, tears on hers. It was as if I saw myself. Like in a
looking-glass (WSS, 24) [27].

But while themselves not English, and indeed outcastes, the Creoles
are Masters to the blacks, and just as Brontë's book invites the reader
via Rochester to see Bertha Mason as situated on the human/animal
frontier ('One night I had been awakened by her yells. . . . It was a
fierce West Indian night . . . those are the sounds of a bottomless pit',
quoted TWT, 247–8), so does Rhys' novel via Antoinette admit her
audience to the regulation settler view of rebellious blacks: 'the same
face repeated over and over, eyes gleaming, mouth half-open', emitting
'a horrible noise . . . like animals howling but worse' (WSS, 32 and
35) [25, 23].

The idiosyncrasies of an account where Antoinette plays the part of
'the woman from the colonies' are consequences of Spivak's decree that
imperialism's linguistic aggression obliterates the inscription of a native
self: thus a black female who in WSS *is* most fully selved, must be
reduced to the status of a tangential figure, and a white Creole woman
(mis)construed as the native female produced by the axiomatics of imperialism, her death interpreted as 'an allegory of the general epistemic
violence of imperialism, the construction of a self-immolating subject
for the glorification of the social mission of the colonizer' (TWT, 251).
While allowing that Christophine is both speaking subject and interpreter to whom Rhys designates some crucial functions, Spivak sees her
as marking the limits of the text's discourse, and not, as is here argued,
disrupting it.

What Spivak's strategy of reading necessarily blots out is Christophine's inscription as the native, female, individual Self who defies the
demands of the discriminatory discourses impinging on her person.
Although an ex-slave given as a wedding-present to Antoinette's mother
and subsequently a caring servant, Christophine subverts the Creole
address that would constitute her as domesticated Other, and asserts
herself as articulate antagonist of patriarchal, settler and imperialist law.
Natural mother to children and surrogate parent to Antoinette, Christophine scorns patriarchal authority in her personal life by discarding
her patronymic and refusing her sons' fathers as husbands; as Antoinette's protector she impugns 'Rochester' for his economic and sexual
exploitation of her fortune and person and as female individualist she
is eloquently and frequently contemptuous of male conduct, black and
white. A native in command of the invaders' language — 'She could
speak good English if she wanted to, and French as well as patois'
(WSS, 18) [12] — Christophine appropriates English to the local idiom
and uses this dialect to deride the post-emancipation rhetoric which
enabled the English to condemn slavery as unjust while enriching

themselves through legitimized forms of exploitation: 'No more slavery! She had to laugh! These new ones have Letter of the Law. Same thing. They got Magistrate. They got fine. They got jail house and chain gang. They got tread machine to mash up people's feet. New ones worse than old ones — more cunning, that's all' (WSS, 22–3) [15]. And as obeah woman, Christophine is mistress of another knowledge dangerous to imperialism's official epistemology and the means of native cultural disobedience.[3]

Christophine's defiance is not enacted in a small and circumscribed space appropriated within the lines of dominant code, but is a stance from which she delivers a frontal assault against antagonists, and as such constitutes a counter-discourse. Wise to the limits of post-emancipation justice, she is quick to invoke the protection of its law when 'Rochester' threatens her with retribution: 'This is free country and I am free woman' (WSS, 131) [96] — which is exactly how she functions in the text, her retort to him condensing her role as the black, female individualist: 'Read and write I don't know. *Other things I know*' (WSS, 133; emphasis added) [97]. In Spivak's reconstruction, Christophine's departure from the story after this declaration and well before the novel's end, is without narrative and characterological explanation or justice. But if she is read as the possessor and practitioner of an alternative tradition challenging imperialism's authorized system of knowledge, then her exit at this point appears both logical and entirely in character:

> 'England,' said Christophine, who was watching me. 'You think there is such a place?'
> 'How can you ask that? You know there is.'
> 'I never see the damn place, how I know?'
> 'You do not believe that there is a country called England?' . . .
> 'I don't say I don't *believe*, I say I don't *know*. I know what I see with my eyes and I never see it.' (WSS, 92) [67]

This articulation of empiricism's farthest reaches spoken by a black woman who *knows* from experience that her powders, potions and maledictions are effective in the West Indies, undoes through its excess the rationalist version valorized by the English, while at the same time acknowledging the boundaries to the power of her knowledge. Officially condemned and punishable in Jamaica — 'Rochester' tries to intimidate Christophine with mention of magistrates and police — this other wisdom of the black communities is assimilated into Creole culture — Antoinette calls on and has faith in its potency. But when the novel transfers to England, Christophine must leave the narrative, for there

3. For a discussion of the correlation, see Sandra Gilbert, 'Rider Haggard's Heart of Darkness', *Partisan Review* 50:3 (1983).

her craft is outlawed, which is why after making her statement, 'She walked away, without looking back' (WSS, 133) [97].

Spivak's deliberated deafness to the native voice where it is to be heard, is at variance with her acute hearing of the unsaid in modes of Western feminist criticism which, while dismantling masculist constructions, reproduce and foreclose colonialist structures and imperialist axioms by 'performing the lie of constituting a truth of global sisterhood where the mesmerizing model remains male and female sparring partners of generalizable or universalizable sexuality who are the chief protagonists in that European contest.'[4] Demanding of disciplinary standards that 'equal rights of historical, geographical, linguistic specificity' be granted to the 'thoroughly stratified larger theatre of the Third World' (238), Spivak in her own writings severely restricts (eliminates?) the space in which the colonized can be written back into history, even when 'interventionist possibilities' are exploited through the deconstructive strategies devised by the post-colonial intellectual.

* * *

JUDITH RAISKIN

England: Dream and Nightmare†

I come so far I lose myself on that journey.

— Jean Rhys, "Let Them Call It Jazz"

I am the little Colonial walking in the London garden patch — allowed to look perhaps, but not to linger.

— Katherine Mansfield, *Journal*

The displacement Jean Rhys's characters experience under British cultural and political domination on the islands is compounded when they "return" to their "mother country," the home of some or all of their ancestors. * * *Such is the journey made by many Caribbean fictional characters, such as Clare Savage in Michelle Cliff's *No Telephone to Heaven* and Tee in Merle Hodge's *Crick Crack, Monkey*. Others, like Samuel Selvon's characters in *Lonely Londoners*, journey to England after World War II hoping for work. For those whose parents or grandparents came from Great Britain, their trip is often considered a "return" to the "mother country" although they themselves may never have been there before. Rhys's stories such as "Let Them Call It Jazz"

4. Gayatri Chakravorty Spivak, 'Imperialism and Sexual Difference', Oxford Literary Review 8:1–2 (1986): 126.
† From Judith L. Raiskin, Snow on the Cane Fields: Women's Writings and Creole Subjectivity (Minneapolis: University of Minnesota Press, 1996) 144–52. Reprinted by permission of the publisher. Page numbers have been changed to correspond to this Norton Critical Edition.

and "Temps Perdi," her novel *Voyage in the Dark*, and part 3 of *Wide Sargasso Sea* continue her exploration of West Indians' relationship to English culture, but in these works the confrontation takes place on English soil. Christophine's assessment of England as a "cold thief place" captures the alienation and economic exploitation that Rhys's women experience in England and France. As Rhys makes clear in her depictions of "alien" women, selfhood depends not only on cultural reflections of one's experience and environment but also on economic agency. Rhys shows the ways in which cultural colonialism, operating through myths of home and family, is particularly implicated in the economic impoverishment and social exploitation of the colonized woman.[1]

We can recognize Rhys's fictional depictions of West Indians in England within a central theme in Caribbean literature (and even more generally in Anglophone postcolonial literature): the alienation of the colonial-born character in England after World War II. Typical of this genre are Samuel Selvon's and George Lamming's writings that focus on the adventures and difficulties of male West Indians in England trying to find work, love, and dignity in a racist society.[2] Rhys's work is specifically and adamantly about *female* West Indians from a variety of racial backgrounds. Because these characters are white or partially white Creoles, they make the journey to England a kind of "homecoming." While Rhys's analysis shares much with those of male Caribbean writers of her time, her work adds the crucial variable of gender to the relationship of colonialism, capitalism, race, and exile. In most of the critical surveys of West Indian literature of the 1960s and 1970s, when Rhys was writing her later work, she is the only woman represented.[3] Caribbean literature of the 1950s and 1960s was largely written by male writers depicting primarily male experience.

Following Phyllis Shand Allfrey, who wrote the novel *The Orchid House* (1953), Rhys was one of the first West Indian writers to focus on West Indian women. Her novels and short stories repeatedly articulate the complex social position of the "strange woman" for whom

1. Critics such as Helen Tiffin and Erika Smilowitz have pointed out that Rhys creates powerful parallels between colonialism and sexual exploitation; indeed, Rhys exposes colonialism as a particularly pernicious rhetoric and practice for women. See Helen Tiffin, "Mirror and Mask: Colonial Motifs in the Novels of Jean Rhys," *World Literature Written in English* 17, no. 1 (April 1978), pp. 328–41; Erika Smilowitz, "Childlike Women and Paternal Men: Colonialism in Jean Rhys's Fiction," *Ariel: A Review of International Literature* (special edition: Commonwealth Women Writers) 17, no. 4 (Oct. 1986), pp. 93–103.
2. Both authors produced a series of novels relating to this experience. Their first novels are: Samuel Selvon, *Lonely Londoners* (1956; reprint, Harlow, England: Longman, 1985); George Lamming, *In the Castle of My Skin* (New York: McGraw-Hill, 1953).
3. For example, see Kenneth Ramchand's *An Introduction to the Study of West Indian Literature* (Middlesex, England: Thomas Nelson, 1976); Bruce King, ed., *West Indian Literature* (Hamden, Conn.: Archon Books, 1979). This trend is changing, and Simon Gikandi's recent work *Writing in Limbo* has chapters on Merle Hodge, Paule Marshall, and Michelle Cliff (see *Writing in Limbo: Modernism and Caribbean Literature* [Ithaca, N.Y.: Cornell University Press, 1992]).

being "down-and-out," as are most of Rhys's characters, is an experience that differs significantly from that of her male counterparts in fiction and journalistic exposé.

Antoinette's ultimate disempowerment and impoverishment in *Wide Sargasso Sea* is facilitated by a fetishized representation of the British Empire grounded * * * in myths of family loyalty and safety. For Antoinette, who is passed from guardian to guardian — from mother to nurse to step-father to church to step-brother to husband — the stability of familial relations represented by the title of the dining room picture, "The Miller's Daughter," is an attractive alternative to the confused girlhood she lives. Rochester, who did not enjoy but rather suffered an English childhood, recognizes Antoinette's idealization for the colonial dream it is:

> She often questioned me about England and listened attentively to my answers, but I was certain that nothing I said made much difference. Her mind was already made up. Some romantic novel, a stray remark never forgotten, a sketch, a picture, a song, a waltz, some note of music, and her ideas were fixed. About England and about Europe. [56]

Although * * * the English cultural domination of colonial education in many ways makes England more "real" to the native Caribbean than his or her native land, there always remains the intriguing mystery of the metropolis, the unsettling attraction of the unfamiliar:

> England, rosy pink in the geography book map, but on the page opposite the words are closely crowded, heavy looking. Exports, coal, iron, wool. Then imports and character of inhabitants. Names, Essex, Chelmsford on the Chelmer. The Yorkshire and Lincolnshire wolds. Wolds? Does that mean hills? How high? Half the height of ours, or not even that? Cool green leaves in the short cool summer. Summer. There are fields of corn like sugar-cane fields, but gold colour and not so tall. After summer the trees are bare, then winter and snow. White feathers falling? Torn pieces of paper falling? They say frost makes flower patterns on the window panes. [67]

A great part of Antoinette's education has very little to do with her actual lived experience. The English place-names she learns are mythical sounds to her, and she can only guess what cornfields or snow might look like by comparing them with what she knows about her Caribbean world. In contrast to Antoinette's confusion, the girl represented in "The Miller's Daughter" seems quite at home in this mythical world. Antoinette's identification with that girl requires that Antoinette regard her own surroundings and experiences as insignificant, less than real.

In her novel *Crick Crack, Monkey* (1970), Merle Hodge movingly expresses this feeling of inauthenticity and cultural doubleness experienced by those inculcated with the imperial dream. Her heroine, Tee, growing up in Trinidad, creates for herself an English double named Helen, who, like the Miller's Daughter, is quite comfortable with her English surroundings:

> She was my age and height. She spent the summer holidays at the sea-side with her aunt and uncle who had a delightful orchard with apple trees and pear trees in which sang chaffinches and blue tits, and where one could wander on terms of the closest familiarity with cowslips and honeysuckle. Helen loved to visit her Granny for then they sat by the fireside and had tea with delicious scones and home-made strawberry jam. . . . Helen wasn't even my double. No, she couldn't be called my double. She was the Proper Me. And me, I was her shadow hovering about in incompleteness.
>
> For doubleness, or this particular kind of doubleness, was a thing to be taken for granted. Why, the whole of life was like a piece of cloth, with a rightside and a wrongside. Just as there was a way you spoke and a way you wrote, so there was the daily existence which you led, which of course amounted only to marking time and makeshift, for there was the Proper daily round, not necessarily more agreeable, simply the valid one, the course of which encompassed things like warming yourself before a fire and having tea at four o'clock; there were the human types who were your neighbors and guardians and playmates—but you were all marginal together, for there were the beings whose validity loomed at you out of every book, every picture (often there were Natives and Red Indians and things, but these were for chuckles and for beating back, to bring you once more the satisfaction that Right prevaileth always just before THE END), the beings whose exemplary aspect it was that shone forth to recommend at you every commodity proposed to your daily preference, from macaroni to the Kingdom of Heaven.[4]

It is not coincidental or accidental that for Hodge literature and advertising occupy the same position and have the same effect on Tee's consciousness. English literature *is* the advertisement for the benefits of English rule. Dionne Brand, who is from Trinidad, makes much the same point about American popular culture and U.S. imperialism when she compares the Dallas Cowboys with the U.S. Marines.[5]

Because much of their daily experience goes unreflected in the literature, art, and racial ideology that surrounds them, Rhys's characters suffer from an inability to articulate, let alone take control of, their political situations. The myth of England and of the colonials' spiritual

4. Merle Hodge, *Crick Crack, Monkey* (1970; reprint, London: Heinemann, 1985), pp. 61–62.
5. Dionne Brand, "I Used to Like the Dallas Cowboys," in *Sans Souci and Other Stories* (Ithaca, N.Y.: Firebrand Books, 1989), p. 115–29.

and racial relationship to it contributes to their feelings of inauthenticity both at home and in England. The doubleness of their identities— as both Caribbean and English while also neither Caribbean nor English—forces them to shift between the two national "realities," much as one must focus on *either* the goblet *or* the women's profiles in the gestalt visual images. Seeing one image necessarily excludes the other; it takes a great deal of mental energy to retain the existence of both simultaneously. As the creole character Anna Morgan in Rhys's novel *Voyage in the Dark* puts it: "Sometimes it was as if I were back there and as if England were a dream. At other times England was the real thing and out there was the dream, but I could never fit them together" (*VD*, p. 3).

But it is not only the British Creoles like Anna and Antoinette who struggle to establish a stable lived reality in a place defined psychologically and culturally by myth. Rochester, too, has grown up with a cultural representation of a foreign land—that is, with the English literary creation of the abundant but menacing New World. Antoinette and Rochester represent for each other the seductive yet terrifying differences of the Old and New Worlds invented by European literature and art. The "dream" each of them seeks in the other embodies within it the nightmare of the strange:

> "Is it true," she said, "that England is like a dream? Because one of my friends who married an Englishman wrote and told me so. She said this place London is like a cold dark dream sometimes. I want to wake up."
>
> "Well," I answered annoyed, "that is precisely how your beautiful island seems to me, quite unreal and like a dream."
>
> "But how can rivers and mountains and the sea be unreal?"
>
> "And how can millions of people, their houses and their streets be unreal?"
>
> "More easily," she said, "much more easily. Yes a big city must be like a dream."
>
> "No, this is unreal and like a dream," I thought. [47–48]

For Antoinette, the colonial, England is a troubling double image— the exotic yet comforting England she learns about in school and identifies with as a white person and a place where her dream of violence, one she simultaneously struggles to suppress and to discover, will be enacted.

　　* * * Antoinette finds that her place of escape is also her place of imprisonment; her dream of an England of snow, cornfields, and millers' daughters progressively becomes her dream of violence and destruction. Each time Antoinette has her dream, England becomes more menacing and she becomes more active. This "dream" is never referred to as her "nightmare," for by the end of *Wide Sargasso Sea* the violence

visited upon the English institution (Thornfield Hall) and English literature *(Jane Eyre) is* the dream of the awakened and furious colonized
figure.[6] The one thing Antoinette does not lose in the course of her
journey of disintegration is this dream that progressively reveals England
to be a strange, foreign place, *not* a home or refuge for the Jamaican
Creole. This shifting dream of England and of her place in it is Antoinette's coherent psychological (and later her political) answer to her
loss of agency as she is exchanged between English men. Although in
the convent Antoinette does not yet recognize that the menacing place
in her dream is England, we recognize the prophesy ("This must happen," [36]) building in Antoinette's series of dreams about England and
Thornfield Hall:

> We are no longer in the forest but in an enclosed garden sur-
> rounded by a stone wall and the trees are different trees. I do not
> know them. There are steps leading upwards. It is too dark to see
> the wall or the steps, but I know they are there and I think, "It
> will be when I go up these steps. At the top." [36]

These "different trees" that Antoinette does not recognize are English
trees. Unconsciously she knows that England is not really the place she
will find the beauty and comfort she longs for. Although on some level
she knows the confrontation that awaits her "at the top" of Thornfield
Hall, she cannot yet consciously connect this terror with England. In
fact, Antoinette tells the nun in the convent that she had been dreaming
about hell, not England.[7]

In "Temps Perdi" Rhys again describes England as hell, especially
to the outsider. The narrator of this story * * * struggle[s] against the
"lies" of books and is relieved to find one book that she can use as a
defense against the rest because "all saying the same thing they can
shout you down and make you doubt, not only your memory, but your
senses."[8] The book she finds validates her own experience of England
as a cold, heartless place, and she quotes the passage triumphantly:

> ". . . to conduct the transposition of the souls of the dead to the
> White Island, in the manner just described. The White Island is
> occasionally also called Brea, or Britannia. Does this perhaps refer

6. For Sandra Drake, the struggle for Antoinette's survival, which represents the survival of the
   Caribbean as something other than a copy of Britain, is fought and won at the conclusion of
   the novel. The destruction of Thornfield represents the colonial refusal of European patriarchy
   and empire and the commitment to indigenous cultural materials instead. See Drake, "All
   That Foolishness/That All Foolishness," *Critica* 2, no. 2 (fall 1990), p. 100; and in this volume,
   p. 205.
7. Mary Lou Emery provides a rich reading of Antoinette's dreams by reading them in the context
   of Caribbean cultural motifs and theories about the language and logic of dreams. Like Sandra
   Drake, Emery reads the final dream as Antoinette's spiritual reidentification with black Caribbean culture. See Emery, *Jean Rhys at "World's End": Novels of Colonial and Sexual Exile*
   (Austin: University of Texas Press, 1990), pp. 53–60.
8. Jean Rhys, "Temps Perdi," in *The Collected Short Stories* (New York: W. W. Norton, 1987),
   p. 257; hereafter referred to in text citations and notes as "TP."

to White Albion, to the chalky cliffs of the English coast? It would
be a very humorous idea if England was designated as the land of
the dead . . . as hell. In such a form, in truth, England has appeared to many a stranger." (To many a stranger . . .). ("TP,"
p. 257)

The association of England with hell is humorous to this unnamed
author because it is in such obvious discord with England's own cultural self-understanding. But Antoinette's complex political and cultural
status makes it difficult for her to separate the mythologized England
from the harsh reality of the place. Nowhere is Benedict Anderson's
definition of a nation as an "imagined community" more striking than
in the power such imagination holds over the British Creole. Because
their very identities are dependent on their connection with an imagined English mother country, Rhys's creole characters suffer greatly
when, upon their journey "home," they confront an England that in
its coldness and brutality proves the storybook England to have been a
lie. Antoinette cannot reconcile her hatred of England and her final
defiance against it (her dream) with the Creole's cultural love of
England:

> I must know more than I know already. For I know that house
> where I will be cold and not belonging, the bed I shall lie in has
> red curtains and I have slept there many times before, long ago.
> How long ago? In that bed I will dream the end of my dream. *But
> my dream had nothing to do with England and I must not think
> like this*, I must remember about chandeliers and dancing, about
> swans and roses and snow. And snow. ([67]; emphasis added)

Antoinette remembers her hellish dream when she tells Christophine
she wants to go to England, but she adamantly refuses to make the
connection between her alienation and the mythical England of swans,
roses, and snow. Even at the end, when she is imprisoned in the manor
house she is about to destroy, Antoinette continues to split the idea of
England in two, maintaining an idyllic England separate from the political reality of the England that has denied her freedom and civil
rights. The "real" England in Antoinette's mind is the one in which
she is more than an object of exchange and in which she can exercise
her own economic transactions. In answer to Grace Poole's question
about where she acquired the knife with which she attacked Richard
Mason, Antoinette answers:

> "When we went to England," I said.
> "You fool," [Grace Poole] said, "this is England."
> "I don't believe it," I said, "and I never will believe it."
> (That afternoon we went to England. There was grass and olive-
> green water and tall trees looking into the water. This, I thought,

is England. If I could be here I'd get well again and the sound in my head would stop. Let me stay a little longer, I said, and she sat down under a tree and went to sleep. A little way off there was a cart and horse—a woman was driving it. It was she who sold me the knife. I gave her the locket round my neck for it). [108–09]

England, the "home" and "mother" of the Creole, has betrayed Antoinette. Her response as a split subject—on the one hand, a loyal British subject and, on the other, a Caribbean nationalist of sorts—is a split conception of the England that has betrayed her. That which does not correlate with the myth of roses and bright snow—the manor house, her imprisonment, the damp cold—becomes not-England: "They tell me I am in England but I don't believe them. We lost our way to England. . . . This cardboard house where I walk at night is not England" [107]. Gayatri Chakravorty Spivak reads this "cardboard house" as the actual book *Jane Eyre* in which Antoinette finds herself trapped—the text that demands "a self-immolating colonial subject."[9] It is also, however, Antoinette's attempt to continue believing in a "real" England that matches the cultural mythology while she destroys the England that entraps her. If she must see one England as "unreal" or "cardboard," she maintains the mythical England as real; the one she experiences as the theater prop can be struck at the end of the play.[1] Antoinette's rebellion and destruction are therefore not directed against the British part of herself but against a brutal political reality that threatens her own identity as a British/Caribbean Creole. This reading attributes more ambivalence to Antoinette's act of violence and retribution than does Sandra Drake's or Mary Lou Emery's, both of which interpret the final act as a resolution of Antoinette's conflicted identifications and loyalties and as her commitment to indigenous as opposed to British culture. It is, however, Antoinette's inability to thoroughly dispose of her belief in a benign and motherly England that prohibits her from enacting a conscious and self-preserving resistance.

In contrast to Antoinette's persistent desire for and allegiance to this place, England, Christophine recognizes that England is as much a construct of "belief" as of "knowledge" or truth. Unlike the white Creole, she asserts her identity as separate from its existence:

> "England," said Christophine, who was watching me. "You think there is such a place?"
> "How can you ask that? You know there is."
> "I never see the damn place, how I know?"
> "You do not believe that there is a country called England?"

9. Gayatri Chakravorty Spivak, "Three Women's Texts and a Critique of Imperialism," *Critical Inquiry* 12, no. 1 (autumn 1985), p. 251; and in this volume, p. 243.
1. Rhys was fond of theatrical metaphors, drawing on her own experience as a chorus girl. Anna, who also becomes a chorus girl in *Voyage in the Dark*, describes her arrival in England: "It was as if a curtain had fallen, hiding everything I had ever known."

> She blinked and answered quickly, "I don't say I don't *believe*,
> I say I don't *know*, I know what I see with my eyes and I never
> see it. . . . Besides I ask myself is this place like they tell us? Some
> say one thing, some different, I hear it cold to freeze your bones
> and they thief your money, clever like the devil. You have money
> in your pocket, you look again and bam! No money. Why you
> want to go to this cold thief place? If there is this place at all, I
> never see it, that is one thing sure." [67][2]

When Antoinette changes Christophine's more metaphorical "place"-
England to the political "country"-England, Christophine recognizes
the power of this vocabulary ("She blinked and quickly answered . . .").
As an Obeah woman whose knowledge exceeds the categories of English ontology, Christophine has been forced, at least in appearance, to
acquiesce to the new "belief" system of legal incantations by which the
new English order can imprison her as a practitioner of a competing
code of power. When Christophine distances herself as a black Caribbean from the spiritual "place"-England, Antoinette switches the terminology to one of politics and fealty. Recognizing the threat implicit
in the political terminology, Christophine retreats behind the double
negative ("I didn't say I don't believe"), while countering the white
creole myth of England with the black version of it as a "cold thief
place." The magical word "country," Christophine discovers, only carries power in Prospero's mouth. She tries to use it as self-protection
against Rochester's threats: " 'No police here,' she said. 'No chain gang,
no tread machine, no dark jail either. This is free country and I am
free woman' " [96]. But apparently the political use of "country" is
effective only for the white "children" of the "mother" country. For the
black ex-slave, England is not a "mother" but a "thief," not a protector
but an exploiter.

At the center of Rhys's writing is her extremely powerful deconstruc-
tion of this "family" — the mother country, England, and her children,
the colonies. * * * Rhys's Caribbean characters returning to the
mother country do not find themselves nurtured in the "home" they
have been so persuasively educated to expect, but rather find themselves
once again in exile, this time not on the frontier, but in the heart of
the metropolis.

*   *   *

2. Benita Parry reads this difference between "belief" and "knowledge" as Christophine's challenge to Rochester and Western empiricism: " 'Read and write I don't know. Other things I
   know.' She walked away without looking back" (*WSS*, p. 97). See Benita Parry, "Problems
   in Current Theories of Colonial Discourse," *Oxford Literary Review* 9, nos. 1–2 (1987), p.
   39; and in this volume, pp. 248–49.

Jean Rhys: A Chronology

1890   Born in Roseau, Dominica, to Welsh father (Dr. William Rees Williams) and Creole mother (granddaughter of a Scottish-born plantation owner and a West Indian, possibly Cuban, woman). Named Ella Gwendolen Rees Williams.

1907   Leaves Dominica for England to attend Perse School for Girls in Cambridge.

1908–09   Leaves Perse School and enrolls in the Academy of Dramatic Art; stays two terms and is withdrawn on the basis of an unfavorable report on her progress. Refuses to return to Dominica and joins a touring musical comedy company as a chorus girl. Her father dies. Has a love affair with a wealthy older man who leaves her after 18 months, providing her with a long-standing pension.

1914   Writes manuscript in exercise books of what will be published twenty years later as *Voyage in the Dark*.

1919   Leaves England for Holland to marry Jean Lenglet, a Dutch journalist and poet (pen name Edward de Nève). They move to Paris.

1920   Their son, William, is born and dies after three weeks. Moves with Lenglet to Vienna, then Budapest.

1922   Returns to Paris and gives birth to daughter, Maryvonne, in Brussels.

1923–24   Meets Ford Madox Ford, who encourages her writing. Lenglet is imprisoned for breaking currency regulations in Vienna and entering Paris illegally and is extradited to Holland. She lives with Ford and Stella Bowen in Paris and becomes Ford's lover. Uses this experience for her novel *Quartet*. "Vienne" published under the name of Jean Rhys in the *transatlantic review*, edited by Ford.

1927   *The Left Bank and Other Stories*, with a preface by Ford, published by Jonathan Cape.

1928   *Postures* published by Chatto & Windus. (Published as *Quartet* in the United States).

1929   Lives in London with Leslie Tilden-Smith, her literary agent, while writing *After Leaving Mr. Mackenzie*.

1930   *After Leaving Mr. Mackenzie* published by Jonathan Cape.

1932	Translates *Barred* by Edward de Nève (Lenglet) and helps get it published.
1933	Divorces Jean Lenglet.
1934	*Voyage in the Dark* published by Constable. Marries Leslie Tilden-Smith.
1936	Visits the Caribbean (Martinique, St. Lucia, Dominica) and New York with Tilden-Smith.
1939	*Good Morning, Midnight* published by Constable. Outbreak of WWII.
1939–45	Rhys spends the war years in several small English villages and in London. Her daughter and Lenglet live in occupied Holland and participate in anti-Nazi resistance activities. Lenglet is arrested, imprisoned, and sent to a German concentration camp.
1945	Tilden-Smith dies. Rhys begins work on *Wide Sargasso Sea*.
1947	Marries Max Hamer, Tilden-Smith's cousin, and lives in London.
1948	Rhys arrested for assaulting neighbors and police. Sent to Holloway Prison Hospital for psychiatric evaluation; released after a week and placed on probation. Uses this experience later in short story "Let Them Call It Jazz." Answers actress Selma Vaz Dias's advertisement in the *New Statesman* seeking information about her whereabouts.
1950–52	Max Hamer imprisoned for misappropriating funds from his firm. Rhys lives alone in temporary rooms in Maidstone.
1955	Moves with Hamer to Cornwall.
1956	Selma Vaz Dias finds Rhys again with another advertisement in order to adapt *Good Morning, Midnight* for a radio play, which is broadcast on BBC in 1957. Rhys signs contract with André Deutsch for *Wide Sargasso Sea* and begins professional friendship with Diana Athill, Francis Wyndham, and Diana Melly, who help and encourage her writing for the remainder of her life.
1960	Moves with Hamer to Devonshire.
1961	Jean Lenglet dies.
1964	Part One of *Wide Sargasso Sea* published in *Art and Literature* without final revisions. Rhys has a heart attack.
1966	Max Hamer dies. Rhys has another heart attack. *Wide Sargasso Sea* published by André Deutsch; it wins the W. H. Smith Award for Writers and the Heinemann Award of the Royal Society of Literature.
1968	*Tigers Are Better Looking*, a collection of short stories, published by André Deutsch.
1975	*My Day*, a collection of three autobiographical pieces, published in *Vogue* and in New York by Frank Hallman.

1976   *Sleep It Off, Lady*, a collection of short stories, published
        by André Deutsch.
1978   Receives the Commander of the Order of the British
        Empire for her literary work.
1979   Dies on May 14 in Royal Devon and Exeter Hospital.
        Smile Please: An Unfinished Autobiography published post-
        humously by André Deutsch.
1981   *Quartet* adapted to film by James Ivory and Ruth Prawler
        Jhabvala.
1993   *Wide Sargasso Sea* adapted to film by Jan Sharpe, Carole
        Angier, and John Duigan.

Selected Bibliography

HISTORICAL BACKGROUND

Atwood, Thomas. 1791. *The History of the Island of Dominica.* London: Frank Cass, 1971.

Brathwaite, Edward Kamau. *Development of Creole Society in Jamaica, 1770–1820.* Oxford: Clarendon Press, 1971.

Holt, Thomas C. *The Problem of Freedom: Race, Labor, and Politics in Jamaica and Britain, 1832–1938.* Baltimore and London: The Johns Hopkins University Press, 1992.

Lewis, Gordon K. *Main Currents in Caribbean Thought.* Baltimore & London: The John Hopkins University Press, 1983.

Williams, Eric. *From Columbus to Castro: The History of the Caribbean 1492–1969.* London: André Deutsch, 1970.

WORKS BY JEAN RHYS

Rhys, Jean. *After Leaving Mr. Mackenzie* (1930). Rpt. in *The Complete Novels.* New York: W. W. Norton & Co., 1985.

——. *The Collected Short Stories.* New York: W. W. Norton & Co., 1987.

——. *Good Morning, Midnight* (1939). Rpt. in *The Complete Novels.* New York: W. W. Norton & Co., 1985.

——. *Quartet* (1928). Rpt. in *The Complete Novels.* New York: W. W. Norton & Co., 1985.

——. *Smile Please: An Unfinished Autobiography.* New York: Harper and Row, 1979.

——. *Voyage in the Dark* (1934). Rpt. in *The Complete Novels.* New York: W. W. Norton & Co., 1985.

——. *Wide Sargasso Sea* (1966). Rpt. New York: W. W. Norton & Co., 1982.

Wyndham, Francis, and Diana Melly, eds. *The Letters of Jean Rhys.* New York: Viking, 1984.

INTERVIEWS WITH JEAN RHYS

Bernstein, Marcelle. "The Inscrutable Miss Jean Rhys." *Observer Magazine* (London), (June 1, 1969): 40–42, 49–50.

Cantwell, Mary. "A Conversation with Jean Rhys, 'The Best Living English Novelist.' " *Mademoiselle* (October 1974): 170–71, 206, 208, 210, 213.

Carter, Hannah. "Fated to be Sad." *The Guardian* (August 8, 1968).

Plante, David. *Difficult Women: A Memoir of Three.* New York: Atheneum, 1983.

Vreeland, Elizabeth. "Jean Rhys: The Art of Fiction LXIV." *Paris Review* 76 (1979): 218–34.

CRITICISM AND BIOGRAPHY

• indicates works included or excerpted in this Norton Critical Edition.

Abel, Elizabeth. "Women and Schizophrenia: The Fiction of Jean Rhys." *Contemporary Literature* 20.2 (Spring 1979): 155–77.

Allfrey, Phyllis Shand. "Jean Rhys: A Tribute." *Kunapipi* 1.2 (1979): 23–25.

Angier, Carole. *Jean Rhys: Life and Work.* Boston: Little Brown and Company, 1990.

Baer, Elizabeth R. "The Sisterhood of Jane Eyre and Antoinette Cosway." *The Voyage In: Fictions of Female Development.* Ed. Elizabeth Abel et al. Hanover, New Hampshire: University Press of New England, 1983. 131–48.

Brathwaite, Edward Kamau. *Contradictory Omens: Cultural Diversity and Integration in the Caribbean.* Kingston, Jamaica: University of the West Indies, 1974.

——. "A Post-Cautionary Tale of the Helen of Our Wars." *Wasafiri* 22 (Autumn 1995): 69–78.

Brown, Bev E. L. "Monsong and Matrix: A Radical Experiment." *Kunapipi* 7.2–3 (1985): 68–80.

Bruner, Charlotte H. "A Caribbean Madness: Half Slave and Half Free." *Canadian Review of Comparative Literature* 2.2 (June 1984): 236–48.

Campbell, Elaine. "Reflections of Obeah in Jean Rhys's Fiction." *Kunapipi* 4.2 (1982): 42–50.

Cliff, Michelle. "Caliban's Daughter: The Tempest and the Teapot." *Frontiers: A Journal of Women's Studies* 12.2 (1991): 36–51.

Davidson, Arnold E. *Jean Rhys.* New York: Frederick Ungar Publishing Co., 1985.

• Drake, Sandra. " 'All That Foolishness/That All Foolishness': Race and Caribbean Culture as Thematics of Liberation in Jean Rhys's *Wide Sargasso Sea.*" *Critica* 2.2 (Fall 1990): 97–112.

• Emery, Mary Lou. *Jean Rhys at "World's End": Novels of Colonial and Sexual Exile.* Austin: University of Texas Press, 1990.

• Erwin, Lee. " 'Like in a Looking Glass': History and Narrative in *Wide Sargasso Sea.*" *Novel* 22.2 (1989): 143–58.

• Fayad, Mona. "Unquiet Ghosts: The Struggle for Representation in Jean Rhys's *Wide Sargasso Sea.*" *Modern Fiction Studies* 34.3 (1988): 437–52.

Ferguson, Moira, "Sending the Younger Son Across the Wide Sargasso Sea: The New Colonizer Arrives." *Colonialism and Gender Relations from Mary Wollstonecraft to Jamaica Kincaid: East Caribbean Connections.* New York: Columbia University Press, 1993. 90–115.

Ford, Ford Madox. Preface to *The Left Bank and Other Stories* by Jean Rhys. New York: Harper and Brothers, 1927.

Frickey, Pierrette, ed. *Critical Perspectives on Jean Rhys.* Washington, D.C.: Three Continents Press, 1990. 1–16.

Friedman, Ellen G. "Breaking the Master Narrative: Jean Rhys's *Wide Sargasso Sea.*" *Breaking the Sequence: Women's Experimental Fiction.* Ed. Ellen G. Friedman and Miriam Fuchs. Princeton, New Jersey: Princeton University Press, 1989.

Fulton, Nancy J. Casey. "Jean Rhys's *Wide Sargasso Sea*: Exterminating the White Cockroach." *Revista/Review Interamericana* 4 (1974): 340–49.

Gardiner, Judith Kegan. *Rhys, Stead, Lessing and the Politics of Empathy.* Bloomington: Indiana University Press, 1989.

Gregg, Veronica Marie. *Jean Rhys's Historical Imagination: Reading & Writing the Creole.* Chapel Hill & London: The University of North Carolina Press, 1995.

• Harris, Wilson. "Carnival of Psyche: Jean Rhys's *Wide Sargasso Sea.*" *Kunapipi* 2.2 (1980): 142–50.

Harrison, Nancy R. *Jean Rhys and the Novel as Women's Text.* Chapel Hill: University of North Carolina Press, 1988.

Hearn, John. "The *Wide Sargasso Sea*: A West Indian Reflection." *Cornhill Magazine* 1080 (Summer 1974): 323–33.

Howells, Coral Ann. *Jean Rhys.* New York: St. Martin's Press, 1991.

Hulme, Peter. "Dancing with Mr. Hesketh: Jean Rhys, Dominica, and the Last of the Caribs." *Sargasso* 7 (1990): 18–27.

———. "The Locked Heart: The Creole Family Romance of *Wide Sargasso Sea*." *Colonial Discourse/Postcolonial Theory*. Ed. Francis Baker, Peter Hulme, and Magaret Iversen. Manchester: Manchester University, 1994.

———. "The Place of *Wide Sargasso Sea*." *Wasafiri* 20 (Autumn 1994): 5–11.

James, Louis. *Jean Rhys*. London: Longman Group Ltd., 1978.

———. "Sun Fire — Painted Fire: Jean Rhys as a Caribbean Novelist." *Ariel: A Review of International English Literature* 8.3 (1977): 111–27.

Kamel, Rose. " 'Before I Was Set Free': The Creole Wife in *Jane Eyre* and *Wide Sargasso Sea*." *Journal of Narrative Technique* 25.1 (Winter 1995): 1–22.

Kloepfer, Deborah Kelly. *The Unspeakable Mother: Forbidden Discourse in Jean Rhys and H. D.* Ithaca: Cornell University Press, 1989.

Koenen, Anne, "The Fantastic as Feminine Mode: *Wide Sargasso Sea*." *Jean Rhys Review* 4.1 (1990): 15–27.

Le Gallez, Paula. *The Rhys Woman*. London: McMillan, 1990.

Leigh, Nancy J. "Mirror, Mirror: The Development of Female Identity in Jean Rhys's Fiction." *World Literature Written in English* 25.2 (1985): 270–85.

Loe, Thomas. "Patterns of the Zombie in Jean Rhys's *Wide Sargasso Sea*." *World Literature Written in English* 31.1 (1991): 34–42.

Look Lai, Wally. "The Road to Thornfield Hall." *New World Quarterly* (1968): 17–27.

Luengo, Anthony. "*Wide Sargasso Sea* and the Gothic Mode." *World Literature Written in English* 15.1 (April 1976).

Mellown, Elgin W. *Jean Rhys: A Descriptive and Annotated Bibliography of Works and Criticism*. New York: Garland Publishing, Inc., 1984.

Mezei, Kathy. " 'And It Kept Its Secret': Nation, Memory, and Madness in Jean Rhys's *Wide Sargasso Sea*." *Critique* 28.4 (Summer 1987): 195–220.

Nebeker, Helen. *Jean Rhys: Woman in Passage*. Montreal: Eden, 1981.

Nunez-Harrell, Elizabeth. "The Paradoxes of Belonging: The White West Indian Woman in Fiction." *Modern Fiction Studies* 31.2 (Summer 1985): 281–93.

Oates, Joyce Carol. "Romance and Anti-Romance: From Brontë's *Jane Eyre* to Rhys's *Wide Sargasso Sea*." *The Virginia Quarterly Review* 61.1 (Winter 1985): 44–58.

O'Connor, Teresa F. *Jean Rhys: The West Indian Novels*. New York: New York University Press, 1986.

• Parry, Benita. "Problems in Current Theories of Colonial Discourse." *The Oxford Literary Review* 9.1–2 (1987): 27–58.

• Raiskin, Judith. *Snow on the Cane Fields: Women's Writing and Creole Subjectivity*. Minneapolis: University of Minnesota Press, 1996.

Ramchand, Kenneth, introd. *Tales of the Wide Caribbean: Stories by Jean Rhys*. London: Heinemann, 1985. 1–21.

• ———. *An Introduction to the Study of West Indian Literature*. Middlesex: Thomas Nelson and Sons Ltd., 1976.

———. "Terrified Consciousness." *The West Indian Novel and Its Background*. 2nd ed. 1970; London: Heinemann, 1984.

Rodriguez, Ileana. "Jean Rhys: Island/Nation — *Hortus Conclusus* in House/Garden/Nation: Space, Gender, and Ethnicity in Post-Colonial Latin American Literatures by Women. Trans. Robert Carr and Ileana Rodriguez. Durham, North Carolina: Duke University Press, 1994.

• Rody, Caroline. "Burning Down the House: The Revisionary Paradigm of Jean Rhys's *Wide Sargasso Sea*." *Famous Last Words: Changes in Gender and Narrative Closure*. Ed. Alison Booth. Charlottesville: University of Virginia Press, 1993. 300–25.

Smilowitz, Erika. "Childlike Women and Paternal Men: Colonialism in Jean Rhys's Fiction." *Ariel: A Review of International Literature* (special edition: Commonwealth Women Writers) 17.4 (October 1986): 93–103.

Smith, Angela. Introduction to *Wide Sargasso Sea* by Jean Rhys. London: Penguin Books, 1997. vii–xxvi.

- Spivak, Gayatri Chakravorty. "Three Women's Texts and a Critique of Imperialism." *Critical Inquiry* 12.1 (1985): 243–61.

  Staley, Thomas F. *Jean Rhys: A Critical Study.* Austin: University of Texas Press, 1979.

  Sternlicht, Sanford V. *Jean Rhys.* New York: Twayne; London: Prentice Hall International, 1997.

  Tiffin, Helen. "Mirror and Mask: Colonial Motifs in the Novels of Jean Rhys." *World Literature Written in English* 17.1 (April 1978): 328–41.

- Thorpe, Michael. " 'The Other Side': *Wide Sargasso Sea* and *Jane Eyre*." *Ariel* 8.3 (1977): 99–110.

  Visel, Robin. "A Half-Colonization: The Problem of the White Colonial Woman Writer." *Kunapipi* 10.3 (1988): 39–45.

  Webb, Ruth. "Swimming in the Wide Sargasso Sea: The Manuscripts of Jean Rhys's Novel." *The British Library Journal* 14.2 (Autumn 1988): 165–77.

  Wilson, Lucy. " 'Women Must Have Spunks': Jean Rhys's West Indian Outcasts." *Modern Fiction Studies* 32.3 (Autumn 1986): 439–48.

  Wolfe, Peter. *Jean Rhys.* Boston: Twayne, 1980.